MORE PRAISE FOR *HOLLYWOOD, INTERRUPTED*

"Fearless. Vicious. Hilarious. Andrew Breitbart and Mark Ebner prove conclusively that radical family values + infinite financial resources + cultural idol worship = moral chaos.

Celebrity is the modern American version of aristocracy. *Hollywood, Interrupted* shows that our celebrities are every bit as mad, corrupt, and unaccountable as their Medieval European counterparts (albeit with better teeth). And like the old aristocracy, they really are one big, incestuous family.

What you don't understand—what you could not possibly understand—is that not only are these people nuts: They're nuts who all know each other. Hollywood is the most dysfunctional family in the history of the world and *Hollywood, Interrupted* reads like a transcript of their therapy session. It's cheeky, sophisticated, and authoritative."

Jonathan Last, *Weekly Standard*

"Hollywood hypocrites are going to simmer with fury at the painful barbs, backed up by plenty of facts, that these two sleuthing authors toss at some of the industry's most beloved stars and wags. If you love Larry King and Oprah, you'd better get ready to defend their honor, because this book deftly melts the shine off their armor."

Jill Stewart, "Capitol Punishment" syndicated columnist, radio and television political commentator

"'The rich are not like you and me,' F. Scott Fitzgerald said. *Hollywood, Interrupted* demonstrates that the rich and famous are not like anybody—at least anybody you'd want to be, or even shake hands with. In the deliriously scandalous tradition of Hollywood Babylon, Breitbart and Ebner's juicy dispatch from the spiritual capital of the Porn Belt reveals Tinseltown to be a glorified cathouse populated by collagened sociopaths. These also happen to be the people who drive American popular culture. Be afraid, be very afraid."

Rod Dreher, *Dallas Morning News*

"In *Hollywood, Interrupted* Breitbart and Ebner dig deeply into the very heart of our greatest export—pop culture—as produced by Hollywood, the movie industry and the people who affect and infect America. You cannot take a more fascinating or terrifying trip. There are tales of the fabulously famous here you would never know if not for their work. *Hollywood, Interrupted* is a book you have to put down frequently in order to catch your breath. Absolutely riveting."

Lucianne Goldberg, Publisher, Lucianne.com
News Forum and Talk Radio Network host

"This book blew me away. It's more than I wanted to know, but I couldn't stop reading it."

Orson Bean, actor

"Reading *Hollywood, Interrupted* is like sitting on a stakeout and having a telescopic view into the darkest reaches of the corruption and perversity of today's celebrity culture.

From the very first page to the last, Breitbart and Ebner's probing reporting spells out in graphic detail how Hollywood lives by a set of norms the rest of America finds appropriately appalling—and endlessly fascinating. The authors have the unusual courage to take on Scientology. They provide revelations about Michael Jackson's sickness that go beyond even today's headlines. They rip the phony veneer off the political correctness of Rosie O'Donnell and Barbra Streisand. They give readers a behind-the-scenes understanding of how snooping private eyes and ruthless information brokers feed scoops to the tabloids. And, in one riveting chapter, they document how a young woman in the AOL backroom unmasked the bizarre fetishes of some of Tinseltown's top names. *Hollywood, Interrupted* is no 'E' channel fluff. It's disturbing stuff. But it's all too real and it's utterly riveting."

Richard Gooding, investigative reporter

HOLLYWOOD, INTERRUPTED

Insanity Chic in Babylon— The Case Against Celebrity

Andrew Breitbart and Mark Ebner

WILEY

JOHN WILEY & SONS, INC.

Published by John Wiley & Sons, Inc., Hoboken, New Jersey.
Published simultaneously in Canada.

For general information on our other products and services, or technical support, please contact our Customer Care Department within the United States at 800-762-2974, outside the United States at 317-572-3993 or fax 317-572-4002.

Wiley also publishes its books in a variety of electronic formats. Some content that appears in print may not be available in electronic books.

For more information about Wiley products, visit our web site at www.wiley.com.

ISBN 0-471-45051-0

Printed in the United States of America

10 9 8 7 6 5 4 3 2 1

Dedicated to
Benjamin Geza Affleck

CONTENTS

ACKNOWLEDGMENTS

The authors would like to thank the following people without whose contributions this book would not have been possible:

Marc and Michelle Atlan; Lori Depp; Carrie Fisher; Matt Drudge; Bret Osterberg; Ed Dunne; Malissa Thompson; Katherine Durant; Xan Converse; Jonah Goldberg; Jonathan Last; Jordan Kitaen; Ken Neville; Adrian Otto; Jane Hamsher; Jim Mauro; Scott Slayton; Mickey Ramos; Matt Stone and Trey Parker; Jennifer Howell; Paul Barresi; Brian and Tracey Karadizian; Pamela Anderson; Boba; John Lavachielli; Mike and Diane Silver; Will Hornaday; Lance and Lotte McCloud; Paul Hughes; Melanie Graham; Lucianne Goldberg; Nelson Handel; K.J. Doughton; Rebecca Rivkin; Simone Missirian; Jim Salz; Paul Raff; Jack Hughes; Lisa Derrick; Paul Cullum; Jack Cheevers; Christian Logan Wright; Richard Rushfield; Alex Smithline; John Irwin; Seth Jacobson; Gary Hewson; Mickey Kaus; The Fat Pack; Robert Howell; The Enrights; Kristen Stavola; newsgroup: alt.religion.scientology; Ann Coulter; Dr. Jeffrey Gandin; Ariana Huffington; David Greenfield; Michael Haile; Tim Hale; Arlene and Gerald Breitbart; Suzanne Hansen; Deb Weiss; Andrew John Ignatius Vontz; Jane Bussmann; John Connolly; Pamela van Giessen; Helene Godin; Shana Larsen; Xenu; Roxie and Poorboy; The Backstreet Detectives (Dan Hanks and Fred Valis); Bill Bastone and The Smoking Gun crew; Rick Ross; Nipper Seaturtle; Silkonat; The Breitbarts (Susie, Mia, and Samson); The Beans (Orson, Max, Zeke and Alley Mills); Mary and Dr. Herbert Ebner; Carolyn Maxwell; David White; and Lenora Hewson.

AN INTERVENTION

This book started writing itself on the America Online Instant Messenger network. If you don't already have it, get it—now. Save *Freddy vs. Jason,* it's the best work the ill-advised AOL Time Warner merger has put out, and better yet, it's free.

As passing professional acquaintances (Ebner being a 20-year, bleeding heart investigative journalist, and Breitbart a conservative, first generation internet news junkie working for Matt Drudge) our political differences kept us at a distance until we discovered we had one thing in common: our mutual disgust with the state of popular culture. We would chat online from time to time to communicate entertainment-based story leads and to discuss trends in film, music, and television. Sometimes we would simply alert each other to tune into the latest tripe being fed to us through more traditional media outlets.

In September 2001—a few days before *that* day, when things trivial were of heightened concern—we late-night web dwellers turned

Anne Heche's alien confessional with Barbara Walters into a frantic all-night online chat, mocking the distress in which Hollywood now finds itself:

MarkEbner59: You've got to be kidding me! This is about the most insane thing I have seen on TV--ever. And not because of that opportunistic, rat-faced Heche. I can't believe that ABC is running this for an hour under the guise of NEWS!

Bodiaz: Did you notice when Heche spoke in her space alien language Walters never asked her to repeat what she said. That would have exposed if she were a fraud.

Bodiaz: Either Walters dropped the ball BIG TIME, or she wanted to keep the ruse going. She would have lost her kooky scoop.

MarkEbner59: What did Heche say anyway? I missed the alien language thing.

Bodiaz: Something like, "Sorten ooken uden carnuha vachoo anachnu... Eeden ahn duhoot, der uhten hagen spiel... Achnen tood amalyoo..."

MarkEbner59: Good god.

Bodiaz: I think you should pitch a magazine piece. Call it "Hollywood, Interrupted"--a play off the award-winning Jolie/Ryder real life nutcase review. Celebrities are now reveling in their madness, and for the first time in history getting paid big dollars to be anti-role models. It's "insanity chic."

MarkEbner59: Actually, I think it would take a book to do the story justice...

Hollywood, Interrupted is not a carefree romp through Tinseltown's glory days, nor is it a simple laundry list of celebrity flameouts; American Media Inc. (the National Enquirer, Star and Globe) has that dime store paperback market cornered, and, for the photos alone, we heartily recommend *FREAK!—Inside the twisted world of Michael Jackson* by Nick Bishop.

This book was composed as a cautionary tale for the rest of the planet, at once examining the utterly debauched causes and conditions of excessively bad behavior in Movie City that, unfortunately, adversely affects mass culture.

As of this writing, accused participatory kiddy pornographer/soul singer R. Kelly, suspected spouse killer Robert Blake, and an allegedly murderous rock producer named Phil Spector walk the streets. The despicable Spector dances directly into a fawning Esquire profile penned by a writer so smitten, so blinded by his nostalgic romance with this psycho's Wall of Sound accomplishment of yesteryear that he refused more than passing acknowledgment to the dead girl (actress Lana Clarkson) in question. Accused boy-lover Michael Jackson still operates his merry-go-round in Neverland, and around it goes.

"Yesterday's news," you say? Maybe so, but "R," Bobby, Phil, and Jacko are simply the most glaring, recent examples of a generation's worth of insanity fallout gone unchecked. And while the details of those dinosaurs' deviance bleed into back-page crime blotters, Hollywood—now utterly devoid of creativity—insists on telling us how to live, what to eat, who to pray to and who to vote for. Like pigs in a trough, the collective cult of celebrity for Century 21 sidles up to the all-you-can-eat Hollywood buffet that spoons out a psychotic smorgasbord of creepy reality shows, self-indulgent award shows, and rancid talk show soup from a menu designed to at once dazzle and further demoralize us. What next?

Bodiaz: AP reporting: It has taken five months, but Roman Polanski finally has in his possession his Best Director Oscar for the Holocaust drama "The Pianist." Polanski's friend, actor Harrison Ford, hand-delivered the statuette to the filmmaker at the Deauville Film Festival in France. Polanski was not at the ceremonies in Los Angeles in March because he faces prison time if he returns to the United States from Paris. He fled to France in 1977 to avoid sentencing for drugging a 13-year-old girl and coercing her into having sex.[1]

Bodiaz: Han Solo emerges as Hollywood's unquestioned Ambassador of Bad Will--The Fugitive handing a fugitive statutory rapist an Oscar. And look at this--Agence France Press reports: "At a safe distance from his homeland, veteran Hollywood actor Harrison Ford launched a broadside at US policy on Iraq, his country's gun laws--and the film industry for producing "video games" for teenagers."[2]

Bodiaz: As told to Germany's *Stern* magazine, Johnny Depp says: 'America is dumb, it's like a dumb puppy that has big teeth that can bite and hurt you, aggressive.'

MarkEbner59: So, now we have self-appointed emissary Ford joining Johnny Depp and his traveling *Folies Bergere* revue, blasting our government from foreign shores. Depp is probably crying in his vintage Bordeaux about no one hand-delivering *him* an Oscar...

Bodiaz: Yeah, and Depp's "patriotic" back flipping when confronted by the American press is like a botched audition for Cirque du Soleil. Of course, no one points out that entertainment is the U.S.'s second biggest export after aerospace equipment, and examines why craven stars pander to foreign markets, tapping into their worst anti-American tendencies.[3] Meryl Streep got it right in *The Wall Street Journal*: "We export the crap. And then we wonder why everybody hates us and has a distorted picture of what Americans are..."

MarkEbner59: Are the end times upon us?

Bodiaz: Perhaps.

   Hollywood, Interrupted is also a red flag warning to you to not believe what you read in glossy entertainment magazines, "arts and entertainment" newspaper inserts or see on E!. We can debate political bias in the media all day but no one has even touched on the bias that almost all media seem to have toward celebrities and Hollywood.

While "insider" media promises daring glimpses into exclusive enclaves of power and privilege, they never acknowledge that *access is a function of control*. Hollywood publicists—

MarkEbner59: No offense ladies!

—have long shielded their celebrity clients from confronting legitimate journalism, and as a result their clients' lives become a collection of puff pieces strung together to create a sugar-coated mythology. Upon a star's inevitable flameout, the ever-reliable entertainment journalist is there to spin the hell-and-back, redemptive tearjerker. Sophocles would be proud, but sadly, the malleable talent invariably comes to believe these lies created by flacks and complicit journalists. In no time, known commodities like Ben Affleck are trapped in their larger than life personae with no place to go but down. And that's insanity, baby.

At its core, the relationship between "entertainment journalism" (an oxymoron if there ever was one) and celebrity is, in their own therapy-speak, "co-dependent" and "dysfunctional." Any entertainment hack worth his saltpeter understands that he is compromised—effectively neutered from word one. To get the big interview, conditions are met with the publicist, contracts are often drawn, and the writer is expected by his editor to 1) write an "edgy," readable piece, and 2) not burn a bridge with said celebrity and bankrolling studio. Burn the publicist, access denied. This puts the reporter into a cyclical, ethical quandary: In order to succeed he or she must become a contradiction by creating a fiction that reads controversial, yet still keeps the celebrity team happy. *In toto*, entertainment journalists are disgruntled; they are professionally castrated. And to top it off, these masochists are, in turn, castigated, and hated by the stars they've just fluffed up.

Bodiaz: It's the "news journalists" who protect these
Hollywood crybabies and by extension promote their
insanity. These media types are married to them.
Their kids go to school with each other. They vacation
together. The KNOW they're out of control, yet
they protect them when they are exposed. If Erin
Brockovich ever decided to pull her award winning

shenanigans on her new Hollywood friends, they'd have her living back in a trailer park faster that she can say *Final Justice*. The whole thing is so incestuous, and sick.

MarkEbner59: Tell me about it... I can't tell you how many times I've had a solid Hollywood investigative piece killed in a back room editorial barter agreement with some star the magazine needs for their cover. And don't get me started on being bound and gagged from telling the whole story because the raw truth is too gory for a "family publication..."

Bodiaz: REUTERS Reports: Calling himself a "smut peddler who cares," porn king Larry Flynt has formally announced his bid for California governor but acknowledges that voters might not be able to stomach his sleazy background...[4]

MarkEbner59: Leave the gold-plated wheelchair-bound pornographer alone.

Bodiaz: Are you kidding me? I could write a book about Hollywood's re-birthing of Larry Flynt. This is a man whose own daughter accused him of sexually abusing her though he countered that she has "serious mental problems."[5]

MarkEbner59: And?

Bodiaz: Is Hollywood that hard up for heroes? He's a known drug abuser who publishes a magazine that isn't even a titillating turn-on to red-blooded men, unless they're seriously sadistic...[6]

MarkEbner59: So?

Bodiaz: Shut it, Ebner. The guy is lauded as a First Amendment angel in *The People v. Larry Flynt*. Masquerading as a defense of the "free speech movement,"

Hollywood crafts clever political statements rejecting
normative family values and crams an aggressive
pornographer and rank decadence down the world's throat.
Of all the people in the world to lionize, Hollywood
cognoscenti chose an unrepentant scumbag who then ended
up using his newfound cultural cachet to become
Clinton's sanctified defender during the Lewinsky saga.
How poetic is that?

MarkEbner59: --Andrew, I write for *Hustler*. Larry is not
so bad. I mean, at least he's not a hypocrite like some
of the others. Say, Hugh Hefner...

**Bodiaz: On this we will have to disagree. Flynt
personifies a Hollywood where anything and everything
goes, except for self-respect and human decency. I know
you have a soft spot for the underbelly of Hollywood.
But I have to raise my children here.**

MarkEbner59: Look--I empathize with people like Larry
because these people are at least honest about who they
are, what they do. I know all this because investigating
the sick, the depraved, the godless, it kinda takes one
to know one. I mean, look what we're covering in this
book! I've detoxed on the Cedars Sinai psychiatric
flight deck with a liver-load of hepatitis C. I was
raised by nannies. I've been tossed out of some of the
finest liberal academic institutions, I've sold pans to
pay the rent (and I may have to do it again). You don't
even want to hear about the illicit sex...

**Bodiaz: You're right. I don't... Wanna see the latest
Governor Schwarzenneger nude photo?**

MarkEbner59: Dude... Uh... You really need to get
offline, and get out of the house more. Come see the
Babylon! See how life is really lived in this town. See
how cults kill, Dr. Feelgoods flourish, celebrity kids
shoot speedballs and your neighbor runs a brothel.

Bodiaz: That's exactly why I stay in. I'd rather be with my family than out catching social diseases with you.

MarkEbner59: Okay--your family is great. Unfortunately, there are no visiting hours for me at the dumpster behind Planned Parenthood.

Bodiaz: Damn. What will my "vast right-wing conspiracy" think of that?

MarkEbner59: I don't care! Listen, I recognize disease when I see it. When it comes to weighing in on the overt insanity of Hollywood today, I understand this pit of degradation like my own dirty laundry. I'm sick and tired of the public falling for all the Hollywood lies.

Bodiaz: Pop culture matters. It infects everything. Ultimately, I guess we're kinda on the same page. The degradation of society by the cult of celebrity may be the one subject on which both liberals and conservatives can agree.

❑ ◼ ◼

The entertainment media circle-jerk that has worked so well and for so long for the Industry keeps churning, and the somnambulant celebrities and publicists are still going about their business as if it is always going to be that way.

"YOU'VE GOT MAIL!"

With the Internet, talk radio and cable news, the entire entertainment industry is now fair game for scrutiny, criticism and *mockery* at a global level. And, as hopeful harbingers of the death of the cult of celebrity, we bring you the alarum that is *Hollywood, Interrupted*.

Bodiaz: ☺

MarkEbner59: ☺

IT'S A FAMILY AFFAIR

PART I

Where Marlon and Ryan and Melissa and Brian
(among others) procreate and have children.
Nannies are hired. Children go to school.

A New Weird Order

Leggo My Ego!

Why do Hollywood stars, the most attractive, admired, and highly compensated citizens of the world, have families more screwed up than even the notoriety-driven mongrels loitering around the green room at the Jerry Springer show?

The short answer is *ego*. Insatiable ego. Constantly massaged ego. 24-hour-a-day concierge ego. 400-thread-count linen at the five-star luxury dog kennel ego. Trading in your prefame spouse for a world-class model ego.

Ego. Ego. Ego.

For every celebrity, by design and necessity, is a narcissist. The desire to become a star requires an incredible appetite for attention and approval. To achieve fame and its accoutrements takes laser-like focus, and a nearly commendable ability to stay self-centered in the service of the dream. Maintaining celebrity is a 24-hour-a-day process requiring a full-time staff to solidify the star's place at the top of the social pecking order. An impenetrable ring of "yes" creatures— including assistants, publicists, managers, agents, hair and make-up artists, stylists, lifestyle consultants, Pilates instructors, cooks, drivers, nannies, schedulers, and other assorted caretakers—work round-the-clock to feed the star's absurd sense of entitlement. Celebrities focus on the minutiae of self all the time—and they make sure that no distractions like airplane reservation snafus or colicky babies interrupt this singular focus. This often extremely lucrative self-obsession invariably becomes downright pathological.

That is why Los Angeles is a veritable triage center for psychiatry, and why the industry responds so well to Woody Allen's neurosis-driven films when the public at large barely registers his openings. It is also why psychiatry's arch-nemesis, Scientology, has made Hollywood central to its base of operations (more about the "church" of L. Ron Hubbard and its hold on Hollywood later!). The competition for the dollars of damaged celebrity souls is stiff—may the best man win, Freud or Hubbard.

Massive ego and narcissism may be the primary ingredients for achieving and maintaining Hollywood success, but they are also the number one cause of the grandiose foibles in their storied, disastrous personal lives. The full-time job of parenting requires absolute self-lessness. In contrast, the full-time job of celebrity requires absolute selfishness. The two by definition do not naturally coexist. Yet, because of their fame, money, and social power, stars somehow think they can defy the odds and maintain a high level of professional success, and still raise healthy families in the process.

No wonder so much rotten fruit is hanging from the dysfunctional celebrity family tree.

Celebrity Bumfights

The exotic personal exploits of celebrities are fascinating to read about, and presumably to live through, but by all accounts Hollywood is not the proper environment to raise children. Divorce notwithstanding, Bruce Willis and Demi Moore (1987–2000) seemed to have their priorities straight when they moved to Hailey, Idaho, to raise their children.[1] Sissy Spacek raised her kids in Virginia[2] and has all but kissed the LA life goodbye. Sam Shepard and his life room-mate Jessica Lange also opted for a simpler life for their family in Minnesota.[3] Likewise, Michael J. Fox and actress wife Tracey Pollan share time at homes in rural Connecticut and Vermont.

"If we're [in L.A.] all the time, our life is about me. Our life is about my job or the way people react to me. Everywhere we go, businesses this, dinners that, lunches that. I don't want my family to be about me. I want it to be about us, and I can do that better here," Fox told USA Today Weekend in 1997. "I know what it's like to eat with the Queen of England. And it doesn't mean as much as sitting on the floor today with my kids."[4]

These examples represent a small but hopeful trend toward celebrities pursuing a sense of normality for their kids—despite the odds against their parents being able to weather the storm away from the logical epicenter of their egos' home, Hollywood.

Sadly, a cottage industry has thrived in which the flotsam and jet-sam of celebrity misbehavior, usually the offspring, air the family's dirty laundry in the pursuit of achieving something they never had growing up—a sense of self-worth—because their parents larger-than-life accomplishments and minute-to-minute needs too often eclipsed their own.

Books like Christina Crawford's Mommy, Dearest and the late Gary Crosby's Going My Own Way offered sensational, firsthand accounts into the family lives of Joan Crawford and Bing Crosby, proving that even in the industry's Golden Age, Hollywood idols did not make top-notch parents. Nor most likely do their own children, comfortable perform-ing literary blindsides on their star parents in the pursuit of their own 15 minutes of fame. It's a vicious cycle. These stories took time to come out, usually not until after Mommy or Daddy entered the ranks of the dearly departed, and as postmortem tell-alls did not allow their famous parents much opportunity to wage a defense.

In the current Hollywood scene, it's not just the kids but also the parents publicly airing the secret family tittle-tattle, often in real time and for large sums of money. Celebrity reality television in the form of "The Osbournes" has expedited and streamlined the process by which celebrities share their innermost secrets and lay out their personal family turmoil. Waiting until the end of rehab to tell Stone Phillips about the road to hell and back is simply too late now.

While actor Jake Busey ("Shasta McNasty") is trying to make a name for himself in his father's erratic shadow, he must compete with dad's on-screen reality antics in "I'm with Busey." To sell the show, Comedy Central posits the born-again rehab alumnus as more unpredictable than Ozzy Osbourne. In an interview with *Maxim* magazine Gary Busey promotes the show by sharing his drugged-out low point: "I came home one day, took off my windbreaker and three bundles of cocaine fell to the floor. Well, my dog Chili, who has short hair, came in and lay on her back with her legs in the air and she rubbed all the cocaine on her back and side. So I got a straw and I started brushing back her hair and snorting where I saw the cocaine. Back, butt, side—not a spot was left. It took me 25 minutes to snort all the cocaine the dog had on her coat."[5]

So transparent is the network suits' desire to chronicle the domestic meltdowns of the rich and famous, VH1 slated princess of the damned Liza Minnelli, daughter of Hollywood's most glamorous suicide, Judy Garland, along with her short-term wax show husband David Gest (2002–2003) to star in their own televised journey to hell. When Minnelli attempted to hijack "The Liza and David Show" and make it into an extended "Larry King Live Weekend," replete with old timers like Steve and Edie belting out standards around the bizarre couple's home piano, VH1 immediately dropped the idea. Dueling lawsuits between the parties ensued with personal details coming from both sides reminiscent of a divorce proceeding.[6] If Minnelli couldn't realize that her path to career rebirth was exposing herself and her bizarre husband of the moment to raw exploitation, that was her problem. Not Viacom's.

The saddest aspect of E! Channel's ratings bonanza "The Anna Nicole Show" is reluctant costar, Daniel, Anna Nicole Smith's Nirvana T-shirt–wearing adolescent son. "He doesn't like the cameras," the plus-sized head case told "Good Morning America." "He's doing it for mama."[7]

As if it isn't hard enough going through the awkward teen years as the offspring of a demented single mother, Daniel is forced to withstand the public viewing of what mom calls her "rollercoaster" of a life.[8]

"Hold on," Smith warns viewers, Daniel be damned.[9]

Alt.Family.Hollywood

Is it too late for Hollywood families who have already flamed out to tap into the burgeoning market for celebrity-driven reality TV? Stars can't live off the proceeds of "E! True Hollywood Stories," you know.

Some past vignettes of the familial eruptions of the down and out and famous would surely whet the appetite of parasitic network suits today if they could only rewind time, and get a guarantee in writing that the stars have no intentions of pursuing their dignity anytime soon.

Marlon Brando heads a family so damaged its story line wouldn't make the cut on a Brazilian soap opera. Over the years he has helped to create a series of nine children with four different women.[10] In 1990, son Christian killed Dag Drollet, the Tahitian lover of his half-sister Cheyenne, who later committed suicide by hanging herself in French Polynesia, where her father sent her to recover from chronic depression.[11] "I have come to despise my father for the way he ignored me when I was a child," Cheyenne once publicly stated.[12]

After a few years in the brig, Christian then got involved in a paternity squabble with Bonny Lee Bakley, the future wife (and future murder victim, allegedly) of actor Robert Blake, who proved to be the father in question. We all know what happened next.[13]

Marlon Brando ballooned while holed up in his Hollywood Hills home, and local food deliverymen acclimated to the clandestine rituals of getting the icon his daily caloric bounty—including throwing McDonald's hamburgers over the gate.[14] In a rare public appearance on "Larry King Live" in 1994, filmed at his home, Brando babbled incoherently and declared "Hollywood is run by Jews."[15] To top it off, Brando planted a slobbering on-screen kiss on King.

"This is a false world," Brando once opined. "It's been a struggle to try to preserve my sanity and sense of reality taken away by success. I have to fight hard to preserve that sense of reality so as to bring up my children."[16]

We're thinking that Marlon lost this particular fight.

Oscar-nominated Ryan O'Neal (*Love Story*) and his Oscar-winning daughter Tatum (*Paper Moon*) have both flourished in the trade, yet both—along with Ryan's doomed son Griffin (*Attack of the Killer Bimbos*)—have withstood so many self-inflicted life traumas it's no small wonder they are still alive. Ryan's battles with the bulge and cancer,[17] along with his stealing of Farrah Fawcett from his best pal Lee Majors,[18] make for a compelling script, perhaps better than any the three O'Neal burnouts have read in the last two decades.

Tatum's career tanked as she couldn't stay off heroin long enough to keep custody of her kids spawned by temperamental tennis icon John McEnroe.[19] Tatum repeated the cycle of her mother, Joanna Moore, who, according to Tatum, was more interested in getting high than caring for her own children.[20]

Brother Griffin has said that the O'Neal children were "traded like dogs" between Ryan and his estranged wives,[21] contributing to his inevitable drug and anger management problems. Griffin was tried for manslaughter in the death of Francis Ford Coppola's son, Gian-Carlo, who was decapitated in a drunken speed boating accident. He was found guilty of a lesser charge and admitted to drinking at the time of the accident.[22] Subsequently, an ex-girlfriend took Griffin to court alleging he said he'd kill her for breaking up with him and proved he had attempted to do so when he rammed his Ford Bronco into her parked car as she sat inside fearing for her life. He was en route to her home when police later arrested him.[23] Griffin pleaded no contest and was sentenced to one year in a drug and alcohol treatment program.[24]

Kids of Hollywood royalty seem much more susceptible to tragic downfalls than their peers in the general population:

- Paul Newman's son Scott died of a Valium and alcohol overdose in 1978.[25]
- Mary Tyler Moore's 24-year-old son Richie accidentally shot and killed himself in 1980—the same year his mother starred in the wrenching *Ordinary People*.[26]
- Carroll O'Connor's son Hugh killed himself in 1995 after a 16-year battle with drug addiction.[27]
- Barbara Eden's son, Matthew Ansara, died of a heroin overdose in 2001.[28]

How many people do you know whose children have died of substance abuse or suicide? Add to the Hollywood death count the names of the Hollywood kids, like the O'Neal clan, who narrowly averted tragic endings after struggles with drugs, alcohol, and celebrity parents, including Charlie Sheen, actress Mackenzie Phillips ("One Day at a Time"), and Carol Burnett's late daughter Carrie Hamilton (who struggled with drugs and later died of cancer in 2002).[29] We'd list even more, but you get the point.

The female progeny of the Beach Boys' cosmically disturbed Brian Wilson hooked up with the daughter of infamous hedonist John Phillips of the Mamas and the Papas to create Wilson Phillips. "I know that there is pain, but you hold on for one more day and break free the chains," the saccharine pop trio sang in the 1990s single *Hold On*, from their eponymous debut album that garnered four Grammy nominations.

The biggest casualty of the musical union was Carnie Wilson, a big-hearted soul with a magnificent voice. The group's career took off, but Carnie was surrounded by people obsessed with her Rubenesque figure, especially in contrast to her thin sister Wendy and super slender Chynna Phillips. The all-important music videos that pushed the band's success all but ignored her visage. It didn't help that hovering above her was the spirit of Mama Cass Elliott, who died in 1974 at the age of 32 from a massive heart attack brought upon by her excessive weight.

In an interview with Wilson, conducted by her "lifestyle consultant" and her psychologist before her stomach reduction and broadcast live on the Internet, she brought up the psychological factors that led to her morbid obesity, including bonding with her father over large bowls of Raisin Bran and half-and-half gobbled up in the middle of the night. "It was so damn good, it was so good."[30]

Dad's all-encompassing, mostly LSD-induced insanity caused him to hand over "total therapeutic authority" to Dr. Eugene Landy, a controversial psychologist, who famously exerted total control over every aspect of his patient's life for years.[31] Well, not total. Dr. Landy didn't take over as Carnie or Wendy's father.

Chynna's half-sister, Mackenzie Phillips, tells how dad, "Papa" John Phillips, instructed her in the art of joint rolling at 10 and injected her with liquid cocaine at 17. "To any normal, decent person reading this, that probably sounds horrific," Phillips said. "But dad didn't know any better. To him it was all part of being cool, being a 1960s dude. I paid the price for that. For years I felt bitter, but I forgave him on his deathbed."[32]

Family friend Mick Jagger slept with Mackenzie when she was a mere 18 years old—with dad in the apartment at the time fully aware of what was happening. According to Mackenzie, Jagger told her, "I have been waiting for this since you were 10 years old."[33]

Phillips was at one point Hollywood's most notorious recurring waste case—before Robert Downey Jr. broke all land speed records—and could not keep up with her maternal duties during her bouts with cocaine addiction. Now positioned as one of the town's clean-living spokespeople, the actress currently stars as the mom on the Disney Channel series, "So Weird." Indeed, it is. But not by Hollywood's standards.

"The Kennedys are the royal family of America. But if you want to talk about true glamour, scandal, and just a true collection of interesting and wild celebrities, that applies far more to my family," J. Paul Getty Sr. once bragged.[34]

The oil-rich, commonsense-poor Gettys bestowed upon Los Angeles a world-renowned, heavily endowed art museum and a semitalented actor named Balthazar. The son of J. Paul Getty III (the one who was kidnapped, known to friends as Paul) and the grandson of J. Paul Getty Jr.—former heroin addicts alike, he also descended into a junkie's life not long after his *Lord of the Flies* success at the age of 17.[35]

Balthazar spent much of his adolescence under the tutelage of his now ex-junkie, HIV-positive aunt, Aileen Getty, the former daughter-in-law of the Queen of Dysfunction, Elizabeth Taylor.[36] Balt, as his friends call him, is fond of letting his penis fall from his pants at inopportune moments, according to an LA-based journalist, causing his pals to urge him to "set some boundaries."[37]

By age 16, dysfunctional wunderkind Drew Barrymore had written a tell-all book, *Little Girl Lost* (Pocket Books, 1991), in which she described the pain of growing up in a famous household. Grandfather John had drunk himself to death, and her father had a long history of drug abuse to go along with the family trademark drinking. "Until I was five years old my father and I were very close. When my parents separated I had a nervous breakdown," she admitted. "I was nine at the time. By the time I was eleven I was drunk. By the time I was fourteen I had my first joint. . . ."[38]

Her first marriage to a bartender lasted 19 days. Now divorced for the second time from comedian Tom Green, Drew proves money and success can often obscure high-octane dysfunction.[39] Today she is one of Hollywood's most bankable young actresses and has a production company that ably produces the bland *Charlie's Angels* moneymakers.

Viva la dysfunction!

Alternative Family Ties

The twisted values of fame are born not only from nepotism or from up-and-coming stars lured into the fast lane acquiescing to Hollywood peer pressure. Some stars were born and reared as destiny's children, conceived and raised by hippies, oddball nonconformists, and other Age of Aquarius rejects, many who now feel compelled to carry on their nutty lineage by altering society via their artistic gifts.

There is no shortage of celebrities raised in nontraditional, radical settings who have accumulated enough personal wealth and power to obscure the fact that they are not philosophically on the same page as the majority of us. Some of them were raised in communal settings, sent to alternative schools and mind-bending summer camps, and indoctrinated throughout life to see the suburban nuclear American family structure as somehow suspicious and corrupt. These people believe the rest of us are brainwashed (think: *The Matrix*) and only they possess the infinitely open minds that allow them to sense the entire scope of the human experience (think: *Hair*). It's a distinction we couldn't understand unless, of course, we opened our minds, accepted their orthodoxies, and joined the psychedelic circus.

Since *People* and *Us* magazines and other publicity venues in which celebrities share their backgrounds and promote their careers tend to have a nice working relationship with the industry, these unconventional back stories tend to be glossed over or put into the best possible light. A case in point is the late alleged future savior of mankind, River Phoenix (*Running on Empty, The Mosquito Coast, My Own Private Idaho*).

"We believed we could use the mass media to help change the world and River would be our missionary," eulogized Heart Phoenix, formerly Arlyn Sharon Dunetz from the Bronx, at her son's funeral following his not-so-holistic overdose from cocaine, heroin, Valium, ephedrine, and marijuana on Halloween in 1993.[40]

Any cursory examination of the life and death of River Phoenix exposes the crash-ridden intersection of Hollywood waywardness and the mostly sycophantic, loony, and enabling entertainment press. The institutional imperative to maintain unfettered star access helps to wave off red flags, while the so-called open-mindedness of the journalists serves to soft-pedal questionable alternative life choices. Some might call it a codependent relationship, with the media acting as the enabling, subservient partner.

River Phoenix represented a Baby Boomer media ideal—he was a young, talented, successful, sensitive, outspoken (yet nonthreatening) peacenik love child, cultural icon, and environmental activist. A spokesperson for the cause. A messenger.

And what of River's drug problems?

"What problems? There weren't any problems," said brother Joaquin, two years after River's death when queried by *USA Today*.[41]

The media also turned a blind eye to River's drug problems because they loved what he represented. If River Phoenix was ever in peril during his meteoric rise, which he clearly was, the intrepid entertainment press was not predisposed to tell. Had they offered the straight dope, so to speak, and not doled out a predictable feel-good, soul-searching narrative, Child Protective Services would have probably possessed a compelling case to swoop in and take away Joaquin Rafael (a.k.a. Leaf), Libertad Mariposa (a.k.a. Liberty, Liberty Butterfly), Summer Joy, Rain Joan of Arc (a.k.a. Rainbow), and River Jude from hippie hell parents John and Heart Phoenix.

"We never treated them like children but like extra added friends," Heart reportedly said. "And they have always held up their part of the deal. It was never like 'We know better because we are the parents.' It was more like 'This is the first time we've ever done this too. What do you think?' And the children were so wise. If we made a mistake, we made it together. But if you open yourself up, a way presents itself. You find the right path."[42]

Please—don't try that at home!

John met Heart in 1968 at the commencement of the Summer of Love when the sometime gardener picked up the 23-year-old former secretary hitchhiking.[43] Heart was kicking off a "spiritual journey" soon after renouncing her background as a "clone" and divorcing some poor schlub back in New York. "We just knew we had similar desires," Heart recalled.[44]

One of the paths Heart and John took on the back roads to enlightenment was jumping from commune to commune, Oregon to Colorado to Texas, mostly under the influence of intense drugs, and popping out kids under circumstances that have gotten impoverished, drug-addicted black women jailed. "I fell in love with LSD," Heart once said in a typical fawning press interview, written without any sense of moral outrage for an audience apparently too jaded to raise an eyebrow. "Grass was plentiful and cheap and together they were an essential part of our journey."[45]

John and Heart soon became "missionaries" for the Children of God,[46] a cult founded by David Berg, who, according to sociologist David Van Zandt, encouraged sex among its underaged members.[47] Though not compensated for the work, John was given the lofty title Archbishop of Venezuela and the Caribbean. The family settled outside Caracas where five-year-old River and his three-year-old sister, Rain, distributed cult pamphlets while performing music on the streets for handouts.[48]

River's memory painted a bleaker picture of the early years. "It was disgusting," he said of a "shack" he once called home. "It had no toilet and was rat-infested."[49]

Mother Heart maintained her faith. "We had a vision that our kids could captivate the world," the Phoenix family matriarch remembered, repetitively conveying a messianic obsession to use her children to reach the Promised Land—Hollywood.[50]

Bumming a free ride back to America on an ocean freighter in 1978, the destitute Phoenix family took refuge at Heart's mother's place in Florida, relegating Heart to leech off the middle-class teat she had renounced nearly a decade before.[51] Soon thereafter, Heart Phoenix had yet another vision that predictably cast her children in the starring roles.

After entering the kids in numerous talent contests around Florida, seeking to win favor of the clone-like judges, a Phoenix family friend sent a letter to actress Penny Marshall describing the Phoenix family's stage charms. Through an employee Marshall sent a perfunctory letter encouraging the Phoenix clan to stop by the set of "Laverne and Shirley" if they ever came out to Hollywood.[52]

Like God speaking to Moses, Heart heeded the calling and again uprooted the family. Forty places in 20 years, she once boasted. With John's inability to work due to a recurring back problem and a dearth of archbishop work in the States, the Phoenixes of Caracas by way of Florida headed to Los Angeles.

"I figured I'd play guitar and sing with my sister, and we would be on television the next day," River said. "We were really naive."[53]

Soon the kids soon found their way into one banal acting role after another: *Space Camp* for Leaf, "Growing Pains" for Summer, *Kate's Secret* for Liberty, *Maid to Order* for Rain. And glory be, Heart Phoenix, vegan activist, nomad without peer, and advanced human spirit, became her kids' manager—an earth stage mother, if you will. Nirvana is apparently found bypassing progressive child labor laws and creating a vegan gravy train for parents who think hard work is for the birds.

Hollywood is the one place, save Marin County, where the Phoenix clan blended right in. "We were in competition, at the same auditions," recovering heroin addict and River's *Stand By Me* costar Corey Feldman once said. "We got to know each other's families. He was a normal kid. We were both normal kids who were in the business."[54] If this quote were entered into the court record, the prosecuting attorney would then say, "Your honor, I rest my case."

Rob Reiner, who directed River in *Stand By Me*, noted without irony, "It's clear he's been loved by his parents, who are people who have been able to maintain what was good and pure about the 1960s—morality without the garbage."[55] And that morality translated into something that would raise the eyebrows of even the most open-minded flower child. When River, who claimed to have lost his virginity at the age of four(!), once set out as a teenager to have sex with a girlfriend, the Phoenix family hosted a pagan ritual, constructing a love tent for the occasion. "It was a beautiful experience," Heart later said.[56]

"I'm glad I did it when I was young," River once said, perhaps trying to justify the unjustifiable. "But I didn't want those young vaginas and different body parts [penises?] that were in my face to make me perverse when I was older, so I blocked it all out. I was completely celibate from 10 to 14. You're just born into that reality, and you accept it."[57]

At 23, the much-ballyhooed great white hope River Phoenix reached a dead end on the wayward path his family had led him. Brother Joaquin, the Phoenix family's latest commodity, who along with sister Rain was with River the night he died, placed the fateful call to 911. "I'm thinking he had Valium or something," he told the dispatcher. He was only off by about four or five drugs.[58]

Hollywood, for all its love of gritty reality and overwrought drama, has yet to produce the sexy and compelling tragedy of the family Phoenix. Unlike the Jerry Springer show freaks—who ostensibly teach us important life lessons about humanity—the River Phoenix cautionary tale hits too close to the bone for Hollywood to exploit.

Perhaps if Joaquin's career starts hitting the skids, Heart Phoenix can reinvent herself again, option the sucker, and put her only living son in the starring role.

Prada-Wearing, Pharmaceutical-Happy Tepee Sisters of Love

"Turn on, tune in, drop out," Dr. Timothy Leary, Winona Ryder nee Horowitz's godfather, famously said.

Ryder, the convicted shoplifter of high-end designer fashion, was raised by hippie "intellectuals" in northern California who heeded the good psychedelic doctor's advice and opted to live on society's edges. Rejecting the allure of middle-class life, the family lived at times on an electricity-free commune in Mendocino, California, and traveled the land in a psychedelic bus named Veronica.[59]

Dad runs Flashback Books in the tie-dyed community of Petaluma located 45 miles north of San Francisco, a specialty bookstore dealing exclusively in materials related to the drug experience. And mom is a "video artist"—whatever that is. Her folks together penned the scholarly work *Shaman Woman, Mainline Lady: Women's Writings on the Drug Experience.* "It's great," Ryder told hometown cheerleader, the *San Francisco Examiner.* "It's about famous women writers like Louisa May Alcott and Edith Wharton who used opium or whatever while they were creating their masterpieces. It goes all the way up to Patti Smith."[60]

Like the Phoenix family, Winona's brothers and sisters were also given F-U names: Sunyata, Jubal, and Yuri, who was named after a Russian cosmonaut.[61] The family's rejection of consumer culture's creature comforts peaked when the family opted to become one with their oppressed spiritual kin, the native American Indian, by living in a tepee.[62]

The Horowitz tribe?

"Whenever I've had choices to make," Ryder said, "I've known how to make them. I don't know if that comes from the 60s or if it comes from something else. But it's a wonderful thing to know."[63] Wonderful indeed. One imagines that master choice-maker Ryder, inspired by 1960s Yippie Abbie Hoffman's counterculture tome *Steal This Book*, will soon begin penning her own alternative life guide tentatively entitled *Steal This $525 Black Leather Dolce and Gabbana Purse with Metal Eyelets and Leather Fringe.*

Perhaps not so strangely, Ryder befriended Courtney Love, her sister in the aristocracy of tabloid queens. Love also called a tepee home during her similarly nontraditional path to adulthood with parents as transparently nutty as Winona's.[64] To Love's credit, she paid lip service to rejecting her parents' ways, but created and marketed her own patented dysfunctional lifestyle that will likely traumatize parents for decades to come. Yet somehow no intrepid journalist has taken the time to investigate how Hollywood's royal screw-ups, products of households that rejected wealth on philosophical grounds, could become iconic fashion plates ready to wear the sashes of the New Materialism.

Desperately Seeking Insouciance

The acting Arquettes epitomize the anti–nuclear celebrity family that emerged from the Sixties: Father Lewis (J.D. Pickett on "The Waltons") smoked pot with the kids; the family lived for a time on a commune and spent a summer at a nudist colony.[65]

The result? David "Mr. Courtney Cox" Arquette is a recovering heroin junkie.[66] Brother Alexis flaunts his gender identity issues as "Eva Destruction" and "Amanda B. Reckonedwith" in drag shows around LA.[67] Sister Patricia prefers 16 hours of sleep daily, and says a nudity phobia causes her to bathe in the dark.[68] Courtesy of Camp Wannaseemytushee, presumably.

Sister Rosanna hit it big in *The Executioner's Song* opposite Tommy Lee Jones and *Desperately Seeking Susan* with Madonna. Dating Steve Porcaro from Toto made her name a truly bad early MTV-era rock music anthem.

In an October 1985 *Playboy* "20 Questions" Q&A, the actress activist labored about one of her causes, abortion—one of fertile Hollywood's secret weapons of the trade—and at one point blurted out the following in response to the question of whether she had ever had an abortion: "Well, as a matter of fact, yes. And my mother went to have an abortion when she was pregnant with me. I mean, she was on her way, and then the nurse told her to go out through the back door because the place got raided and the doctor got arrested because it was illegal. This was during the Fifties, when women used to go to these old buildings and someone would do it with a knife and a newspaper. I mean, some butcher. I've had two abortions: one when I was much younger and one two years ago. I was deeply involved with a man the second time. We made the decision together that it wasn't the right time for us to have a baby. It wasn't a pleasant experience. We were going to get married but the moment just wasn't right. The abortion ended up being OK, because I broke up with that person. So, you know, I wouldn't want to have the marriage break up and have a two-year-old running around."[69]

Was Arquette completely oblivious to the fact that abortion's illegality at the time saved her life, as she sang the praises of her two choices on purely selfish and not medical grounds? Or doesn't she care?

Cognitive dissonance aside, had Arquette achieved greater success in her acting career—instead of being relegated to the position of pay cable male fantasy, repeatedly flashing her admirable breasts on screen—and continued to advocate for women's issues as she did in *Playboy*, it is likely women would have eventually lost the right to vote. Arquette's stunningly candid answer, representative of Hollywood's utilitarian approach to the issue, exposes the rift not between pro-choice and pro-life camps, but between pro-abortion Hollywood and pro-choice America. The average person can see Hollywood's pro-abortion stance not as a philosophical abstraction born of altruism and a passion for women's rights, but as a necessary evil for actresses who must stay nubile to remain employable in a business not keen on putting pregnant or nursing women in nude scenes. Just ask "Melrose Place" evicted tenant, Hunter Tylo. The best way for actresses to assuage their guilt is to put on the hat of strident pro-choice activist claiming to be fighting for the civil rights of the masses, the very people they mock in their artistic work and treat with contempt in their daily lives.

Arts of Darkness

The airline industry has not declared war on the American family. Nor have the great steel companies in the Rust Belt produced any grand proclamations demanding fundamental changes to the institution. Professional sports leagues, from the NFL to the NBA to Major League Baseball, have remained tactfully silent on the subject as well. So have taxidermists, timber folk, and assorted pharmacists, dog groomers, and independent candy store operators. But somehow entertainers, people whose job description is to divert our attentions, feel compelled to traumatize us with their insane interpretation of family—both on screen and off.

Hollywood, run and inhabited by Baby Boomers and their Generation X progeny, is on a mission to obliterate the ideal of the nuclear family and to undermine traditional child-rearing practices. The entertainment landscape is littered with high-end product that demeans the family unit, and in their own lives, celebrities fail to set a good example. Shamefully, they are rewarded for rejecting middle-class American mores.

Entertainment executives may argue that they are giving the public what they want when they find new and nastier ways to expand trash TV into the familial realm, but the same cynical, exploitative, anti-family strain is also evident in critically praised films and pay cable series.

On the big screen, *American Beauty* captured the imagination of the members of the Academy in 2000 when it received the Oscar for Best Picture. The Alan Ball-scripted film captures perfectly the elite point of view that Middle America is a wasteland inhabited by conspicuous consumers, twisted souls, and bad parents.

The only time Hollywood presents the family unit as sympathetic is when it seeks to normalize the abnormal through artistic propaganda. Case in point: HBO Films' *Normal*, starring acclaimed actors Jessica Lange and Tom Wilkinson, depicts a couple who after 25 years of marriage must deal with the husband's desire to have a sex change. Middle America is the setting in all its drab décor, as the story arc and message fall in line to present the family's acceptance of the father's untraditional desire. The prepubescent daughter in the film represents the unspoiled, open-mindedness Hollywood wishes were commonplace, as she loses no sleep over her father's out-of-nowhere desire to become a woman, while she is struggling with becoming one herself.

"To me, the essence of the piece really was the definition of love," Lange said while promoting the film. "Can you look beyond the external and actually see into the heart of another human being? What happens when you have the external suddenly going through this extraordinary and kind of unnatural transformation?"[70] Typical patronizing pedagogy on the art of sensitivity from artists who think they are the last defense from the rest of us going on a transgender hate-crime murder spree.

Aired in March of 2003, the film preceded the June report by gossip columnist Liz Smith that Larry Wachowski, one of two brothers behind *The Matrix* films, was rumored to be going through the same process with his wife, Thea Bloome.[71] Bloome was apparently less forgiving, as divorce papers unearthed by "The Smoking Gun" web site showed. She noted that her husband "has been extremely dishonest with me in our personal life" and that the couple's separation was "based on very intimate circumstances concerning which I do not elaborate at this time for the reasons of his personal privacy."[72] Perhaps actress/activist Jessica Lange can hold a private screening of *Normal* for Bloome to show her that her reaction was not so normal.

Television programmers' idea of a functional family—ignoring the ridiculous canned-laughter sitcoms and half-hearted "Little House on the Prairie" clones crafted to appease the Family Research Council's G-rated guidelines—is best represented by Alan Ball's other critically acclaimed creation, HBO's "Six Feet Under." The show chronicles the Fishers, a twisted family in the funeral business, each member mired in dysfunctional subplots—an abusive gay relationship, the revelation of the family matriarch's infidelity to the now dead father, forays into group sex, etc. Ask anyone that watches it and they will swear by it. But an exemplar of the ideal family, it is not.

"Sex and the City," a pox on Sarah Jessica Parker's house, will have long-lasting deleterious effects on those women who bought into the hype, thinking that living as successful working women leading promiscuous sex lives well into their thirties will ensure a happy ending. These trash-talking metropolitan sluts get away with cultural murder saying and doing that which would have a male show with the same premise slapped with a misogyny label.

The truth is the show is in large part penned by liberated gay male writers who are putting their sexual politics into the mouths of babes—an X-rated version of what the *Look Who's Talking* movies did by putting adult voices in the mouths of children. Will our families, let alone the sexes, ever recover from the horror?

Dan Quayle Was Right

"Hollywood thinks it's cute to glamorize illegitimacy. Hollywood doesn't get it," Vice President Dan Quayle railed in 1992.[73] "It doesn't help matters when prime time TV has Murphy Brown, a character who supposedly symbolizes today's intelligent, highly paid professional woman, mocking the importance of fathers by bearing a child alone, and calling it just another lifestyle choice," Quayle further complained.[74]

Quayle's comments ignited a firestorm from Hollywood, and the former vice president became the laughingstock of almost everyone, except those trying to raise children outside the nannybelt. "Murphy Brown" producer Diane English snidely responded on the evening Hollywood bestowed Emmys to the show, "As Murphy herself said, I couldn't possibly do a worse job raising my kid alone than the Reagans did with theirs."[75]

Anyone with a smidgeon of common sense knows that Quayle was, in essence, right. But the absolute power of the Hollywood PR machine was relentless in mocking Quayle and his message. Candace Bergen herself years later agreed when she told the *Los Angeles Times*: "My family has always come first—by a mile . . . I had a very difficult time playing Murphy the first year after the baby, as a distant second priority. It was very distressing to me, and I couldn't get them to change it. Just hated it, and even [my daughter] hated it when she would watch certain episodes. I didn't think it was a good message to be sending out."[76]

In post-Quayle real-life Hollywood the damage is done. The traditional family unit is regularly contorted and lambasted by sitcom creators. The one-two punch of having too much money and too little common sense instigates atypical life choices that trigger a predictable chain of media events. The life decision is 1) announced through the alternative lifestyle-friendly entertainment press, which 2) features kudos from their peers in the industry as a means to 3) downplay the raised eyebrows from the majority of common folk elsewhere whom they play for bigots.

It's a proactive form of damage control that works because Middle America has traditionally had so few means to respond, other than through boycotts. Most people would have to live in a pop culture isolation ward if they were forced to respond to every star's public life choices. Plus, most Americans could care less what entertainment industry folks do in their private lives; they just don't like Hollywood's agenda to undermine ideals they take seriously and are trying desperately to underscore at home.

So celebrities benefit from a virtual détente in which they get to publicly push the cultural envelope in a conspicuous way, and the rest of the world, for the most part, has to cross its fingers and hope the rot doesn't spread.

Celebrity Adopto-Babies

Assuming a female's child-bearing years are between the ages of 18 and 44, an actress, model, or singer is likely to be toiling in her demanding career as her biological clock ticks away oblivious to her Q rating. Instead of settling down with a long-term suitor, a starlet is usually juggling a buffet of hunks, or dames in the lesbian chic era, further pushing her away from the traditional motherhood route.

There is almost no incentive for the typical celebrity to lay down traditional roots, so Hollywood players not in committed relationships have taken it upon themselves to make their public adoption of children a high public relations priority. "I was adopted purely for publicity purposes," Christina Crawford recalled in an interview. "My entire childhood was made public. I was trained on how to smile for the camera, how to answer reporters' questions. I had special clothes worn only for photo sessions. And when the press left, (my siblings and I) became less valuable."[77]

The more alternative a lifestyle, the more noise the celebrity adoption brings. Few know about the adopted children of Jamie Lee Curtis and her husband Christopher Guest (until she wrote her best-selling children's book on the subject, *Tell Me Again About the Night I Was Born*) or Steven Spielberg and Kate Capshaw, yet celebrities like Angelina Jolie and Paula Poundstone have made their accumulation of children a made-for-television lesson for society to behold. However, according to Dr. Laurel Bernau, a therapist in Santa Barbara, there are special issues endemic to the celebrity adoption. Dr. Bernau told *The Washington Times* of one famous client's high-profile adoption of a baby girl. "When the child grew older and her legs didn't look as shapely as her mother's, the narcissistic woman began telling all her friends, 'Of course she doesn't look like me—she's adopted.'"[78]

In 1997, an unknown 30-something, unmarried woman named Calista Flockhart got her big break when David E. Kelley gave the stage actress the title role in the television series "Ally McBeal." No one put a gun to Flockhart's head when she opted for career over settling down and having children.

Flockhart's adoption of a baby boy in 2002 came as a surprise to the legion of middle-class fans who related to the show's morality tale about the sacrifices single working women make. Her Dachau chic physique had already telegraphed a distress call that the stress and 16-hour workdays of a successful TV star had taken their toll; her collapsing on the set from exhaustion confirmed it. What made her think she could carry the added burden of a child—sans partner?

"Ally McBeal" costar Dyan Cannon told "Access Hollywood," "She needs something to love when she gets home and on her days off."[79] The obvious rejoinder, of course, lost on anyone within a 50-mile radius of Flockhart and Cannon's moral code, is that a child needs someone to love them full time.

Lara Croft Womb Trader: Anatomy of a Celebrity Adoption

Actress Angelina Jolie showcased her most irresponsible life choice when she boasted on ABC's "20/20" in July 2003 of her new role as an adoptive single mother to a Cambodian orphan. The twice-divorced, Oscar-winning actress—herself a product of celebrity family dysfunction (her father, actor Jon Voight, and her mother, French actress Marcheline Bertrand, divorced when she was 3)—discovered the boy during a stint as Goodwill Ambassador for the United Nation's High Commission for Refugees. Considering the *Gia* star is a refugee from her own family, her new UN role seems tailor-made for her.

Voight revealed to the E! Channel in 2002 that he is estranged from his daughter since they starred with one another in *Lara Croft Tomb Raider* and claimed that his daughter has "serious emotional problems." "She's been staying away from me because she knows I've been trying to reach her to get help," he said to an audience of millions.[80] Jolie later called his comments "unforgivable."[81]

Jolie's career has flourished despite (or perhaps because of) a public persona emphasizing the bizarre. She brags of blood rituals, a history of self-mutilation, and an obsession with the funeral sciences.[82] Her marriage to four-time divorcee and fellow Oscar winner Billy Bob Thornton earned the couple the status as King and Queen of the Hollywood Goth Prom. Tales of Jolie's unconventional upbringing—apparently her mother allowed for her to have a live-in boyfriend at age 14—paired with Thornton's phobias and colorful past created a portrait of a modern Hollywood couple unwilling to conform to societal norms.[83]

The media was agog with their madness and the lurid tales of bloodletting and wild physical interludes. Earlier, Jolie's behavior at the 2000 Academy Awards exposed her to a flood of gossip when she passionately kissed her "date" after winning an Oscar for her role in *Girl, Interrupted*, offering the jaw-dropping line: "I am just so in love with my brother! He just held me and said he loved me ... I have nothing without you. You are the strongest, most amazing man I've ever known, and I love you."[84] Up until that point, all assumed her date was her boyfriend or her husband and not her brother. The odd sequence of events in front of a billion people watching on TV around the world forced a PR defensive that only served to expose her untraditional background to further scrutiny.

Cut to Cambodia. Jolie, in a role of her own making, seeks sanctuary through a child—a child she names Maddox Chivan Thornton Jolie, abandoning his given Cambodian name of Rath Vibol. "Maddox was the last child I saw," Jolie confided to Barbara Walters during their "20/20" interview. "And he was asleep. And they put him in my arms and he stayed asleep. And then he opened his eyes and he smiled. He stared at me for two minutes, and then he smiled. And I cried and felt like this kid is okay being in my arms and he accepts me. He never cried. And ... we just hung out and became friends."[85]

Maybe when he's older, like say, four or five, the two can cut themselves and wear amulets around their necks filled with the other's blood—a show of unconditional commitment to one another.

To acquire Maddox, Jolie says she and Billy Bob had to undergo a rigorous background check administered by the U.S. Immigration Service to see if the two would make fit adoptive parents. "As an actor, it's always weird," Jolie complained. "You're being evaluated, and then you've got these crazy stories about you. And you're being evaluated whether you can be a parent and they say that you're nuts."[86]

The bumbling bureaucrats must have forgotten to ask Thornton if he had any intention of being a father to the kid. They also missed a *Rolling Stone* cover piece that described the couple as "America's most dangerous marriage." Additionally, they failed to translate one of Jolie's tattoos—"*Quod Me Nutrit Me Destruit,*" which means "That Which Feeds Me Destroys Me"—and, in the end, signed off on the high-profile, high-risk adoption, anyway.[87]

Lara Croft Womb Trader, like all dysfunctional starlets with a sudden urge for immediate unconditional love, was awarded legal custody of Maddox, who quickly became the catalyst for the demise of the storied alternative couple. "Billy and I just became very different people," Jolie lamented as scenes of a mohawk-sporting toddler played in the background. "I started focusing on traveling a lot, and really wanted to, and knew Cambodia, and really wanted to adopt a child. . . . and that was before Maddox even came home. And, by the time Maddox came home, we were kind of living apart."[88]

"I never had the feeling that they were going to make it because of both of their serious problems, and they've both been very public about them, so I never really held out any hope," Voight said. He wasn't alone.[89]

Jolie boasts of a master plan to raise Maddox on her own, splitting time between the United States and the mystical Cambodia to enable Maddox to stay in touch with his native heritage. Missing from Jolie's strategy, however, is a father for young Maddox, as she has ruled out getting married again or having a child with another man—or woman. "I think now having a child would mean that this person would become a father to my son, and that would have to be permanent, and I haven't had a good experience with that, and with my father, or with the men in my life, seeing long relationships. So, I don't want to have a temporary father for my son."[90]

Why is there no concern whatsoever on placing a full-time male role model permanently in his life? Didn't Anthony Perkins's star turn as Norman Bates lay out the inevitable ending of that horror story line? Given her estranged relationship with her father and now Billy Bob Thornton, the one male in her life who looks to be front and center for the kid is Uncle James Haven. Maybe Jon Voight can utilize some of his reserve Hollywood cache to save the kid and cast him in a celebrity reality series entitled "Run, Maddox, Run." Only in celebrity sycophant Barbara Walters's hyperbolic chamber of inverted values and nonjudgmentalism could the expressions of a twisted sensibility escape without journalistic scrutiny.

And why is Maddox's ethnic background worthy of creating a sanctuary for him in a country noted for genocide within the last generation? Had the child been abandoned in a less PC and less exotic environment, like Appalachia, would Jolie be setting up a compound in the hills of West Virginia so Maddox could be close to his moonshine-distilling people?

It might be safer. "They've removed 48 unexploded land mines so far," Jolie divulged to *People* magazine. "I'm sure some people will question why I'm bringing my son into an area with land mines. When I looked around, I saw other families and thought, 'Why shouldn't *I*? *I'm* happy there.'"[91] And, really, who wouldn't be happy waking up to a panoramic view of *The Killing Fields*? Hopefully, what remains of the Khmer Rouge has grown more open-minded to the role of the artist in society, and will leave the naive new neighbors in peace.

The "C" in Designer C-Section Stands for...

Liz Hurley sure knew how to start her son Damian's life off on a demonic note. First, she got impregnated by film producer Steven Bing (whose credits include, naturally, the film *Why Men Shouldn't Marry*), a man who didn't want to have a child with the actress in the first place (though he's subsequently offered child support).[92] According to at least one British tabloid, even private dick to the stars Anthony Pellicano publicly questioned Hurley's claims of paternity on Bing's behalf. Bing, a close pal of Bill Clinton, appropriately, would have been more subtle yelling, "Slut!" in a crowded theater.[93]

Second, Hurley had the controversial C-section. For some celebrities—it is unclear whether Hurley fits in this category—it's a fatuous vanity procedure having questionable medical benefits.[94] In the past, the surgical procedure was relegated to medical emergencies, yet it is now being scheduled a week or two in advance of more than a few self-absorbed stars' scheduled delivery as a means to avoid stretch marks and other post-natal aesthetic inconveniences. In the case of Hurley, Mike Myer's costar in the first *Austin Powers* flick, she reportedly had her incision made below her "bikini line."[95]

Yeah, baby!

"She scheduled the tummy tuck right after the C-section," Knight-Ridder Newspapers reported, citing "inside sources." Hurley showed up less than two months after her delivery at a charity function wearing a show-stopping skintight gown, a coming-out ritual now customary for postpartum sex symbols showing they still have it.[96] Obsessed with her postnatal physique, Hurley told the British media, "I have killed myself to try and shed the pounds—all 53 of them."[97]

The elective C-section, as it is clinically known, is clear evidence of the self-obsessed behavior exhibited by some celebrity mothers finding new ways to push the narcissistic envelope. Someone should deliver the heartbreaking news to these vain expectant mothers that most doctors agree by that time the damage is already done. "The abdomen is already stretched out by that time," Boston doctor Sharon Margulies said in an investigation into the trend by NBC's San Francisco affiliate KNTV. "It isn't safe to do an elective C-section. If you could avoid perhaps the last three months, that would make a difference, but obviously that wouldn't be safe for the baby."[98]

Perhaps it's just a coincidence but Victoria "Posh Spice" Beckham, Zoe Ball, Melanie Blatt, and Catherine Zeta-Jones also had C-sections. Are they UK tarts on the vanguard of a transatlantic trend, or are they simply statistical anomalies who actually required the procedure?[99] Incidentally, while eight months pregnant with her second child, Mrs. Michael Douglas performed a strenuous song and dance number from the hit musical *Chicago* at the 2003 Oscars, as an ambulance waited outside in case her water broke during a particularly high note or difficult move.[100] Anglophile Madonna scheduled her C-section based upon her reading of the Kabbalistic calendar.[101] Oy gevalt!

"Mother's love" is supposed to be the definitive example of selfless love, but celebrity women now bastardize that notion. In Hollywood, mother's love refers to the mother's love of herself, and their postpartum hard bodies, in particular. Thankfully, some are willing to criticize the idiotic behavior. "If they are willing to have children," one mother told NBC, "they should go the 40 weeks, or however long, without worrying about their image."[102]

If only America had Fleet Street where Victoria Beckham's designer C-section was met bluntly with the scornful populist headline: "TOO POSH TO PUSH."

Sarah Jessica Parker, Cindy Crawford, and Hurley are cited as adherents of Pilates and yoga as a means to get their tummies back to award show–acceptable size. Parker was seen flaunting her washboard waistline and wearing a black corset top at the Golden Globes two months after giving birth to her first kid, James.[103] "The supermom syndrome has expanded from working and having kids, to working and having kids and having a body like this," Dr. Jan Christilaw, a Vancouver-based OB-GYN and in charge of the specialized women's health at British Columbia Women's Hospital told the *National Post.* "It is not attainable in most women's lives—nor should it be."[104] But incredibly, influential female role models in Hollywood, with their priorities up their increasingly tighter derrieres, are sending out the message that it is.

My Kid's Mom: Passing the Parental Buck

Cultural elites and the suburban mother are at war, and populist bullets fly daily on the Dr. Laura Schlesinger radio show. The show's slogan, parroted by many female callers, "I'm my kid's mom," is an affirmation of stay-at-home motherhood, and a not-so-subtle attack on the feminist movement's promotion of nannies and day care over primary mommy care.

In Hollywood, however, there is no debate. The nanny is not only a foregone conclusion, but a central parental status symbol, along with sending the kids to the right trendy school and creating "play dates" with the right trendy kids of other celebrities and industry moguls. Many celebrity parents employ multiple nannies to oversee the daily grind, often on a one-to-one basis, or one better. Tom Cruise and Nicole Kidman (1990–2001) employed one nanny for each kid and a full-time nurse.

Demi Moore and Bruce Willis employed four nannies for their three children Rumer, Scout, and Tallulah. One, Kim Tannahill, took the couple to court claiming the couple "shamelessly exploited and abused (her), through fraud, deceit, oppression, intimidation, threats and force."[105] Tannahill lost the case, but even if the charges weren't true, for three years Moore and Willis entrusted the lives of their daughters to a woman who they claimed, in their own court filings, was "...a dishonest and disloyal employee who, among other things, misappropriated moneys... improperly billed personal expenses to plaintiffs' accounts, failed to follow instructions and, on occasion, improperly performed her duties in dealing with the children."[106]

Apparently mishandling the children as a celebrity nanny isn't sufficient grounds for firing, but woe to the Hollywood hired help who "work and tell," violating nondisclosure clauses by revealing private details of their employers' twisted lives and value systems.

A Modest Proposal

It is a melancholy object to those who witness an industry filled with rich and famous people possessing no hint of common sense, and exhibiting pathological parenting behavior.

It may sound harsh, like no-smoking laws at bars, or requiring catalytic converters to cut down on vehicle emissions, or China's one child policy, but in time people will realize it is for the greater good: Celebrities should not be allowed to have children. Period.

Women entering Hollywood and getting the all-important Screen Actors Guild card should immediately have the controversial Norplant birth control device implanted in their upper arm. Men should be given vasectomies. Both procedures are reversible, and upon giving up their glamorous pursuits, for whatever reason, they should then be granted full reproductive options.

Nor should celebrities be allowed to adopt—whether through private attorneys, trips to Third World nations, or utilizing in vitro surrogate wombs for rent. The celebrity family tree should be contained until a generation of self-obsessed and self-indulgent overgrown toddlers learns to live within the liberal parameters of what constitutes an emotionally healthy life, and proves they can exhibit rational behavior for a prolonged period of time. We'll let the electorate decide when that time comes.

This is not just to protect kids from celebrities, and celebrities from themselves. This is about stopping the most prominent role models in the world from hastening the demise of Western civilization. Celebrities simply can't perform in the role of parenthood.

The law for those celebrities who now have children, like Madonna, will be grandfathered. Lourdes and Rocco are spared—for now. But child protective services should be on her and Guy Ritchie or whomever and they should be on an especially short leash, just like other suspect classes. Angelina and Maddox Jolie of Phnom Penh by way of Malibu may have to lay low in the Mekong Delta until the coast is clear.

We profess, in the sincerity of our heart, that we have not the least personal interest in endeavoring to promote this necessary work, having no other motive than the public good of our country.

2

HOLLYWOOD NANNIES

The long hot celebrity news summer of 2001 began with a splash on Saturday, June 16, as the pop music festival Wango Tango arrived at Dodger Stadium in Los Angeles. Hosted by Britney Spears, and featuring Ricky Martin, the Backstreet Boys, and the Bee Gees, the kiddy pornish concert didn't cause any scandal, but found itself at the center of a tragedy that exposed the dark side of Hollywood parenting, where neglected children are handed off to inept nannies and babysitters while the parents go about their business of being self-important.

That Saturday, rocker Tommy Lee, former drummer of the band Motley Crue and costar of a pornographic honeymoon video featuring former spouse Pamela Anderson, threw a birthday party at his Malibu home for his five-year-old son, Brandon Lee. Among the 15 preschoolers and their guardians invited were four-year-old Daniel

Karven-Veres, son of actress Ursula Karven and James Veres, along with his caretaker, German au pair Christian Weihs.

Opting to leave the party early to attend the Wango Tango festival, Weihs asked another nanny, Judith Zeihm, to look after Daniel. "Don't worry," the au pair told Daniel's mother, when he arrived at her home at 2:30 PM to get ready for the concert. "He's out of the water." Karven, according to her testimony in court during a civil suit against Tommy Lee, said, "What water?" and testified that this was the first time she had heard about water.[1]

While host Tommy Lee talked with his "life coach"[2] and stand-in nanny Zeihm was out walking her dog, another party guest, 20-year-old Janelle Harris, stepped into the pool and onto the body of Daniel Veres. Tommy Lee called 911, and other adults tried vainly to resuscitate Daniel, but by the time the paramedics arrived, the boy was a corpse.[3] Therein lay the crux of the Veres's lawsuit against Tommy Lee. They felt life vests should have been provided, a lifeguard should have been on duty, and more responsible adults should have been poolside.[4]

Yes, indeed, adults more responsible than au pair Christian Weihs—who fled home to Deutschland several days after the accident, and could not be located for months, arriving on the stand in a Perry Masonesque flourish.[5] Perhaps adults more responsible than dog-walking "child watcher" Judith Zeihm should have been left in charge of young Daniel.[6] Or maybe, on learning that an adult-sized swimming pool was involved and that her child's minder was on the way to rock out at Dodger Stadium, maybe the stunning blond Ursula Karven should have at least made a phone call, or driven the few miles to Tommy Lee's Malibu estate to keep an eye on her beloved son.[7] Alas, none of these scenarios occurred, and young Brandon Lee's birthday party memories now include flashbacks of news helicopter footage and televised court reports.

The wrongful death civil lawsuit was filed February 21, 2002, and dismissed April 17, 2003. It would appear that during that time, the distraught mother costarred in the made-for-TV movie, *Never Say Goodbye*, airing just 10 weeks before the final verdict.[8] Who looked after her other child while Mrs. Veres was pursuing her career in Canada? Who knows? But actress Ursula Karven and her husband—

a "former national champion swimmer" who dabbled in film and television production and acted in minor roles in the 1970s and early 1980s—are no different from hundreds of Hollywood families who employ hired help to raise their children.[9]

In Hollywood, the two main castes that employ nannies are stars and the people who make them. When hired by these people of privilege, many nannies are required to sign nondisclosure or privacy agreements, threatening huge lawsuits should the nannies reveal even the brand of baby lotion used in their employers' household. However, we found more than one professional child-care worker whose employers neglected to get their signatures, and their stories provide a horrifying look at child rearing among the rich and famous.

Mary Poppins

Once an actress has plastic surgery, Golden Globe awards, a private jet, and several homes, what's left? "The most fulfilling role of my lifetime," spout many a toothy star on any given talk show: "Motherhood." If pregnancy might get in the way of another role of a lifetime—say a potential Oscar-winning role—or interferes with a shooting schedule, there's always adoption. And if conception is a problem, well, surrogate mothers or in vitro fertilization are available and expensive ways around that problem. As Hollywood nanny number one, "Sunny" (whose continuous employment in celebrity child care depends on her anonymity and concealment of her past employers) says, "It's not enough for Steven Spielberg to have four [children] of his own, he has to go buy more."[10]

Explains Sunny, a veteran nanny in her thirties whose clients have included some of the heaviest players in Hollywood on both sides of the camera: "Celebrities see their kid as an accessory. And the novelty wears off exactly the same way the novelty wears off their new plane, their boat, and their second house. And so, those kids are abandoned."[11]

Maybe Katherine Hepburn was right. In essence, the venerable actress revealed in her biography *Kate Remembered*: You cannot do everything, and you have to decide what it is you want to do. So, she made an appropriate choice by not having children. But today's stars and starmakers lack the wisdom of the late Kate. States Sunny, "These people are greedy. I mean, that's what it all boils down to, they are greedy beyond words. Somebody else has a kid? They have to have one."

Dragged out for photo ops, expected to keep their mouths shut and look pretty, these star spawn endure the horrendous indignity of listening to their parents on talk shows talking about how "fabulous it is being a parent," and how much they "love" their children while the objects in question—and they are treated as such—sit at home with the hired help.

At 18, Suzanne Hansen trained at the Northwest Nanny Institute in Oregon. Reflecting on her late Eighties foray into Hollywood family life, at 35, she has written a self-published memoir, *You'll Never Nanny in this Town Again,* largely about her thinly veiled experience with then Hollywood royalty, the Michael Ovitzes. In this breezy narrative she recounts a story about another nanny who purposefully used a hand vacuum to eliminate an actor's stash of cocaine in the bathroom. "It wasn't the cocaine snorting that got to me. It was watching him on a talk show... telling the understanding host about the evils of drugs," said the Dirt Devil-wielding nanny. Once she heard that story, Hansen began to watch daytime talk shows featuring her past employers or the employers of nannies she knew. Hansen was stunned to hear how the stars' descriptions of their child-rearing and home-making abilities were so fantastically different from the events she experienced and those related by her colleagues. If the truth came out, writes Hansen in her book, the nannies would have to be placed in a witness protection program.[12]

What does it tell a kid when the secretary to the mother comes to a parent-teacher conference, or when the Hispanic maid who can't speak English does the child's homework for him because the mother is getting hair extensions put in, and it takes all day? Sunny, who worked for a dashing television actor and his movie star wife during one of their marriages in the early nineties, recounts an appalling story: "I went with [the movie star mother] on a school interview one time, and the headmistress asked her what kind of play her daughter was into—was she into Barbies, make-believe, art? There was no possible way that [the mother] could answer that because she never, ever spent any time with her daughter. And, her answer was, 'You're just going to have to find out.' That was her answer to the question. She didn't even know her child."[13]

Sunny was outraged by her employers' lack of care and affection for their children. "With one of the families I worked for, the kids were in therapy—and I had to go with them once a week. Do you think that the parents were going to go? No."[14]

While traveling with the TV star and movie star family, Sunny was outraged to discover the parents doing drugs on an airplane flight with their children in tow. It was her job to keep the kids happy and quiet while the parents flew high—very, very high. When that mother's middle child went into rehab at 17, mommy dearest actually went public, admitting the fact that she smoked pot with him and stating, "I thought it would be good if we did it together." Sunny has a point, albeit far more radical than our argument for mandatory Norplant and vasectomies: "When you get your Screen Actors Guild card, you should get sterilized."[15]

Sunny says of her stint as a nanny to some of Hollywood's most powerful people, "Almost all the kids that I know of ended up in rehab, usually more than once. One of the kids tried to kill herself and she is now only 22 years old. She was in psychiatric hospitals for [attempted] suicide, and drugs and alcohol." Hollywood children end up lousy students as well. "Three of the kids that I took care of have been to more than one college," says Sunny of her privileged charges. Luckily, their wealthy and well-placed parents can afford the huge donations (read: bribes) necessary to admit and keep their kids in four-year liberal arts holding tanks away from home with the hope for humanity that maybe the youths will develop into anything but them.[16]

While the children of stars can be sad and difficult, it's the offspring of executives that are the real brats. According to Sunny, who worked for a major producer-director, and Hansen, who nannied for former Hollywood alpha-male agent Mike Ovitz's three children, the little darlings are never, ever reprimanded. Sunny shakes her head in disbelief and says, "Nobody ever said, aside from the nannies, 'That's unacceptable behavior.'" Adds Hansen, "[Judy Ovitz] did not command for him [the six-year-old] to be respectful at all to any adults."[17]

It was the staff who received the brunt of abuse from the children. "First of all, I can't tell you how many times I've been threatened by a child about being fired," says Sunny.[18] At Ovitz's house, Hansen claims the children continually told the staff (including Hansen) that they'd "have Daddy fire you."[19]

Hansen says that the children learn by example from their parents on how to treat the adults in the household. "Because the man treated the staff very disrespectfully, and would say very inappropriate, adult things to the child such as, 'Oh that stupid Maria! She makes me so mad when she does that. I can't believe it. I hated that other Nanny we had. . . .' Saying inappropriate things that you should not be telling your children about the staff led him to know that we were paid workers."[20] In her book, Hansen recounts that the six-year-old of one Hollywood honcho would scream at her, saying, "I hate you. You're an idiot," while the child of another Hollywood heavy would repeatedly tell his nanny, "You're fat and ugly."[21]

Sunny shakes her head, "You never hear a mother coming in and saying 'Uh-oh. Please don't talk to her like that. She is a valuable member of our family. She's taking care of you, she's ironing your clothes, she's driving you to school, she's helping you with your homework—you don't speak to someone like that. . . . And, she's an adult and she deserves some respect.' But no, no, no—that would never happen. The parents would laugh and think it's hilarious [when the kids would abuse us]."

Explains Sunny about many Movie Town families, including some she worked for, "A lot of Hollywood couples remain married because it is too expensive to separate. They can't afford it. So they stay together and hate each other. They hate each other, but the thought of splitting up? It's not going to happen. Nobody wants to part with whatever material things that they have—because that's far more important than anything else. So, they kind of come to some kind of bizarre peace where they are civil to each other, and they run their marriage like a [business]."

Suzanne Hansen noticed this as well. The level of communication and what couples would share with each other wasn't present, and the actual amount of time Hollywood couples interacted with each other was limited because of their schedules.

Nowhere is this more obvious than the following heartfelt note Hansen says Michael Ovitz sent to his wife through the CAA office.

> *Dear [Judy]:*
>
> *We don't get the chance to talk or see each other that much. I just wanted to take this opportunity to express my gratitude for the professional and thorough job you did on the premier. Your efforts in such matters are appreciated.*
>
> *Love,*
>
> *[Michael]*[22]

There were no flowers, nor a piece of jewelry included with the note; just the cold formal words sent out from the office.

Once married, these sad women have kids as fast as they can and they pawn them off on the nannies. They don't always care what kind of nanny they get as long as that nanny will keep the kids out of their hair, away from them, quiet, and, in effect, not in their lives. Or, as Suzanne Hansen found out when she attended a "nanny support group" in Beverly Hills, nannies are, for the most part, poorly educated and poorly paid, making as little as $150 dollars a week (the going rate today is less then $300) as full-time housekeeper/nannies.[23]

Once a child is born to a family of wealth and questionable taste, an around-the-clock baby nurse is hired. Often older women, very rigid in their ways, their job is to get the baby to sleep through the night. During the six weeks they take care of the baby 24 hours a day. These nurses are also called *doula*, a word that, ironically or appropriately, comes from the ancient Greek and means "most important female slave" in a household. Nowadays doulas' jobs range from prepartum care to being present at the birth through long-term postpartum care, though most Hollywood households opt only for the latter aspect.[24]

And then, after Austin or Madison is sleeping through the night, it's time for the nannies to step in and take over. But by this time, the damage to the parent-child relationship has already started. "Does he know I'm his father? I'm not sure he does," reportedly pondered Ovitz once looking at his eight-month-old son before going off to a hard day at CAA.[25] "How do you put him to bed? What do you do? Can I rock him after he's had his bottle?" the super agent's wife asked of the same baby several months after the child had been born.[26] According to Hansen, it was her first time ever attempting to attend to her baby.

Once the child is left in the hands of an employee, the birth mother is free to do what she does best—organize charity benefits,[27] exercise (one of the rules in the Ovitz house was that neither parent could be interrupted during their workout), or shop. And after a hard day at Barney's and Saks, they're too exhausted to be with their kids.

"Their addictions are so huge, and they are addicted to *things*. They're shop-a-holics like you cannot imagine. There is a whole sub-culture of Hollywood mothers who do nothing but shop. I mean, that's their job," says a shuddering Sunny.[28]

In Sunny's experience, the mothers are addicts; the professional shoppers are pushers. "At all the stores there are special contacts, associates who do nothing but cater to these women. And, if you don't work in a house like this, you can't imagine the crap that is sent over on a weekly basis. Neiman Marcus, Saks, Fred Segal—any of them— they will, on approval, send over a whole closet thing full of crap for women to look pretty."[29] Considerately, the stores remove the price tags so the hired help won't see a blouse or undergarment priced at about their entire month's salary.[30]

And while the lady of the house shopped either from her Frette sheeted bed or on Jimmy Choo–clad foot, it fell to the nanny to do the normal things a parent should do. Sunny recalls her stint at the director-producer's house. "The therapist would actually tell me that the nine-year-old 'needed to be hugged and shown affection.' And that clearly wasn't my job, yet I did it. Yet, I was completely replace-able."[31] The transient nature of nannies made things all the more dif-ficult for Sunny. She saw a pervasive attitude in Hollywood where people were completely replaceable and expendable. "When you bring someone into your house, be it an immigrant or a college stu-dent, or an older person—whoever you get to care for your child, that is an important role. And it's really, really damaging for this child to see, over and over again, people getting fired, people leaving, people being abused. What does that tell that kid?" she asks rhetorically.[32]

One result seen by all the nannies was a lack of toilet training culminating in defiant territorial peeing—children literally pissed off.
One of the TV star/movie star brood, reports Sunny, "was wearing
diapers at five, while another family has one child that urinated wherever she felt like it and the other was also wearing diapers at five."[33]

Such stories are endemic, explains Sunny. "Almost every kid that
I've taken care of, or been involved with at that level, they all have
these weird peeing or shitting problems. All of them . . . . I have so
many stories about bathroom problems that are bizarre. Some of
them up until they were like 18 years old."[34]

Ovitz's six-year-old son urinated in the front yard on a tree, and
Suzanne Hansen recounted that she reprimanded him for doing that
in public. "Mom said I could," whined the bad seed, body waste
dripping on his loafers. Hansen shook her head in disbelief. "Oh, you
don't know anything!" the little demon screamed. "My mom said
I could, and my mom is in charge of you, I can have you fired." And
indeed, according to Hansen, Mrs. Ovitz had okayed the outdoor
toilet stop, confirming her son's outburst as she strolled up. "Oh yes,
Suzy, I told him it was okay. We're in a hurry and I don't want him
to go all the way back to the house."[35]

Things were similarly bizarre and destructively permissive with
Sunny's charges in Brentwood at the home of the highly paid, highly
successful director-producer. All three children were doing poorly
in school. The nine-year-old was scared of his own shadow and he
wet his bed constantly. The 12-year-old was breaking into the neighbors' house, while the four-year-old threw horrible temper tantrums,
destroying her room, pulling all of her clothes out of drawers, tip-
ping over furniture. When Sunny would tell her that she'd have to
clean up the mess she'd made, the mother would step in, saying,
"Awww, honey. You're having a bad day." Sunny's response, "No, she's
not having a bad day, she's having a temper tantrum." Her advice,
"She needs to get back into her room and clean it up," was met with
blank stares.[36]

Every time the four-year-old would have any kind of problem—
she'd hurt herself, done badly in school, or gotten into a fight—her
mother would immediately give the kid a candy, or ice cream, or
Popsicle. That would get her and the other kids addicted to a sub-

stance one nitrogen atom away from cocaine,[37] using food as a reward. "I used to say to the mother all the time, "Don't do that! You are making an addict. You're also teaching your kid that whenever she does something wrong, she is rewarded," explained Sunny, to no avail.[38]

According to Sunny, this mother had a horrible drug problem, and when she would have a nightmare, she would come into the kids' rooms and wake them up announcing, "Let's have a party in my bed!" They would come into her room in the middle of the night and she'd give them sodas and chocolate, and let them watch a movie, regardless of the children's early morning school schedules.[39]

Another job showed Sunny the hypocrisy of Hollywood. While regularly making fun of Sunny's conventional belief system, the mother would have consultations with plastic surgeons. Then, she'd get the doctor's birth date and time of birth for her astrologer at a thousand dollars a pop, in order to get her doctor's chart to see if he was the right doctor for her nose job, boob lift, or tummy tuck. Another mother spent $600 an hour for a "psychic massage" where someone would stand over her and not even put their hands on her. "What's up with that?" asks Sunny. "To have someone come over and wave their hands over you for $600??? I don't think so."[40]

But it was while working for the well-known director-producer that Sunny saw the greatest hypocrisy. Her employers were heavy contributors to the Democratic Party. Like many deep-pocket donors, they were invited by President Clinton to join him in Washington, D.C. The husband was too busy to go, but Sunny traveled with his wife.[41] "We had dinner at the Gephardt's house, dinner with the Speaker of the House. I mean, you can't imagine—sitting at dinner with Barbra Streisand and Barbara Boxer."

At the time the big-issue political talking point was insurance for small businesses, and how American insurance and medical care was out of control. At one point during a meeting, Secretary of Health and Human Services Donna Shalala was "talking about how horrible the Republicans were because people can't get adequate medical care because they don't have insurance." Sunny's boss turned to her and said, "We're going to change this. Thank God Clinton is in office." The nanny was appalled. "Here I am, working for these multibillionaires. Billionaires! In that home they had nine full-time staff members. Not one of these people had insurance. I said, 'Well, why don't you start with your house by getting everybody that works for you insurance?'" Her suggestion was not taken into consideration.[42]

After a series of disastrous vacations with the Ovitzes, Suzanne Hansen began to realize that despite another year on her contract, she could no longer continue to work in an environment where she claims that her employers expected her to be on call 24 hours a day, six days a week, except on holidays when she worked a full seven days around the clock; where there was no laughter; where threats from six-year-olds were de rigeur in a household where the art work was more important than the children[43]; and where the ruler of the household was "a sad pitiful shell that in reality had nothing but things."[44]

When she screwed up the courage to tell her employers she was quitting, she says she felt the full wrath of Michael Ovitz, head of Creative Artists Agency. "Could you wait until after the Aspen trip? Could you wait until she gets back from the Golden Door," asked the concerned husband about his wife's trip to an expensive health resort/spa. "She deserves this."[45] Then, according to Hansen, he asked, "Do you really plan to work here in this town as a nanny?"[46]

That day, the same day, Hansen says Ovitz asked if she planned on working again, was the day she had to leave the Ovitz house. Hansen's nanny placement agency had found other jobs for her, but she claims that she was effectively blacklisted from the houses of those in the entertainment industry.[47] According to Hansen, in order to allow Hansen to be released from her contract, Ovitz made the agency agree that she could only work in nonshowbiz households.[48]

"Isn't it hilarious that he took so much time to do that? That's hilarious," Hansen laughs now. But at the time, Ovitz was apparently making it personal. "There was talk of getting my sister fired from the Creative Artists Agency," says Hansen. "She worked there in the accounting department, and she is a fabulous employee. And so, I think they knew they couldn't do that—flat out fire her—because there would be a legal issue. Her boss told her that there was 'great discussion about that' though."[49]

Some Hollywood nannies have done quite well for themselves. Robin Williams married his children's nanny after divorcing his first wife and ending another affair that wrecked his marriage; they have two children together, and one from Williams's first marriage. Long before the question arose whether he was married to the mob, Mike Ovitz's personal trainer turned action star/guru Steve Seagal upped the nanny ante while married to Kelly LeBrock. Fascinated by her children's caretaker, Arissa Wolf, Seagal creepily named his and LeBrock's daughter after the babysitter and then left LeBrock for the nanny amid rumors of LeBrock's accusations of spousal abuse. Arissa the elder is still believed to be Seagal's "companion," having born a daughter with him named Savannah.

Suzanne Hansen and Sunny emerged relatively unscathed from their lives as Hollywood nannies. Hansen is now, in a wonderful bit of serendipity, a labor and delivery nurse, a wife, and a mom, happily raising her own brood in Oregon. Sunny does volunteer work and is happily nannying for what she calls a "normal family." Though her boss is a wealthy successful Hollywood personality, there is none of the bedwetting, tantrums, or unchecked addictions that characterized her past posts in the minefield of Hollywood marital dysfunction. As a personal cautionary tale, Sunny remembers the TV/movie star family's mile-high party in the sky. "What was that life?" she asks. "A chaotic mess. And I think my experience, my grace, has been really helpful in that, by example, I have not gotten sucked into that kind of lifestyle." In closing, she tips her nanny cap to Suzanne Hansen. "Wow!" she exclaims with a hint of envy. "Suzanne has something the people I've worked for will never have. She actually got out of Hollywood and found a man and is personally raising her own children that she loves. She's actually making a contribution to the world."[50]

3

If there's any question whether fame and related Hollywood power infect the celebrity gene pool, we need only visit an elite academy where the Hollywood haves dump their offspring, and according to alums, drugs, debauchery, and death collect effortlessly in their wake.

The road to hell is paved with good intentions, but when experimental academia and parents' good intentions jeopardize the lives of students, it's time to take a gander.[1]

> We had spent all week at Ryan's house, and Ryan and I wanted the night alone. . . . We went in to check on Phillip, and Phillip couldn't shoot himself up. I usually do it for him, anyway. I shot him up, and after I shot him up he had this rush. Whatever. I don't even know, but, as I was sitting right next to him at Ryan's desk mixing my batch, Phillip put the song "Heroin" by Velvet Underground on repeat. . . . I felt nauseous, and I went into Ryan's bathroom and stood

at the sink throwing up, and when I went back in the room, Phillip
was like blue and dead, and I guess he had had a seizure and
probably been dying when I was sitting next to him—but I didn't even
look up. I freaked out. He was stiff as a board; his eyes were in his
head, he was all blue. Little trickles of saliva. He was breathing.
I moved him, I tried to give him CPR, but he had swallowd this
tongue....I ran and got Ryan, and we tried everything, but we couldn't
get him back to life....

The narrator of this true scenario—a pretty and pierced teen we'll call Madeleine—didn't get to spend the night alone with Ryan. A friend nearly dying, paramedics, cops, and—oh yeah—parents in absentia, have a way of messing up a high. And high school. Folks, this ain't "Beverly Hills 90210;" it's more like *Less Than Zero.*

Since leaving her elite prep school, Madeleine—sprung from a fractured family of Hollywood elitists—has attended college and has spoken to seventh and eighth graders about her four off-campus drug arrests. The aforementioned incident, and the subsequent dismissal from school, was followed by months of in-patient therapy at a rehabilitation clinic in Minnesota. She was of the best, the brightest. As were her two cohorts, Ryan and Phillip, who were also arrested and then expelled their junior year.

Madeleine was a daily pot smoker in seventh grade. By eighth grade she was smoking bud day and night and binge drinking, and had added amphetamines to the mix. The former straight-A student reflects, "Every time I was on speed I would perk up and lead class discussions, and all the teachers were like, 'Why don't you do this all the time?' I was like, 'What's up? You want me to be speeding all the time?'"

Ninth grade was Madeleine's "hippie faze," which included LSD, hallucinogenic mushrooms, and ecstasy. Her first arrest for possession of drugs (LSD and marijuana) and a trespassing charge went down that freshman year. When she told the arresting officer where she went to school, he commented, "Oh, *that* explains it."

Tenth grade was about any drug she could get her hands on, including PCP. "Every pill under the sun," she says. If a prescription bottle warned, "Do not operate heavy machinery," to her, "Those were directions to take it." During the summer between sophomore and junior years, she first tried heroin.

A typical upper-class school day for Madeleine would begin getting picked up for school at her long-divorced mother's home in a hippie enclave by best friend Ryan. They'd pull over and shoot heroin, and then make first period. Mid-morning snack time was spent sneaking out to the parking lot with heavily trust-funded girlfriends to smoke pot—an activity that would "keep her high until lunch." During lunch period, Madeleine and drug casualty in training Phillip would roll out to nearby Lincoln Boulevard in seedy Venice, where they'd score heroin. If they didn't have afternoon classes (which was often the case), they'd pick up Ryan and head back to Madeleine's house, where, Madeleine explains, "Since my mom wouldn't get home from work until six, we'd shoot up all day. You know, lie around, smoking, putting on music, and shooting up all day." Anticipating mom's arrival, Ryan and Phillip would split and Madeleine would be in bed by 5:30 PM. "I don't know how she put up with me," says Madeleine of her mom, "but I didn't like her, I didn't want to be with her—so, I'd be napping all the time." Later in the evening, she'd sneak out of the house and shoot dope again with Ryan.

The bisexual Madeleine had been Ryan's best friend since they met in seventh grade, and counting him as her last high school boyfriend, she acknowledges that it was heroin that brought them together. Her mom was oblivious to all this. "Uh, she pretty much had no idea, but I had got arrested three times in a period of three months for heroin, so she was kind of sort of clueing in."

While Madeleine's parents were patently clueless, Ryan's movie industry folks seemed to have slept through much of his golden rule days. "The night Phillip overdosed, they were upstairs sleeping," says Madeleine. "We had the paramedics in there, we had the cops in there, and they were all milling about for about a half hour thinking that Ryan owned the house because Ryan was trying to manipulate the situation so they wouldn't find out that his parents were upstairs sleeping. Finally it was evident that he was a kid, he was in school, he was 17, and, uh, they went up and woke the parents. But they would have slept through the whole fucking thing."

Crossroads—A Distinctly Progressive School

Nestled smack in the middle of a Santa Monica, California, barrio is the $20,000-a-year college preparatory institution called Crossroads School for Arts & Sciences. Except for those who feed the conflux of mostly white, hip-hop–styling, happy-hippie, stoned surfer, beglittered rave mavens, few Latinos are found on the campus constructed as a gilded ghetto around an alley. A few African-American students are spotted sporting letterman's jackets, and the orchestral Asian faction tote their violin cases around, circumventing a *kaffeeklatsch* of rich Los Angeles Jewish kids sprinkled with a token lot of goyim.

In his touching eulogy to a Crossroads administrator we'll meet later, *Vanity Fair* editor/Crossroads alumnus Matt Tyrnauer describes his alma mater best:

> Crossroads—which, I know, sounds like a drug-rehab center—
> is a unique institution. . . . Crossroads was (and is) a cradle of
> Limousine Liberalism . . . founded in the 1970s on radical,
> hippish principles overtaken (or taken up) by radical chic
> Hollywood. It is the kind of place Tom Wolfe or Joan Didion
> would have had a field day writing about. It was [a] . . . funky and
> somewhat out of its mind place. . . . This was a sensitive, hippie
> school, filled with hot house flowers, coddled children of
> McGovern liberals; faculty who were members of the SDS [the
> radical Students for a Democratic Society]—people given to
> over-reaction. . . .

Another Crossroads alum, Hollywood journalist (*Vanity Fair*) and fiction writer (*On Spec*, St. Martin's) Richard Rushfield shares: "It used to be that everyone at Crossroads was either Jewish, Baptist, or Buddhist. The Baptists and Buddhists were all on scholarships. The white goyim were the ones on the baseball team." His television writer (CBS sitcom "The Stones") sister Ali Rushfield quips, "The black people that weren't on the basketball team were also Jews."

The Crossroads administration ardently claims diversity at the school (they have an adjacent academy courting inner-city kids called New Roads), but what really makes this place unique is that, in the last quarter century, it has prepped an entire generation of "young

Hollywood." Some—including actress Zooey Deschanel, (*Elf*) roots rock singer-songwriter Gillian Welch, A-list movie director Michael Bay (*Armageddon, Pearl Harbor*), that guy with the metal plate in his head's progeny actor Jake Busey, comic actor Jack Black (*School of Rock*), actress Kate Hudson, *Lord of the Rings* trilogist Sean Astin, and "Saturday Night Live's" Maya Rudolph—now play in the star-studded fields of the entertainment industry.

Other Crossroads alumni are dead before their time: Holly s (1997), killed in an environmental education course skiing mishap[2]; Morgan Leslie Segal, Class of 1985, a post-graduate suicide casualty[3]; and Daisy L. Sampson, 1987—self-inflicted gun-shot–destroyed daughter of actor/suicide victim, Brian Keith.[4] Some alumnae are in and out of scrapes with the law. For example: Marxist ex-faculty member Jeff Cooper's son, the currently incarcerated Zeke Cooper, Class of 1986, and Victoria Sellers whose (pre–Heidi Fleiss association) main postgraduate achievement was posing for *Playboy*. Also, *Die Hard* director John McTiernan's stepson Ethan Dubrow, who accidentally blew away his best friend with a shotgun blast at a dinner party.[5] (When we last checked, Crossroads has no elective course on gun safety in their curriculum.)

While many from these kids' parents' generation have had the dubious luxury of living long enough to see friends wind up dead or in jail, these kids are often doomed to the same fate accelerated, or survive to make movies about it. One girl, writer Jessica Kaplan (who recently perished in a tragic private plane accident that ironically displaced a Hollywood creative community living in the apartment building destroyed in the crash),[6] tried to capitalize on the latter route.

Equal parts Lolita/Anaïs Nin, the late Jessica Kaplan at 16 penned an unproduced movie called *The Powers That Be*, which was promptly picked up by REM rocker Michael Stipe's hip film company before she began her senior year. Although Kaplan, in an interview held a few years before her death, coyly counted her screenplay as more of "a look at media and pop culture," her story of rich white kids emulating hip-hop culture to tragic, if not soap-operatic, ends definitely seems Crossroads-inspired, or, at least prep school–prophetic. The *Los Angeles Times* noted that, in Kaplan's script, "a young male teacher helps the script's heroine deal with the crises it [kids involved with gangsta culture] causes." Interestingly, the young male teacher in Kaplan's story has sex with the 17-year-old heroine *and* the school's headmistress.

Small wonder the character that gets his head blown off for trying to be hard in the face of a real gangsta in classmate Kaplan's screenplay is surnamed "Kessler." Her creative nemesis from the same class is filmmaker and college student, Eric Kessler, Class of 1997.

"I've read some of her [Kaplan's] script," sneers Kessler, "and it's a direct result of her surroundings. And the denial of that makes her seem ridiculous, you know?" This synapse-exploding savant describes the Crossroads scene: "[Crossroads] is like an opium den," Kessler explains, yet, ironically, at present, he seems safer from chemical temptation on the street than he did under the care and protection of Crossroads where AA meetings and drug testing are part of the mysterious extracurricular scene. "I think there's more drugs at Crossroads than 6th & Bonnie Brae [a notorious downtown Los Angeles heroin corner]. I call it the Bonnie Brae Gift Exchange," he says of the spot where he squandered much of his Bar Mitzvah money. "There's a ridiculous amount of drugs [at Crossroads]," he laughs. And that would include heroin? "Sure." Cocaine? "Oh, yeah." Hallucinogens? "More like with the seventh and eighth graders." He describes a favorite Crossroads party game, called "Daddy's a Doctor": "You'd go to a party and go to the dad's medicine cabinet and steal his drugs. I've eaten a lot of Zovorax, you know what I'm saying?" Well, frankly, no. "It's a herpes medication." Does it get you high? "Not at all, but I've never had herpes." Lucky him. STDs and even AIDS are seen as a rite of passage for Crossroads students.

When touring the Crossroads campus, the avuncular Headmaster, Roger Weaver, steers you to the computer-filled classrooms, fancy arts center, and well-stocked library named for the school's idealistic founder and trustee emeritus, Paul Cummins.[7] Weaver is quick to point out all the academic challenges offered, and Crossroads kids clearly do get an education rivaling liberal arts colleges—but with that challenge comes the pressures of the privileged class.

Crossroads film guru Jim Hosney, known for markedly changing the lives of his flock of young cinéastes called "Hosneyites," will show his high schoolers films he screens for postgrad-level students he also teaches at the American Film Institute, but he'll draw the line with hardcore adult fare like *Salo*, or *Last Tango In Paris*, because he feels his kids will find them "too emotionally devastating."

While Hosney agrees that the average Crossroads student is capable of doing college-level work, he worries that "they are doing so much, it almost drives them to the brink of a nervous breakdown." Along with the traditional Crossdressing Day and the Ménage à Prom for which students purchase tickets in groups of three, Crossroads curriculum has what they perceive as a holistic outlet for the pressure-cooker academic environment—the new age Mysteries Program.

Fostering Mystery and Joy

We are the weavers....She is the weaver and we are the web....she is the needle and we are the thread....She changes everything she touches.... Everything she touches changes....Ki-yay-wha-tay-lay-nyo-ma-ha-tay-hi-lo-hi-lo-hi-lo....We are one, with the infinite sun.... Forever, and ever, and ever....

A "talking stick" is passed, and a young girl begins to share an innermost secret. The others murmur "Ho" to express their approval. No, this isn't a peek into a secret session at a movie studio retreat, but it is less than a generation removed.

Though what you hear here, who you see here, ought to stay here—if you close your eyes, and imagine a gorgeous sunset...you are almost there.... Now, the magic words: Ho-meta-qui-asan....

Described in a school brochure as a course that "facilitates and honors each student's passage into adulthood," Mysteries (a required grade 6–12 course within the unique Crossroads Human Development Department) has sparked much controversy on and off campus.

A film executive and heir to Mary Tyler Moore Productions original owner Mel Blumenthal, Jason Blumenthal (1986), loved Mysteries, benefiting from all its guided imageries and self-discovery rituals, which culminated into a senior class rite of passage retreat to a hippie commune in Ojai, California. While he was developing Jean-Claude Van Damme and Brad Pitt movies, he actually pined for the time as a teenager spent meditating in class "in the middle of a crazy high school day."

In contrast, Blumenthal's contemporary, writer Jim Gibson (son of "Laugh-In" joke man Henry Gibson) regards Mysteries as "a crock of shit." "It was so bizarre," says Gibson. "We would pass around this gourd, and everyone would have to say what they were feeling."

Although the Mysteries course is required, at least one lucky student got out of it because her parents felt it "interfered with her analysis." Fifteen years later, Gibson still resents having been "force-fed" Mysteries as a requirement, taking up valuable time for elective courses he would have preferred to take.

Hollywood writer Richard Rushfield (class of 1986) describes Mysteries as basically "group therapy, a self-realization class," where you "sit in a circle, and you sometimes do guided imagery: turning off the lights, closing your eyes, and imagining that you're floating down a river with eagles flying overhead." He describes a typical session:

"You'd pass around a gourd, and only the person with the gourd could talk. If you're not holding the gourd, the only thing you can say is 'Ho.' 'Ho.' You can only say 'Ho' to express approval. If you disagree, you say 'Oh.' So, one day [a female student] had the gourd, and started telling a story about her best friend's boyfriend cheating. And the story goes on and on and my friends and I are straining, sweating, gritting our teeth not to laugh. And 10 minutes later, [she] brings the story to a close: '. . . and so, I told my friend and she didn't believe me, and now none of my friends will talk to me, and, I guess it's just like Billy Joel said—Honesty really is . . . a lonely word.' At which point we burst out laughing."

A local newspaper reporter witnessed a 17-year-old Crossroads student's turn with "the speaking stone." On his five-day experience in Ojai, after careful thought, he gushed: "I was lost, but now I'm found." Amazing. Might this be the kid who was treated to a faculty member's academic report that basically said he'd be doing better in *class*, if he "got his head out of Ojai"? There's a good chance.

Another less amusing Mysteries story involves an overweight, less than attractive girl who confessed to being pregnant in session, only to have students talking behind her back for the rest of the semester— wondering aloud "how anyone could even touch such a hideous pig, let alone fuck her?"

The Mysteries Program was originally developed in 1983 and run by Jack Zimmerman, who had previously professed at The Oakwood School—often described as "a little Crossroads in the Valley." After leaving Oakwood in 1975, he founded the experimental school Heart Light in 1980, which at its peak, had no more than 30 students. After three years of experimenting on children, Zimmerman's vision unfolded. "I didn't realize what Heart Light was about until about 1983," says the liberal arts PhD. "Then I began to see that what it was really about was this program which we called The Mysteries Program. You know, it was a full school, but the real juice of the school was this program."

Crossroads founder Paul Cummins taught under his guru Zimmerman at Oakwood before he founded Crossroads, and when Zimmerman's Heart Light dissolved, Cummins invited him to Crossroads to help the students get in touch with themselves. The bone thrown to Zimmerman was that he could direct the on-campus program and run the excursions that concluded each senior year at The Ojai Foundation—a hippie commune where the kids would camp in yurts for five days, and learn how to chant.

The Ojai Foundation was once run by, as alumnus Rushfield describes him, "a person named 'Brother John', who apparently thought he was a guru, or a prophet." Rushfield's favorite anecdote about Brother John took place in 1986 when two teachers were cleaning out the sweat lodges after use by students. As they were clearing branches, huge rats came scurrying out, causing the teachers to scream in terror. Brother John, overseeing their work from a hill nearby, chirped, "Oh, look at the little field mice!"

The regimen that the Class of 1986 was treated to include vegetarian meals, sweat lodging, and clearing the land for the hippies. "Free slave labor," is how Gibson and other grads describe the work detail. An example of down time, as observed by Rushfield, was spent in ménages à trois in a medicine teepee where a case of venereal warts germinated in threesomes, later spreading to other students upon return to civilization.

Rushfield's sister, writer Ali Rushfield, says she was freaked out on day 3 of her Ojai trip. "I ran out of cigarettes, so I convinced one of the Hawaiian shirt-wearing commune dwellers to take me and a friend to the Circle K store in the town of Ojai. For some reason he had to take us at 4 AM, and he told us to meet him at the sweat lodge. And, when we found him, he and all the rest of the Ojai people were dancing naked around a fire. He saw us, and got dressed and drove us into town,... and he had this Tupperware thing of pot on his dashboard." According to Ali, she and a friend brought back cigarettes and candy to the commune, and one of them made a mistake of leaving a candy wrapper on the ground. The next morning they awoke to utter mayhem, because "someone had discovered there was like normal food on the premises."

Richard Rushfield recalls a teacher reading an evaluation that honcho Zimmerman had written about a student: "Stuart is having trouble getting in touch with his coyotes this semester." "Coyotes," laughs Rushfield, "refer to the laughter and the wild man inside of him."

Eric Kessler sums up his Ojai rite of passage: "Well, I fucked like every girl on the Ojai trip, and I smoked crack, and they [the faculty] didn't give a shit. It was like 'free will.'" Another graduate recounts an Ojai session in a sweat lodge when an adult got hold of the gourd and "recounted having an erotic dream of a lesbian affair with the student beside her."

"Thankfully," writes one ex-X-Roader on her alumnae web site, "My shrink wrote me a note to get out of that Ojai brainwashing trip. Oh, I know... It was a life altering experience for many of you. Watching from the outside (or alley) all I noticed was that people who had never spoken to one another in 6 years came back hugging (and whatever else—hey: possible topic "what happened in Ojai?"). The friendships, hugging and what all lasted about three days—maybe a week, and then everyone ignored one another again.... It is possible I just wasn't evolved enough for the experience."

White punks on therapy? Yes, and dope, and social diseases, and syringes passed like so many exams—none of which is detailed in the Crossroads literature, but still, alumnae stories abound. Ex-Director of the Crossroads Upper School, the late Jake Jacobusse (who left in 1991, and mysteriously died of yellow fever in 2003) reflected on the Crossroads emotional experience from his last academic outpost in

Holland, Michigan—the Black River School, an upstart charter public school he had fashioned in the Crossroads image. He admitted to mixed feelings about the Mysteries Program: "The line between teacher and counselor is so very thin, and you really can't breach that line, because when you breach it you're in territory you don't belong. . . . Especially," he emphasized, "when the faculty, by and large were not licensed therapists." On public humiliation resulting from group sharing, Jacobusse said, "Those examples are probably two of dozens. . . . When children are privy to private info, it can be hurtful . . . if not out and out destructive."

The current Crossroads Mysteries coordinator (Zimmerman was put out to pasture as a "consultant/advisor"), drama teacher Peggy O'Brien, thumbnails the program as "a human development curriculum that Crossroads offers, that's a required class basically from grades six through twelve. It focuses on the health of the child in terms of well-being in all aspects. Not just academic life, but emotional, physical, spiritual, and mental development." While both O'Brien and Zimmerman are quick to insist that the ancient ritual-based program is not designed as therapy, Zimmerman peppers his course description with words like "therapeutic," "healing," and "magic," refusing to acknowledge the inherent dangers involved when children disclose private, intimate details of their lives to judgmental peers. His solution is to bring the breach of confidence back into the circle and discuss it.

Is Anyone Paying Attention to Their Kids?

Mysteries aside, Jacobusse squarely shifted the blame for emotionally troubled Crossroads youth to the parents. When the daughter of a well-known television star was having trouble with grades at Crossroads, Jacobusse found himself straddling the fine line between counselor and administrator. He explained, "she had a tough time in school because, you know, her personal life was tough." When he recommended a transoceanic sailing trip as a way out for her—"a way to try and have a fuller life, separate from everything that had gone on before"—she balked, because, he explained, she was so dependent on her analyst that she didn't dare go.

One of Jacobusse's fondest, most hilarious memories of oblivious Hollywood parenting comes from a phone conversation he had with Carol Burnett. Burnett's daughter, former drug addict/singer Erin Hamilton,[8] was about to enroll at Crossroads, and Jacobusse called her mom requesting the teen's transcripts from a school she'd been attending in Hawaii. He describes it best: "We talked business for awhile about transcripts, and then she said, 'Now, what are we going to do about my body?' And there was a long silence on my part—trying to figure out, 'Was this a come-on?' So I didn't quite know what to say, and I said, 'Well, uh, uhh,' and then I said something completely irrelevant, and she went into fits of laughter as only Carol Burnett can, and she said, 'Is this Jake from Crossroads?' And I said, 'Yeah, who did you think it was?' 'Ohhhh,' she said. 'I won't even bother, it's gonna make it worse yet.'" Turns out, Burnett thought she was talking to fitness trainer to the stars, Jake "Body by Jake" Steinfeld the entire time.

Jacobusse once found himself reprimanding O.J.'s son Jason Simpson for telling a math teacher to "fuck off," and went to his deathbed with no forgiveness for Jack Nicholson. According to Jacobusse, Nicholson not only refused to recognize his son Caleb Goddard (conceived with actress Susan Anspaugh on the set of *The Last Detail*) by saying a few words at the kid's graduation, but the angry actor did not even show up for the event. "What kind of shit is this?" asked Jacobusse of the actor. "It's your own son."

Cher and aging rocker Greg Allman's son, Elijah Blue (now of the aptly named rock band *Deadsy*), was a Crossroads student, but "that Allman twit," as Jacobusse called him, "wasn't present." "I mean, that was part of Elijah's problem," he lamented. "I think Cher was a wonderful mother, but the Allman guy would come into town and not even call. I mean, what kind of life was that for Elijah?"

Another "twit" in Jacobusse's book was Elliot Gould—Crossroad's grad, actor-director Jason Gould's father. "Again, Barbra [Streisand] had to be a single mother," he complains. "Gould was never around." If Gould's absence was a result of his busy schedule doing dinner theater and the occasional movie cameo, Jacobusse agreed that Barbra's success and Gould's failure is cosmic justice. "It all comes around," he said.

And around it goes. Of the twenty ex-Crossroads students contacted, most offered that they would send their children to their alma mater, *and* donate money to the school—if only to insure that the next generation of Hollywood cell-phone kids can meet at the Crossroads. Maybe their offspring will be featured in some entertainment rag or perennial network examination of "Young Hollywood."

What Happens after Graduation

There is a saying amongst Gen X-Roaders: "With the exception of the Menendez murders, every major LA scandal has touched familial with Crossroads." There are OJ's kids Jason and Arnelle (Class of 1987); Bob Evans' (of cocaine abuse and the Cotton Club murders) son, Josh (Class of 1989); and Heidi Fleiss's top girl, Peter Sellers' daughter Victoria Sellers (Class of 1981), whose latest project of note was a featured appearance in Ryan Broomfield's documentary, *Heidi Fleiss—Hollywood Madam*. Heidi's money-laundering father Paul Fleiss was the pediatrician for several Crossroads kids, and alumnus Andrew Gross's brother, Richard Gabriel, was a jury consultant for the defense on the OJ and the Heidi Fleiss cases, and actually discovered the jury tampering that got the prostitution part of Heidi's case dismissed. Suspected wife-murderer Robert Blake was also a Crossroads parent, and Jordan Chandler, the kid who richly settled molestation charges against Michael Jackson, was also a student.

Although not a student, former sex videographer Rob Lowe [9] was a star of the annual Crossroads Cabaret, during the rehearsals of which he got to know a cast member. When he was arrested for his Atlanta encounter, the police raided his house and his costar from the Cabaret (class of 1990) received a call from the Malibu police, informing her that a videotape of her visit with the young Brat Packer had been found at his home. She was in eighth grade at the time of this event. Another West Winger, Martin Sheen, campaigned at Crossroads, reportedly shaking hands with a lineup of disinterested kids, repeating, "Hello, I'm Martin Sheen." Finally, Gary Coleman, the pint-sized former child star whose adult problems are legion and legendary, was a Crossroads student and a 2003 California gubernatorial recall candidate. Hidden behind the Crossroads six degrees of separation sitcom and yesterday's headlines is the aforementioned gang of three juniors expelled for heroin. And there's a former faculty member's son, Zeke Cooper, who, fresh off a state prison bid for armed robbery, went on the lam again while his father, it's told, was off fighting in the *Intifada*.

To summarize the plight of many Crossroads kids, it's almost too easy to point to the concept of diminished expectations—children coming up without a chance in hell they'll ever achieve success commensurate with that of their parents. What we're observing here are cases of child abandonment in direct conflict with the Crossroads philosophy, which states in part: *To be effective with young people, teachers and parents themselves must continue to learn so that they may perceive the young accurately and treat them wisely.* Clearly, when a group of children abandoned by the nature of their parents' deference to careers and social whirls are dumped into an environment where the crystal-chompers are setting the curriculum and building an environment that is the only environment these children know, it's bound to twist some heads.

Hollywood Sony Pictures studio executive, Amy Pascal, representing the first graduating Crossroads class (1976) has fond memories of her high school years: "Starting the day with Latin," then "sitting on the ground having a big talk about sex education," and then "backpacking trips." Although not associated with the school any more, her analysis of the Crossroads value system is "about being the best you can be, and not trying to be like anybody else." Interesting word choice given the Army-like slogan about a value system that should be set by parents, who—in the current Crossroads era—are, by and large, not there. Sure, most alumnae would send their kids to Crossroads, because that is the only sense of familial bonding they had as they came of age.

Pascal implies that a value system should be taught in a school that in effect replaces the home environment. Would that value system include, as recounted by Ali Rushfield, teenage girls being subjected to naked adults on field trips on which they are isolated from society—let alone the classroom—for five days? Girls encouraged to disclose details of pregnancy in a group setting, and then ridiculed later?

Teachers, not licensed therapists, leading these sessions? Sorry, but when students are exhausted by confessionals in a group with rules of communication masked in hokey ritualistic chanting under which dogma is pushed, resulting in punishment by humiliation, you have the makings of a dangerous situation if not a cult-like environment.

To be fair, Pascal had left the school before Mysteries had arrived, as had action film director, Michael *The Rock* Bay (Class of 1981), who frowns on the fact that Crossroads has become "the star place," and suggests, "It may have lost its innocence." From the twisted head group of a recent graduating class, writer-filmmaker Kessler explains it all for us. On the nature of guruism in a school where students worship their teachers to the point of idolatry, Kessler theorizes: "A cult sort of depends on emotionally insecure people who aren't very knowledgeable about a subject, and they have a guru who becomes worshipped." He believes the theory applies to Crossroads. "They [the students] are very insecure, not very educated, stupid kids who want to know everything and want to be the best without doing any work. So, you have these half-witted know-it-alls who become self-proclaimed authorities, and they become worshipped."

The functional environment where children learn math and science in the classroom and look up to and learn values from their parents at home barely exists, as highlighted by ex-administrator Jacobusse, and explained by Kessler. "Parents of Crossroads kids are egotistical, self-involved people who shouldn't have children," declares Kessler, who, although voted "Most Likely to Be a Thorn in Everyone's Side" by his graduating class, takes more pride in his claim of having introduced crack-cocaine to Crossroads. And although this is just one kid's opinion, Kessler did spend four years at Crossroads, so he's entitled to his opinion: "Let me sum it up for you: Crossroads is a school for overprivileged rich kids whose fathers are pretty intelligent, and whose mothers are pretty, stupid women who their fathers fucked. The products of their loins are stupid kids who think they're smart, but don't read and don't write, and sort of assume knowledge." To Kessler, apathy seems the rule among Crossroaders. "It [apathy] runs rampant at Crossroads. I mean, you go to school in such a sheltered environment that you don't even realize the shit that's going on politically outside the school—socially, economically, and culturally." Got it. What does the future hold for dumb, apathetic Crossroads youth? "They're fucked if they don't have a trust fund," says Kessler. "If they don't have a trust fund, they'll be homeless in less than 10 years."

Even the occasional suicide attempt by a student—one girl reportedly ate 48 ibuprofen capsules in an unsuccessful try, and another allegedly banged her head against a hallway wall repeatedly while threatening to cut her wrists—doesn't phase Kessler, who offers instructions on the art: "If you really wanna kill yourself, get like fucking 10 grams of fucking coke, three or four grams of heroin, and fucking do it in about a half an hour and you'll be dead."

Or perhaps firing a .22 pistol into the back of your head might do the trick. It worked for Daisy Keith, class of 1987. After an argument with her boyfriend in 1997, she decided to get the last word in by blowing her brains out in her bathroom with a gun reportedly given to her by her father as a present. Her pop, Brian Keith of "Family Affair"—riddled with cancer—also shot himself, following his daughter's lead. It was a family affair.[10]

When told the tale of a student's apparent breakdown in 1986 when, dressed as a pirate, he interrupted a Crossroads awards assembly featuring the secretary of education, and declared himself "Emperor of Crossroads," Kessler takes to the director's chair. "Excellent, cinematic, genius," he waxes. But that kid, who also staged an impromptu "tortilla toss" from the roof of an administration building, clearly fell apart in front of an entire school that encourages "wacky behavior." "I won't disagree with that," concedes Kessler. "Have your fucking breakdown, but capitalize on it, you know what I'm saying? Have your breakdown, but make sure you get it down on paper and get it to your agent by Monday morning so she can send it out."

When the idea of channeling psychoses, in effect capitalizing on one's breakdown doesn't sit well at the table, Kessler leaps up, indignant. "What are you talking about? He knows what's going on. Don't you understand? The insane people are the people who have been enlightened." Kessler is flying now, but does he ever come down? Does Kessler ever crash? "The thing about me is that I've learned to control myself in the last several years because there's so much money at stake." Well, all that self-control found Crossroads postgraduate

Kessler homeless as predicted—strung out on heroin in a last-chance Valley drug rehabilitation center. He eventually got clean and sober and enrolled in college.

Zeke Cooper wasn't allowed to participate with his fellow classmates on graduation day, 1986. He missed Headmaster Roger Weaver's reflections of the academic year past: "Trying to get students down from buildings delivering iconoclastic speeches ... [students] studying to Black Flag," and his encouraging of grads to "develop further [their] innate weirdness." Cooper wasn't present for the processional march through the alley to the song "Happy Trails," and a gospel rendition of "Que Sera, Sera." The diminutive, 5-foot 6-inch, 120-pound, half white-Jewish/half African-American kid, described by his only high school friend as "a social outcast, a clown puppet for everybody," was suspended from school a few weeks before graduation for cutting a kid on the arm with a knife.

Cooper grew up in seedy South Central Los Angeles, and had his father Jeff not been on the political science faculty at Crossroads, he might not have ever *seen* the ocean, let alone this private school by the shore. "The criminal minded thing was ingrained in him from the start," says his friend. Within a month of the graduation day he was barred from, Cooper was arrested for burglary in June of 1986, for armed robbery in November, for grand theft auto the following January, and for minor possession of alcohol in March. He was busted for taking a vehicle without the owner's consent in April. Almost a year to the day from his first arrest, Cooper was popped again—this time for receiving stolen property (a gun)—and subsequently saw his probation on an earlier robbery charge revoked. He was sent to state prison on a two-year bid.

After his first stint in prison, Cooper briefly went on the straight and narrow. He worked at a university, got into a relationship, and attended college. Since Independence Day 2002, Zeke has been a third-striker facing life in prison, prominently listed as "America's Most Wanted"'s 716th capture. Current charges on his post-Crossroads resume: Attempted murder of two Los Angeles Police Department officers.[11]

A friend of Zeke's describes their relationship: "I was Zeke's side-kick and we did a few bad things when we were in school, but, you know, we were just kind of bored and we didn't feel accepted by the rich kids, and we didn't live in their same neighborhood, and we just lived the way, you know, kids from South Central lived."

When Cooper showed up with that knife at school, he was clearly crying for help. His incriminating comments to an arresting police officer that found a stolen handgun on him echo the early cries. When asked why he was carrying the gun, according to his arrest sheet, he actually confessed, "It's my buddy's gun... both of us uses the guns when we do our robberies." Then he threatened, "Some Bloods jumped me in Hollywood last night. If I see them again, I'm gonna do them."

"The robberies *were* a cry for help.... We were outcasts in school," concurs Cooper's pal. "He was a small kid. He ended up in prison and hooked on crack because he was the smallest kid who had to live up to the OGs [Original Gangsters]" And he was an outcast at Crossroads, a place where individuality was encouraged as long as it was practiced as a whole. Cooper's friend agrees: "As long as you were respectable to some certain standards, then it was okay to do whatever you wanted, and I guess it depended on how much money your family had, or whatever."

Zeke Cooper could not even raise money to hire an attorney. Where was his father, who is best described as a political science guru with his own following? *Hollywood, Interrupted* couldn't find him, but a former student recalls, "Jeff Cooper once arranged an all-school assembly featuring a pro-Palestinian speaker. Paul [Crossroads founder] wanted to include a speaker on behalf of the Israeli side, and Jeff flipped out. He got on stage in front of the whole school and said that there was no freedom of speech at Crossroads. Paul followed with a rebuttal. He was furious. It is the only time I have ever seen Paul angry. Jeff was either fired or quit soon afterward." Another Crossroads alumnus recounts, "I think he was fired, or in Hollywood-speak, he "retired" because it was time to do some soul searching. Jeff was a brilliant but way off base Communist lunatic who brainwashed everyone in our ethics class. I was a twelfth grade Communist who spouted off theories of Mao while driving a red Nissan 200SX convertible with tinted windows...." "Maybe it is true," laments Zeke's only friend, "that Jeff didn't think to show him how to think about the outcome of things."

The Road Less Traveled

The Crossroads School takes its name from a passage in Robert Frost's poem, "The Road Less Traveled." Unfortunately, with divergence comes a body count. There are plenty of schools like Crossroads. Most start up and fade away like Zimmerman's Heart Light, but Crossroads is embraced and supported by the wealthy Hollywood community—adults wanting to be hip and alternative at the expense of their children. So-called alternative education can be a frightening place where serious boundary violations can occur, because it's all about the parents and where they send their kids. So, the problem really isn't Crossroads as much as it is the parents. Crossroads is but a symptom, much like television, CDs, and DVDs. Parents don't want to parent, so they foist the responsibility off on the media and other people who do, without questioning the motives or methods of the "other people who do." Kids under pressure start thinking of themselves as adults, and start playing adult roles. Soon, they are beating the hell out of themselves for mistakes they think they made.

Crossroads alumnae suicide victims aren't coming back. No second chances and no amount of therapy will help the dead, or heal the more devastating emotional scars. But the other kids mentioned here *can* survive in spite of the dysfunction foisted upon them by parents and academics. Hell, the little junkie girl fresh out of a halfway house (Madeleine) already completed college way ahead of the class she was expelled from. With continuous sobriety, Eric Kessler may well wind up the next Joel Silver.

When will things improve? When Crossroads parents and administrators learn that *teachers* have no business treating a maladjusted child in a nonconfidential environment filled with other judgmental students. When parents are required to take a class in parenting to learn to treat their kids with at least the courtesy reserved for celebrity pets. Maybe then things might improve. A little.[12]

FEAR AND LOATHING IN LOS ANGELES

PART II

Where besotted stars fail to heed the warnings of the past and Dr. Feelgoods run rampant. Celebs get carried into rehab for a little equine therapy or to their graves.

SCREWBALL TRAGEDY

Hollywood has been a morass of drugs, alcohol, petty crimes, and mental illness since its inception. From the Golden Age of movies beginning in the 1930s, there have been countless stars who got by and possibly even succeeded because of their outrageous behaviors. Frances Farmer was lobotomized, Vivian Leigh was bipolar, Judy Garland famously overdosed on diet pills, Gene Tierney had shock therapy, and James Coburn dropped acid for fun.

In Hollywood's glorious past, the studio system acted as a firewall between entertainer and public, finely controlling the artist's public persona. Certainly the stars of yesteryear were just as prone to deviance and mental lapses, but back then the studios worked overtime to project the image of wholesomeness. Many a scandal was kept under wraps to keep the studios' investments intact.

Martin Grotjahn, the late psychiatrist to the stars, once opined, "Actors have no proper identity. When someone assigns them an identity, they can do that very well. But when they get off the stage, they collapse....Even actors who seem to be the exception really are not." The late Peter Sellers confirmed this dark revelation when he said: "If you asked me to play myself I wouldn't know what to do. I do not know who or what I am. There used to be a me, but I had it surgically removed." None of this was lost on Freud, who declared, "The artist has an introverted disposition and has not far to go to become neurotic."

Madness has manifested itself in film lore and legend, from the Silents through the Golden Age of Hollywood, on up through the 1960s and 1970s. And through a study of the legendary behind-the-scenes PI's, problem solvers, and film industry fix-it men, the classical studio system was able to hush up its scandals and sordid controversies before the civilian press could get hold of them.

The Reign of Bedlam

Let's witness first hand how similar Hollywood today is to the freak shows of yesteryear. Imagine yourself stumbling onto a time machine. You hop inside, fumble with the antiquated control console, and find yourself transported to England, circa 1680.[1] Passing by two women as they gawk and giggle at an increasingly dense population of dirt-spattered street beggars, you enter Bedlam Hospital for the reasonable admission fee of one penny. Over 100,000 sensation-starved citizens—including British nobility—will visit this Moorfield sanitarium over the year, hungry to view English society's poor, unfortunate souls—the insane.[2]

The lunatics and maniacs on display inhabit rows of drab, cramped boxes, each abode smaller than a coat closet. Many are naked, shackled to dungeon walls with heavy, clinking chains, while others run amok, desperate to escape the whips and taunts of their "caregivers." Some rant aloud about an unjust government, while others cower in shadowy corners, faces covered in hands, whimpering. Like the mother of all peep shows, or the ultimate carnival freak show, Bedlam will pack 'em in and exceed an annual income of 400 pounds for this popular diversion.

Things haven't changed much since the reign of Bedlam as an entertainment hotbed for the jaded and curious. Three centuries later, society's cravings for absurd, unusual, and excessive behaviors are stronger than those of a nicotine addict on a smoke-free flight from LAX to Europe. The Moorfield asylums have been reformed, providing exceptional care to the mentally ill since their days as geek-show fodder, but now we have washed-up celebrities mewling and puking on their own reality shows. And supermarkets of the Western world boast the pulp equivalent to seventeenth-century patient watching: tabloids, with their sordid stories of celebrity addiction, eccentricity, and romantic instability. Hollywood is the contemporary Bedlam, dishing out blatant tales of insanity that would put its English counterpart to shame.

It wasn't always like that.

Let's assume that the gloomy Bedlam scene is not to your liking, and you reprogram the time-travel vehicle for the Golden Age of Hollywood. It's 1948, and Anatole Litvak's film, *The Snake Pit*, is slithering into the limelight. Donning the prestigious logo of 20th Century Fox and starring bankable leading lady Olivia de Havilland, *The Snake Pit* bravely spearheads a movement toward dignified, respectful depictions of mental instability. Commercial Hollywood is finally dipping its reluctant toes into unknown waters, leading viewers past the locked gates of Juniper State Hospital and into the New York institution's bleak wards—indeed, human "snake pits" where staffers are as cold as lizard's skin and psychotic patients lash out like venomous rattlers.

Olivia de Havilland plays Virginia Cunningham, a New York writer wrestling with paranoia. Afraid of his wife's morphing moods and increasing suspicion, Virginia's husband dumps her into the noxious Juniper State Hospital stew of unstable residents and tyrannical nurses. After being taken under the saintly wing of Dr. Mark Kick (Leo Genn), one of the cinema's first on-screen advocates of Freudian psychoanalysis, Virginia confronts the demons of her past and reclaims her sanity. In addition to its pioneering examination of an individual gaining insight through probing "talk therapy" sessions, The Snake Pit denounces frightening physical treatments such as electroconvulsive shock, hydrotherapy, and lobotomy. Reflecting society's desperation for kinder, gentler mental health treatments, and its consequent embrace of "talk therapy," *The Snake Pit* suggests that America's mental health system is in need of a major overhaul.

How to upgrade this dysfunctional jumble of bureaucratic, indifferent hospitals? The image of a thoughtful, sympathetic psychiatrist-as-saint, painted by the film's stoic healer, Dr. Kick, suggests that shrinks are society's new heroes. Favoring lab jackets and spectacles over blue spandex pants and red capes, psychiatrists become the supermen of American culture. And unlike Clark Kent, whom many resembled, shrinks of the mid-1900s don't require a phone booth to make their transformations. Just a couch.

Capitalizing on this positive image, real-life practitioners quickly jockey themselves into position to treat Hollywood's elite, but not always with such happy endings. Karl Menninger was known for catering to LA's rich and famous, his Menninger Clinic a high-profile treatment center. Consequently, scandals surface, like those surrounding the alleged mistreatment of Robert Walker, star of *Til the Clouds Roll By* and *The Clock*. At the insistence of MGM Studios, Walker admits himself to a sanitarium, following the actor's arrest for drunk and disorderly conduct. On August 28, 1951 (foreshadowing the modern-day "Doctor Feelgoods" we'll discuss later), the actor dies following the ingestion of barbiturates allegedly given by Los Angeles psychiatrist (and Menninger Clinic trainee) Frederick Hacker.[3]

Time-travel framework aside (after all, we're not delusional here, are we?), the examination of Hollywood's Golden Age as a bastion of actors and actresses grappling with the frayed ends of sanity is as labyrinthine and complex as any of the screen's great dramas. Whether they're fictionalized, on-film depictions of madness, or true-life dances with disorientation and dementia, these stories act as a startling contrast to the way that movie star madness is handled as a means of commerce today.

Apologies, Frances

Take, for instance, Frances Farmer's mind-boggling slide down a slippery psychiatric slope that culminated in torture, neglect, and a possible lobotomy. As *The Snake Pit's* cinematic depiction of institutionalized patients premiered, Farmer was enduring a real-life hospitalization at Western Washington State Hospital that lasted over five horrific years, depicted in the movie *Frances* starring Jessica Lange in the title role.

Perhaps the ultimate tale of Hollywood Insanity, Farmer's legend continues to gain momentum even as the story retains a certain unexplainable mystery. Fellow Puget Sound resident and Nirvana band frontman Kurt Cobain immortalized Farmer's plight in the 1992 song, "Frances Farmer Will Have Her Revenge on Seattle," while emphasizing the pull that this tragic icon's story has on the actresses' followers to this day. Meanwhile, the saga boasts a wild, larger-than-life canvas of twisted supporting characters (including an Evil Matriarch and a Mad Doctor) that makes the volatile actress seem tame and resigned in comparison. It's no accident that our heroin heroine Courtney Love was rumored to have worn a Frances Farmer original dress at their wedding, and the crazed couple, in fact, named their heroin baby Frances Bean.

A deep political vein runs through Farmer's macabre series of misfortunes, in which a stubborn, outspoken beauty from West Seattle angered a myriad of Forces That Be and suffered dearly.

The first strike against this outspoken attorney's daughter arose in 1931, during her junior year of high school, when Farmer wrote a controversial essay entitled, "God Dies,"[4] marking her as the poster girl for "Pagan youth."[5]

Four years later, during her enrollment at the University of Washington, Farmer again succeeded at pissing off her countrymen and further exacerbating her already tense relationships with hometown critics by fleeing Seattle for several years, to accept a trip to Russia, sponsored by a radical student newspaper called *Voice of Action*.[6] She toured the Soviet Union, and although the fledgling actress repeatedly whined, "I'm not a Communist," insisting that her motives were merely to sample the country's theatre culture and admire Russia's exotic landscapes, anti-Red sentiments were thick in the Puget Sound area. A hotbed of labor reform disputes between radical labor reformers and conservative politicians, Seattle soon branded Farmer a trouble-making Commie.

Upon her return to America, Farmer took up residence in New York and performed in Broadway productions. Later, she was snatched up by a perceptive Paramount Pictures talent scout and replanted in Southern California. Her Hollywood star rose nearly overnight: in 1936 alone, Farmer's intense onscreen stare and deep, commanding voice marked four film appearances, most notably in Goldwyn's *Come and Get It*, where the versatile knockout played both a sultry tavern singer, *and* the crooner's young daughter.

Farmer appeared in 14 films between 1936 and 1942 in spite of blacklisting allusions. Despite this fast track towards Tinseltown fame, complete with critical comparisons to Greta Garbo,[7] Farmer grew tired of the celebrity "schmoozing" routine she was encouraged to partake in by studio honchos. Early 1940s Hollywood was like an ocean-sized medicine cabinet chock full of amphetamines, its starlets gobbling down such chemicals like moppets touring a candy store. Not only did hip diet pills like Benzedrine help to melt the pounds away by suppressing one's appetite, but they were also easily attainable, and not yet recognized as an addictive scourge. Farmer was no stranger to diet pills, and she also brought her rebel persona up several notches by smoking and drinking to excess. She broke the mold of pristine Hollywood princess, blithely denouncing enemies as "cocksuckers" while living in freewheeling, warts 'n all slovenliness (complete with beater car and humble, ramshackle homes) through a string of divorces, and one known affair with playwright Clifford Odets. This against-the-grain volatility would prove to be Farmer's undoing.

On October 19, 1942, a motorcycle policeman stopped Farmer in Santa Monica for erratic driving.[8] Resisting arrest, the confrontational actress was promptly jailed. Three months later, she slapped a studio hairdresser with enough force to break the woman's jaw.[9] Meanwhile, Farmer neglected to pay a fine related to the Santa Monica arrest, and was soon back in the clink, kicking, flailing, and hurling obscenities every sordid step of the way. A criminal hearing ensued, in which she was sentenced to 180 days in jail. According to film critic and author Leonard Maltin, "When she was refused a phone call upon leaving the court, she became hysterical, punching and kicking, and was sent to a cell in a straight jacket."[10]

Farmer spent time at several institutions, culminating in a five-year stint at Western State Hospital in Steilacoom, Washington. Between May 5, 1945, and March 23, 1950, Farmer was confined to the oppressive mental health facility and "treated" with cold-water immersion and insulin shock therapy.[11] Farmer's 1972 autobiography *Will There Ever be a Morning?* suggests that she was sexually abused by orderlies, and other books and films documenting her confinement share this view.

Late in 1948, the same year that *The Snake Pit* premiered at theaters, Farmer was visited by Dr. Walter Freeman,[12] a famed neurologist who boasted the dubious distinction of being America's first lobotomy expert.[13] Written descriptions of the doctor give him the aesthetic appeal of a sinister Nazi from some Indiana Jones action spectacle, noting his goatee, spectacles, and balding bean. Freeman's unfettered enthusiasm for neurosurgery interventions only added to his creepy, mad scientist aura.

"Lobotomy gets them home" acted as a kind of personal catch phrase for Freeman, a Washington resident who boasted a record of nearly 3,500 lobotomies performed over his lifetime. Pursuing each consecutive skull-encased brain with fervor, Freeman worked his cranium-impaling magic at over 55 hospitals across America. The doctor was particularly fond of transorbital lobotomies, which severed nerve networks connecting the brain's thalamus to its frontal lobes, allegedly neutralizing the "overactive emotions" that characterized insane individuals. The procedure involved shocking a person unconscious, jamming an ice-pick-sized instrument called a leucotome through a tear duct, and then hammering it another inch and a half through bone and gray matter (on at least one occasion, Freeman used a construction mallet to ram the spike home). Through all of this, Freeman never attained any type of certification in surgery.[14]

According to Arnold's biography, the tall goddess whose blonde curls and sultry lips had wowed viewers of 1936's *Come and Get It* was hauled into an isolated treatment room during one such visit by Freeman, and jolted with electric shock until she lost consciousness. "No one will ever know what happened next," Arnold confesses, "but the overwhelming conclusion drawn by the people of Steilacoom at the time was that the doctor lifted her right eyelid and stuck a needle into her brain. Because when she came to, Frances Farmer was not the same person she had been, and she would never be the same person again."[15]

Even as Farmer's lobotomy has become an assumed part of her legend, rendering her story the classic, tragic Hollywood weeper, more recent accounts of her commitment at Steilacoom continue to debate whether Farmer was among Freeman's surgical guinea pigs.

"I'm sure Frances Farmer didn't have one," claims Beverly Tibbets, a Western State Hospital employee from 1947 to 1982. "I worked on all the patients who had lobotomies, and Frances Farmer never came to that ward."[16]

It's easy to see why Cobain, who died in 1994 by a self-inflicted shotgun blast to the head, would consider Farmer a spiritual comrade. As a fellow Pacific Northwest entertainment icon whose mindset put her at odds with the establishment, Farmer's insane lifestyle has much in common with Nirvana's nonconformist musical contributions. Her ties to Communism coupled with her contemptuous view of Hollywood's smug insincerity seemed the impassioned traits of a "creative artist" marching straight to her grave to the beat of a different drummer.

After her ordeal, Farmer likened her experiences as a mental patient to those of a Bedlam-era untouchable. "Never console yourself into believing that the terror has passed," she warned ominously, "for it looms as large and evil today as it did in the despicable era of Bedlam. But I must relate the horrors as I recall them, in the hope that some force for mankind might be moved to relieve forever the unfortunate creatures who are still imprisoned in the back wards of decaying institutions."[17]

If insanity can be portrayed as cool, dark, and artistic, then our celebrity nutcases can continue to live life on the edge in public with the self-aggrandizing hope that we will lionize systematic, bizarre behavior as an act of "artistic rebellion."

Privately Bipolar

In contrast to Farmer, the earthy, blonde nonconformist, Vivien Leigh embraced Hollywood royalty and proudly aligned herself center stage among the town's pampered elite. If Farmer's "insanity" legend, as created by the intense political climate of the times and the harsh retribution that was handed celebrity iconoclasts, is to be believed, Leigh's brush with the tree of madness came from an entirely different synaptic branch.

Born Vivian Mary Hartley on November 5, 1913,[18] Leigh was already performing onstage at age three under the encouraging wing of Gertrude, her devout Catholic mother.[19] By 1935, she had married Leigh Holman, given birth to her only child, Suzanne, and starred in a number of English plays. Fate intervened with even more dramatic transition, when Leigh starred alongside Laurence Olivier in the stage production *Fire Over England*. The two costars became lovers, in a union that would become one of Hollywood's most celebrated romances. Their relationship would also hold the key to Leigh's 1938 role in *Gone With the Wind*, after the smitten actress traveled to America to visit Olivier (then filming *Wuthering Heights*). While "Larry" completed the production, Leigh met the Selznick Brothers, participated in a screen test, and won the role of tempestuous heroine Scarlett O'Hara, despite tough competition from Paulette Goddard, Lana Turner, and Norma Shearer.[20]

In 1939, Leigh's star shined brightest of any Tinseltown actress, as *Gone with the Wind* premiered to ecstatic acclaim and claimed a Best Picture Oscar. Meanwhile, the celebrated woman's mysterious, cat-like performance—accented by those piercing green eyes—won her the Academy Award for Best Actress; she won a second Oscar in 1951 for her performance in *A Streetcar Named Desire* opposite Marlon Brando. Meanwhile, she sealed her affections for Olivier by marrying the actor in 1940 (having left first husband Holman in 1937).

Although Leigh didn't embrace the rebel role that Farmer came to symbolize, she flaunted her "illicit" romance to Olivier, a definite no-no during the highly regimented image control that marked the studio systems of that era. According to Anne Edwards's 1977 biography, *Vivien Leigh*, MGM studio head David Selznick pleaded with the couple that they "use discretion" and avoid being seen in public together prior to their marriage.[21] She was also a heavy chain smoker, inhaling four packs' worth of ciggie smoke a day during production of *Gone with the Wind*.[22]

Leigh also struggled with bipolar disorder, which manifested itself in attacks of hysteria and depression beginning in the early 1940s. Leigh and Olivier managed to contain the volatile mood swings associated with bipolar illness, with low-profile periods of relaxation at Notley Abbey, their pastoral, 69-acre estate in Buckinghamshire. According to Edwards, Olivier became a studious observer of warning signs hinting that perhaps his wife's manic depression would intensify.

"He was beginning to note a pattern," the author described. "For a few days prior to an attack Vivien would be exceptionally nervous, all of her reactions—speech, laughter, gestures—accelerated. Then would come the insane outburst, lasting several hours, followed by a severe depression, and finally a humble, embarrassed contrition."[23]

As if to reinforce the couple's discreet handling of Leigh's fragile condition, Edwards also noted, "If Vivien's behavior indicated, as he thought it might, an attack of hysteria to come, he wanted to control her and keep the matter private." Such descriptions make it difficult to envision Olivier pushing "blow by blow" press releases on his wife's fluctuating condition through an overworked fax machine to salivating publicists, as many of today's celebrities might consider doing.

According to Gavin Lambert's essay concerning his relationship with Leigh as her screenwriter for 1961's *The Roman Spring of Mrs. Stone*, the actress was matter-of-fact and unpretentious concerning her health challenges. "Two weeks before shooting started," he recalled, "Vivien announced that she felt herself going 'dry,' and that she would take a shock treatment the next day. She mentioned this to . . . me with no more fuss than someone with a headache asking for an aspirin. Her lack of self-pity was touching and elegant."[24]

A whiner, Mrs. Leigh was *not*.

The Fixing Enablers

Hollywood's Golden Age was also a time of "fixers." Minimizing a star's struggles, eccentricities, and health woes in the public eye was the demanding job of these public relations flacks, who dutifully concealed the fallout of breakdowns and blowups. Each studio had a "crisis management" expert to follow its stable of stars and mop up their messes. Perhaps the most famous studio cleanup man was MGM's Howard Strickling. According to *Variety* writer David Bloom, Strickling "routinely cleaned up after bad boys Clark Gable and Robert Taylor. Little tricks like providing studio talent for the Culver City police and fireman's balls ensured cooperation when he needed official discretion over a star's arrest."[25]

"He would blithely reinvent the biographies of young stars," writer Peter Bart revealed of Strickling, "complete with new names and often new sexual orientation. He was able to move at lightning speed to suppress news stories about the indiscretions of his stars—arrests for pot possession or assignations with underage girls."[26]

Bloom also cites Fox's Harry Brand as another skillful fixer who utilized family connections to veil wrongdoings committed by his celebrities. "His brother was a judge; his wife Sybil was so tight with the Los Angeles County Sheriff's Department that it named the women's jail after her."[27]

While the regimented, controlling studio system of Hollywood's Golden Age might have maintained the celebrity community with protection from potentially devastating publicity, this firewall of image alteration could also be a curse. Substance abuse issues played a central role in the passing of Judy Garland, whose addiction to barbiturates was manifested through attempts at weight control and increased energy. As her drug ingestion increased, Garland's behavior became more erratic, culminating in MGM's termination of her contract.[28]

Swallowed by a quicksand of divorces, breakdowns, and suicide attempts, Garland's abandonment by her studio seemed especially brutal, considering the many subsequent allegations that MGM had actually *fostered* her chemical habits. "Her grueling schedule at the studio led to a dependency on pep and sleeping pills that was to dog her for the rest of her life and eventually end it," stated Leonard Maltin in his *Movie Encyclopedia*.[29]

Meanwhile, Garland confirmed the studio's enabling push towards addiction, stating, "[MGM] had us working days and nights on end. They'd give us pep pills to keep us on our feet long after we were exhausted. Then they'd take us to the studio hospital and knock us cold with sleeping pills.... Then after four hours they'd wake us up and give us the pep-up pills again so we could work another seventy-two hours in a row."[30] Garland died in 1969, after ingesting her final, fatal dose of barbiturates.[31]

Caught up in a separate wave of pill popping and studio neglect, Marilyn Monroe also died next to an empty bottle that housed the barbiturates she'd swallowed before fading to black.

Gene Tierney was one of Hollywood's many A-list actresses hospitalized for severe depression. Known for her sexy overbite and striking cheekbones, Tierney turned in classic performances in such unforgettable Golden Age films as *Laura*, *The Ghost and Mrs. Muir*, and *Leave Her to Heaven* (for which she was granted a Best Actress Oscar nomination in 1944). However, this consistent streak of celebrated output would come to a screeching halt as Tierney was chewed up and spit out by the unsparing Tinseltown movie machine. "Her acting performances were few in the 1950s," reveals the Internet Movie Database, "as she battled a troubled emotional life that included hospitalization and shock treatment for depression."

Such controversies did little to deter Hollywood's hunger to align itself with the hip practice of psychiatry, which many would later blame—alongside neglectful, exploitative studio practices—for spinning this web of pills, quiet rooms, straightjackets, and wasted celebrity lives. As the studios pushed their clients through relentless schedules like so much expendable cannon fodder, couch-hugging, psychiatrist bedfellows profited from the resulting bouts of superstar neurosis.

However, the failure of psychiatry to rescue such icons as Farmer, Leigh, and Garland—accompanied by the challenging, rebellious social defiance that marked the late 1960s—would see shrinks quickly fall out of favor with Hollywood filmmakers. "The American cinema began responding heartily to the cultural upheavals of the 1960s, questioning the old ideas of sanity and conformity, and turning against the champions of these redefined concepts."[32]

Consequently, movie mind doctors and mental hospitals would become unsympathetic symbols of an old guard authority that repressed creativity and required upgrading. Rebel psychiatry critic/ Scientology apologist Thomas Szasz, once a professor of psychiatry at the State University of New York, became renowned for his controversial view that mental illness did not exist. "Mental illness is a myth whose function is to disguise and thus render more palatable the bitter pill of moral conflicts in human relations," Szasz insisted in his classic essay, "The Myth of Mental Illness."

Such popular viewpoints helped to shape a stereotype of insanity as "an enlightened expression of rebellion against a crazy society."[33] Soon, the floodgates were opened for depictions of crazy people as more rational than their "sane" peers (*King of Hearts*), and mental hospitals as cold, callous holding tanks run by sadistic dictators (*One Flew*

Over the Cuckoo's Nest). This attitude of giving the finger to authority and bucking the system through nonconformist nuttiness saw 1960s stars acknowledging their "ids" with reckless abandon.

Big-toothed, shallow-cheeked *Our Man Flint* icon James Coburn got in touch with the wild and wooly warrior within, through liberal doses of hallucinogens. "I did like LSD, peyote and other psychedelics," the actor confessed to *Playboy* in 2000. "They were interesting. They cleared my head. We used to chew some peyote, go up into the desert around Joshua Tree and run around, jumping from rock to rock, thinking we were great gazelles. I came away understanding a lot more about myself and life."

Meanwhile, counterculture cronies like Dennis Hopper and flat out burnout Peter Fonda sowed their wild oats during *Easy Rider*, inhaling phony drugs and snorting ("powdered sugar really hurts"), but more often puffing real reefers. According to the 2001 documentary *Shaking the Cage*, the film's crew received a kilo of marijuana for recreational toking, while "all interviewees confirm that any time you see someone smoking a joint on-screen, it was loaded with the kind bud."

Suddenly, the rampant abuse of diet pills had given way to a host of more diverse chemically induced behaviors. Uppers, downers, pot, acid, heroin, speed, and other instant insanity potions launched a new generation of celebrities flaunting their highs even as they struggled to remain coherent on their production sets.

Today's hybrid of celebrity insanity is an even more aggressive strain. Free agents no longer shackled by the censoring hands of studio watchdogs—or held back by such outdated concepts as integrity, manners, and dignity—the New Millenium's shameless den of A-list attention seekers boasts more freaks, fiends, and fetishists than the *Rocky Horror Picture Show* on Halloween night, apparently unmoved by the warnings voiced by Frances Farmer and her more sympathetic Golden Age peers.

5

DOCTOR FEEL GOODS

In Hollywood, money can't buy you love, but it can buy you medicine. Not only the kind you would expect—world-class specialists and round the clock nursing when you are sick—but also the kind that feeds illness: drugs. Since the early days of the entertainment industry, there has been a cadre of medical practitioners willing to trade their Hippocratic Oaths for gargantuan fees, a brush with celebrity, and a taste of the high life. But in the last 20 years, as the culture of celebrity began to dominate American discourse and the dollars grew astronomical, more and more doctors are now for sale.

By the 1970s and 1980s, recreational drug use was in full swing in Hollywood. So-called "set doctors" were more than likely to be tricked out in the garb of your average drug dealer, with their black bags filled with marijuana, cocaine, hallucinogens, methamphetamines, and downers. Casual drug use was widely ignored by everyone and indulged in by many. Cocaine especially became a "line item" in many film budgets, masquerading there as entertainment expenses or special director perks.

But as careers went up in smoke (or up the star's nose), the cultural attitude began to change. Studios, whose megabucks were riding on increasingly erratic talent, began to crack down. Illegal drug use went underground, no longer hip and increasingly uninsurable. But Hollywood's taste for the stuff did not, and as the 1990s rolled around, celebrities increasingly turned to prescription medicines to fuel their habits and cure their imagined ills. Suddenly, the medical profession found themselves playing a new role, that of drug suppliers to the stars. Dr. Feelgood now came with a legitimate medical degree and a license to dispense, leading some of today's biggest stars down a torturous spiral of abuse that left careers on the rocks, lives shattered, and corpses strewn about the finest mansions on the hill.[1]

One Director, Two Doctors, Two Deaths

When super producer Don Simpson—who with partner Jerry Bruckheimer was responsible for such hits as *Top Gun* and *The Rock*—was found dead, slumped on his toilet in 1996, the LA County Coroner found traces of 21 different drugs in his body, only one of which—cocaine—was illegal. Although they ruled that cocaine caused the massive coronary that killed him, police at the scene of his death found more than 2200 pills strewn about his Bel Air estate.[2] Ironically, the book found at his side was a biography about noted drug abuser Oliver Stone.[3]

Simpson collected doctors like J. Lo collects husbands, but three-quarters of those pills were prescribed by one doctor, his "friend," Stephen Ammerman. They had met in a Santa Monica gym a few years before and Simpson, sensing an opportunity, quickly struck up a friendship.[4]

Ammerman was an emergency room doctor with a bag load of addictions himself—binge eating, yo-yo dieting, and a serious drug habit, fueled by his ability to write his own prescriptions. But Ammerman had a more dangerous addiction, one that would prove his downfall: He was addicted to celebrity. Despite being a brilliant trauma room doctor and the inventor of several successful medical devices, Ammerman was seduced by the wealth and power of the entertainment industry around him. Overweight though he was, he desperately wanted a piece of the big pie.

He wrote a screenplay about a doctor addicted to drugs, and another about a bear called "Kodiak."[5] When luck struck and Ammerman met Simpson, it was a match made in heaven. Ammerman wanted to get into movies; Simpson wanted drugs. Let's do lunch. It was a relationship that put them both in early graves. Ammerman died in the pool house of Simpson's estate in August of 1995 and Simpson overdosed just five months later.[6]

The who-what-where's surrounding the twin overdoses are murky at best. Charges of sloppy police work abound. Notorious Hollywood fixer Anthony Pellicano, a private investigator with alleged Mafia connections,[7] a propensity for being linked to the threatening of journalists,[8] and a brand new criminal rap sheet of his own,[9] was on Simpson's personal payroll at the time. Various accounts of both events have Pellicano "sanitizing" the death scenes before the police were called in order to save his client from embarrassment.[10] Conspiracy rumors abound, pointing to murder by various other powerful people who stood to gain from Simpson's end, including his then ex-partner, Bruckheimer. Various journalistic accounts seem to have been suppressed by various Hollywood powerhouses.[11]

But what seems to be clear is this: In 1993, Ammerman was treated for four months by infamous "psychopharmacologist" Dr. Robert H. Gerner for attention deficit disorder. During that time, and despite Ammerman's history of addiction and drug abuse, Gerner treats Ammerman with over 700 pills including various amphetamines.[12] Not long after, Gerner is brought up on charges of overprescribing meds and for sexual assault of his patients, including a certain female patient he allegedly took to fondling during something he called "rubbing therapy" (thus giving new meaning to the old definition of a therapist as "the rapist").[13] Gerner is suspended for a time and given a seven-year probation. Soon after, Ammerman is arrested twice for increasingly bizarre behavior, including climbing through a neighbor's window naked and growling at policemen trying to restrain him.[14] Oddly, the state medical board does nothing to prevent this obvious madman from treating trauma patients, but at least they get him into detox.[15]

Laughing as he leaves the hospital, Ammerman quickly pursues more meds, but old reliable pill doc Gerner is serving out his suspension, so Gerner deals Ammerman to one of his protégés, Dr. Nomi Fredrick.[16] Fredrick was a young pup fresh out of her internship. Ammerman plays her like a violin, denying ever having substance abuse problems and claiming to be a Harvard grad. She whips out her pad and sends him off with perscriptions for Ritalin, Prozac, and more of his favorite upper, Dexedrine.[17]

Meanwhile, Simpson has extricated himself from the tomb constructed by the box office failure of *Days of Thunder* with the back-to-back-to-back successes of *Bad Boys*, *Crimson Tide*, and *Dangerous Minds*. But while climbing out of a professional grave, he was backsliding into his real one. Drugs are taking over his life, and although everyone in Hollywood knows it, the pressure of saving face prevents him from pursuing the help he needed.[18] Instead, he does what good producers do: He does it his way.

In short order, Simpson installs Ammerman in the mansion on the hill as his full-time live-in doctor, with orders to craft a full-scale detox and rehab program on the premises.[19] Such is the prerogative of power, leavened by an unhealthy dose of sick dependency. After all, Ammerman was still doing active battle with his own demons. Physician, heal thyself.[20]

Nurses, medical equipment, and a mountain of drugs quickly pour into the estate,[21] followed in short order by Ammerman's new doctor, Nomi Fredrick. At the time, Fredrick was living the dream. A poor Puerto Rican raised in the Bronx housing projects, she had paid her own way through college and med school, and clawed her way through a five-year residency that she believed had delivered her to the doorsteps of big-time success. As a star protégé of Gerner's, a life of treating the best of the best lay before her.[22]

Fredrick tells Simpson the home detox paradigm is lousy, but it's the only treatment her new star client will agree to. Unwilling to lose the fees, she feels it's better to do something rather than just watch the slow-motion train wreck grind inexorably to its doom. For a period of a few weeks, she aggressively prescribes opiates and other drugs in a way she now admits was far outside of then-established medical practice. During this time, she grows to loathe him and his image of himself. But she believes, in her neophyte way, that it would be wrong to terminate his treatment. It's a belief that will ultimately lead to her own tragic downfall.[23]

Two or three weeks into Simpson's treatment, Fredrick gets a panicked early morning call from the Simpson estate. Ammerman is dead in the pool house, the victim of a massive overdose of self-prescribed morphine. She rushes over to find the house full of cops. According to Fredrick, also in the circus ring stands Anthony Pellicano, again, the private eye notorious for his ability to fix celebrity problems by making them go away.[24] Pellicano, long on Simpson's payroll and friends with the cops, denies that Simpson and Ammerman had any real relationship; Fredrick says Pellicano described Ammerman as a "hanger-on." According to Fredrick, he also denies that Ammerman was Simpson's doctor.[25]

There's such chaos that the LAPD leave the scene without gathering evidence that would be crucial to resolving the unanswered questions surrounding Ammerman's death. Immediately upon their departure, Fredrick says she witnesses Pellicano "sanitizing" the estate, effectively removing all traces that tie Simpson to Ammerman, and by extension, to Fredrick, including most if not all of the many meds that Fredrick prescribed Simpson. This fact will become important in the confusion that followed a few months later.[26]

But in the immediate aftermath of Ammerman's death, Fredrick's star patient is suicidally depressed. Fredrick spends a couple of days at the estate, manning a suicide watch, for which she charges the obscene sum of $500 per hour, 24 hours a day. What the hell, she thinks, I hate his guts and he's filthy rich. It was her passive aggressive way of getting back at him. Wrong? Perhaps. But faced with a client who she hated, and who had unlimited resources, she did the typical thing for a girl on the move.[27]

To clear his drug-addled mind, Simpson decides to jet off to Hawaii to detox again,[28] and with Ammerman gone, he takes along Fredrick, putting her up in the room down the hall. All the while, her meter is running. $500 bucks an hour. Cha-ching.[29]

Once ensconced in her Hawaii hotel room, Fredrick refuses to write Simpson more prescriptions. He throws her out of the hotel room. Thus spurned, Fredrick's animus leads her to another mistake.

She goes downstairs and gets a massage, and then buys her mother some jewelry. She spends about $2500 that she charges to the room, which Simpson is paying for. When she checks out the next day, she pays for the gifts herself.[30]

A week later, Simpson leaves her and Hawaii and returns to the care of one of his former physicians. Fredrick has treated him for a total of about five weeks.

Five months later, Simpson is dead of an overdose. Of the 21 drugs in his system, only one—used to treat upset stomachs—was given to him by Fredrick. But his death threatens to blow the lid off prescription medicine abuse in Hollywood, a vicious problem that had already claimed the lives of Margaux Hemingway and others. Someone had to shoulder the blame, and that someone turned out to be Nomi Fredrick.

The *Los Angeles Times* published a series of blistering reports laying the blame for Simpson's death squarely on Fredrick's shoulders, despite the fact that she hadn't treated him for over five months. In addition, she claims that all the drugs she had prescribed had been removed from the Simpson estate after Ammerman's death. The obvious contradictions not withstanding, the *Times* series wins a Pulitzer Prize for investigative reporting.

This draws the attention of an ambitious state's attorney in Sacramento, who begins a three-year investigation of Fredrick that includes a multiforce invasion of her home and office in search of incriminating records.[31] The eventual prosecution before the state medical board takes five years and costs Fredrick $250,000. In the end she loses her license for a few dumb mistakes, and for being in the wrong place at the wrong time with the wrong sick celebrity.[32]

Today, Fredrick is a ruined woman. She tells us that she can't pay her lawyers, who feel so badly about the injustice done to her that they are pursuing her multiple appeals pro bono, over her protestations. She owes the state $83,000 in reimbursement to pay for her prosecution. She's broke, fighting cancer and lupus, and struggling to raise her kid alone.[33] Hollywood needed a fall guy, and Fredrick was a sitting duck. Too new, too unconnected, too inexperienced in the ways of power, and too seduced by celebrity to understand what was happening to her. Fortunately, in November 2003, a judge reversed the revocation of Fredrick's license, allowing the possibility for her to practice medicine again.

(Shop)Lifting Your Spirits

Dr. Feelgood is often lurking in the shadows of your favorite tabloid travesties. On the very day that Winona Ryder was sentenced for shoplifting, her $500-per-hour Feelgood lost his license.[34] Although her taste in purses (she lifted five) got most of the press after her light-fingered jaunt through trendy Beverly Hills Saks Fifth Avenue, police also discovered a veritable pharmacopoeia of prescription meds in her seemingly bottomless marsupial pouch. Most bore the name of the most recent pill doctor to the stars to fall from grace, Jules Lusman.

Like Ammerman, Lusman was apparently obsessed by "the life." He came to LA from South Africa, where he lost his medical license under questionable circumstances. He found California all too willing to issue him a new one. Looking to build a practice, he left flyers at some of the towns toniest hotels, and was soon rubbing elbows with the kind of people who could afford to stay there. Whether his famous clientele—including walking chemistry experiment Ozzy Osbourne, the late Anthony Quinn, and Courtney Love—found him through a hotel or from his quickly growing reputation as the fastest prescription pad in the west is open to debate. In one press report, Lusman himself said, "I made myself available, and word got out that I was available."[35]

Lusman was quickly a welcome fixture at the houses on the hill, charging that big $500-per-hour fee (including drive time) to cure what ails you, but also availing himself of party invitations and tickets to screenings. Anything for a taste of *la vie*.

In June 2001, Lusman visited the home of Winona's good friend Courtney Love. Love was complaining of what must have been excruciating pain from a bee sting. Just three months earlier, Love had told *US Weekly* of her love for the prescription painkiller Vicodin, saying, "Who isn't doing them? I did it. I loved it. And I also ended up in rehab." Lusman must have missed the issue because he whipped out the pad and gave the Vicodin junkie a prescription for Vicodin.

A pain reliever commonly prescribed after major surgery given for a bee sting? "Doctors write prescriptions," Lusman reportedly said at the time. "What is excessive to one doctor isn't necessarily excessive to another doctor."[36]

Word of Love's new supplier quickly made it to her gal pal Ryder, and in September of that year, Lusman started treating Sticky Fingers as well, breaking the law in a way that has become standard practice for doctors who prey upon the famous by opening up a file for her under a fictitious name, Emily Thompson. Prescriptions for Vicodin, Valium, and state-of-the-art painkiller Endocet soon followed.[37]

When Ryder was arrested three months later, her personal survival kit contained the opiate Demerol, Endocet, Vicoprofen, and Vicodin— and that was just her walking-around stash. It was enough medication to stop a small rhinoceros in its tracks. To be fair to the overly generous Lusman, he wasn't the only quack being played for a goose by Ryder. Court documents reportedly claimed that she had received 37 different prescriptions from 20 different doctors between 1996 and 1998.[38]

Like Nomi Fredrick before him, Lusman took the fall, although unlike Fredrick it's pretty clear he earned it. The judge, Joseph Montoya, who revoked his license, cited four other patients to whom Lusman had grossly overprescribed powerful pills, and said in his decision, "The scenario was that of a doctor catering to the demands of wealthy and/or famous drug-seekers for prescription narcotics which would otherwise have to be obtained on the street, the doctor in question working on a cash-and-carry basis."[39] (Needless to say, Lusman wasn't billing too many insurance companies.)

In true Hollywood tradition, all drug charges against Ryder were dropped.

"The Point Is to Stay as Healthy as You Can up to Death" —Nick Nolte to the *Evening Standard*

There are doctors, like Ammerman, easily seduced by the glitter of Hollywood. They come to believe that their lives and contributions are insignificant in comparison to the High Life. Others, like Fredrick, are naïvely cowed by the power of money. Some, like Lusman, are content to ride the wave for whatever profit they can harvest. But our fourth house call is to a doctor for whom celebrity is but a weakness ripe to be preyed upon for profit.

For Dr. Christian Renna, the foibles and vulnerabilities of the entertainment elite are spreading grounds ripe for the planting. Throughout his long career, this "osteopath" has ridden society's fears, vanities, and vulnerabilities in the face of death into a stable of lucrative, quasi-medical businesses based around his two practices in Dallas and Beverly Hills.

Renna's point of entry, chaperone, and meal ticket into the tea parties of the cultural dysfunctionals was the grandmaster of gonzo filmmaking, Oliver Stone. Whether they were Vietnam War buddies or met later is unclear, but what's certain is that their public association began in 1988 on the whacked-out set of Stone's Ron Kovic biopic *Born on the Fourth of July*.[40]

A family osteopath practicing less than a decade[41] when Stone's traveling big top hit Dallas in 1988 to begin shooting the film, Renna signed on as company medic. Film companies routinely employ a medic on set, especially when there are stunts or large crowd scenes to manage. Renna's wife, Miranda, also got a bit part in the film as a sexy barmaid, one of many locals hired to fill out the cast.[42]

Renna proved himself indispensable, and quickly found himself palling around with Stone and Co. The friendship stuck, and when Stone was back in Dallas two years later to film *JFK*, Renna was again at his side, this time carrying the title of "Production Physician," an otherwise unheard of credit in the movie industry. To wring a little more juice from the pie, Renna double-dipped into the production budget by appearing in a bit role as a Bethesda doctor.[43]

Renna continued to carry the unconventional credit on Stone's next two films, *Heaven and Earth* and *Natural Born Killers*, but by *NBK* Renna's duties had expanded far beyond treating the ill. Almost everyone from actors to top to bottom production personnel who worked on these films knew of Renna. As one key production person said, "I never knew his name. I just knew him as Dr. Feelgood." According to the source, at the end of particularly grueling work days, Stone was known to call out, "Where's Chris? I need my medication!" In addition to his on-call servicing of Stone, it's alleged Renna routinely administered B_{12} shots to the tired cast and crew. According to one performer who couldn't sleep, the highly addictive downer Restoril was there for the asking.[44]

Shortly after the recounting of Renna's drug dealings on *Natural Born Killers* was reported by the Ebner half of *Hollywood, Interrupted* under the pseudonym CC Baxter in *Spy* magazine, the good humor doctor responded thus:

Spy, June, 1995
Letter to Spy
Natural Born Enemas

> *You are truly the burlap of scandal rags. Not only was what you wrote about me, Oliver Stone, and Natural Born Killers (out on video) incorrect {THE INDUSTRY, February}, but you failed to dig up the real stuff, which was much more scandalous and despicable than the cheap, stupid stuff you reported.*
>
> *First, how original was it to smear me with the title "Dr. Feelgood"? Which of your imbecile staff captured that prize quote? I mean get wired SPY, Feelgood was what they called Elvis' Doctor! If you couldn't find someone to give you a "Dr. CHem-man" or a "Dr. Jumpstart" quote you should have done what you usually do and make up something Spy-cheesy like "Dr. Delight."*
>
> *Next, the comment about Oliver surrounding himself with people with less than dignified backgrounds implies that our backgrounds are somewhat close to dignified. I hope you didn't mean me! I used a II-S deferment to dodge five, count 'em, five years of draft eligibility and inhaled and masturbated at the same time.*
>
> *Indiscriminate B-12 shots! No way. V-8, sometimes I.V., and always from rusty cans. There was no way the company was going to pay for real B-12 for such last-stop hacks as Harrelson, Downey and Lewis, not to mention Tommy Lee and Sizemore. And certainly not for an equally untalented and derelict crew. I had to use V-8, and they were lucky to get that uncut.*
>
> *Your next paragraph contained the biggest laugh. You said I was licensed in two states. Incredible! I want to know, have you or any of your sources ever seen my license? Has anyone even tried to verify that I have a license? Are you prepared to back that license thing up? If I were a real doctor, or even a D.O. for that matter, I'd be tempted to come over and do a procto exam on C.C. Baxter [Ebner] so I could locate his head and laugh in his face. You idiots actually think I'm a doctor! Oliver hired me to tell Tom Cruise (a.k.a. Ron Kovic) he'd never walk or have sex again, but at the last minute he gave*

the lines to Bob Gunton because he liked his beard. The problem was he'd already paid me SAG minimum. Now you, of all ragscum, know that Oliver has a reputation of being brilliant, clever, and always getting his money's worth. Without any lines, I'd been overpaid; so he made me pay him back by acting like "the-doctor-on-the-set" for all his subsequent films. I can't believe you junior sophisticated went for it hook, line, and sinker!

. . . I'm . . . just some star-serving-fake-doctor giving out V-8 shots and living on a movie set. I'm surprised you guys even noticed, but then again, some guys are whores for whispers, aren't they?

Chris Renna
Dallas, Texas

C.C. Baxter [Ebner] responds: Hey Chris, can I get a high colonic with that procto?

Renna would perfect his role on most of Stone's next pictures, including *Nixon, U-Turn,* and *Any Given Sunday* (where he was credited as "production consultant," presumably because of his osteopathic experience, despite the fact that his osteopathic specialty is in family medicine, not sports medicine). He would also frequently double-dip into the production budget by playing small roles, often a physician of some sort (except *NBK*, where he thought it would be cool to portray a prisoner with a swastika tattooed on his forehead). His wife also made a small career out of taking checks as a bit player on Stone films.[45]

But Stone was just Renna's ticket into the world of celebrity medicine. When asked by a Dallas business newspaper what was the most important decision he made that led to his success, Renna replied "going into preventative medicine."

Preventative medicine. The practice of healing people who aren't sick. The perfect practice for a snake oil salesman like Renna. His first big money idea was fat people. When doctors started experimenting with the combination of over-the-counter uppers, commonly know as "fen-phen," to treat obesity, Renna jumped on the train like it was the last one out of Saigon in 1975. Sure, the pill combo helped some who were chronically obese, but far more patients were of the "I'd look better in a swimsuit if I was 15 pounds, lighter" variety. For a country generally thought to be overweight, and certainly one so dosed with images of 105-pound models that they felt that way whether it's true or not, getting on the miracle diet train was a gold mine. In 1996 alone, there were 18 million prescriptions written for fen-phen.[46]

The rush of cash must have blinded Renna to the increasingly obvious deleterious side effects of this untested drug cocktail. Even weeks after the FDA began putting out warnings that fen-phen use led to an increased risk of a potentially fatal and incurable heart valve defect, Renna was out front cheerleading for the meds. In July 1997, after the FDA had already issued two strong warnings of the drug combo's dangers, *The New York Times* reported that "Dr. Christian Renna, a doctor with offices in Dallas and Los Angeles who says he's prescribed fen-phen for hundreds of patients, said, 'I am not worried about the use of these medications.' Rather, he said, 'I am worried about the public's reaction.'" Eight weeks later, the FDA recalled the drugs, and a massive class action suit was filed due to the link to the heart valve problems.[47]

Seemingly, desperate for a new fad on which to capitalize, Renna tried his hand at a number of get-rich-quick schemes. He became spokesman for a company called Protective Factors, endorsing a product called Smoke Defense. Smoke Defense was a blend of herbal antioxidants that claimed to significantly reduce the incidence of smoke-related diseases. Renna goes on record, quacking that "Taking Smoke Defense on a daily basis is an easy, effective way for smokers to protect themselves against the harmful effects of smoking." Not surprisingly, the company itself soon goes up in smoke.[48]

Ever willing to explore areas outside of his bone-cracking expertise—especially lucrative ones—Renna stumbles on the oldest snake oil in the business, the Fountain of Youth. Renna embraces the religion of antioxidants and starts the LifeSpan Clinic, a practice that specializes in "life extension therapies," basically cashing in on people's fear of death through hGH, human growth hormone, a controversial synthetic hormone known to accelerate the growth of existing cancers.[49] It's a regimen he had tried out on Stone years before.[50] But now it was his ticket back to the big bucks.

What more fertile field for cultivating the seeds of youth than beauty-obsessed Hollywood? Stone sums up Hollywood's vainities in a November 2000 interview with *The Evening Standard*. "Why do we have to die at 75?" he said. "Why not 100? It got me thinking. I think I look younger, but feeling better is the issue." Renna quickly becomes the latest in a series of faddishly fashionable gurus singing the praises of a healthy diet and vitamins as a way of raging against the dying of the light. Stone, always looking for a new kick, swallowed Renna's line like a starving salmon. He quickly swears by Renna's regimen of vitamins and supplements, a hodgepodge of known and folkloric remedies of no scientifically proven effectiveness.

With Stone as his calling card, other celebrities like Mickey Rourke, Chuck Norris, and Red Hot Chili Peppers frontman Anthony Kiedis quickly sign on. Most famously, Renna hooks up with human chemistry set Nick Nolte. In May 2001, yo-yo rehabbing Nolte joins Renna on the CBS newsmagazine "48 Hours." Nolte discusses his diet regimen (including raw asparagus for breakfast), the 60+ pills he takes every day, his obsessed study of his own blood under a microscope, and of course, the tens of thousands of dollars he spends each year trying to stay young. Renna earns his keep by performing a rash of "tests" and then vaguely proclaiming that "Nick is definitely functioning like a younger person."[51] Months later, Nolte is arrested driving wildly on the Pacific Coast Highway under the influence of the date rape drug GHB, clearly dysfunctioning like a younger person.

And Renna? He goes on, pumping aging Boomers full of hormones and vitamins, leaving them no younger but lighter in the wallet. Did Stone pollute Renna, making him into what he is today? Or was Renna just a leech waiting for a ripe-veined animal from whom to feed. One can't tell for sure. Clearly, they make a symbiotically sick combination, doctor and patient, director and actor, and . . . friends.

But when the hypocrites of the Hippocratic Order meet the desperate needs—drugs (comfort), beauty (immortality), and oblivion—of the rich and famous, money changes hands, as do the ethics that serve as the bedrock of a moral society.

Hide and Go Sikh

Hepatitis C infects well over 4 million otherwise ordinary Americans. Known as the "silent killer," the virus also rages through the royal bloodlines of Hollywood's incestuous entertainment community. In a cozy, company town where bodily fluids are mixed like so many

Cosmopolitans, anonymous Hollywood "heppers" are as likely to be chairing a movie studio meeting as they are a Beverly Hills 12-step congregation.

Not since AIDS surfaced in the early 1980s has a pox on Movie City put so many of the glitterati on a par with a vast proportion of the bulk California prison system, unfortunate Vietnam veterans, and Skid Row junkies sharing syringes with everyone.[52]

The largely faceless Hollywood hep set is an apt risk group, comprised of the legions who have shared drug needles (including spoons and cotton) and/or shared straws or bills to snort street drugs. Some have had tattoos or piercings applied with contaminated inks or needles, had unprotected sex with multiple partners, or had a history of sexually transmitted diseases.

The hep C blight plaguing Hollywood might easily be written off as some sort of karmic retribution for youthful indiscretion. But, "Just speaking for me," says junkie memoirist Jerry Stahl (*Permanent Midnight*), "I deserve a lot worse. Hepatitis C? I got off easy. I should be strung up . . . with my liver hanging out of my nostrils for the shit I did."

Somber entertainment industry professional Buddy Enright bleeds: "My response to these moral referees declaring that people deserve hepatitis C is that this is bigotry's finest hour if this is the position the world is going to take. It conveniently excludes, or actually disregards the fact that these people—whether they're [the late] Mickey Mantle, Naomi Judd, Larry Hagman or me—are somebody's brother or sister, or somebody's mother and father. We are somebody's children. These are not just statistics. We are people who are going to be disappearing from the entertainment scene, the music scene, the nursing scene, and the teaching scene."

That said, hepatitis C is not necessarily a death sentence. A small percentage of the infected clear the virus on their own, and pricey new interferon-based treatments are now available that suppress the insidious virus into sustained submission in up to a remarkable 60 percent of test trial cases. While leading liver disease specialists are reluctant to claim an absolute cure is afoot, they are witnessing positive results from what they cautiously call "sustained responders," or patients who have remained clear of the detectable virus for six months after completion of their treatment regimens.[53]

But where are the infected Armani-clad movie execs, starlets, and young MTV rockers when hep C research, on the cusp of a cure (or at least a vaccination), could use a pop culture booster shot most? Where are the lily-livered counterparts to the outspoken Parkinson's-afflicted Michael J. Fox, the diabetic Mary Tyler Moore, and the HIV-infected Magic Johnson? They are hiding. And whispering.

An anonymous, infected Disney executive shrugs and says, "Hep C is not exactly the disease of loving." This VP-striped ex-junkie is not likely to helm a hep C charity benefit any time soon. And a pretty working actress who fears she'd lose roles, "especially those involving love scenes," should she come out as a Hollywood hepper won't be sporting a yellow ribbon at her next audition.[54]

Unfortunately, when celebrities with hepatitis C are hushed to the point of mounting whispering campaigns of self-preservation, they flock to the gurus and mountebanks offering up quack cures which might result in celebrity silence equaling death for lack of better care.

The aforementioned Disney exec claims a Beverly Hills–based Sikh physician cured him. He notes that his prescribed tonic of herbs "cost [him] a fortune." But the Sikh in question, internist and "functional medicine" specialist Dr. Soram Singh Khalsa, twice refused interview requests—his Hippocratic Oath bounding him to treat the sick to the best of his ability notwithstanding.

Not surprisingly, when we got the report that Red Hot Chili Pepper front man about town Anthony Kiedis was sharing his alternative hepatitis C success story to a number of desperate heppers, the source of his purported cure led right back to Dr. Soram Khalsa's door. Unfortunately, the rocker's healer, Sat Hari Khalsa (who also did not return repeated phone calls) had recently stopped working out of the Khalsa Medical Clinic—the Beverly Hills-based home to Dr. Soram's internal/functional medicine office. Clinic administrator Siri Bhrosa Kaur Khalsa sternly offered that not only did Sat Hari no longer work there, she functioned not (as some of her patients were led to believe) as a registered nurse, but as an "assistant."

Sat Hari, an apostate Sikh, has been administering a controversial treatment known as ozone therapy to Kiedis (who likewise did not respond to interview requests through his publicist and management). She reportedly tours with his band and tends to a select, word-of-mouth–referred group of carefully screened, wealthy hep C patients when time allows.

One former Sat Hari patient is motion picture transportation co-ordinator (responsible for all the Teamsters, drivers' vehicles, and coordination of every aspect of the mammoth task of transportation on a movie production) Vic Anderson. Having twice undergone debilitating interferon treatments, leading to common side effects like head and muscle aches, fever, chills, nausea, irritability, insomnia and depression, Anderson—after months of waiting for a call-back from Sat Hari—holed up at wealthy Los Angeles entrepreneur Gerald Schamales's Brentwood estate for a series of ozone treatments.

Ozone therapy, not FDA-approved, involves the intravenous re-moval of blood. The blood is then thinned using several agents, mixed vigorously with ozone, or O_3—an unstable, "supercharged" form of oxygen falsely rumored to kill viruses—then run through ultraviolet light (another falsely presumed blood-cleansing agent), and finally injected back into the patient's system.[55] Anderson and Schamales underwent months of daily ozone therapy at $150 a pop. Their health did not improve. In fact, both of their virus levels, as tested in a more clinical setting after the ozone treatments, rose quite dangerously.

Anderson is unfazed by the failure of Sat Hari's ozone treatments, even though both he and Schamales took the therapy to the limit—resorting to self-injecting measured doses of ozone directly into their veins. Anderson shrugs. "She [Sat Hari] never claimed that this was a cure. She said that Anthony [Kiedis] had been doing it, and he had responded to it very well. But," according to Anderson, "she had never seen a blood test from him, she only took him at his word." Bottom line? "She never made the claim that this was going to be the solution to my hepatitis C problem."

Then why do it? "I've read things that said 'Hey, this works,' and I've heard things that said 'Hey, this works.'" He sighs. "When you're sick, you're going to opt to try and take advantage of this stuff."

Schamales is a bit more blunt regarding his failed ozone experi-ment. "I was disappointed," he says. "They [ozone therapists] don't know what they're doing."

Nevertheless, Red Hot Chili Pepper Anthony Keidis most recently appeared in a "behind the scenes" *Rolling Stone* magazine feature. In a photo, the pop icon is depicted kicking back on his tour bus, shirtless, with a huge hypodermic needle applied to his vein by an anonymous feminine hand. Taking no issue with the efficacy of ozone treatment, *Rolling Stone* irresponsibly shared dubious, quasi-medical speculation from a rock star with about a million readers when they published the following photo caption credited to Keidis:

"The first line in the second verse of 'Can't Stop' sings the praises of being treated with ozone. It's a gas that our nurse administers through the vein. Cleans the body of viruses and bacteria. New medicine on the cutting edge."[56]

"Don't Worry About a Thing"

Details magazine dubbed hep-infected Pamela Anderson "the poisoned pin-up," and "Saturday Night Live's" Tina Fey recently joked that Anderson and her former (or maybe current, maybe not) fiancé Kid Rock (she dumped him at one point because he "drinks too much") were bridal-registered at the Centers for Disease Control. Anderson, best known for her breasts, "Baywatch," and her best-selling, widely inseminated honeymoon video, shrugs off the jabs. The mother of two is used to public ridicule, and considers herself an outcast from the elite Hollywood circles sharing news of the latest elixirs.

In fact, Pamela's main source of fellowship was a homeless guy who confronted her at the grocery store. "He just dragged himself into the store," marvels Anderson. "And he was all dirty, and he goes, 'Pamela, don't worry about a thing. I have hepatitis C.'" She replied: "I won't worry about it any more. Thank you sir. We're in this together." And then she walked around the corner in her Prada blouse. "But it was so endearing," she gushes. "He was really reaching out to me. He was like, 'Don't worry, I'm okay.'"

Reportedly also on and off and on again with her former husband, the ripe-for-a-reality show rocker Tommy Lee, who she claims infected her via a shared tattoo needle, Anderson battles the disease with humor. "You have to have a sense of humor," she insists. "That's how I'm dealing with it. I'm going to make 'Liverace' T-shirts for everybody."

Anderson is not ready for the latest debilitating Western medical treatments. She's too busy raising her kids as a single mom and working on a self-referential animated show called "Striperella" with Marvel Comics legend Stan Lee. Her hope for a cure lies in the hands of her matronly homeopathic healer, Wendy Hewland. The remedy specifically tailored for Anderson, according to Hewland, consists of "70% plant sources, 20% minerals and mineral composites, and 10% animal sources such as lion's milk and bugs and butterflies and all sorts of things."[57]

A dual-infected (HIV and hepatitis C) *New York Times* journalist pooh-poohs the herbs and the ozone. "It all sounds like the beginning of AIDS," says the scribe, who is about to go on a cutting edge "combo therapy" called Peg-Intron. He asks, "With so many promising treatments in the pipeline, why waste your time?"

Why? Like most Hollywood product, it takes time, trial, and foolish error for the players to come around to what really works.

6

FROM REHAB TO DETOX

Detox? There's a bargain. $13,000 for a three-and-a-half week treatment. And, folks, I don't want to sound like a casual user or anything, but if you can come up with $13,000, you don't have a problem yet!
—Sam Kinison

The second step in the Alcoholics Anonymous big book blueprint for living sober reads: *Came to believe that a power greater than ourselves could restore us to sanity*—a sweet, simple, spiritually dressed up way of telling celebrity 12-step stumblebums that they are, indeed, insane—a fellowship of cracked, deranged, disordered lunatics. They are mad, maniacal, non compos mentis nuts. They're reasonless, screwy, unbalanced, unsound, wacky, witless, and irrational—in short, a bunch of brainsick Bedlamites, unfit for human interaction outside of the loony bin. Still, a common, if not clichéd definition of insanity clung to in Hollywood is Einstein's "doing the same thing over and over and over again and expecting different results." "I can control my drinking and drug use," spout besotted celebrities from time to time, as they are rehired time and time again, and, from time to time, they lose control and break out in crime.

In the Golden Age of Hollywood, press agents worked overtime to hide their star clients' frequent visits to the drunk tank, or more fittingly, insane asylum. Today, celebrities opportune to stay mad by marketing their madness. Such strategy keeps them in the spotlight. Waving the rehab white flag at just the right moment—usually timed for a movie premiere, record release, or comeback platform— has become a time-honored right of passage, a badge of honor, ulti- mately played out in publicist-controlled chitchat with Diane Sawyer or Barbara Walters.

To wit, in the turgid ballad "On My Own" off her last album titled "Just Whitney," demented diva Whitney Houston sings, "I never had the chance to do things my way, so now it's time for me to take con- trol."[1] Too bad her ill-advised appearance on Diane Sawyer's couch to promote her album and basically announce that she had too much class for crack cocaine was a case study in a fractured life belying the putative substance of her art. In the midst of her very public melt- down, Houston turned up on national television with her husband, criminal crooner Bobby Brown. They came off like a pimp and his pedestrian crack whore in the last throes of denial. According to Whitney, she has "solved her problem," *on her own*, and in a bizarre outburst of Just Say No-ishness, the screaming skull actually announced to ABC news cameras, "Crack is cheap. I make too much for me to ever smoke crack. Let's get that straight, OK? I don't do crack. I don't do that. Crack is whack."[2] If Whitney doesn't realize that the "control" she sings of is her own worst enemy, statistics have her in a box in less than five years.

On a parallel death track of his addictions, tortured actor Nick Nolte recently told the *New York Daily News*, "You keep it under con- trol. Sometimes you don't." In a "share the moment" moment shared from the Kodak Theater in Hollywood, his "dazed and drooling" mug shot, snapped after he took a wrong turn en route to an AA meeting, was beamed as a faux fashion statement around the world courtesy of Oscar ceremony host Steve Martin. Clearly, that was an example of one of those "sometimes you don't" moments for the 62-year-old Nolte. The date rape drug GHB was found in his system the night he was pulled over for erratic driving in Malibu. In the *Daily News*, Nolte further commented, "I asked someone out recently, someone closer to my own age, and she said, 'Oh, no, you're too famous.' I got famous to [get sex], and now I can't. What are you going to do?"[3] Dosing yourself with GBH wouldn't seem to be the right answer.

Interesting that the Academy of Motion Picture Arts and Sciences finds humor in Nolte's self-destruction on the same night they award a fugitive who drugged a 13-year-old girl, anally violated her, and then fled for France to pursue his legacy in the arts.[4]

Nolte = Funny.

Polanski = Genius.

Thank God nobody gave Manson a camcorder in prison. He would possess an Irving Thalberg lifetime achievement award by now.

Currently on probation, yet, in keeping with the Hollywood tradition of rewarding stars for their excessive behavior, Nolte, clean and clear-eyed out of rehab, has a host of studio movies in the pipeline. The other classic reprobate, Downey Jr., turned his revolving door tour—from jail to rehab to retox—into a fresh self-reinvention as a television star on "Ally McBeal," and blew that by getting loaded again.[5]

Fans intoxicated by stardom and charmed by the Hollywood bad boy allure should also note that most of our drug- and alcohol-plagued personalities are parents, begging the question: If they can't manage or control their own lives, how can they manage the lives of their offspring? Oh yeah—in the cross-cultural hands of illegal caretakers.

Rehab California-Style

Like a really, really bad sitcom, in late summer of 2001 (even as "Friends" stooge Matthew Perry was lolling around Cedars-Sinai Hospital detox unit), Robert Downey Jr. and Ben Affleck (who friends had taken to calling "Robert Downey Jr. Junior") found themselves encamped at Promises Malibu, a luxury rehabilitation center overlooking the Pacific Ocean.

After his umpteenth probation violation in July 2001, Downey (*Less Than Zero*) was court-ordered to spend a year at Promises Malibu. Affleck, too, sought help on the cliffs of Malibu, following a Las Vegas booze and gambling binge. Noted Promises alum Charlie Sheen dropped him off for a brief Promises stint in late July.[6] Still, Downey, Perry, and Sheen all shine in their high-paid television appearances.

Posh residential rehab centers like Promises Malibu employ gourmet chefs and personal trainers, and even offer professional babysitter services for slippery celebrities working on life-or-death movie projects. Babysitters, or celebrity chaperones, assist their charges as outpatients in overcoming their deadly diseases, which that are often masked, yet perversely promoted by publicists as "cumulative lifestyles," "personal issues," "exhaustion," and "dehydration."

Requesting anonymity, a music industry veteran shares her experience of strength and hope found at Promises Malibu:

> Someone I'd been seeing—which is a euphemism for having sex with— admitted himself to Promises because he realized he was doing too many drugs, a surprise to me since I hadn't seen him loaded during our six months of doing the deed. He called me from there and asked that I come visit him the next Sunday. Always willing to be of service, so to speak, I did.
>
> I pulled into the private parking lot off a narrow road and saw the place made famous by so many blurry photos in tabloids. The buildings, a large two-story house and a smaller guesthouse, stood on opposite sides of a pool and Jacuzzi. At picnic tables shaded with umbrellas from the hot Malibu sun, residents fraternized with their guests. There was a tee, some golf balls, and a couple clubs on the edge of a shale ridge. "This is our driving range," laughed my substance abusing stud.
>
> My friend, we'll call him Ted, escorted me about and introduced me to his fellow junkies, juicers, hopheads, and coke fiends. One was the CEO of a huge corporation; his family had flown in on a private jet to visit. Another had been on a championship sports team; his family was staying in a hotel nearby. There was also an actor whose excesses were legendary; he insisted that everyone call him by the name he'd checked in under—Larry Blechman, but we all knew who he was. One of his assistants dropped by with some scripts and magazines. Another famously rehabbed actor also came by to visit the inmates, maybe not the best idea. His career was, and still is, so in the dumps it could make anyone turn to drink out of despair. If that's what sobriety does, make mine a double eightball, dude.

First, Ted showed me around the main house where dinner was being prepared—huge steaks, richly marbled, an inch and a half thick were being marinated for the indoor grill; residents took turns cooking, making salad, doing the dishes and so on during their stay. This might have been the only time someone would ever set a table or do dishes—rehab can be so harsh. The ever-vigilant staff kept close eye on the carving knives, more carefully than they did female visitors.

While most people milled about outside, Ted gave me a tour of the guesthouse that he shared with some of the guys. Ladies and some other men were housed in the larger dorm, though this may vary by the number of each sex present at a time. The main room of the guesthouse was a kitchen/family room with a TV, stereo, and plenty of comfy chairs and couches. The messy bedrooms were shared, and Ted felt he should show me the bathroom as well—mainly so he could draw the blinds and have sex with me. "I could get kicked out for this," he smiled afterwards. I walked out of the bathroom first and out onto the patio, and he followed a couple minutes later trying to be as discreet as possible—hell you don't want to blow your $1000 a day detox for some nooky, now do you? Addict answer: Only if you don't get caught. I wonder if he ever shared about that in an AA meeting.

P.S. Ted has been clean and sober now for over six years. While he still enjoys doing it in lavatories, he only indulges with his fiancée, and she's not me.

Back at the recovery ranch before lights out, stars in recovery savor an ocean view in front of a cozy wood-burning fireplace while kicking the habit. Only 28 more days to go before they are released to the pages of *People* magazine in which they'll discuss the joys of newfound sobriety. Problem is, they rarely stay clean and sober, and they damage the otherwise excellent reputation and effectiveness of Alcoholics Anonymous by breaking their anonymity at all levels by broadcasting their membership to press, radio, Internet, or television audiences. A celebrity chronicles his adventures in rehab, announces his AA membership to the world, and winds up soused in public again, giving the altruistic AA program a bad name to those who desperately desire recovery. As a power of example largely unheeded in Hollywood, Bill Wilson, the cofounder of Alcoholics Anonymous, broke his anonymity but once—in his obituary in *The New York Times*.[7]

Although it's often joked that Minnesota with its flagship treatment center Hazelden is "the land of 10,000 rehabs," California is truly the backyard Mecca for inebriated entertainers "in between projects." In 2001, California passed Proposition 36, allowing first- and second-time nonviolent drug offenders to receive substance abuse treatment instead of jail time. So, the number of facilities will only increase to service the conga line of junkie and juicehead celebrities in and out of recovery.

Imagine the horror of being sentenced to the newest sanitarium-by-the-shore. Passages of Malibu boasts: ". . . house and guest house is spacious (15,500 square feet), exquisitely detailed and finished with exotic woods and marble, several fireplaces, two juice bars, a library, chef's kitchen, a dining room to seat thirty people, 12 bedrooms, each with its own private marble bath." This luxury facility also features distractions purposely not found in most rehabs stressing the need for an addict/alcoholic to keep the focus on himself or herself. With its "fully equipped gymnasium, an arts and crafts room, a media room with a flat screen 65 inch television screen, an auditorium with stage for the production of plays and readings that seats approximately 80 persons, and a large living room for informal meetings and relaxation by a fire," Passages offers amusements aplenty. Forget focus. With perks like that, inebriated inmates might easily forget why they are there in the first place.

The Passages founders and facilitators for fun in the sun are the tanned and toned ex–cocaine and heroin junkie Pax Prentiss, and his pop, Chris—a metaphysical writer publishing under the pseudonym swu wei. Unflinchingly, Passages offers the following in terms of treatment[8]:

- Electroencephalograph (brain wave analysis)
- Twice-weekly Acupressure/Physical Therapy, one-on-one
- Twice-weekly Spiritual/Psychic Counseling, one-on-one
- Twice-weekly Psychotherapy Sessions, one-on-one
- Twice-weekly Trainer, one-on-one
- Twice-weekly Hypnotherapy Sessions, one-on-one
- Weekly Reflexology Treatments, one-on-one
- Acupuncture, one-on-one
- Yoga Therapy, three times/week
- Weekly Drama Therapy

- Full Body Massage, three times/week
- Equine Therapy
- Hydrotherapy
- Sauna Therapy
- Nutritional Counseling
- Meditation Instruction
- Metaphysical Training

Equine therapy? Is Passages some sort of hoax intended for sitcom development? Nope, the rehab is as real as its slogan is unbelievable: *"Easy Sobriety. It's a way of life."*

To their credit, Passages does offer weekly one-on-one "12 Step Training," which hopefully includes the collective, cautionary AA opinion, "We thought that we could find an easier, softer way. But we could not." But how in the name of equine therapy is a half-cocked Passages client with a given inability to differentiate true from false supposed to distinguish advice from the AA Big Book from that of Mister Ed?

THE BELIEVERS

PART III

Where Tom and John and Kirsty do battle with
Thetans. Madonna gets vocal. Who's a
Scientologist and who isn't?

KARMA CHAMELEONS

Los Angeles is a land where many want to *believe*. And since so many in the business of illusion are already dedicated to narcissism and self-denial, the Southland has become a seller's market for body cults, New Age spirituality, and fast-food salvation. Yoga is the new A-list religion in Hollywood, as chic yoga studios around town have become reliable places to spot Jerry Seinfeld, Demi Moore, Meg Ryan, Lucy Liu, and Nicolas Cage, among others. Yoga teachers like Yogiraj "Bikram" Choudhury and Gurumukh have themselves become stars. Though no one has admitted affiliation yet, Nude Yoga is said to be a Hollywood rage. The come-on of tantric sex has become a talking point for hemp devotee Woody Harrelson and singer Sting, who brags of five-hour sessions with wife Trudy, information that smacks of over-sharing. Actress Rita Wilson, best known as wife-of-Tom-Hanks, who made a name for herself as producer of the movie *My Big Fat Greek*

Wedding, claims one of her secrets of successful marriage is that "you gotta have lots of tantric yoga sex!"[1]

Madonna, Courtney Love, and Roseanne simultaneously converged on the Kabbalah, a Jewish mysticism that relies heavily on meditative, devotional, numerological, and mystical practices. Quickly falling in line were Sandra Bernhard, Laura Dern, Goldie Hawn, Diane Keaton, Naomi Campbell, Steven Seagal, Porno for Pyros front man Perry Farrell, and Elizabeth Taylor. Guy Ritchie's Madonna penned a children's book on the cult that, in a February 2002 interview with Larry King, Monica Lewinsky said helped stimulate her "mental brain."[2]

"Historically Hollywood and the entertainment industry have been rife with such connections to controversial groups," says internationally recognized cult expert Rick Ross. "Many people view celebrities as 'role models' and may be influenced by their endorsements of such groups."[3]

Bucking the Establishment

Celebrities believe they are the anointed ones. But like mere mortals searching for the meaning of life, celebrities want to know the Truth of Existence, preferably in a really cool, unique, easier, softer setting, from some exotic teacher or guru, so they can be way ahead of the trend curve. By hawking their avatar to the public, celebrities are hopeful they will gain some karma points in the hereafter so they don't reincarnate as the literal jackasses they appear to be in the here and now.

Although the New Age–debunking Catholic Church and hardline Protestant sects have argued otherwise, celebrities' often flaky faiths are for the most part relatively harmless to them. However, when noncelebrities get involved with some of these groups, their experiences can differ significantly from the quasi-spiritual good times had by the more famous. Many innocent citizens are lured into destructive groups by the positive press spun by celebrities to their chosen alternative belief systems. While celebrities are praised, red-carpeted, and pampered within cults, often the civilian members are treated with far less than loving care, a fact that is easily hidden from the oblivious stars.[4]

Some belief systems employ subtle forms of mind control and enlighten by lightening one's wallet, and that's the least of their malfeasance. These cults operate as a group with an absolute totalitarian leader (dead or alive) who has no accountability to anyone and who is himself or herself the defining element of the group. That personality defines the entire group and is its organizational glue. Members of destructive cults give up their ability to think and reason largely for themselves and instead become very dependent on a leader to think for them, to analyze for them, and to make value judgments for them. Combine cult affiliation with celebrity-employed machinery (lawyers, accountants, business managers, agents, publicists, and nannies) and the star in question need not think at all!

Ego destruction is actually part of the formula for a cult mindset, according to deprogrammer and cult expert Rick Ross. By tearing down the members' egos and critical thinking faculties, cults begin to do the members' thinking for them. All responsibility for one's thoughts and actions is turned over to the group's leader; members don't have to think for themselves. The very thing most cults promise is freedom—freedom from worry, from illness, from negativity—and they deliver it in an Orwellian fashion, freedom through thought control.[5]

But in Hollywood, there are scores of actors, directors, and other industry professionals who like to think of themselves as representing free thought, free expression, and freedom in general. They make a point of speaking out on various issues, questioning authority, and general rabble rousing. These same gung-ho-for-their-guru celebs may question the authority of the Establishment in Washington DC, or pay lip-service support to human rights of people all over the world, yet they rarely question the authority of leaders of cult groups with whom they affiliate themselves. These brainwashed tastemakers do not trouble themselves to worry about the living conditions and exorbitant costs for noncelebrity members who may be suffering in the lower rungs. Additionally, they don't really want to hear, or may be shielded from, the voices of former members treated as "evil apostates" who have been abused by the cult. So here we have a group of self-perceived do-gooders who march in lockstep to hell at the order of their personal totalitarian messiah, yet scream "fascism" whenever some government refuses to do what the celebrity feels it should.[6]

There are a grossly disproportionate number of Hollywood celebrities who are involved in cults, but then again, compared to the rest of the cities in the United States, Hollywood also has a disproportionate number of young blond bimbos with 36C-cup bras and 17-inch waists. The insecurity of stardom, the itinerancy of only being as good as your last picture, and the ever-popular excuse of low self-esteem make for vulnerable, support-needy groups of people in Hollywood, who are by nature and nurture emotionally starved. Religio-spiritual groups find they can prey on that helplessness, attracting celebrities with ease, especially when one successful star speaks out on behalf of a belief system. Once indoctrinated, the entertainers' egos are massaged, their needs are met, and they are assured that they have found *the Way*, because darn, they are special—and especially valuable.

Cults aggressively recruit celebrities, or "opinion leaders," because they see them the same way that Madison Avenue does—as a pull for further sales by endorsing their product. Combine that recruiting with the stars' vulnerability, and you have a recipe for Cult-o-mania California style—a litany of luminaries involved in one group or another, flogging their chosen faith of the moment. Frankly, it's hard to keep up with these celebrity cult-hoppers who run from one guru to the next in the futile search for the Antidote for Boredom.[7]

If It Sounds Eastern, It Must Be Hip

Hollywood's fascination with exotic religions dates back to the 1920s when stars rubbed shoulders with Krishnamurti, a handsome young Indian mystic who frolicked with the likes of Greta Garbo, Charlie Chaplin, and writers Aldous Huxley and Christopher Isherwood on the banks of the Los Angeles River.[8]

But by the mid-1960s, sages and gurus were as plentiful as lice in a North Beach flophouse. Zen was extremely popular as the precursor to the New Age movement, with literary idols Alan Ginsberg and Jack Kerouac leading Hollywood into its rejection of straight America's rigid and conformist Judeo-Christian orthodoxy.[9]

Speaking of false idols, the San Francisco scene also developed two high proto-priests, Anton LaVey and Charles Manson. Aside from brief brushes with fame (Sammy Davis Jr. was an honorary member of LaVey's cult) and his publicity-starved claims that he mounted Jayne Mansfield, Church of Satan leader LaVey stayed pretty much below the Hollywood radar.[10] That is until Marilyn Manson (née Brian Warner from Fort Lauderdale, Florida) decided to really *epater le bourgeoisie* by proudly displaying his friendship with the dying Black Pope in his autobiography *Long Hard Road Out of Hell*.[11]

Death dealer Charles Manson, a one-time practicing prison Scientologist,[12] lured homeless hippie chicks from the Haight into his filthy bed.[13] Like many young rock star wannabes, Manson used his bimbo brigade to gain access to stars. Manson lived with Beach Boy Dennis Wilson before the murders for about six months, and Wilson rewrote and recorded Manson's composition "Cease To Exist" as "Never Learn Not to Love."[14]

While Charlie Manson was California dreamin', the Beatles became more popular than Jesus and proceeded to find God in the form of a bearded Indian, the Maharishi Mahesh Yogi. The Maharishi taught a groovy form of enlightenment called Transcendental Meditation (TM), which involved mumbling a mantra, a secret word that the Maharishi had chosen especially for the individual, a word never to be shared with another person. Later it would be revealed that you weren't supposed to share your exclusive mantra with anyone else because the Maharishi, in a time saving device, gave everyone in specific age groups the exact same mantra.[15]

Popular stage magician Doug Henning joined TM and went from levitating elephants to self-levitation; followers of TM believe that if they meditate hard enough they will bounce in the air. Henning also unsuccessfully ran for Canadian Member of Parliament as a Natural Law Party candidate. Until his untimely death from liver cancer in 2000, Doug Henning was an ardent supporter of the Maharishi, often working to raise funds for Veda Land, a TM-oriented theme park in Canada.[16]

In the United States, the Natural Law Party, comprised of mainly TM members and graduates of the Maharishi University of Management, attempted to merge with Hollywood favorite Ralph Nader's Green Party.[17]

The Hollywood rallying cry for separation of church and state vis à vis Norman Lear's People for the American Way seems only to apply when the church in question is of a Judeo-Christian orientation. When writing to Georgia State Senator Tanksley regarding Georgia's Senate Resolution 1, which would begin the process of amending the state constitution in order to authorize public funds to be given to religious organizations for certain social service purposes, PFAW President Ralph Neas used Baptists as an example of those who might discriminate against others: "A Baptist group, for example, could refuse to hire Catholics or Jews. And a religious organization could refuse to hire divorced, gay, lesbian, or other individuals based on that group's particular religious beliefs."[18]

Neas specifically targeted Baptists as examples of those who would be intolerant, and then lumped all other intolerants under the blanket label "religious organization." Why, one wonders, did he decline to mention that should this bill be passed, a Dianic Wiccan group could refuse to hire a transgendered person or a man for religious reasons; that some businesses run by certain sects of Islam could prohibit a menstruating woman from working; and that employees of businesses run by Scientologists could force employees to run the business under the Church of Scientology's principles and undergo Scientology training?

Media mogul Ted Turner flashed his anti-Christian bias when he referred to Catholic staff members as "Jesus freaks" at a meeting in the Washington newsroom prior to a party for departing broadcaster Bernard Shaw, which took place on Ash Wednesday. According to news reports, the Mouth from the South explained, "I was looking at this woman and I was trying to figure out what was on her forehead," he reportedly said. "At first I thought you were in the [Seattle] earthquake. I realized you're just Jesus freaks." The comments prompted CNN business anchor Stuart Varney to quit the network,[19] Turner divorced his wife Jane Fonda when she became a born-again Christian, stating in an interview with *The New Yorker* magazine, "She just came home and said: 'I've become a Christian.' That's a pretty big change for your wife of many years to tell you. That's a shock."[20]

Judeo-Christian faith has never been big on Turner's list of loves. The Mouth described Christianity as a "a religion for losers,"[21] and suggested that adultery be removed as sin from the Ten Commandments.[22] In 2002 he implied in an interview with the London-based *The Guardian* that the Palestinian suicide bombers were justified.[23] In 1999 he suggested that it's time that Pope John Paul II "get with" the twentieth century; in the same speech he called the pontiff "a Polish landmine detector."[24] He eventually apologized for and/or recanted most of his antireligious rants.[25]

Turner's religious bias seems to only point towards the West. At the United Nations Millennium Peace Summit in 2000, funded in large part by Turner, who had made headlines with his donation of $1 billion to the UN, the rambling media cowboy blasted his own religious upbringing in a Christian sect and went on to praise indigenous religions, butterflies, flowers, and nature.[26] He recalled leaving the Christian faith of his childhood because the denomination of which his family were members "... taught we were the only ones going to heaven.... That confused the devil out of me. I said heaven is going to be a mighty empty place with nobody else there."[27] The summit was opened by an Incan priest and Turner delivered the keynote speech in which he expressed his belief that there is one god who manifests "himself" in numerous ways. Turner has yet to apologize to feminists for stating that god is male.[28]

In the unholy marriage of Eastern religion and Western celebrity, we find the spiritual roots of today's hypocritical Hollywood evangelism. Enlightened celebrities preach touchy-feely egalitarianism, yet live in completely oblivious transcendental opulence. Because they are so darned exotic, Eastern religions have a strong pull for Westerners trying to be cool. And since it's part of a celebrity's unspoken job description to be as esoteric as possible, many turn blindly to the East, as romanticized by commercials, fashion, and golly-gee recruitment movies (*Ghandi, Kundun, The Last Emperor,* and *Golden Child*) for answers instead of just doing what those religions suggest: looking within for the Answer.

In the 1990s Deepak Chopra quickly became the celebrities' guru du jour, combining health, wealth, and spirituality into an easy-to-swallow combo platter that paraded celebrity converts. And thanks to Oprah, the public gobbled up his books, wondering if they were living and eating in accordance to their "dosha," or body type as explained by Deepak in his books on health. For those in need of dosha balancing, Chopra offers Integrated Medical Consultations with David Simon, M.D., the Medical Director of the Chopra Center for Well Being conveniently located an hour and a half south of the Paramount lot at La Costa Resort and Spa near San Diego. There, on the other side of the world from Chopra's impoverished homeland, the three-day Perfect Health Seminar (including "primordial sound meditation," yoga, and vegetarian lunches) costs $595. For the athletically inclined, the Center offers Golf for Enlightenment—"the ultimate weekend workshop on leadership and golf" which includes yoga and meditation along with "General Sessions with Deepak Chopra on Soul of Leadership," meals, a massage, and a round on the links. At the height of his popularity, the country club guru's adherents included Demi Moore, Linda Gray, Cindy Crawford, Naomi Judd, Michael Jackson, Steven Seagal, Madonna, Bonnie Raitt, and George Harrison, many of whom later became adherents of Dr. Philip Berg's Kabbalah Center. In the case of Steven Seagal, the martial arts trainer-turned-actor discovered a whole new side of himself.[29]

In 1997, Seagal was anointed a tulku, a high holy man, upsetting the reverence many in Hollywood had toward Tibet. "I think he's on his own trip there," laughed Richard Gere, an outspoken Tibetan Buddhist, friend of the Dalai Lama, and advocate for freeing Tibet.[30] Gere established himself as the avant-garde, poorly coached defender of the mountainous, mythic country during his speech at the 1993 Oscar awards ceremony. The gentle actor blasted Deng Xiaoping, mispronouncing the Chinese leader's name while urging, unilaterally, for him to withdraw Chinese troops from Tibet.[31] Gere is expressly grateful if anyone's "so-called celebrity status" helps raise awareness of Tibet. As the reincarnation of a holy man, the baby sitter–boinking Seagal made his name and dubious career on rumors of a career in the CIA, and wound up in trouble with the Mob.[32]

While Tibetan Buddhism is a relatively new trend in Hollywood, Nichrin Shoshu of America—the U.S. branch of the Shoku Gai sect of Buddhism (which is behind the third largest political party in Japan, Komeito, or "Clean Government") has been circling around celebrities for several decades. Singer Tina Turner credits NSA and its annoying high-pitched, nasally chant "Nam myoho renge kyo" with giving her strength to launch a comeback career composed of repeat "retirement" tours.[33] Celebrity chef John Sweeney, who strangled the life out of actress Dominique Dunne on her front lawn, carried a Bible to court in a successful bid to sway the jury into a manslaughter charge. He then converted to NSA, at least while he lived with his NSA girlfriend in a West Hollywood bungalow, after serving less than half of his six-and-a-half-year prison term.[34]

Downward Dog to Vocal Tones

Guru-hopping model Christy Turlington, who has flowed from runway to floor mat with her books and pricey line of yoga apparel, is into Swamis Muktananda and Satchidananda. She's also into Yogi Bhajan.

Designer Donna Karan promoted Swami Satchidananda's yoga studio and his Integral Yoga Institute in an April 1999 *Vanity Fair* magazine insert. Maybe she should have done some fact checking: In 1991 numerous female followers alleged that Satchidananda had used his role as their spiritual mentor to exploit them sexually,[35] charges he denied, "They know it is all false," said Satchidananda, founder of a Virginia retreat called Yogaville nestled on 700 acres of land given to him by singer-songwriter Carole King. "I don't know why they are saying these things. My life is an open book. There is nothing for me to hide."[36] Satchidananda died in August 2002 and was buried in a $2 million shrine in Yogaville. One of his former students, painter and pop artist Peter Max, who pleaded guilty to tax evasion in 1998, commented, "From my young adulthood, he set my feet upon a spiritual path imbued with love and service."[37] The year of Satchindananda's death, Karan flowed her allegiance over to yoga instructor Rodney Yee and showed yoga pants in her heavily hyped August 2003 runway collection.[38]

Gucci has a $350 yoga mat, perfect for the upscale students at the Bridge Institute in Los Angeles, where the white-garbed, turban-wearing Gurumuhk Kaur Khalsa teaches stars, including Madonna and Courtney Love, how to do fittingly named poses like "the cobra" and "the corpse." Gurumuhk has been teaching Kundalini yoga for over 30 years, and the past decade has seen her move her classes (which include members of the Red Hot Chili Peppers, Roseanna Arquette, and David Duchovny) from her living room in West Hollywood to the Golden Bridge Nite Moon [sic]. Courtney Love professes that the methods taught by Gurumuhk are "better than Prozac" but has not yet compared the practice to prescription painkillers like her favored Vicodin. Love performed at a $200-a-ticket benefit at Johnny Depp's house of death, the Viper Room, to help fund-raise for the center's launch. Cindy Crawford was trained by Gurumuhk, "the prenatal expert Hollywood has come to trust" to deliver her babies at home, drug free. No word on what pose Gurumuhk recommends for breech births, or what mantra will untangle the umbilical cord from around a choking fetus's neck.[39]

Gurumuhk herself is a member of Sikh Dharma, a.k.a. 3HO (Healthy, Happy, Holy Organization), a group that rose to prominence in the mid-1970s. Its members—who are not affiliated with the Sikhs from the Punjab region of India—wear gauzy, all-white dresses and white cotton leggings, doffing Q-tip shaped turbans. Members are drawn primarily from upper- and middle-class whites who are encouraged to spread the word of Yogi Bhajan. Many followers become chiropractors, yoga instructors, and in some cases, outright quack healers; one follower was indicted for smuggling marijuana from Thailand over a four-year period, money laundering, and arms dealing.[40]

One of the prime tenets of 3HO is that its members are the "pure ones." Part of that purification comes from rising at 3 AM, praying, meditating, and taking a cold shower. Diet is strictly vegetarian, and there are fasts and special diets that may be "necessary." It's also necessary to do yoga and to chant repetitively. According to cult experts, chanting and meditation, combined with dietary restrictions, can produce pliable mental states, making an individual more susceptible to group-think, a mindset reinforced by the continual emphasis on their unique position as the "pure ones."[41]

Madonna has blithely promoted yoga and Hinduism by sporting a dot on her forehead and henna-painted hands. Yet her historic MTV performance combining Eastern mysticism with Western hedonism, "did not sit well with sincere Hindus, Vaishnavas and yoga practitioners around the globe," according to a statement issued by the World Vaishnava Association. The WVA was mainly protesting the karma chameleon's wearing of a see-through blouse and Hindu facial markings at the MTV Music Video Awards. Madonna's response, issued through her publicist, was swift and proved Madonna to be less an enlightened one, and more a posing cobra. "The essence of purity and divinity is non-judgment. They should practice what they preach. If they're so pure, why are they watching TV?"[42]

Although Madonna, the Mother Superior of Perpetual Self-Indulgence, briefly shilled for Shiva, she is famously first and foremost loyal to Kabbalah, or at least the form of Kabbalah as taught at Rabbi Philip Berg's Beverly Hills–adjacent Kabbalah Center. Kabbalah is "very punk rock," Madonna says, oxymoronically adding, "It teaches you that you are responsible for everything," proving conclusively that Madonna was never punk, merely a poseur.[43] Madonna reportedly bought her "punk rock" religion a £3.5 million (um, like $5 million?) house as its London center.[44]

Madonna is not alone in her devotion to the mystical tradition popularized (some would say degraded) by former (secular) insurance salesman Berg, née Feivel Gruberger.[45]

Roseanne Barr and Madonna's ex-stage girlfriend, once funny comedian Sandra Bernhard, are also converts to spiritual insurance salemen Berg's version of Kabbalah, which combines astrology and New Age aphorisms with merchandise like "Kabbalah water." Rabbi Yehuda Berg, the son of the Kabbalah Center's founder, claims this water is charged "with positive energy, so that it has healing powers."[46] The Center also hawks $26 lengths of red string worn around the wrist to protect one against the "evil eye."[47] Explains Bernhard about her Kabbalistic experience, "My DNA has changed—my whole way of being has changed. My energy, my understanding, my compassion, my level of tolerance and patience is something I never dreamed I was capable of."[48] Excellent news. Bernhard's DNA shift has finally knocked her off the fringes of the star map.

Barbra Streisand and Liz Taylor have shown up at posh Kabbalah-cues, and aging actresses Linda Gray and Goldie Hawn have been spotted at the luxe Kabbalah temple and adjacent gift shop. Demi Moore lived up to her nickname "Gimme More" when she requested a Kabbalah Center rabbi get the mystic ball rolling for her by making holy house calls. On the flip side, Madonna has said the star-studded Kabbalah center is "the one place I don't feel like a celebrity."[49] Madonna's husband, Guy Ritchie, is definitely acting like a Hollywood diva with regards to his Kabbalahist conversion. According to the *New York Post*, "Sony was interested in producing Ritchie's new project, *Revolver*, a crime caper set in Las Vegas. . . . But when studio execs saw the script, they balked because it was loaded with kabbalah references." The *Post* goes on to quote a "Hollywood suit" (executive): "Kabbalah is seen as a kind of cult in some circles and no one wanted to be associated with it. Guy's agents told him to rewrite *Revolver* [without the Kabbalah plugs] and maybe it would sell." According to the *Post*, Ritchie ended up doing a rewrite to everyone's satisfaction, only to call his agents at William Morris a few days after it was submitted, fire them, and let it be known the rewrite would be scrapped. "Guy apparently felt he had to be true to his kabbalah beliefs and not stick with the rewrite," claimed the *Post*'s informant. "He was apologetic but felt he had to go to CAA—where Madonna's agent [Bryan Lourd] was and where they would support his kabbalah vision for the movie."[50]

To prepare herself for a grueling week of Paris fashion shows, supermodel Naomi Campbell volunteered her precious time at the Kabbalah Center,[51] where scrubbing toilets is considered a "mitzvah" or a good deed leading to blessing.[52] How touching to think that Campbell might actually get her perfectly manicured hands grubby by doing some honest manual labor instead of abusing her assistants.[53] It's also a blessing to buy a Hebrew language *Zohar*, the thirteenth-century text that is the foundation for Kabbalah. At Berg's Kabbalah Center the most mitzvah-ed of the editions costs over $400; at Borders or Barnes and Noble you can get a paperback version in English for under $20.[54]

The Kabbalah Center's touchy-feely version of the ancient mystic tradition, which they claim "is much more than an intellectually compelling philosophical system," suggests that simply running your fingers over sacred texts and touching the letters will provide plenty of powerful Hebrew hoodoo with the least amount of effort. Rabbi Robert Kirschner, of the Los Angeles Jewish Cultural Centre, says: "It [Berg's Kabbalah] is meant for people who want simplistic answers to the world's problems."[55] Indeed, the Kabbalah Center's web page reads, "With its vision of bringing Kabbalah to anyone and everyone who has a desire to learn, the Centre is dedicated to revealing the ancient wisdom of Kabbalah . . . to helping people to improve their lives personally, professionally, and spiritually . . . and to ridding the world of chaos, fostering true peace, and bringing about the spiritual transformation of all mankind."

It's just a matter of time before many pop culture icons are spotted wearing the Kabbalah Center's official T-shirt printed with three Hebrew letters that are "part of an ancient code known as the 72 Names of God—the recently revealed Kabbalistic antidote for whatever ails us." The Kabbalah Center urges adherents to "simply focus your eyes on the letters, then visualize destroying your ego." How utterly perfect for Hollywood! As Kabbalah cutie and New Age victim Alanis Morissette whines, "Isn't it ironic?"[56]

Fleecing the Flocks

One of the first religions to promise freedom, if not in this life, then in the next, began nearly 2000 years ago. The gospel of Jesus Christ has changed the lives of millions over the past centuries. Unfortunately, some take Jesus's name in vain, utilizing the good will of the Good Word to fleece their flocks, with that money going to prop up the preachers' celebrity life style. Televangelism, or religion by Ronco, preys upon the lonely, the shut-ins, and the desperate, fueling hopes that monetary "love offerings" given in exchange for cheap gewgaws like key chains and prayer cloths will improve their lot in life. Didn't Jesus cast out the moneychangers from the temple?

Jim and Tammy Faye Bakker caught legal wrath for swindling their followers; tarantula-eyelashed Tammy Faye became a talk show host, gay irony icon, and the star of an autobiographical documentary (*The Eyes of Tammy Faye*), proving that Hollywood does forgive, although the jury is out on God's judgment.

Currently the biggest Christian superstars, whose power and influence far outshine the Bakkers, are Pat and Jan Crouch, founders and owners of Trinity Broadcast Network. The couple, who promote a controversial aspect of Christianity called Word of Faith, rake in over $100 million a year for their TV ministry,[57] and draw on a pool of Christian celebrities who promote their faith and current projects to audiences who share their beliefs.

Because TBN is the largest Christian broadcasting network in the world, it provides an unprecedented platform for celebrities, politicians, and others to reach their fellow Christians. Unfortunately, many of these guests may not know that their presence on the Crouch couch lends legitimacy to a minstrel show that has received major criticism from fellow Christians and the secular world. The image of Christianity portrayed on TBN is criticized as a blasphemed take on the Word of God.[58] And then there are the financial issues.

In 2000 the Crouchs bought a $5 million home in Newport Beach, California. Mrs. Crouch was quoted as saying that she wanted more room for her dogs. However, her attorney Colby May clarified the purchase, stating that the couple's ministry bought the house, and—despite Mrs. Crouch's desire for a larger dog run—the mansion would be used as a pied à terre for out-of-town visitors.[59]

In July 2000, the Crouchs were sued for $40 million by a West Virginia minister, Sylvia Fleener, for plagiarizing her published 1997 novel *The Omega Syndrome* and turning it into the hit movie *The Omega Code,* starring Trinity Broadcast Network regulars Michael York, Casper van Dien, and Catherine Oxenberg. The Crouch's son Matthew and TBN synergistically produced the movie. The suit was settled for an undisclosed amount in Ms. Fleener's favor, because after all, thou shalt not steal.[60]

Celebrity guests on TBN have included Chuck Negron of Three Dog Night, soap opera ("The Bold and the Beautiful") star and two-time *People* magazine "Most Beautiful People in the World" Hunter Tylo, and the repeatedly repentant drug addict Gary Busey. There have been numerous appearances by rapper-turned-reverend MC Hammer, and lots of requests for "love offerings" via checks, money orders, or credit cards.[61]

A frequent TBN guest is the ditzy Dyan Cannon, late of the series "Ally McBeal" and the execrable movie *Kangaroo Jack,* who has started up her own ministry called, with plenty of hubris, God's Party with Dyan Cannon and You. God's Party features Dyan's preaching and her Pentecostal-style laying on of hands healing.

There are no hors d'ouerves served at God's Party, but it is "come as you are." Cannon calls on everyone with a "black hole," whose dreams have not come true, and who feels lost and alone to come on down because "da party starts here." In this case, "here" is in a soundstage on GMT Studios in culturally dormant Culver City. God's Party was formerly held at CBS Studios; however, the ongoing bash got cancelled at that location when an Orange County woman, Melody Traylor, and her husband sued Cannon and CBS for negligence and "loss of consortium" when Mrs. Traylor was allegedly injured during a healing.[62]

After some music, after a dance troop gets down for God, but before donations are solicited, there's a chance for healing at the hands of Dyan herself who, like an old-time tent show preacher, will place her manicured mitts on the afflicted so God's power can cure their ills. Traylor claims she was called up on stage for healing and "instructed to fall backward," but was not caught by a member of staff. Oops.[63]

God's Party seems to be the current rest home for Cannon on the road much traveled. Her other flirtations with faith have included dalliances with nearly every self-help fad to trundle through Hollywood including watermelon diets, hypnosis, LSD, and climbing inside an Avis van and pounding its walls.[64]

Out on a Limb

While Cannon's faith is vaguely rooted in the Word of God, some stars have found the words of disincarnate entities far more comforting. In the 1980s, actress Sally Kirkland and musician Carl Wilson of the Beach Boys were entranced by John-Roger, a former Rosemead High School English teacher who called himself Dr. John-Roger Hinkins, and later Sri John-Roger. Offering followers hope of escaping from the wheel of rebirth and karma by ascending Earth's negative realms into "a totally positive state of being" called "soul consciousness," John-Roger taught that reaching the "soul realm" is virtually impossible without the assistance of the Mystical Traveler Consciousness. MTC is a metaphysical power John-Roger claimed to embody, along with the mantle of the "Preceptor Consciousness," an even more powerful presence said to exist on Earth only once every 25,000 years. This mumbo-jumbo, especially accessing the "Mystical Traveler Consciousness," was not cheap or easy, and being the Preceptor Consciousness seems to have worn out John-Roger; currently his classes and workshops are being lead by one John Morton, but health permitting, J-R himself might manifest.[65]

While accepting her 1987 Emmy award, actress Sharon Gless of "Cagney and Lacy" fame gave special thanks to Lazaris, the spiritual entity that Los Angeles resident and former insurance salesman Jach Pursel says inhabits his body. At the peak of his popularity, Pursel claimed more than 25,000 followers in Southern California and around the world, and counseled celebrities such as Gless and actress Shirley MacLaine.[66]

During the past decade, MacLaine, once the most outspoken of all New Age celebs, the mother—or at least midwife—of these cultural and theological abominations, has been curiously absent from the current crop of craziness, ducking the Deepak pack. MacLaine isn't decking the halls with Kabbalah's glory, or enjoying the latest trend, talking to dead people. In this case, it's the recently deceased who are chatting up has-been stars, as opposed to the 5000-year-old warrior Ramtha who so entranced MacLaine, fellow actress Linda Evans, and Evans's ex paramour, New Age musician Yanni.

Ramtha, channeled by former cable TV installer J.Z. Knight, was the ruler of Atlantis until the idyllic island's inhabitants did something bad with technology and blew themselves up, a not so subtle antitech warning that has been floating around the myth of Atlantis since the discovery of the steam engine. Prior to the Scientific Age, Atlantis had supposedly disappeared because of an earthquake or because of the gods' wrath, depending on the expert. Given to foot stomping and goofy phraseology, Ramtha began to body hop, appearing with the corporal help of a German woman. Knight subsequently sued her, claiming she, J.Z., was the only human through whom Ramtha deigned to speak.[67]

This wasn't the only drama in which Ramtha and his vehicle Knight were involved. Ramtha urged followers to move to Yelm, Washington, and to invest in Knight's horse-breeding farm. The investments were not very surefooted, and Ramtha's reason for the mass move—impending natural disaster—failed to manifest, leading to disgruntled, poorer, and very vocal ex-believers. While many of the shorn sheep left Ramtha's teaching, the facial massage machine touting Evans has remained touchingly faithful.[68]

Ramtha was also involved in a child sex abuse case; voice instructor Wayne Allen Geis and his common-law wife, Ruth Beverly Martin, allegedly confessed to statutory rape of a 15-year-old girl after being questioned by Ramtha before 800 astonished students at The Ramtha School of Enlightenment. The couple were subsequently arraigned on 10 counts each of sexual misconduct with a minor.[69] At the time, Deputy Prosecutor Andrew Toynbee said he didn't think Knight would be called to testify.[70] While Ramtha was present in J.Z. Knight's body, J.Z. herself was in a trance and did not recall the revelation. Apparently it's difficult to astrally serve a subpoena on a 35,000-year-old Atlantean warrior.

The ancient dead may have fallen out of favor, but contacting the dearly departed via medium John Edward is a favorite celebrity pastime. Skid Row singer Sebastian Bach; talk show host and former PETA-phile Rikki Lake; *Devil In A Blue Dress* actress Jennifer Beals, "Touched By an Angel's" Roma Downey; and author Anne Rice are just some of the name guests who've used the sloe-eyed, Long Island-accented medium to transmit messages from the Other Side.[71]

Dubbed the "world's biggest douche bag" by stage magicians Penn and Teller,[72] Edward delivered few surprises when he got hold of Rice's dead daughter; the poor kid has been exhumed in every interview and article about Rice since *Interview with the Vampire* went paperback, and there isn't a Goth kid worth their black hair dye who doesn't know that Michelle Rice died at age five of leukemia and that her death inspired her mother's multimillion dollar legacy of vampire, witch, and bondage novels.[73]

A celebrity's job is to act, to shine in his or field. And whether they gain success from dabbling in spooky Santeria like Jennifer Lopez, Eric Estrada, and the late Desi Arnaz; by worshipping the goddess in her many forms; by ignoring religion all together; or by following a mainstream belief system, that's their personal life. Religion, a private matter, should not be shoved down the public's throat, and celebrities, with their high flake factor, don't necessarily make the most convincing proselytizers.

Former drug addict Gary Busey says he's sorry on TBN, but keeps getting into scrapes. Tibetan Buddhism stresses peace, yet alleged holy man Steven Seagal packs a pistol under his brocade Nehru jacket. It's nice that celebrities have faith to get them through those long nights when the bad reviews come in. It's rather reassuring that they have something larger than their egos in which they can believe. However, despite a plethora of good old-fashioned etiquette books reminding us that religion and politics should not be discussed at the dinner table, stars are strangely compelled to chew and choke on their karma with their mouths wide open.

8

SHILLING FOR SCIENTOLOGY

I WANT YOUR BODY—THETANS

"Celebrities tend to be creative and spiritual people," fawns the former folk singer Reverend Heber Jentzsch, now president of the Church of Scientology International. "As the human spirit is the source of all creativity, rekindling the artist spiritually enhances his creative potential, restores to him high ethical standards and other- wise helps him to forward his work in the creative arts. I think this is why many artists are drawn to Scientology."[1]

Once hooked and drawn, many find it near impossible to leave Scientology. Christopher Reeve is an exception. According to his auto- biography, *Nothing Is Impossible: Reflections on a New Life*, as a young actor, Reeve took a free Scientology personality test outside a super- market, followed by an introductory course, which only cost him "a few hundred dollars." But after that initial processing, he was pres- sured into "auditing," which he describes as "outrageously expensive."

According to the actor, Scientology wanted $3,000 in advance for that service, which was billed at "$100 an hour in 1975."

In his book, Reeve goes on to explain that the auditor used the fabled E-Meter. It didn't take x-ray vision for Reeve to conclude that the "E-Meter was basically a crude lie detector." Reeve developed a "growing skepticism about Scientology," so he decided to do his own rundown on the E-Meter's accuracy. He recounts how he told his auditor a long story about a past life, but his former life was a complete fabrication, based upon a Greek myth. However, according to Reeve, the highly trained auditor didn't detect the actor's prevarication. That prompted the Man of Steel to be done with Scientology. Reeve writes, "The fact that I got away with a blatant fabrication completely devalued my belief in the process."[2]

Essentially a confessional, auditing is one of the main services of Scientology, the sect that began calling itself a church at conveniently the same time the Internal Revenue Service started demanding tax payments. For decades Scientology fought the IRS, until an odd thing happened in 1993—the IRS capitulated and granted Scientology tax-exempt status after one of the group's high ranking officials had an unscheduled, closed-door meeting with the then head of the IRS.[3]

Along with their tax-exempt status, Scientology can boast that they have more visible celebrities than any other denomination in the United States. They are also the most litigious church in the world, and it is claimed that they are notoriously slow to pay outstanding judgments against them.[4] Currently, Scientology is embroiled in a notorious wrongful death civil suit, which they are vigorously contesting.[5]

Pulp science fiction author L. Ron Hubbard created Scientology in 1950 as Dianetics. Hubbard, who is referred to within Scientology as "The Source" or "The Commodore," was mustered out of the Navy when he began hanging out with a group of sci-fi authors and Bohemians at the home of Jack Parsons, a founder of Pasadena's Jet Propulsion Laboratory. Along with his work on rockets, Parsons also practiced ritual magic and followed the philosophy of Satanist Aleister Crowley, the self-styled "Beast" and "Wickedest Man in the World." Hubbard performed ritualistic sex magic with Parsons, ran off with Jack's girlfriend, and swindled the scientist out of thousands of dollars. Hubbard would later spin the sordid truth, claiming that his actions were under orders of Naval Intelligence. He boasted that he had broken up a black magic sex ring and rescued a girl from their clutches, though why it took him three years of sex magic and swinging parties to accomplish this has not been explained. He would later marry the girl he "rescued," Betty Northrop, although his divorce from the first Mrs. Hubbard was not yet final.[6]

In 1955 Hubbard made an interesting proposal to his followers: They should pick a celebrity and try to get him or her to join Scientology. However, they were responsible for all expenses incurred during the pursuit. Hubbard admitted that luring stars like Groucho Marx, Greta Garbo, Milton Berle, and even Walt Disney into his clutches would be difficult, but encouraged his flock to reach celebrities by any means necessary. "Put yourself at every hand across his or her path," wrote Hubbard. He ordered his adherents to not permit "discouragement or no's or clerks or secretaries to intervene in days or weeks or months to bring your celebrity in for a formal auditing session."[7] Nowadays, that behavior is considered stalking.

Scientology today has a veritable mass of celebrities shilling for it. John Travolta, who in 1983 expressed his doubts about high-level Scientology management, now credits Scientology with helping him make $20 million a picture. "I would say that Scientology put me into the big time," the portly actor has said.[8]

Lisa Marie Presley, whose mother, the taut Priscilla, is also a Scientologist, married within her faith once, to Danny Keogh, by whom she has two children. Accused child molester Michael Jackson, her second husband, showed no interest in Scientology; the couple divorced after less than two years of marriage. Lisa Marie, who has finally released an album—featuring an anti-psychiatry single echoing Scientology's refrain that shrinks are evil—on Capitol Records, then married Nicolas Cage. However, she couldn't coax him into the group, and the marriage ended in less than four months.[9]

As international spokesperson for the Scientology-sponsored Citizen's Commission on Human Rights (CCHR), Lisa Marie has joined a long line of Scientology celebrities parading before Congress to state Scientology's mantra that psychiatric drugs are harming children.[10] One wonders how seriously her position as a children's advocate was taken by Congress, considering that as the mother of two young children, Danielle and Benjamin, she married a man who publicly admits to sharing his bed with young boys.

Because Scientology requires a large investment (reaching the top levels can cost upwards of $300,000), it's possible that some of the money made by the Presley estate, including sales of memorabilia and admissions to Graceland, is funneled into Scientology coffers. "I wish that he knew what Scientology was before he died," the ex-wife of The King, Priscilla Presley, moaned, adding that Scientology's staunch anti-drug policies could have "helped Elvis a lot" in fighting his addiction to prescription drugs.[11]

Elvis is swiveling in his grave. According to a close associate, The King once said, "...Fuck those people! There's no way I'll ever get involved with that son-of-a-bitchin' group. All they want is my money." Another old Elvis crony said, "He'd shit a brick to see how far Lisa Marie's gotten into it."[12] But at least she gets awards and titles.

Along with being the spokeswoman for the "anti-psych" group CCHR, Lisa Marie was recently presented the World Literacy Crusade's Humanitarian Award at their tenth annual celebration of Martin Luther King's birthday by fellow adherents Isaac Hayes and Chaka Khan.[13] The World Literacy Crusade is another Scientology front group, which uses the Study Technology of L. Ron Hubbard.[14] Study Tech teaches kids phonics and other logical learning methods, including the standard elementary school practice of rereading what they don't understand and looking up words in a dictionary.

The E-Meter challenged by Christopher Reeve is used extensively in the Study Tech setting. Students are periodically subjected to questioning on the meter to ascertain if they have any disagreements or misunderstood words they have not looked up. Students who refuse to submit to meter checking are routed to "ethics," where they receive further auditing or are required to write confessions of all their transgressions as a student. Those confessions, of course, become property of Scientology Inc.[15]

Applied Scholastics, whose spokesperson is the Lifetime Network regular and prominent Scientologist Anne Archer, is licensed to promote Study Tech. The group is run by Scientologists, as is Bridge Publications, the outfit publishing the Study Tech books along with all of Hubbard's tomes including the turgid *Battlefield Earth* saga.

Applied Scholastics is, in turn, part of the Association for Better Living and Education (ABLE).

An umbrella organization, ABLE coordinates social betterment projects used to generate positive publicity for Scientology, and thereby assist it in making inroads into conventional society. The programs ABLE oversees are Narconon, for which Hubbard developed his Purification system (which we'll get to next); Criminon, which disseminates "church" propaganda in prisons; the Way to Happiness Foundation, which "sponsors programs you can implement for real-world results for the individual, the family, in schools, in businesses, in communities and in police and criminal rehabilitation programs"; Applied Scholastics; and the World Literacy Crusade.

At various points, Scientologists have lobbied to have Study Tech used in public schools, with much public uproar and not a lot of success. "I have some fairly serious questions about the constitutionality and, from a public-policy standpoint, the propriety of using these materials in public schools," said Douglas Mirell, a board member of the American Civil Liberties Union of Southern California. Mirell has examined some of the study-skills books and compared them with materials from the church. "It seems like the books go out of their way to use terms that have a technical definition within the religion."

Fortunately, legislators agree with Mirell so far. Indoctrinating students into the Study Tech's unconventional language and world view, with its implied acceptance of L. Ron Hubbard as authority figure, would do much to soften them up for future recruitment into Scientology itself—apparently the real goal of Applied Scholastics.[16]

Sweating It Out

The Study Tech also espouses a detoxification program called the Purification Rundown, developed, naturally, by L. Ron Hubbard, for use on adherents, the public, and in the Hubbard-created Narconon program (not be confused with the altruistic Narcotics Anonymous).

Enlightened golf and nude yoga pale beside the hocus-pocus of the "Purif," which many celebrities publicly endorse and credit for their stunning careers and happier lives.[17] Participants visit a Scientologist doctor, then begin using "a combination of exercise, vitamins &

minerals and time spent sweating in the sauna." It's claimed by Scientology that the program participants are "able to rid themselves of toxins previously exposed to."[18]

Scientology's reasoning behind using the Purif within the confines of education is "When a person has had years of exposure to toxins his/her ability to study is affected."[19] Purif participants build up to doses of 5,000 mg of niacin, gradually increasing the amount they take over a period of days or weeks. These mega-doses of niacin cause an intense skin flush, almost like sunburn, which adherents are prodded into believing is the flushing of radiation and drug residues from their bodies.[20] Scientology's insistence that radiation is water-soluble and that radiation damage can be "run out" by this process is based on Hubbard's word; he actually wrote a ludicrous book entitled *All About Radiation.* Hubbard's ill-informed assertions contradict medical science. The facts are that people sweat out water and trace minerals in saunas and the only thing large doses of niacin can cause is skin flushing and liver damage.

Now famous for her televised outburst "Scientology Rocks!" to a flabbergasted Barbara Walters, Travolta's wife Kelly Preston endorses the Purification Rundown, as does Kirstie Alley, who physically belies L. Ron Hubbard's ridiculous assertion, "There is no such thing as a fat cell."[21]

Danny Masterson, who embodies the sleazy, amoral, stoner Steven Hyde on "That 70's Show," explains his enjoyment of the flush and sweat program, "I have been acting since age 4. I have always been working and I have always been in Scientology my entire life. (I was born into it.) Each service in Scientology is something I have added to my toolbox of data for living. The Purification Rundown lifted a cloud off my head and enabled me to think and see clearly."[22]

Scientology versus Science

One of Scientology's major goals is the eradication of psychiatry, with the church's publicly stated goal—not met, though not for lack of their trying—of wiping out psychiatry by the year 2000.[23] Beyond that failed endgame, the Study Tech books proselytize against psychology, stating, "The subject of psychology began its text by saying they [sic] did not know what the word means. So the subject itself never arrived. Professor Wundt of Leipzig University in 1879 perverted the term. It really means just a study (ology) of the soul (psyche). But Wundt, working under the eye of Bismarck, the greatest of German military fascists, at the height of German war ambitions, had to deny man had a soul. So there went the whole subject! Men were thereafter animals (it is all right to kill animals) and man had no soul, so the word psychology could no longer be defined."[24]

The use of this anti-mental health diatribe—a fundamental part of Scientology's belief system—in a children's textbook is not out of character for Scientology, even though the book in question is part of what is promoted as being entirely secular "study materials."

An outspoken supporter of Scientology and thus a hater of all things psychiatric, the heterosexual Tom Cruise used his celebrity to promote Scientology's anti-psych agenda by attacking the mental health profession. Interviewed while filming the movie *The Last Samurai* in Australia, the heterosexual Cruise complained, "Today in America I know they are so quick to put children on drugs because they are not learning well." The heterosexual Cruise's comment was an apparent reference to medications like Ritalin, which are prescribed for children with certain learning disabilities, most notably attention deficit disorder.[25]

The heterosexual Cruise claims he was helped regarding his own supposed learning disability, dyslexia, through Scientology's Study Technology. In an exclusive *People* magazine interview hyping Scientology and its literacy programs, the heterosexual Cruise raved about L. Ron Hubbard's Study Tech and how the paunchy guru's methods made it pos-sible for him to read and learn to fly an airplane. How nice for him, but that was his personal experience with dyslexia, not with Ritalin or ADD, and thus has no bearing on his anti-psychiatry, anti-Ritalin argument. Oddly, the heterosexual Tom Cruise had previously denied his dyslexia; in 1992 he told New York celebrity journalist Marilyn Beck that he'd started reading faster after studying a Scientology manual. "And that convinced me," he said, "that I had never been dyslexic."[26]

The majority of medical opinions on dyslexia state that this learning difficulty cannot be cured by the use of drugs, including the heterosexual Cruise's Scientology induced bête noire Ritalin, and, in fact, psychiatric drugs are not recommended for dyslexia, although the drug is often prescribed for attention deficit disorder and attention deficit hyperactive disorder. The effects of dyslexia can be alleviated by skilled specialist teaching; however, no independent, peer-reviewed evaluations have been done on the effectiveness of the Study Tech on the syndrome.

In fact, Scientology does not invite peer review or double-blind studies of any of its programs. J. Thomas Viall, Executive director of the International Dyslexia Association says, "When an individual of the prominence of Tom Cruise makes statements that are difficult to replicate in terms of what science tells us, the issue becomes what other individuals who are dyslexic do in response to such a quote-unquote success story. There is not a lot of science to support the claims that the teachings of L. Ron Hubbard are appropriate to overcoming dyslexia."[27]

Give Us Your Money and You'll Find Out What a "Thetan" Is

The heterosexual Tom Cruise and John Travolta have achieved the state of "clear," joining the ranks of, according to Scientology, about 50,000 whom came before. These stars have also learned the great $350,000 secret of Scientology.[28]

Over 75 million years ago, in a universe far, far away, evil alien overlord Xenu captured all the rebel souls by calling them in for tax auditing and, after injecting them with a mixture of glycol and alcohol, they were transported in B-1 bombers to earth and flung into volcanoes. Then the volcanoes were exploded with neutron bombs. The souls of these immolated aliens, called body thetans (thetan is L. Ron's word for souls), now cling to us like nasty body lice, through reincarnation after reincarnation, and can only be removed through hours of auditing at a cost of hundreds of thousands of dollars.[29]

Travolta and the heterosexual Cruise, like other "clears," are supposedly immune to illness and in Scientology lingo, free of their "reactive minds"; they function solely on their "analytical minds." As advanced operating thetans (supersouls) with their god-like abilities fully restored, the heterosexual Tom and John can now create life;

they can create universes; they have cause over matter, energy, space, and time; and they are free of the bonds of the physical—functioning totally on the spiritual. Of course, this does not explain such dire fare and box office flops like the heterosexual Cruise's *Far and Away* and Travolta's *Battlefield Earth*, but maybe even good thetans can goof once in a while.[30]

Lawsuits, Libel, and Cover-Ups

Hubbard wrote in 1976, "The purpose of the [law] suit is to harass and discourage rather than to win. . . . The law can be used very easily to harass, and enough harassment on somebody who is simply on the thin edge anyway, well knowing that he is not authorized, will generally be sufficient to cause his professional decease. If possible, of course, ruin him utterly."[31] This sentiment, a sacrament of Scientology since it was written by The Source, is observed with astounding regularity by the heterosexual Tom Cruise, thereby creating a thrill ride for lawyers quick to play party to such a lucrative religious practice.

However, while the heterosexual Cruise usually wins his cases, his church has been losing. When Scientology sued the *Washington Post* for violating trade secrecy laws by publishing parts of Hubbard's wacky upper level cosmology, they not only lost the suit, but were forced to pay the *Post's* attorneys fees. The presiding U.S. District judge Leonie Brinkema had this to say about the sect's suit: "The court finds the motivation of plaintiff in filing this lawsuit against the *Post* is reprehensible. . . . Although the [Religious Technology Center, an arm of the Scientology Church] brought the complaint under traditional secular concepts of copyright and trade secret law, it has become clear that a much broader motivation prevailed—the stifling of criticism and dissent of the religious practices of Scientology and the destruction of its opponents."[32] After a best selling *Time* magazine cover story critical of Scientology ran in June 1991, the church not only sued the magazine for libel, it also sued former member Steven Fishman and his Florida psychiatrist for $1 million each for "defamatory" comments they'd made that appeared in the article.

Attorneys for Fishman came up with an ingenious way to fight back: At a Christmas party held at the Scientology Celebrity Centre, several stars—including Juliette Lewis, Kelly Preston, and Isaac Hayes—were subpoenaed by servers dressed as elves. Not long after, Scientology lawyers dropped their suit against Fishman, and *Time* won the protracted lawsuit against them.[33]

Editors and publishers have been contacted about one *Hollywood, Interrupted* jouranalist and sent voluminous "dead agent" files aimed at disgracing and disparaging him when it seemed the writer was pitching an unfavorable story on Scientology. Attempting to interview a Scientology star, he was ordered by PR flacks to avoid asking questions about Scientology.[34] And this from a church with a creed reading, in part, "All men have inalienable rights to think freely, to talk freely, to write freely their own opinions and to counter or utter or write upon the opinions of others."[35] In other words, you can write freely, unless you criticize Scientology. If you dare to criticize, they will sue you, or, in Hubbard's own doctrine as articulated in his "fair game" policy against perceived enemies, you "may be deprived of property or injured by any means by any Scientologist without any discipline of the Scientologist. May be tricked, sued or lied to or destroyed."[36] Scientology even has its own intelligence arm charged with enforcing Hubbard's policy of harassment. These sailor-suited swabs, drawn from the "elite" Sea Org who have signed a billion-year contract indenturing them to Scientology, are known as the Office of Special Affairs.[37]

Spreading the Word—In Creative Ways

Kirstie Alley has delivered numerous testimonials regarding her recovery from drug addiction through Narconon, a rehabilitation program based upon Scientology teachings. Alley must be following Hubbard's directives. She has been through years of Scientology training, including numerous Purifs and tons of classes, which have helped her in her career trajectory from highly paid sitcom star to the spokeswoman for Pier One, a down-market home goods store. She recently opened a literacy center housed in the Beverly Hills Mission of the Church of Scientology that utilizes, with no great surprise, the "breakthrough study methods developed by author and humanitarian L. Ron Hubbard." Alley hopes to draw upon "community and faith groups, neighborhoods and schools" to meet her pledge of training 2,000 tutors to follow the totalitarian teaching methods of The Source.[38]

Unlike many of her fellow parishioners, Greta van Susteren didn't lose a dime when unlicensed investment broker and Scientologist Reed Slatkin, co-founder of Internet service provider Earthlink, was busted for running a pyramid investment scheme. Slatkin, an ordained Chaplain in the Church of Scientology, made sure his star Scientology pals made back their investments at over 10 percent, while falsely promising the same returns to the public and rank-and-file Scientologists. According to Securities Exchange Commission Litigation Release No. 16998, dated May 11, 2001, from 1985 to April 2001, Slatkin used the civilian and ordinary church members' money to pay off the celeb Scientologists. When the bubble burst, many found they had been cheated out of their entire life savings by a man who was a highly revered member of their church—an organization claiming to be made up of only the "most ethical people" on the planet.

Interestingly, Van Susteren's home network CNN, and later Fox, staged a virtual news blackout on Slatkin when it might have been worth a news scroll beneath the commentator's plastic surgery–altered mug, if only to report the fact that she and her husband, damages attorney John Coale, profited off of one of the biggest Ponzi schemes of all time.[39]

"Celebrities are very special people and have a very distinct line of dissemination. They have comm[unication] lines that others do not have and many medias to get their dissemination through," wrote L. Ron Hubbard in May of 1973.[40]

With that in mind, Scientologist Milton Katselas runs a popular acting school called the Beverly Hills Playhouse—like Criminon, Narconon, and on and on—another subtle recruiting ground for the church. Katselas is careful not to label his methods as Scientology tenets, but the church's influence seeps into the playhouse, creeping out many acting students.

"I've learned many things in my life, and I apply them," Katselas says ingenuously. "But am I teaching Scientology? No, that's not what happens." Yet the advice that Katselas dispenses to his actors is loaded with Scientology jargon: There are "suppressive people" (those who, consciously or unconsciously, make things go wrong and hurt others), "roller coasters" (people whose lives take alternating turns for the better and the worse), and "potential trouble sources" (those who make trouble for themselves and others around them).

Classes at the Playhouse are run on strict Scientology principles: Words are looked up in a large dictionary, and students who are too sick to attend classes must report to one of the class's "ethics officers." Having ethics officers in the classroom is an idea borrowed directly from Scientology. According to one former student, "The ethics officers stand around like monitors against the walls with note pads and take notes: who's late, who's talking, who's dating, who's chewing gum."

One young actress loved the Beverly Hills Playhouse when she first arrived to study there. She felt a sense of community and found "instant friends." But after eight months of workshops and classes, she says that she began to realize that Katselas, his students, and his Scientology-based philosophy consumed her life. "There was never an overt feeling that Scientology was being taught, but by the time I left, I started to feel as if there was a cult atmosphere." She continues, "It wasn't about acting as much as a way of life. You had to do precisely what they said or you wouldn't get ahead in your career. You had to become a disciple of their philosophy or you would fail. It was like Big Brother was watching over you."

Scientologist and former star Jenna Elfman likes the ethics officers, the rigid atmosphere, and Scientology's subtle influence. "In Milton's classes, the ethics officers are there to make sure that things are going well so that you can flourish, so that you don't get in your own way."

Elfman says that those who find the most fault with Katselas tend to be the ones "who are just not doing as well as they could be" with their careers and are looking for a scapegoat. Her personal Waterloo may have been hiring a posse of her Scientology buddies to work on "Dharma & Greg"; the show was cancelled after that season.[41]

The Scientology Celebrity Centre publishes a glossy magazine cleverly entitled *Celebrity* that promotes its various stars and their Scientology-focused causes. Scientology media darlings grace its covers, touting the Purif, Study Tech, and other wonders of their wacky religion, though Xenu and Reed Slatkin are curiously absent from its pages. Awards created by Scientology organizations are given to celebrity Scientologist humanitarians and recorded in *Celebrity*'s glossy pages in order to make the plebe members feel like they are part of the most wonderful, ethical, special group of people, um, thetans, on earth.[42]

Faith?

Why are Scientology celebrities so gung-ho for all things Hubbard? One reason may lie in the 60-page deposition of Andre Tabayoyon, who declared that Scientology leaders keep special files on the stars that contain supposedly confidential information derived during auditing sessions. Tabayoyon went on, "It is my opinion, based on my Scientology training, education and experience, that such information is collected by the Scientology organization in order to be able to exert control and influence over people such as [the heterosexual] Tom Cruise or John Travolta should they ever attempt to leave the Scientology organization."[43] Other sources repeat Tabayoyon's depiction of a dichotomous world at Scientology's security-obsessed Gold Base camp in Gilman Hot Springs, California, pointing to celebrities' receiving perks like an apartment with a $150,000 gym and private chef; a Mercedes convertible, two motorcycles, and a motor home; and a $200,000 celebrity-use-only tennis court.[44]

Obviously, celebs are given special treatment, and a couple hundred thousand dollars isn't a huge outlay for an organization that rakes in untaxed millions. But this money comes from legions of lost souls coerced into shelling out every dime they can squeeze from their credit cards.

On the other side of the Gold Base gulag, out-of-standing members toil in the Rehabilitation Project Force (RPF), working off their ethics violations. This practice of using labor as punishment—either for breaking the rules or failing to meet work quotas—is widespread in Scientology, and reeks of Maoist re-education camps. Banishment into the RPF can last several months, during which time members may not speak unless spoken to; must perform menial, often degrading tasks; often subsist on a diet of rice and beans; endure terrible living conditions; and wear armbands denoting their lowly status.[45]

Some of the actions and beliefs of Scientology could be dismissed as just faith-based flackery, except for the horror stories about the RPF and the chilling statements from Hubbard, which reflect on every action Scientology takes.[46] "We are not even vaguely propitiative [sic] toward medicine or psychiatry, and we are overtly intent upon assimilating every function they are now performing," wrote The Source in 1955.[47] In another article Hubbard discoursed on democracy, "Watching the U.S. and Australia fight Scientology with blind fury while supporting oppressive mental and religious practices proves that democracy, applied to and used by people [deviated from reason], is far from an ideal activity and is only democracy [deviated from reason]."[48]

Hubbard's plan for world domination states that Scientology will be successful by, "Bringing continuous pressure to bear on governments to create pro-Scientology legislation and to discourage anti-Scientology legislation of groups opposing Scientology. . . . The action of bringing about a pro-Scientology government consists of making a friend of the most highly placed government person one can reach, even placing Scientologists in domestic and clerical posts close to him and seeing to it that Scientology resolves his troubles and case."[49]

That statement, put into action in Germany by Scientologists, is why Scientology is not recognized as a religion there, leading to John Travolta's impassioned pleas before Congress to sanction Germany for religious oppression. Travolta, other Rondroid celebs, and Hollywood powerhouse attorney Bertram Fields rallied a host of non-Scientology bigwigs to sign a letter protesting Germany's "religious intolerance." The German government claimed Scientology is largely a profit-hungry group that seeks world domination and threatens democracy, sentiments echoed by *The New York Times*, which in an investigative report on Scientology, noted that critics worldwide regard Scientology as "a cult and money machine intended to bilk the faithful."[50]

As a "clear," Travolta will be immune from Hubbard's desire to eliminate those who don't meet Scientology standards. Hubbard has stated that his intention is to "clear the planet," in other words make everyone a Scientologist, or else.[51]

CALIFORNICATION

PART IV

Where hookers—transvestite and otherwise,
gay lovers, porn producers, and
Swing Kids do a dance.

Pornotainment Wonderland

The geographical protuberance of the Hollywood Hills physically divides the mainstream film industry from its baser hard-core porno analogue in the San Fernando Valley. But ideologically, culturally, and in praxis, the barriers between these seemingly divergent worlds are evaporating and a new breed of highly profitable, hyperpornographic mainstream products is popping up to establish and then feed the urges of a sex-crazed nation that is aggressively stepping out of the prude closet and throwing down huge chunks of their discretionary income to sate the appetites that would have sent previous generations sprinting for the nearest available confessional.

Thanks to the creative minds at some of Hollywood's biggest entertainment and marketing conglomerates, consumers no longer have to face the embarrassment of standing in front of a cute girl at the counter at the local Video Mart with an X-rated movie in hand.

Instead, they can simply log online, turn on the TV, pick up some of the most popular magazines in America, head to the local sporting goods store, kick back in the comfort of a hotel room, or cruise down to the local art house or Cineplex.

"Pornotainment" has proven a winning, multibillion dollar formula in the marketplace. Pornotainment shamelessly merges hard-core pornography with everyday, banal entertainment products aimed at everyone from children to senior citizens. Whether you're a child, tween, teen, adult, or Metamucil-chugging senior citizen, the Hollywood pornotainment machine has got you covered.

It's a brave new pornotainment world out there, a world where Hollywood's marketing and branding power ensures that no child will be left behind. You want your kids to be ready to navigate the rapidly changing cultural currents they're sure to face in life. Luckily, Hollywood is ready to help. So why not start them off with an anatomically correct action figure of hard-core porno superstar Jenna Jameson replete with a "heartbreaker" tattoo on her derrière for a mere $19.99? What? Junior doesn't like blondes? No problem. Why not turn his displeasure into a multicultural learning experience by giving him an action figure of African-American porno seductress Midori instead?[1]

Once they've completed their pornotainment boot camp in the sandbox, little Suzie and Bobby can move on to Vince McMahon's hugely popular WWF and WWE television wrestling programs and pay-per-view events where they can watch silicone-injected super-women that look and act like porn stars wrestle in platform shoes, tear each others' clothes off, and allude to every sex act under the sun. And they can always pick up superstar wrestler Chyna's photo spread in *Playboy* or load up on sex advice and photos of half-naked women in the most popular men's magazine in America, *Maxim*, or any of its innumerable imitators.

When snow is falling and it's time to hit the slopes, why not set the whole family up on Sims Fader snowboards featuring images of Vivid video porno stars Kobe Tai, Briana, Chasey Lain, and Kody? Available at specialty shops and major sporting goods chains across the nation, Fader boards will keep you riding a little higher in your soft-backed boots because you'll know you have the strength of the pornotainment industry beneath your feet.[2]

Thanks to Ascent Entertainment, a property of mainstream cable magnate John Malone valued at $755 million, lonely travelers in major hotel chains across America can soothe themselves with in-room pornography for ten bucks a pop at the push of a button.[3]

Nowhere is the convergence of porno and Hollywood more evident than on the marquees of the local $10-a-ticket grind house. Mainstream films like *Boogie Nights* gave porno a patina of cool, mainstream palatability and box office cachet that opened the floodgate for porno-related Hollywood flicks wide enough that even shoe-gazing, cred-obsessed indie directors have jumped on the pornotainment train. In director Katherine Breillat's *Romance X*, Italian porno stallion Rocco Siffredi penetrates his costar Caroline Ducey for the camera in a sex scene that's nearly as graphic as Siffredi's XXX work. French director Gaspar Noé literally drove the audience at Cannes to nausea in 2003 with the agonizingly long anal rape of the *Matrix Reloaded* starlet Monica Bellucci that opens his film *Irreversible* while critically acclaimed actor and director Vincent Gallo elected to cap off his sophomore effort *Brown Bunny* with hipster-turned-star Chloe Sevigny sexually favoring him orally for a full-on 15 minutes. Porno and sexual extremism of all sorts are now run-of-the-mill narrative tropes that directors of all stripes deploy in their quest to shock, awe, and cinematically connect with mainstream audiences.

Thanks to Hollywood, we're living in an ever more open, sexually charged, and salacious pornotainment world. Sexual lifestyle tourism, deviance, and wholesale experimentation have become the norm across the fruited plains, from sea to shining sea, one nation under satellite television, indivisible, with liberty, justice, and pornotainment for all.

There's a Whorehouse in Your Neighborhood!

Every Wednesday afternoon without fail a call comes in to the *Hollywood, Interrupted* offices from a mysterious Asian fellow calling himself "Anderson Chan." Rifling through his Rolodex, his greeting is clipped, his message, staccato: "Hi, buddy... We've got 25 beautiful performers tomorrow... 9:30... Bring your friends, and jackets required, okay?" The message never varies—only the venue.

A few years ago, the dapper Mr. Chan was the frontman for a hard-core, unlicensed, late-night lap dance club in one of the most unlikely spots imaginable: Orsini—a staid, Italian restaurant long favored by the Beverly Hills blue-haired ladies-who-lunch crowd. Management counted former First Lady Nancy Reagan as one of its prized patrons, but the thought of Mrs. Reagan settling into a banquette festering with residual DNA from the prior evening is not exactly an appetizing amusement.

Anyway, Orsini-after-dark closed shop after less than a year of underground operation above the law. Seems that the glare of the tabloid television spotlight and the prying eye of private eyes and the law were too much for Chan and his remarkable guest list.

Fox Undercover/Fox Files was, at one time, preparing a show called something like "There's a Whorehouse in Your Neighborhood." The West Los Angeles Police Department's Vice Squad simultaneously issued an investigation into Orsini of their own, culminating into a meager police report on licensing issues filed with ABC (Alcoholic Beverage Control).

"I don't think they [ABC] did anything," says West Los Angeles vice cop, Sgt. Sasso, about the report filed. However, at one point, there was a joint investigation of Orsini's loosely planned and coordinated between Fox, West LA vice, and private Backstreet Investigations detectives Dan Hanks and Fred Valis.

Sgt. Sasso confirmed that his department was going to be part of the Fox operation. "Yes. Basically, we backed out of it. We didn't go in with Fox." Why not? "I'm not clear why." Private dick Dan Hanks reports, "West LA vice was going to go in with us [along with Fox Undercover] and get one of the girls to go for the okie-doke, but somehow Chan got tipped off."

Hanks contends, "There was someone on the inside of the LAPD who tipped off Chan the night of the operation, and the LAPD backed out at the last minute. "When confronted on the possibility of a mole within his department, Sgt. Sasso sighs and admits, "The department is a big place; we're not immune."

Although the implication of the LAPD participating in a sex crime cover-up seems the real smoking gun in this situation, it would pale in comparison to the overall legacy of Los Angeles police corruption.

Besides, there's still ample breathing room to document how the sex-for-pay climate of Hollywood has shifted from the Beverly Hills madams dispatching whores-to-doors, to on-site delivery of services rendered.

During a dry spell following the shuttering of Orsini-after-dark, Chan would relentlessly phone with news of new public spots to meet no less than 25 lovely ladies, like the Los Angeles jazz club Lunaria, or the ritzy Argyle hotel on the Sunset Strip.[4] These soirées seemed set up as scams—social networking events at which moneyed men could meet and mingle with the siliconed set, with zero possibility of on-site sex. *Hollywood, Interrupted* simply waited for Chan to go underground once again.

It took less than a year for Chan to plumb prime property, offering sexual encounter events at a rotating selection of pricey real estate in and around Beverly Hills. "It's big business," acknowledges Sgt. Sasso, fully hip to Chan's commercial sexcapades. "They're called mansion parties, [run by] people that are in financial straits making between 5 and 15 thousand a pop. They'll hide behind, 'It's a charity event.' Hiding behind keywords. But," explains Sasso, "the bottom line is the property owners make bucks and the promoters [Chan] make beaucoup bucks."

The worst things that can happen at Chan's venues according to Sasso are "sexual assaults," but the easier softer way for the LAPD to deal with these fly-by-night brothels is to treat them as zoning violations. "We establish that they're charging to get in—operating as a business. "Then you can go in for a shutdown . . . costs, fines to the owner . . ."

And what happens to guys like Chan? "Talk about being a predator," says Sasso. "He can just up and leave." Sasso says Chan was kicked out of the San Fernando Valley several years ago. Backstreet Detective Dan Hanks corroborates: "Yeah, absolutely. Different houses every time, different locations. What he [Chan] was doing was, he'd charge the girls like a hundred bucks to get in, and charge the guys to get in. It was like an evening of Plato's retreat—people [having sex] on a coffee table in the living room."

Until the vice squad pays another impromptu visit, for now, Chan's prurient parties seem settled in a 19-room million-dollar home with a million-dollar view, located on a jasmine-scented cul de sac high above the sultry Beverly Hills flats, situated atop a gilded ghetto of abutting cliff-side mansions.

A stealthy, black-clad bouncer type greets you the gate, requesting that you park on a side street below the mansion, so as not to disturb the neighbors. By 10 PM glistening Jags and Mercedes and an array of SUVs line the silent street. Saunter up a narrow sidewalk to the residence gate, where the bouncer ushers you in to a Dionysian pool-side patio area where cigar-smoking men mingle with the evening's "entertainment."

Real estate records reveal that the home was built in 1962, but the two-story nouveau chateau has been remodeled and retrofitted as a porno pad, affecting an *Eyes Wide Shut*–meets–*Boogie Nights* motif. The reflection pool overlooking twinkling downtown Los Angeles and Century City is guarded by gaudy lionine statues, complemented by a raised hot tub bubbling in anticipation for the debauchery to come. Another bouncer, sporting the requisite earpiece/ microphone headgear, signs you in and collects your $40 entrance fee, and the owlish Anderson Chan, in a ridiculously dated black leather suit, greets you, promising "more girls" by midnight. He'll flit off to greet others.

Who is Anderson Chan? Although once thought of as some sort of Asian Mafia type, and that these special evenings were his brainchild, as we watch him scurrying about greeting people and emptying ashtrays—it becomes clear that he's nothing more than a glorified *maitre d' brothel*. The real pimp daddy here in the hills is the owner of the manse—a puffy, bespectacled, middle-aged Armani-wearing man of Arab heritage, puffing a Cuban cigar while fondling a blonde in a tight black stretch skirt, inviting you to "enjoy the view."

This house party starts with a $40 entry fee at the door; then—as the beefy bedroom bouncer Chris explains: "There's a common room for your topless women, for $40 a song—literally: when the music ends, so does the other entertainment. And you also have a one-on-one room for $50 per song, both rooms with a $10 entrance fee. And," he continues, "What you're paying for is the room to yourself with the girl—chairs, a couch, hot tub, and a view." $60 dollars all-in? "Per song," concludes Chris.

Sex, or the possibility thereof, sells, and simple math, for what appears a slow night, makes for at least a mortgage payment on the place. Thirty guys might get serviced by about a dozen females tonight, so that's a cool $1,200 at the door. Figuring these horny cats cadge an average of four songs with the girls, tag on $6,000. A couple of $10 drinks for the boys and girls adds another $1,200, and we've got the house grossing near $8,000 for the evening, assuming that the girls work for a bare minimum percentage of the dance fees, plus generous tips for "extras."

A brief tour downstairs in the plush living room area finds a cocktail party of odd sorts is in full swing. There's everyone from legendary pornographer Hugh Hefner's personal physician to b-boys, to b-actors, to Hollywood writers doing "research," to "old Hollywood" dinosaurs—all attentive to the come-on from the lithe lovelies working the crowd. Some sumo-sized sack of depravity is getting a lap dance on a couch beside a conical fireplace. A gaggle of scantily clad Vietnamese war babies bounces by. "They're the massage parlor girls," informs a young sport with a New Jersey accent who has been coming to these house parties for months now.

A young LA rapper with a cue ball head going by the name Amir sidles up, declaring, "I just get the first dance, and then I ask if there's gonna be some extras. If not, then, I'm out." Amir starts hyping his record label, Dope Fiendz. He starts rapping—

> *Death Squad and Dope Fiendz*
> *Definition what dope means*
> *Park the Benz*
> *And blow scenes*

—and it's time to head back inside towards the feminine fray. An aging, anorexic hooker with a fake French accent named Dominique is getting passed around like an Uzi on a couch crushed with drunken young Israeli guys. She moves to another sofa, peopled with rug merchants who eagerly inspect the merchandize.

Upstairs, we find Sky—a magnificent, leggy, strawberry-blonde creature in a white lace Victoria's Secret peek-a-boo ensemble. Sky quickly offers the advantage of a deserted cut-rate common room—actually, a converted screening room, with soft leather club chairs and couches. As some smooth hip hop–inflected R&B song begins blasting, Sky slips out of her lingerie and writhes seductively. Within 30 seconds of the precious time allotted, she reveals that she's a bookkeeper from Michigan, currently residing in Orange County. Instinct suggests that the bookkeeper has become just another California hooker.

"Would you like another song?" sings Sky for her supper. "Four songs for $200, six for $400," calculates Sky, sexual services included. The only thing missing in this setup is a cash machine. Those two-minute songs are obviously piped in to tempt the timid into laying out more cash.

It's 2 AM, and still no sign of the vice squad. Back outside, the jasmine smells strange. It's a short ride home. Michigan, however, is many miles away for some lost girl named Sky, Chan might one day get deported back to Hong Kong, the mansion owner could face the possibility of 30 months in prison for pandering, and Dominique will one day wind up in a dumpster.

Week in/week out, Chan's offerings are what's happening in the fabled hills of 90210. Pathetic really. But that's only half the story of the sadness of sex in this city.[5]

Swing Kids

We should be praying for ourselves, for we have sinned. Big time. Hollywood has shifted the moral landscape beneath our feet, and a sexual geography that would make Caligula blush has emerged. Nowhere is this change more apparent than in Los Angeles's tawdry Swing Kids subculture.

Thanks to documentaries like "The Lifestyle," HBO's "Real Sex" series, and embellished "America Undercover" visits to Nevada bordellos that depict out-of-shape middle-aged men swigging Coors Light while their partners fornicate with strangers, most people regard swingers as a geriatric, anomalous, and repulsive anachronism resigned to Holiday Inn convention centers and the back rows of seedy RV parks.

While conventional thought posits that swinging is a throwback to the 1970s that died around the same time that Plato's Retreat was shuttered, "Three's Company" went off the air, and everyone's parents quit smoking, a new generation of adventurous, educated, and professionally successful twenty-somethings is embracing the partner-swapping lifestyle to its fullest in homes, illegal clubs, and private parties in venues around the country and Los Angeles, the physical, philosophical, and corporate locus of the pornotainment industry. Hollywood Swing kids wholeheartedly embrace sexual deviance and the opportunity to effortlessly score with really good looking strangers.

For an inside look at the Bacchanal of Hollywood young blood, we dispatched daring, young writer Andrew Vontz into the underbelly of Swingtown.

I needed a Virgil. And it had to be a woman, because as I would quickly learn, if you don't come to the Swing Kids table with a dish for everyone to share, you won't be dining at all. I found my Virgil in "Vanessa," a hot twenty-something whose father is a prominent Los Angeles professional. Vanessa had a refined fashion sensibility, the latest drum'n'bass tunes spinning on her stereo, a good job in the film industry, and more than enough game to score a ride on any given weekend night.

She agreed to show me the way and so a week later I found myself pulling into the parking lot of a warehouse in an industrial district of downtown Los Angeles, a stone's throw from Skid Row. Given the decidedly trashy image of swinging I'd seen portrayed in the popular media, I was stunned to find row after row of Escalades, Navigators, and six-figure German automobiles riding on dubs crowding the lot nearly to capacity. I maneuvered my 1994 Taurus GL into one of the few available spaces, took a deep breath, and headed inside.

Licensing a sex club in Los Angeles is a complicated, legally challenging affair and doing so is sure to draw the scrutiny of the vice squad. To make an end run around these hurdles, the prominent "lifestyle" club that sponsored the weekly partner-swapping party that I was on my way to attend allegedly didn't charge an entry fee to their establishment. During the week the club's promoters hired out the more than 20 themed rooms in the warehouse for porno shoots and claimed on their web site that the weekend events were "casting" mixers where curious couples could mingle, enjoy an open bar and a fully functional night club, and if they so opted, "audition" to appear in future porno productions in a room equipped for taping.

When Vanessa and I got to the door, the club's manager demanded eighty bucks for both of us and the ruse was up. It was pay to play all the way, but there was no turning back now and so we made our way down a long hallway covered in porno photos and bad erotic art until we arrived in the night club area, where dozens of young hotties sipped drinks and gawked at the bodies gyrating on the dance floor. There were a few remnants of the swing scene of yesteryear, but for the most part these guys and gals were good looking, fit, and judging from the cars in the parking lot, rolling in dough.

After grabbing a beer at the open bar, Vanessa and I made our way through the meet and greet area adjacent to the dance club, which closely resembled your average chain restaurant dining room, and cruised into the back area where the real action was going down. The musty smell, radiant heat, and primal sound of no-holds-barred sex smacked us with the force of a steroid-fueled homerun stroke the moment we stepped into the gateway to the sex area, a room festooned with several variations on the classic sex sling that I'd seen in so many swingers documentaries.

Thanks to modern chemistry an erection is now possible at the drop of a pill—even in high-pressure situations such as orgies with complete strangers, which may be one reason more young men are swinging. "Everybody has performance problems, even porn stars" says Swing Kids scenester Dave, who estimates that up to 95 percent of the men he meets who swing take Viagra, himself included. "If you're at a club, there's no privacy. You should expect that. If you're in a group of people, they're watching you. You're performing."

What we were watching was definitely a pornographic performance (why rent porno flicks when you can be in one!), but its sheer entertainment value was negligible. It was disturbing more than anything else. Farther back in the space, we explored room after room of revelers enjoying each other and performing for the crowds. There was a simulated doctor's office, a room with a small tent-like structure with holes cut into it for anonymous play, a maze-like crawl space, an Arabian nights–themed room, a fully functioning locker room, a large room filled with mattresses , and—you guessed it— a hot tub room. Upstairs, we wandered into a fully equipped dungeon that was oddly deserted. Baskets of lube and condoms were within arms reach of every surface suitable for play and on platforms throughout the hallways as well.

There were hot young couples galore, the kind of people that you might see in the break room at the office, lifting weights and pounding the treadmill at Crunch, or hoisting a Grey Goose martini next to you at the hot/right now hipster watering hole of the week. These were normal, everyday people who drove nice cars, dressed well (when they weren't cavorting naked with strangers), and were productive members of society.

What we were witnessing were the effects of pornographic consumption writ large in living, breathing flesh. Similar scenes of youthful excess are unfolding with increasing frequency across America and the Western world every weekend. Indeed, veteran old-school swingers marvel at the influx of nubile young Swing Kids on the once stagnant partner-swapping scene during the past two years. "I'd say a good 25 to 30 percent attending these events are under thirty," says Tony Lanzaratta, 53, executive director of the national swinging organization, NASCA (The North American Swing Club Association). *Swinging has gone so overground that a recent episode of the Fox sitcom "Keen Eddie" focused on hot young couples at a swing club and Jon Bon Jovi is set to star in* One Wild Night, *a wife-swapping flick for Universal.*

In New York, erotic event promoters Grego and Palagia are throwing high-end parties geared exclusively to young, attractive, successful couples and single females that have grown so popular they're virtually impossible to get into. In Texas, The Velvet Curtain club throws similar parties and there's been a sharp increase in the number of young couples among the thousands of people who attend the Lifestyles Conventions swinging summits held annually in Vegas, Miami, and Acapulco. A swinger I met who acts as a host for the organization that throws the party I was attending estimates that the proportion of hot young couples at swing parties has grown to 80 percent of the total patrons during the past year.

Unlike the swingers of yore who embraced partner-swapping as a life-long commitment and guiding philosophical principle, the new school of swingers is young, sexually adventurous, and open to dabbling in tantalizing erotic experiences just for the fun of it. "It's brought an extra element of surprise and vitality to our relationship," says a 28-year-old corporate drone by day and a swinger by night with his long-term girl-friend. Bi-curious women like Vanessa, sexual tourists, and young couples simply looking to spice up their sex lives are new variations on the old-school committed couples swingers paradigm that have sprung up in the Swing Kids community.

"The parties that I've been going to lately have a mix of gay, straight, lesbian, bi, transgendered—it's all over the board," says Tristan Taormino, 32, a partner-swapping veteran, Village Voice sex columnist, and author of Down and Dirty Sex Secrets: *"Everything and anything is going on and you can barely figure out who is doing what to whom."*

Everything and anything was just what Vanessa and I witnessed as we wandered through the sexual romper rooms at the back of the club and soon we'd seen enough. I'd never seen anything like it. It should have been shocking. But it wasn't. It was almost boring because clearly everyone at the club regarded their sexual escapades as transactions no more complicated, involved, or intimate than making a withdrawal at an ATM inside the local Quik-E-Mart.[6]

Hef: A Viagraphy

Hugh Hefner reclines supine on the keystone of the American Dream—a self-made man surrounded in a Peter Pan fantasyland of voluptuous blondes. But a twitch of the nose, a tilt of one's floppy ears reveals that there's something rotten in Rabbitland, a stench of hypocrisy, a whiff of something funny, bunny. Sure, Hef seems wholesome—why, he's in *Stars of Star Wars*, a documentary about the most white bread space movie! And he's always able to wink at his image, playing himself in such varied feature films as *Citizen Toxie: Toxic Avenger IV* and *Beverly Hills Cop II*, not to mention a Carl's Jr. commercial and a drop-in on a British kiddy show—breakfast in bed, anyone? But Hugh Hefner's pleasure-soaked Xanadu is more mirage than oasis, wherein we find plenty of decay.

He's a satyr, a sybarite, a satin pajama-ed sex machine, and a Pfizer-fueled symbol of the American Dream. A fossilized relic embalmed in nostalgia and Viagra, cosseted and cuddled by seven interchangeable, indistinguishable blondes. He's "Hef."

Hugh Hefner (who declined to respond to questions) grew up in the Depression, a descendent of the Puritan founders of America. Their rigid views trickled down to his parents who, according to Hefner, were neither emotionally or physically affectionate; he has claimed that his lifelong compulsion to overcompensate was a re-action to his barren childhood. A virgin through military service and into his twenties, Hefner's desire to overcompensate was exactly what drove him to create *Playboy*.

In 1951, Hef got the job that was perfect for a young man dream-ing of greatness—writing promotional copy for *Esquire* magazine. When *Esquire* readied itself to move its offices from Chicago to New York, the young would-be executive asked for a raise, and was refused. Hef either quit or was fired. The incident left him with an "I'll show them" attitude and the desire to start a magazine of his own—one that would reflect the views of the postwar generation—a sophisti-cated magazine, full of beautiful women and Beat philosophy trans-lated through a GI Bill education—a magazine that would stimulate both the brain and the libido.

To insure his success, he bought the rights to use the most famous photograph in the world—Marilyn Monroe's nude cheesecake shot from the now famous 1951 calendar. Never mind that the photo was now four years old. It was a proven commodity that would sell.

In 1959, Hef purchased the first Playboy Mansion in Chicago, where the plaque on the door read, "*Si Non Oscillas Noli Tintinnare*," which translates roughly from the Latin as "If You Don't Swing, Don't Ring." The first Playboy Club opened in 1960. Chicago police arrested Hef on obscenity charges after *Playboy* published a pictorial called, "The Nudest Jayne Mansfield" in 1963. The trial resulted in a hung jury that voted 7 to 5 for acquittal.

That year Hef began hosting a syndicated television show called "Playboy's Penthouse"; guests included Lenny Bruce, Ella Fitzgerald, and Harry Belafonte. He would later create and host "Playboy After Dark," which was syndicated for two seasons.

In 1971 the magazine was selling 7 million copies, Playboy Enterprises went public, and Hugh Hefner moved out west. Los Angeles was the hub of the film industry and Hefner loved the movies, calling them "the major source of the American Dream." He would go on to produce future statutory rapist Roman Polanski's *Macbeth*, Monty Python's *Now for Something Completely Different*, and *Saint Jack* and *The Crazy World of Jules Vrooder*.

However, in a marketplace where explicit and graphic sex is commonplace and, of course, extremely lucrative, the once financially strong Playboy empire is floundering. The proposed stock offering for Playboy.com was cancelled in March 2000 after the dot-com crash, delaying Christie Hefner's goal of turning Playboy into a $1 billion corporation. Things looked slightly better in 2001, with the company projected to lose 10 cents per share versus the year 2000 loss of 90 cents per share. The company posted a first quarter 2001 net loss of $11.8 million. In 2003 Playboy.com posted scant profits, but the overall picture for Playboy Enterprises as a whole was still described as "iffy."[7]

In a last-gasp effort to withstand the overall decline in ad revenue for magazines, *Playboy* did what every other glossy once worth its salt and celebratory tequila shots has been doing: In 2003, *Playboy* magazine desperately refashioned itself as yet another knuckleheaded "lad mag" knockoff under the editorial direction of former *Maxim* chief James Kaminsky. Playboy may withstand, and even rise above the glut of these lad mags, but there is still the grumbling among the Playboy shareholders about the cost of Hugh Hefner's lifestyle to consider.

"The cost of maintaining the zoo was more than the cost of the New York office, including salaries," says a former employee who worked at the corporation until the turn of this century. Hefner, who was paid $810,230 in 1999, invested $617,000 in rent on the Holmby Hills Mansion in Los Angeles, according to the most recent financial data available. The same documents say that the annual expense of maintaining the Mansion was $4.4 million.

Luckily for the finances of Playboy Enterprises, Hugh Hefner's passion for filmmaking ran parallel with America's desire to watch soft-core pornography. Once Playboy launched its video division and the cable channels, Playboy and Spice, the bucks were rolling in; the cable division is the company's most profitable. And it hides a dirty little secret according to former Playmate, Miss April 1986, Teri Weigel.

"When you are shooting hard-core porn, they yell 'cut' and have you do it for Spice," explains Weigel. In other words, as hard-core porn is shot, it is being repurposed for Hefner's pocketbook with a subtle lift of an actors' leg or arm to disguise the nasty bits, and then the camera rolls on over parts damp and turgid, insuring a stiff return on the investment.

In July 2001, Playboy purchased The Hot Network, The Hot Zone, and Vivid TV from the owners of hard-core porno outfit Vivid for $92 million. The adult entertainment industry trade paper *Adult Video News* reports: "The Hot Network and The Hot Zone have shown, and will continue to feature movies cut to a 'double-X' standard." Now, there's a bang for your buck.

In an astonishing display of spin gone wild, Playboy Entertainment Group president Jim English told AVN, "Everyone is running around saying 'Playboy is going porno' but it's not Playboy that's going that way." He reasons, "Playboy is what Playboy is in each of its venues. Magazine, Online, and TV are all different, but all quality, and have their different messages that they deliver to their consumer base."[8]

Moreover, the type of porn is pretty extreme. The late repentant porn star Linda Lovelace, star of the 1972 vintage porn hit *Deep Throat*, wrote in her 1981 best seller *Ordeal* that she was taken up to the Playboy Mansion and told by her husband to do the dog or else. Lovelace claimed to live in fear of her husband/manager Chuck Traynor. "In *Ordeal*, Lovelace wrote, 'Hefner said that while he liked *Deep Throat,* he was more interested by the movie I'd made with a dog . . .' 'Oh, you saw that one?' Chuck Traynor said. 'Oh, that was terrific,' Hefner said, 'You know, we've tried that several times, tried to get a girl and a dog together, but it has never worked out.' 'Yeah, that can be very tricky' Chuck said, 'the chick's got to know what she's doing.' 'That's something I'd like to see,' Hefner said, 'I think I've seen every animal flick (sic) ever made but—' " Then Chuck offers Linda as a "willing" participant. Lovelace described kneeling down in front of Hef and some of his buddies trying to get the horny hound to hump her. The dog wandered away disinterestedly.[9]

Bestiality wasn't the only genre said to be in Hef's purview. Along with his vast porn collection, Hef allegedly had a very private, very personal collection. "There are cameras everywhere," says former Playmate Teri Weigel, a legend that is backed up by Hef's former girl friend, Playmate Carrie Leigh. In an interview with the *Washington Post*, Leigh says that Hefner videotaped himself having sex with his myriad partners, and she says that he would run footage of himself having sex with someone else while she and Hef copulated. Free-thinking, swinging Hef told her that her jealousy was "outdated" when she told him that his replayed rutting hurt her feelings.[10]

Hefner allegedly destroyed his vast collection of guests getting it on after Leigh lifted one of the tapes in the mid-80s, realizing that these volatile videos could end up in the wrong hands and cause injury. However, guests to the Mansion nowadays still feel the camera's eye. "Your Polaroid is taken when you walk in, if you are a girl," explains a fromer frequent visitor, the pseudonymous "Russ." "There are so many nooks and crannies, and you know you are being watched." One Playmate that Russ encountered in the grotto jacuzzi was a little out of hand, a bit too "drunk and sloppy." Baffled by the unwritten rules of behavior at the manse, Russ says that the next day Hefner personally called the Playmate and told her that that sort of drunken behavior would not be tolerated and that if she ever wanted to come back to the Mansion, she should not let that side of her personality out again. Being "off the list" at the Mansion is a fear that looms over everyone. In an exclusive interview, former Playboy Mansion butler-turned-comedian/actor Tim Bagley recalls that girls would rotate through every six months and then just fade away. "Sometimes I'd be in the pantry, and a girl who had been a regular would come into the kitchen weeping 'I'm not on the list anymore, I snuck in to see what I had done. I just had to get back in.'"

Playmates entertain and amuse Hef's pals, serving as eye candy, "and celebrities are there to keep the girls happy," explains Russ, who has attended over a dozen high-profile Mansion parties including Mid-Summer's Night Eve and Fourth of July. But there is a darker side to the Playmates. Often, according to Bagley, they are requested as private amusements for high-profile celebrities, as in "Go see Movie Star in bedroom 4." Former Playmate-turned-porn star Teri Weigel claims that while she worked for Playboy from 1985 to 1990, Playmates would be offered promotional assignments. While some were legit jobs, appearing at car and boat shows that paid $500 or so, other jobs were less well defined.

"I went on a promotional assignment from Playboy Promotions with some other girls from Playboy. I usually only did modeling work, which was through Playboy Models; they were my agents. All offers for movies, television, print work all had to go through Playboy because I was under contract for five years." Weigel says she took the promotional assignment from Playboy Promotions, and flew to Atlantic City, only to discover that her "job" was to sit next to a high roller in the casino and keep him happy while her fellow Playmates kept their respective "hosts" amused.

"I was so happy because I got $700, and then on the plane I found out that the other girls got $5,000 or more! I thought maybe he didn't think I was cute enough. And then it dawned on me. I asked the girls if they had [done] these guys and they were all, 'No,' but that's the only thing that made sense. Still I got $700, which I needed, and didn't have to fuck this fat guy." Weigel insists that prostitution, sanctioned by Playboy or not, was a common occurrence, as was drug use, although she says she never took part in either while a Playmate.

Shannon Tweed, 1982 Playmate of the Year, who lived at the Mansion as Hef's girlfriend, was allegedly evicted from her position and Hef's bedroom when the mogul discovered she had been abusing cocaine,[11] a story that former butler Bagley more or less confirms. "I was there the night they had the big fight. The door was closed, but I was supposed to be filling up candy jars, so I stood outside and I overheard them fighting. There were words about drugs, that Shannon had been doing them in the sunbathing room."

Hefner's intolerance to drugs stems from the 1973 suicide of his long-time executive assistant Bobbie Arnstein. Indicted, tried, and convicted for cocaine trafficking, Arnstein was being pressured by the government to help them indict Hefner on drug charges. Facing a 15-year sentence, the loyal, emotionally fragile Arnstein overdosed on pills.[12]

Nowadays at the Mansion during parties security is omnipresent to make sure that guests don't violate the host's firm no-drugs policy, but there are ways around it, claims actor/party boy Russ. "If you're a girl, you can usually wheedle your way back in." According to him, a Beverly Hills television actress/heiress and her date were caught smoking a joint at the Mansion. They were both evicted, but she was able to talk her way back into Playboy party good graces; however, her date was permanently banned.

But who needs drugs when you are in the Pleasure Palace, the hump house that Hef built? "George Clooney, who can [do] any girl he wants, is there with a shit-eating grin on his face," laughs Russ. "In the grotto, it's insane. I was in the Jacuzzi and a former Playmate-turned-actress is making out with some guy while another girl is going down on him."

According to Russ, The Mansion, with its legendary past, is building a reputation in the present, with guests like Courtney Love, Leonardo DiCaprio, antiwar rocker Fred Durst, and long time Hef pal, suspected spouse murderer Robert Blake. "I have a picture of me dancing at a party there and in the background you can see Blake and his [now] dead wife." Russ shakes his blond locks in amazement.

Russ says that the décor, complete with the painting over the fire-place of Hef as a Renaissance prince, is unchanged from the 1970s. And many of the faces holding court are still the same—James Caan, Jack Nicholson, and Robert Culp.

To make sure his own needs are met, Hef, the prince of porn, has more than doubled his ration of blondes. One for each decade, explained Hef when he unveiled them at New Years 2001. He explained to the press, "Picasso had his pink period and his blue period. I'm in my blonde period."[13]

If Hefner also had his blue period, it would have to have been the 1980s, which began with a bang when Playmate of the Year Dorothy Stratten was shot-gunned by her estranged husband, who then raped her corpse before turning the gun on himself. Hefner had the unpleasant task of calling Stratten's boyfriend and his then friend, director Peter Bogdanovich and telling him that Stratten had been murdered. Bogdanovich then wrote a scathing indictment of Hefner, the Mansion, and the Playboy lifestyle in *The Killing of the Unicorn*. In his *Mean* magazine interview Hefner attributes the stress from Bogdanovich's revelations (which Hefner disputes) as contributing to his stroke.

Dead Playmates with hostile boyfriends aside, the freewheeling 1960s and sexy 1970s gave way to the conservative Reagan-Bush era, and Attorney General Edwin Meese was eager to stamp out porn, as he understood porn. "*Playboy* wasn't porn, we were told that all the time," says Teri Weigel. "We weren't doing porn, we were doing art, that's what the courts had said." But the courts had said that in 1963. Twenty years later, *Playboy* was under fire. In 1986, Weigel found herself a victim of Meese's antiporn war. "I kept being told you're gonna be Playmate of the Year, dump your boyfriend, keep dating Prince Albert [of Monaco], it'll be good for the magazine, you want to be Playmate of the Year! Then *Playboy* got banned from the 7–11s in North Carolina, which was a huge loss, and so to get back at the state, *Playboy* picked a Playmate from North Carolina to be Play-mate of the Year, just to show them and get even with them!"

The female former Playboy Enterprises employee supports Teri Weigel's implication that Hefner is responsible for choosing the

Playmate of the Year. "It's supposed to be a readers' poll, but it's not. Hefner is in charge." Although, adds the ex-employee—who wishes to remain anonymous because *Playboy* looks good on her resume— during the nine years (1989–1998) Hefner was with his second wife, Playmate for Life Kimberly Conrad Hefner, Mrs. Hefner had a very firm hand in the decision.

There have long been allegations that the way to become Playmate of the Year was to sleep with Hefner, allegations that are supported by the former employee. "You sleep with Hef, that's the deal." Weigel isn't sure about that. "I never slept with Hefner." But then again, she never made Playmate of the Year.

The 1980s were filled with domestic drama: The Shannon Tweed and then Carrie Leigh imbroglios[14] were followed by the publication and serialization of Bogdanovich's book and Hefner's stroke. Meanwhile, the Playboy Clubs were phased out and Hefner faded from public eye. There were still parties, but they were more subdued, with only old cronies coming by and the Playmates trying to keep Hef amused.

Butler Bagley claims that the Playmates who stayed at the Mansion would be sent to Chippendales dance club with cash in hand to pick up the male dancers and bring them back for orgies so that Hefner could watch. And according to Bagley, who worked at the Mansion during the 1980s, condoms were not used. "I was in charge of filling candy dishes, putting out towels in the bathrooms, making sure that there was plenty of baby oil, but never condoms." Teri Weigel says AIDS was never an issue. "We never thought about it. It was something that affected people from a different social group."

Bagley says that there were other things to worry about. "I was so afraid of the grotto. Everyone called the Jacuzzi the herpes pool. I was so naïve, I didn't know what herpes was, but it sounded awful. I was afraid that while I was putting out the towels and bathrobes, I would fall in and get herpes!"

Exchange of bodily fluids was de rigeur for guests at the Mansion. "I had to get the rooms ready for a party," explains Bagley. "The door to the blue room, off the game room, was locked, and I knocked and knocked. Finally someone unlocked it, and three people ran to the showers. On the floor were panty hose that had been shredded to ribbons. The bed sheets were on the floor soaked with baby oil and every body fluid you can imagine, every one of them."

AIDS awareness didn't hit Hef's world until 1994 when Miss September 1986, Rebekka Armstrong, told the *Advocate* magazine that she was HIV positive. Quickly Hefner and the Playboy Foundation moved to provide grants to Rebekka as part of a College Campus Safer Sex program. "It wouldn't have looked good to have a Playmate die broke from AIDS, and she was in real danger of that," says someone who knew Rebekka before the *Advocate* article came out.

"*Playboy* had to help her," says Teri Weigel. "They didn't help me in 1990, and look what happened!" she laughs. In 1990, Weigel was in a car accident that left her unable to work for a spell. Her *Playboy* contract had expired, and both she and her husband were broke. Desperate, she turned to hard-core porn. It was a move that would, ironically, turn Hefner against her forever.

No porn, no drugs are the mantras recited to Playmates even today, as their Freudian father figure hosts grotto groping and baby oil orgies, swallowing Viagra to rally himself for another round of blonde boffing.

Or does he? Does Hef really fornicate like the certain endangered marsh rabbit given the scientific classification of *Sylvilagus palustris hefneri* in his honor? When Brande Roderick appeared on the "Howard Stern Show" to promote both Playboy and her role in "Baywatch Hawaii," the shock jock grilled her unmercifully about her sex life with Hefner. Brande deflected questions with stammers and "I don't know."

"You can't talk about Hefner," explains the former employee. Teri Weigel agrees that while under the five-year contract, Playmates must keep quiet about the goings-on at the Mansion.

But Playboy's former employee, who worked in the New York, Chicago, and Los Angeles offices, feels no such compunction to silence. "Even though Hefner turned *Playboy* over to his daughter, he still runs the magazine. And even though Playboy makes a big deal out of having a 60 percent female workforce, they are very sexist company."

When hired, this woman was warned that she would be working in a very sexual environment. She says that she didn't have a problem with that. However, when the sexual veered into sexual harassment and discrimination, she felt it was time to move on.

"I would get called into an executive's office to fix his computer since that was my job, and he would have a porno tape on the whole time, and he would be commenting about the actresses' breasts and how they compared to mine. And it wasn't even Playboy videos he was watching, either." So much for company loyalty!

When Hef married Kimberly Conrad, it seemed like the wild bachelor had been tamed. He turned the running of his empire over to daughter Christie and put a CHILDREN AT PLAY sign alongside his winding driveway after his sons Marston and Cooper were born. Then in 1998, the happy Hefners separated. Mrs. Hefner and the boys moved onto an estate that Hef bought right next door to the Mansion.

Then came the greatest revelation for Hefner—Viagra. Hef happily announced that Viagra came out the weekend before his birthday, and no doubt for him it is the greatest gift ever. Second only to Viagra was the rediscovery of Hefner and the Playboy lifestyle as both camp nostalgia and an aspiration. Explains actor Russ, "It's part of the whole pimp/player culture. It's acceptable to be a dog. Also, you get a chance to have your picture taken with Hefner. That's huge; you can send it back home. Girls will call their dads once they're inside and go 'Guess where I am!'"

And where you are is surrounded by celebrities and bare-bellied babes. You know you've arrived. "The Mansion has a way of breaking people down. If you are there, you must be cool. There's no I'm-a-celebrity-you're-not-a-celebrity thing," says Russ. And of course, there is the Playboy mystique, the sex-soaked atmosphere, the walls varnished in years of orgy butter. During a party, Hefner might make an appearance, walking down the staircase from his suite, dressed in pajamas with a satin robe, a Diet Pepsi in hand, perhaps escorted by his gaggle of giggling girls, perhaps alone. He greets those he knows, is introduced, is photographed with guests by the always-present documentarians, and then takes to the dance floor to do the geriatric shuffle version of the hustle. It's the same dance he will do in nightclubs across Hollywood when he goes out with the boob brigade, only in clubs an area will be roped off for him so he can dance with his girls while they do their "pseudo-lesbian thing" as one observer calls it.

Gone is the radical intellectual content that made *Playboy* a magazine that men actually read for the articles. As Hef has become a caricature of himself, so has the magazine become a flaccid imitation of a once-vital social force that shaped American society.

Hugh Hefner, once an advocate of free speech, twice turned down the highest award from the Free Speech Coalition, a lobbying organization comprised of First Amendment advocates and members of the adult entertainment business precisely because they are pornographers. After all, he makes art. Well, sort of. Along with his credits as the executive producer on the lofty biographies of such film legends as Clara Bow and Lon Chaney, Hefner is the executive producer of fine works like *Playboy Centerfold Anna Nicole Smith*, *Voluptuous Vixens,* and *Inside/Out*.

And whether he admits it or not, Hugh Hefner reaps the rewards of explicit pornography on the cable channels owned by Playboy. "We shoot hard-core and soft-core at the same time," insists porn actress Weigel. The hard-core gets an X rating and goes into the adult-only section of the video store, while the same footage with a hand here, a thigh there goes straight to Playboy's cable outlets. With smoke and mirrors, Hefner has dressed up porn and taken it to the prom, turning a whore into the girl next door. And of course, according to Hef, *Playboy's Erotic Fantasies* and *Playmate Pajama Party* are art.[15]

And men buy *Playboy* for the articles!

The Heidi Tapes

No foray into Hollywood debauchery would be complete without a peek into the Heidi Affair. How it played out in the media and the truly debauched nature of Heidi and her friends were slightly different. The back story: On June 4, 1993, would-be panderers Ivan Nagy (Fleiss' ex-boyfriend) and his business partner Julie Conatser paid self-styled private investigator Dan Hanks $6,000 to wiretap Heidi's home and base of illegal operations. Hanks put the wiretap bug in place the following day. Over the course of the next two weeks, the gumshoe would retrieve the tapes from a clump of bushes located about two blocks from Heidi's estate.

In August 2003, private eye Dan Hanks of Backstreet Detectives gave us the transcripts and tapes. And he did it for free. Though burglars and police

*turned Hanks' home upside down in their futile attempts to find the tapes,
Hollywood, Interrupted got hold of them the old-fashioned way. We asked
for them. The tapes, recorded over the soundtrack portion of two videotapes,
had been sitting on Hanks' living room bookshelf with his movie collection all
along. In full view, the video box containing the tapes was from the 1937
Shirley Temple classic, Heidi . . .*

Heidi: "Was everything ok?"
Evans: "Really."
Heidi: "With the, the little girl [this last word is drawn out]."

❑ ▦ ■

Evans: "What did that little girl think of me? Did she like me?"
Heidi: "How could she not like you?"
Evans: "No, no. I'm curious."

❑ ▦ ■

Evans: "I was very nice to her."
Heidi: "You were."
Evans: "Very helpful, too. She's not dumb."
Heidi: "No, she's a good kid or I wouldn't—."
Evans: "A good kid who could do well in life or could end up in the
    gutter."

❑ ▦ ■

Heidi: "The first thousand dollars she made I think is the first thou-
    sand dollars she's ever seen in her life."
Evans: "I knew it. And she's a good girl basically. I don't think she
    could—I can be so wrong and naive, but I don't [think]
    she wants to be a full-time hooker."

❑ ▦ ■

Evans: "I'm doing it as an experiment."
Heidi: "Like *My Fair Lady.*"
Evans: "Well, yes, very much so."
Heidi: "Mmmmm."

Evans: "Here's a 17-year-old vagrant who's a fairly attractive girl, who could be very attractive . . . because she has presence and she's not afraid. And she's attractive in an interesting way, and she's sort of sensual too, by the way. That's a good combination. But she has to be able to open her mouth."

Evans: "You, you seen the little girl?"
Heidi: "I will today. I paged her twice."

Heidi: "The little one? She's not returning her pages . . ."
Heidi: "And her ID came in the mail here."
Evans: "What?"
Heidi: "She's been waiting for her ID . . ."
Heidi: "And it's here. And so I'm tryin' to tell her her ID's here and she's not returning her pages. She's a, you know, little kid."

Evans: "I told her I wanted her to come down here. Did she say anything?"
Heidi: "Ah, uhm, she was—I don't know what she was tryin' to insinuate. She said she talked to you and that she'll come down there. When do you want her to?"

Evans: "She seem to like me at all?"
Heidi: "Yeah."
Evans: "A little, eh?"
Heidi: "Yeah."
Evans: "What'd she say?"
Heidi: "She's little and she's so naive to the world so she doesn't quite under—she's asked me so many questions."

Evans: "Okay, put her in a car out here in the next two days."
Heidi: "All right, I'm gonna see her tomorrow, get it taken care of."

■ ■ ■

Heidi: "See, she goes like this, 'Well, what about this check?'" And I
said—I said, "I can't have my name on it, cause—" I said,
"Wait for your ID to come and you go cash it." And I said,
"Here's a couple hundred dollars in the meantime."
Evans: "I ought to give her the cash. Shit."
Heidi: "Okay, well, I'll tell her that."
Evans: "Tell her when she comes down here I'll give her the cash."
Heidi: "Okay."
Evans: "I will, too. I didn't have it then."

■ ■ ■

Evans: " . . . I didn't know she couldn't cash it, see?"
Heidi: "Well, now she can. She has ID. I told her I'm not, I'm not
touching it. With you and me—"
Evans: "Tell her to bring the check down to me and I'll cash it."
Heidi: "I don't want our names even together."

■ ■ ■

Had these rather revealing transcripts never been exposed, the Heidi
Fleiss scandal never would have amounted to anything more than the
shocking revelation that Charlie Sheen, and—Stop the presses!—
Billy Idol, were frequenting prostitutes. With apologies to the *Casablanca* writers, We're shocked, shocked to find prostitution (with
single male entertainers no less) is going on in here!

What is really disturbing here is how the aging movie industry
icon Robert Evans appears to have gotten away with ordering up a
"little one" from Hollywood's favored madam, only to be canonized
recently by the one person who should have crucified him—*Vanity
Fair* Executive Editor Graydon Carter. In a move that would make the
late Leni Riefenstahl proud, Carter was able to produce a completely
one-sided myth-recreating documentary (*The Kid Stays In The Picture*)
about the former Paramount Studios head without having to deal
with this lecherous man's truly dark and unspeakable past. As a
result, the former founding editor of the late lamented *Spy* magazine,

Carter, the ultimate architect of puff pieces framed as "controversy," has sadly become the person he used to love to mock.

One of the *Los Angeles Times* reporters (Shawn Hubler) that quasi-scooped the Fleiss affair in a career making expose admittedly had access to the same wiretap tapes and transcripts from the Fleiss brothel that we were privy to, yet, she avoided reporting on Evans' apparent involvement except in passing: *"I haven't spoken to her {Heidi Fleiss} for some time. Call my press agent," said* "Sliver" *producer Robert Evans. His publicist described Fleiss as a family friend."* Hubler, according the Fleiss transcripts, wound up with a Heidi-proffered $300 bouquet on her desk. Of course, Evans went on to repeat the "family friend" dodge in his very selective Hollywood tell-all book *The Kid Stays In the Picture.* Case closed.

Heidi, in turn, emerged from prison saved—a born-again celebrity, ready to cash in *selectively* (she mostly names dead people, or known celebrity whoremongers) on the contents of her secret "black book." Her black book is actually a veritable "who's who" of Hollywood, chock full of powerbrokers not previously revealed, including the scion of a major corporation that advertises heavily in the *Los Angeles Times.* Heidi launched an underwear boutique (Heidi Wear). She got the requisite plastic surgery, vomited up a tell-nothing book (*Pandering*), and she's now a darling on the talk show circuit with her life story, "Pay the Girl," in development at Comedy Central cartoon character Bob "Kid Notorious" Evans' home studio, Paramount. *That's* insanity chic.

"SEXUAL PERVERSITY" IN LOS ANGELES

10

Michael Jackson and Eddie Murphy are two entertainers with double-decade careers who, despite indiscretions unparalleled, have time and time again ruled the pop charts and the box office. But Jackson is said to be in dire financial straits[1] and Murphy has, at the very least, completely lost touch with the raw comic nerve that made him a respected star in the first place. Such is the result of an appetite for self-destruction gone unchecked. But Hollywood isn't in the business of doling out moral dietary requirements. There are too many greedy mouths to feed.

Eddie Murphy has paid minimal, if any, career consequences for his public missteps. Murphy was stopped by police in 1997 for picking up a 20-year old-Samoan transvestite prostitute in the heart of Boystown in West Hollywood in the wee hours of the morning, while his wife and children were out of town. Despite multiple allegations circulating around Boystown and in the tabloids that Murphy had long frequented she-males of the night,[2] celebrity sleuth Paul Barresi and Hollywood fix-it attorney Marty Singer temporarily stopped the media dead in their tracks. Through legal maneuvers—not to mention the spin planted with the pliant entertainment media—they managed to explain that Murphy was just being "a good Samaritan" by picking up a stranded traveler and giving the "guy" a ride home— conveniently before the Nutty Professor and Dr. Dolittle sequels hit the screens.

Then, even after his tragically unfunny turn in the box-office bomb that was *Pluto Nash*, Murphy most recently raked millions starring in yet another deplorable kid's movie, *Daddy Day Care*. Murphy is considered far too valuable to the movie studio's bottom line so it seems likely that the machinery around Murphy had given him a transgendered eye for the straight guy makeover and the compliant press acquiesced. That's what happens when stars are locked into multipicture deals.

But for all the billable hours lawyers log and hefty retainer fees that publicists pocket from either feeding or fending off the media to their star clients' benefit, there's only so much that can be accomplished on the phone during a manicure. There's a guy trolling beneath their radar in a dark place where celebrity scandal seethes like the SARS virus. The gutter, whether real or metaphorical, is the last place a damage control specialist will look when their celebrity baby goes astray. And by the time they realize where their star spent the night, a hideous dawn of reckoning has arrived that no legal threat or press release can derail. Only when the smut hits the gossip sheets and police blotter will Lucifer recline. Beneath his pillow lie the secrets that no spin can possibly squelch.

The Bagman

He once jabbed a pencil into the throat of a child predator who forced a 14-year-old boy into pornography and prostitution. He shook down a tabloid editor in his office for a long-overdue debt, went home, put his gun away, and wrote a complaint letter to the Better Business Bureau about the tabloid skel and his shady business practices.

He has conducted a regular, consistent, and extremely lucrative business with the tabloids: Eddie Murphy, Michael Jackson, the heterosexual Tom Cruise, Robert Blake, Arnold Schwarzenegger, O.J.—he's brokered information on all of them. He's worked with the mainstream media to expose child pornographers and pimps. He's worked behind the scenes to cover the butts and save or savage the careers of several major stars including Murphy and Jackson. Over the course of 20 years, he has trafficked in the most disgusting troughs of decadence and despair the culture of Hollywood has produced.

Apart from their reputations, he never stole a thing from the rich and famous, even though the opportunity presented itself many times. However, he will confess that he did take a peek into their closets to check out the skeletons hanging there. He has been a porn star and a legit bit actor; he says he's done tours of duty as physical trainer, bodyguard, and/or confidant to the likes of Johnny Carson's wife Alexis Carson, David Geffen, John Travolta, Liberace, Raquel Welch, Joan Rivers, and power agents and managers like the late Stan Kamen (who represented Barbra Streisand, Steven Spielberg, Robert Redford, and Goldie Hawn for the William Morris agency) and Lois Zetter (still active in managing a few special clients and who helped produce films such as *Urban Cowboy*).

He's posed nude in a best-selling issue of *Playgirl*, and exposed the dark side of fame and fortune for the mainstream media. The Los Angeles Police Department came to him for help; so did a rich little old lady who got ripped off by a sleazy boy-toy. And, oh yeah—he may well be the only the Boogie Knight-meets-Magnum P.I. in history to receive a letter of acknowledgement from the FBI for his help in an ugly situation.

He makes his money the old-fashioned way: He earns it. He has a code of ethics emphasizing loyalty and respect, and he follows it. Meanwhile, almost everyone around him—the movie stars and their man-handlers, the power mavens and their procurers, the agents, managers, aspirants, hangers-on, whores, and lawyers—*especially* the lawyers—will do anything they think they can get away with to preserve the reputations of their errant clients.

He can document every relationship he's forged and every job he's ever done. Name a Hollywood scandal in the last two decades and this

Zelig of the Hollywood underbelly played a role in it: If he didn't lever-
age one of the principals, he brokered some of the inside information.
If he didn't know the targets, he knew the grifters who targeted them
or the P.I.s or shysters or crooked cops they turned to to get them out
of it. Because when world-class celebrities come butt-up against the
consequences of their infinite desires—and they will—they will do or
say or pay anything to get out of it.

That's where Paul Barresi comes in. He's the bagman. He knows
this world like he knows his own skin, and its reek and stench are
his oxygen.

Sharing the classic, rugged good looks of a young Burt Reynolds,
Barresi came to Hollywood to be a star. Doesn't everyone? He endured
a childhood in blue-collar mob-ruled Saugus, Massachusetts, with an
ex-Marine dad who beat him regularly and a nun-teacher who did the
same; he did a stint in the U.S. Air Force; and then he hit Hollywood
right in the middle of the swinging 1970's. Lady Luck was on his side,
and she's been a faithful lover ever since. He landed a job as production assistant on the Fatty Arbuckle sex scandal–inspired *The Wild
Party*, and ended up in a scene opposite screen siren Raquel Welch.
Next thing you know, he's being photographed for the March 1974
issue of *Playgirl* with model/actress Cassandra Peterson, now known as
Elvira, Mistress of the Dark. *Playgirl* led to more work in the burgeoning adult entertainment arena.

But pornography wasn't the only acting work that came out of
Playgirl. Barresi signed with a major modeling agency, moved to New
York, ended up touring the country with old-school, fey funny man
Paul Lynde in Neil Simon's *Plaza Suite*, and made a friend for life in
Lynde. He wept when he found him dead. Lady Luck rolled the dice
again, and Barresi settled for good in Los Angeles. Thanks to his affiliation with John Travolta's former fitness craze enterprise called The
John Travolta Dance and Workout Studio, Barresi claims he began
training some of Hollywood's movers and shakers, including Johnny
Carson's attorney Henry "Bombastic" Bushkin and entertainment
mogul-in-training David Geffen. Unfortunately, when Travolta's gym
manager discovered Barresi's background in adult entertainment, he
convinced Travolta to let him go. Barresi reports that he and the danc-

ing queen of the box office at the time met in a coffee shop and Travolta tossed his top trainer severance pay. No matter—Barresi was also working out in the bedrooms of other powerful people.

Along with his acting, on stage and the occasional bit part in mainstream movies, Barresi was realizing another fantasy—he became a real life private eye, and now was solving problems and fixing situations for a fee, using his unique perspective and muscled physique. He was self-made, and molded from his tough upbringing and streetwise savvy—simple as that. Most people wouldn't even think of doing some of the stuff he has gotten involved in, out of fear they might find themselves face down in a gutter someplace with a bullet in the back of their head. That's why he does what he does so well. There are too few fearless gumshoes out there to go around.

Some of Barresi-the-investigator's clients were celebs—like the guy who wanted a specific person's Mercedes worked over with a baseball bat. Others were more prosaic—a rough trade trick that needed roughing up, a debt collection here, a little intimidation there. He helped the FBI capture a criminal on the State of Virginia's most wanted list.

In 1990, the *National Enquirer* ran a cover story based on Barresi's claim that he'd had a two-year love affair with John Travolta. He told the tabloid he'd met Travolta in 1982 when the actor followed him into the shower room of a Los Angeles health club. They later had sex "dozens of times," Barresi said.

Barresi later retracted his Travolta story and sent a letter to the star's lawyer Marty Singer denying that he'd ever engaged in "homosexual activity" with Travolta. Barresi's Hollywood low life was interrupted when copies of the *Enquirer* piece were disseminated amongst his family members, neighbors, and fitness clients. He intuitively blamed Travolta's mother church, Scientology, for that classic "black PR" campaign.

Nonetheless, Barresi still insists on record that Travolta took him on vacation to Hawaii, hired him as his trainer, and helped him get a part in the movie *Perfect*, the homoerotic precursor to *Rolling Stone* publisher Jann Wenner's public coming-out party. Physically fit, Barresi appears in a speaking role in a locker room scene wearing a jock strap. To put it mildly, according to Barresi, Travolta continuously struggled to reconcile his sexuality with homophobic-by-doctrine Scientology.

On probation for "evading a police officer," Barresi caught a strange hand when he sweet-talked his probation officer, and wound up photographed as the personal escort for the future California gubernatorial candidate Arnold Schwarzenegger and Maria Shriver as part of his sentence at an inner-city benefit. He had worked as personal security before, for Mary Hart in Las Vegas.

Barresi's skills as a negotiator working both sides of the gutter run deep. When the Los Angeles Police Department needed some help in uncovering a ring of male prostitutes with clients in some pretty high places, they asked Barresi to step in. According to Barresi, the investigation was derailed because "they [the LAPD] didn't want to touch [a high-ranking member of the Velvet Mafia, Hollywood's cadre of gay moguls]."[3] No matter—Barresi had his sights set on Michael Jackson. For the next decade, the P.I. sat patiently on the fringe, taking notes, as the King of Pop began to self-destruct.

About a Boy

In 1993, Michael Jackson paid a California dentist's son, Jordan Chandler, millions of dollars in an out-of-court settlement,[4] but denied claims he had molested the boy at his 2,700-acre private ranch. But, in a report filed at the time by the Los Angeles Department of Child Services, the child claimed Jackson had molested him. The report of alleged abuse reads like a classic tale of seduction told in the bureaucratese of a social worker.

The child is "the minor." His psychiatrist is the "RP" (referring). The $850,000 Beverly Hills home where the interview was conducted was "clean and well-kept, no apparent safety hazards, all utilities working." The "minor had a difficult time focusing and often went off the topic," but was "consistent in his story." Which was: Jackson called him every day for long conversations about video games and his ranch, that he bought him toys, took him to Las Vegas, and they watched a tape of "The Exorcist" together there.... Both he and Jackson were so scared by the movie that they slept in the same bed, and did so other times at both of their homes. And that after several of these sleepovers, Jackson began kissing him, rubbing up against him, and ultimately engaging in oral sex and masturbation.[5]

These lurid reports filed in 1993 detailed the mouth-kissing, masturbation, and excessive bedtime activities alleged between Jackson and the 13-year-old Chandler, but most damning and curious were the bevy of preteen boys lining up in Jackson's *defense*. While they all claimed that nothing sexual occurred between them and the pop star, most of them admitted sharing the same bed with him. One of them, a then 11-year-old Australian child, told reporters that he had slept with Jackson, "But," argued the youngster, "he slept on one side and I slept on the other. It was a big bed."

Allegations against Jackson led to a formal investigation, and his homes were searched. After scouring the singer's Los Angeles mansion and Santa Barbara ranch, authorities seized a bounty of photographs and videos, yet, reportedly found no incriminating evidence. The investigation was closed; the "big bed defense" prevailed, and "celebrity justice" won out again with a multimillion dollar payoff.

In the ultimate display of insanity chic, Jackson, who was named President George Bush Sr.'s Point of Light ambassador in recognition of his efforts in inviting disadvantaged children into his home,[6] went on to draw huge crowds, win awards, nurture children's charities, and have his celebrity friends, family, and handlers polish his image while his fame and riches made problems disappear.

In the fall of 1993, withdrawal from the rally-around-Michael circle-jerk came from his sister La Toya. At a news conference in Tel Aviv, the self-exiled singer flat out accused her sibling of sexually molesting children, stating, "This has been going on since 1981, and it's not just one child." Though branded a liar by the indecisive Jermaine and Jehovah's-witnessing Jackson family matriarch Katherine, La Toya flat out accused her brother of "crimes against small, innocent children,"[7] and claimed Katherine had shown her checks made out to Michael's alleged victims' parents.[8]

Depending on your point of view, either Michael was an evil pedophile, or LaToya (who, in a fit of dubious self-promotion, subsequently retracted her accusations—which her family long denied— on Larry King,[9] and was seen in the summer of 2003 at Neverland at his father Joe Jackson's birthday bash) was a pathological liar, neither viewpoint reflecting well on the family dynamics and child-raising skills of Katherine and Joe Jackson. And sandwiched into the family bickering was Jackson's lawyer, Bert Fields, who actually told *Vanity Fair* that Jackson "really lives the life of a 12-year-old." Fields admitted that his client shared a bed with the 13-year-old Jordan Chandler, but did not abuse him.[10]

Besides, if we're to believe Jackson's then-manager Sandy Gallin, his super star client's behavior with youngsters is the fault of the public's prurience. "Michael's innocent, open and child-like relationships with children may appear bizarre and strange to adults in our society who cannot conceive of any relationship without sexual connotations," Gallin said in a press release. "This is not a reflection of Michael's character," explained the Jackson handler. "Rather it is a symptom of the sexual phobias of our society." In other words, we the public, have dirty minds, not his famous client.

Another obvious defense of Jackson in the wake of molestation charges was conveyance of the idea that the multimillionaire mega-star was constantly subjected to extortion attempts. Charged with ferreting out the extortionists was the currently incarcerated for explosives violations, bare-knuckle private investigator, Anthony "The Pelican" Pellicano. But the shady, baseball bat-wielding celebrity PI[11] failed to set up the father of Jackson's accuser as an extortionist, so—behind the scenes—according to Baressi, the Pelican hired the self-styled sleuth to find others who were out to damage his famous client's reputation.

Barresi—long self-employed collecting damaging info on celebrities and then soliciting the spoils out to the highest bidder, whether the tabloids, second-party investigators, lawyers, or his own conscience—found plenty of people close to the pop star willing to talk smack.

Jackson has clearly had his problems with the law over his alleged sexual proclivities. He was very vulnerable to blackmail, having already paid out millions to settle one case. A gay pornographer had infiltrated his entourage with the possible goal of setting up the star and then blackmailing him. Barresi says he tipped off the star's lawyers and the Feds, knowing that not only would the lawyers make bank and the Feds make a bust, but that he would have done the right thing—for a fee.[12]

Peter Panderer

It was summer 2001 and Paul Barresi was working steadily producing adult, military-themed films[13] for the gay market. One day the phone rang; it was Barresi's buddy Vaughn Kincey, another skin flick producer, who incidentally was caught up in a breach of contract lawsuit with Michael Jackson's company, MJJ Music.[14]

The story, as related by Barresi and confirmed in an interview with Kincey, goes like this:

> *"Hey, did you hear the latest about Michael Jackson and gay porn?" Barresi waited for a punch line. During the time he'd investigated the allegations of child molestation involving Jackson, he had heard jokes aplenty. And because he's known as an investigator and a guy who can get information out to the right person or the public, he's funneled plenty of stories; most don't pan out.*
>
> *"Okay, I'll bite, what's up?" Barresi asked when no joke materialized. Kincey's reply made him pause. "There's a . . . porn producer working for Jackson, and it's Fred Schaffel!"*

Fred Schaffel was a name Barresi knew well. He was a known sex industry scumbag. His cinematic specialty was gay porn with titles like *Cocktales* and *Man with the Golden Rod*, and he had a predilection for young-looking performers, preferably straight, who he would recruit in Eastern European countries like Hungary and the Czech Republic for both his personal and professional pleasure.

Barresi made a preliminary call to a friend at the *National Enquirer*, but his tabloid contact told him that unless he got some more information, they weren't interested. He'd hoped maybe they'd float him a retainer to check out the story and if it panned out, pay him handsomely. But now that the tabloids were all conglomerating, their hunger—and their expense accounts—had dried up. He had other things to occupy his mind, so he let the matter drop.

The pleasant summer passed into the fall, or autumn of Jackson's career, and Barresi had almost put the Michael Jackson porn rumor out of his mind until one Sunday Kincey called again, and, according to Barresi, told him that after a lot of casually asking around, he had found out that Fred Schaffel was working for Jackson under the name Marc Schaffel, but he wasn't sure in what capacity. Marc Schaffel, Fred Schaffel, it certainly made sense, because Schaffel had used the name Marc Fredricks on the porn movies he made. Barresi did a quick Internet search and hit pay dirt; according to several archived articles, Marc Schaffel was the executive producer of the Jackson fund-raising ballad and video, *What More Can I Give*, which was supposedly going to raise $50 million for victims and families of the September 11 terrorist attack. Some more digging turned up the name of Jackson's public relations firm, Rubenstein & Associates. Barresi didn't waste any time calling their office in New York. Since it was Sunday, they were closed, but he left a terse message on their machine.

According to Barresi, the message went as follows:

"This is Paul Barresi. I have information about an unsavory character under Michael Jackson's employ who, if allowed to continue working for Jackson, would prove damaging to Michael Jackson's career and reputation." He left his number, and then contacted his sometime associate, Dan Hanks. Dan and his partner Fred Valis run a private investigation firm called Backstreet Investigations. Like Barresi, they had received face time on various television programs; unlike Barresi, one of them, Fred Valis, was a licensed investigator, which meant the Backstreet team had access to databases that Barresi (and the average citizen) did not. Backstreet detective Hanks printed up Schaffel's Social Security Number and a list of his past addresses, and Barresi went to work researching compromising information on the porn monger turned heavy Hollywood hitter.

On Wednesday, November 7, as Baressi tells it, there was message on his voice mail. The man's voice was nervous, slightly stammering. "It's Barry Siegel and I was referred by Rubenstein & Associates regarding my client." Barresi had to laugh at his attempt at cloak and dagger—not mentioning the client's name. What a wimp, he thought. And he was right.

Barry Siegel, Michael Jackson's personal accountant/business manager, said[15] he was glad that Barresi had called him back, especially concerning the information about an employee of his client which could assist him in ridding his client of said employee.

Barresi says that Siegel listened receptively to what Barresi had to say, and then asked how much he would charge for information that would lead him to the individual in question. Barresi told him he wanted $1,500 for his help, a relatively paltry sum covering the cost of his time and effort. The PI promised: "In the spirit of my well-intentioned efforts, and as a condition of our agreement, you would not be obliged to pay me a dime until after you conducted your own investigation and found the information I provided you to be absolutely true." According to Barresi, Siegel indicated that he thought Barresi's offer was reasonable and said he would have to get back with him.

Barresi recounted that, Siegel called him later and said he'd pay out the fifteen hundred bucks, but that he [Baressi] would have to sign a nondisclosure agreement. No problem. Barresi says Siegel reiterated his good intentions, but added, "I won't be able to have the papers ready tomorrow." That was fine. Barresi knew from past experience that lawyers sometimes dragged their feet. But Barresi was adamant about one thing. "I don't want to have to deal with [Jackson attorney] Marty Singer because they did not treat me fairly in the past when I did some damage control for their client Eddie Murphy." Barresi says that Siegel assured him that Michael Jackson had several lawyers who handled different matters for him, so it wouldn't be necessary to go through Marty Singer. "We'll settle our agreement on Monday, November 12, at 4 PM," he said, and then hung up.

Barresi made a few calls to Schaffel associates to see what else he could dig up on him, as if the list of films wasn't unsavory enough. A fallen pop star struggling for a comeback after facing child molestation charges and who had paid out millions in settlement money doesn't need the director of *View to a Thrill* working for him.

Barresi says he struck pay dirt with David Aldorf, a former Schaffel associate he'd known for awhile. According to Barresi, Aldorf invited Barresi over for an in-depth chat. "Fred owed me money, fifty grand on a deal that would have made me double that. I called him once I found out what job he has now to demand my money, and I let him know I had a tape of him directing porn with two young boys performing."

Barresi says Aldorf paused for effect, opening his eyes wide and clasping his hands like a silent screen diva. "He wanted that tape, I'll tell you that!" Understandably, he [Schaffel] wanted that tape. No one potentially working a grift with a major star as a dupe wants a tape of them coordinating sex shots with young-looking performers floating around, especially if the star has previously been implicated in child sex charges.

Barresi was floored by the existence of a video with Schaffel and young-looking guys on it, which revolted him—even the possibility of minors on videotape was an anathema to him. He also saw the scope of Schaffel's devious plan, which became even clearer as Aldorf went on. "Fred said, 'Be patient, I'm working on this deal and you are going to get your money. Michael Jackson is a billionaire 10 times over. Twenty-five million is nothing to him.'"

Barresi claims he said, "David, you have to do the right thing. Give me the tape." According to Barresi, the conversation went down like this:

> *Aldorf pursed his lip; he was thinking hard. "If those are underage boys on that tape...." Aldorf asked suspiciously, "What are you going to do with it?" Everyone knew how Barresi had often played lawyers and stars against the tabloids, which might have been an option before he heard about the young boys. Or maybe he thought Barresi was going to turn the tape over to Schaffel for some bank, cash that maybe he could get himself. Either way he was wrong. The instant Barresi heard that kids were involved, he knew what he was going to do. He was not only going to Jackson's people, but he was taking it to law enforcement.*
>
> *Barresi pressed Aldorf. "Okay, let me put all my cards on the table. I am assisting the Michael Jackson people and they would very much like to get a fix on specifically what Fred conveyed to you—how he intended to go about framing Michael Jackson. Is that clear enough for you?"*
>
> *Aldorf was relieved. "Oh, good, you are helping Michael . . . well that makes me feel better, but that wasn't what you were doing originally was it . . . when you first called me last summer?" Aldorf was one of the people he had called earlier in the year, hoping he could dredge up information on what Schaffel was up to.*
>
> *Barresi shook his head, "No, I saw a story somewhere."*
>
> *Barresi asked again, just to make sure. "So you are absolutely certain that Fred intended to do what to Jackson?"*
>
> *"Plant kiddy porn on him," was Aldorf's reply. Barresi had an idea where this was going.*
>
> *"And let's say for the sake of argument Jackson said, 'I'm not going to give you the twenty-five million.' Who would Fred go to, to get revenge?"*

Without hesitating, Aldorf replied, "The tabloids."

This was heavier than Barresi had first thought back in July, or even a week ago, heavier than he could have made it. Schaffel might be setting Jackson up for blackmail, and now the fixer saw a chance to be hero to both the cops and to Jackson.

"What else did he say?"

Laughing, Aldorf imitated Schaffel. "He said 'Girl, when I get that $25 million, I'm going to make Fred Schaffel disappear."

For clarification, Barresi asked, "He, meaning Fred, is going to make Fred disappear—talking about himself?"

Aldorf nodded and sat down his coffee cup. "Right."

But Fred Schaffel was about to disappear as far as Jackson was concerned. And he would be history after Barresi's meetings next week. Or would he?

Armed with the tape from Aldorf and more information on Schaffel's past dirty dealings, Barresi decided to make things more interesting and up the stakes for everyone just a little bit. So he did what any law-abiding citizen would do: on November 12, 2001, he called the FBI and the Juvenile Crimes Division of the Los Angeles Police Department.

It wasn't pure altruism or the desire to be a white knight do-gooder that made Barresi get the law involved. He was upping the stakes, insuring that even if he signed a nondisclosure agreement, Fred Schaffel would sweat a bit, and that he could potentially help crack a child pornography ring.

Along with upping the ante, getting the Feds and the LAPD involved was a calculated ploy to make sure Barresi got his measly fifteen hundred bucks. According to Barresi, Barry Siegel had canceled a meeting with Jackson attorney Zia Modabber, who was presumably drawing up the nondisclosure agreement, rescheduling for the next day. Barresi says he was miffed; so he called and let the poor secretary on the other end of the phone know that the tape he had with "Marc Schaffel" on it was going to law enforcement. Knowledge that Schaffel was under investigation for child pornography by more than one agency might cause the Jackson camp to actually keep an appointment with him.

Barresi claims that, predictably, Siegel called on the November 13, and left another apologetic message saying that the meeting had to be canceled because Jackson's lawyer Modabber was out of town and unable to draw up the papers. Barresi called Modabber direct, and an appointment was set up for the next day. He decided to play nice and give them a copy of the tape before he gave it to the LAPD and FBI— his law enforcement guys weren't too happy about being put off, but he assured them he'd see them on Thursday, November 15.

Barresi says he was ushered into Modabber's office. There were two guys there, one of whom introduced himself as Eric Mason, a private investigator who worked for Jackson. The other guy was the youth-ful, diminutive Zia Modabber. Barresi claims that he gave them everything he had on Schaffel and that Mr. Modabber was thankful, stating, "Down the road, we will be happy, in a very big way that you chose to bring me the information." And Barresi believed him.

Barresi's meeting with the cops and the Feds went well, though they were both annoyed that he had held on to the tape for an extra day. He knew that they would sort out under whose jurisdiction the case would fall. That wasn't his concern. Then things took a weird turn on November 16. Barresi claims he called Greg Shearer, a busi-ness associate and good friend of Schaffel (who is the producer of the international gay porn title *Prague Orgy*[16]), to see what he might know about Schaffel and Jackson. Barresi was trying to get even more information for Modabber and Mason, as well as for the cops. After all, the title of Jackson's song that Schaffel was producing was *What More Can I Give* and he wanted to give his all for all concerned, fig-uring that he'd get something back.

Back home, Barresi says he was treated to an extremely abrupt, threatening, racist phone call from Shearer where he was told to shut up or run the risk that Shearer would physically harm him with some nasty things. Although Barresi has the message on tape, Shearer, known as "Spanky" in the gay porn world, says, "I deny saying those things," but he does admit that he "lost [his] temper." Not only did Barresi visit the LAPD's North Hollywood Division and lodge a com-plaint, in typical fashion, he filed a complaint with the NAACP for good measure.

According to Barresi, Shearer began calling his business associates, making threats to boycott and/or stop purchasing Barresi's video product. One associate told him that Shearer had asked where he lived and what kind of car he drove, making the threats against him seem a lot more credible. Barresi believes that Shearer also phoned private investigator Anthony Pellicano, for whom Barresi had worked for over 10 years, demanding a letter in writing from him stating that Barresi had never worked for him.

Although he will not confirm or deny whether or not he called around town smearing Barresi, Shearer does admit to phoning him with a message that may have been perceived as a threat. "I did return one of his phone calls . . . feeding into Barresi's paranoia," says the cagey pornographer. Shearer also admits to phoning Pellicano, and while The Pelican admitted that he knew Barresi, Shearer says that the PI informed him, "He [Barresi] is not currently working for me." In conclusion, Shearer politics, saying, "In my opinion Mr. Barresi makes some outstanding movies. He's extremely cash register honest with the companies he works for. However, I find that if one is in a business, I find it reprehensible that any individual would dig up stories on people in that business only for personal profit. This type of subterfuge, in the end, only embarrasses the industry and us as professionals." Not to mention Peter Pan and his former personal videographer, Shearer's friend and one-time associate, Schaffel.

Apparently, Pellicano had long valued Barresi as a resource. Barresi could get the goods clients wanted. Say for example, two famous stars are preparing to divorce. Pellicano would hire Barresi to dig up the dirt on the husband, to find out what hookers and hustlers he employs and what bondage parlors and "health spas" he frequents. Maybe the dirt is for the wife, to strengthen her position in a child custody or financial settlement agreement. Or maybe Mr. Top Box Office wants to know what scandals are in the pipeline, so he—via Pellicano or Barresi—can make them go away before Starlet Wife's team finds out.

Barresi says he headed out for lunch with Jackson's private investigator Eric Mason. He was providing Mason with other sources he could contact about Schaffel and additional information on Schaffel's shady business practices, including the tape-recorded interview he conducted with David Aldorf. Barresi says that he also alerted Mason that a videotape existed of Schaffel in Budapest, shooting sex scenes with two young-looking performers.

"How much is it worth to save a pop star's ass?" Barresi says he asked Mason, half jokingly, before informing him that by all indications from both the FBI and LAPD, an investigation on Schaffel would begin once they decide on which agency will be handling the case. "Look, this hasn't been easy for me, Eric. Before I came over to meet you, I had threats on my life from one of Schaffel's pals, who also called business associates of mine and told them they should stop doing business with me . . . . These threats are a direct result of my trying to save your client considerable and irreversible damage to his career and reputation. That's deserving of some reward and if Michael Jackson knew the part I played in this, I'm certain he would feel the same way."

Barresi's thought process was simple, though full of fantasy— Michael Jackson had been spared a horrible fate, and since he was so filthy rich and allegedly such a humanitarian, he'd no doubt want to handsomely reward the guy who'd helped him out. Barresi was admittedly guilty of being seduced by the Jackson mystique, as well as his own avarice, but it didn't hurt to try. He was a hero, wasn't he? Don't heroes get a pot of gold, a castle? The moral of fairy tales is that no good deed goes unrewarded. Right?

Thanksgiving had come and gone, and still no check from Barry Siegel. Barresi's measly fifteen hundred bucks hadn't arrived, but Michael Jackson's thirtieth anniversary (in show business) special had aired. Meantime, Barresi had lost 12 pounds running around for the Jackson camp.

Barresi says that Jackson's PI Mason left him a phone message: "Paul, I've been unable to speak with Zia in regard to your request for compensation because he is in the midst of severing ties with Schaffel and negotiating the quick exit out of that relationship and he is not going to turn his attention to your needs until he is finished focusing on that, which won't be until the end of the week. And, when he is finished focusing on that, I'll then talk to him about your request for compensation."

Modabber must have made Schaffel exit very quickly, because, according to Barresi, Mason called him back within hours and left a bold message saying that it has never been their policy to pay for information, and they weren't going to start now. "So that's it. Take care."

In Barresi's mind, the Jackson camp had played him. They had held him at bay until the Jackson special had aired, thus closing the window of opportunity for him to go to the tabloids, who would have paid big for this story, as long as it was timely. Barresi says he should have known. And he should have realized as well that they were the ones taking credit with Michael Jackson for having saved him from a suspected blackmailing scam, or, at the very least, an avalanche of public embarrassment.

But Barresi did have one happy realization: He had saved millions of radio listeners and MTV and VH-1 viewers worldwide from having to suffer through the music video *What More Can I Give*. It was the least he could do for his fellow man. If only his fellow man, in the form of a Jackson representative, had done something for him.

There was only one option left—Small Claims Court. Barresi filed a claim, and the case was given a date of January 2, 2002. Siegel had the case postponed until February 4. Barresi figured he'd want to just write him a check and get it over with. But the morning of Monday, February 4, rolled around, and there he was, outside of the Small Claims Court with Zia Modabber as his witness.

Small Claims Court in West Los Angeles is held in a trailer, and instead of a judge presiding, there's a pro tem—a lawyer or retired judge who hears the case, thus freeing up real judges for more important business. Since Modabber was an attorney, even though he was appearing as a witness, Barresi asked that the case be transferred to a divisional court, which it was. Barresi recalls that, as they walked over to the courtroom, he told Modabber that out of courtesy he wasn't going to refer to their client by name. Barresi hoped that would make him look noble and upstanding, make them think he wasn't some sort of would-be extortionist.

According to Barresi, the judge in the divisional court looked like a cross between Andy Warhol and Peewee Herman—pale, weedy, with a mop of prematurely silvery gray hair and big thick glasses.

Barresi could feel trouble, but followed the bailiff's instructions and offered his file for discovery to Siegel, who handed him his defense for his discovery portion.

The only document of defense was a typewritten memo from the secretary at Modabber's firm who had taken Barresi's call on November 12 when he told her he was going to the FBI and the LAPD with a copy of the Schaffel tape. It didn't read well; it made him look like a smarmy blackmailer. Barresi wasn't betting on the impartiality of the judge, but he sure as hell knew that Modabber and Siegel would put a spin on the story to make sure he didn't get paid and worse yet, look bad.

Without saying a word, Barresi went into the clerk's office and filed a motion to dismiss his claim, meaning it was over. Case closed, never to be reopened again. "Fuck them," thought Barresi. Modabber was probably making four hundred bucks an hour, billable to Jackson, to help undo a mess the business manager had made.

All Barresi wanted was his $1,500. Even more, he wanted Michael Jackson to know his name, that he was the man who had rescued him. But Barresi was not going to hold his breath waiting for a thank you note from the King of Pop.

Pop Goes the King

On July 14, 2002, in *USA Today*, Jackson spokesman Dan Klores denied Jacko's affiliation with gay pornographer Schaffel[17]: "It's unfortunate that old stories like this are being leaked to the media in order to further hurt Michael. The perpetrators of this leak have known for months that Schaffel has had no relationship with Michael Jackson."

Earth to Dan Klores! In 2001, Jackson had already pledged his affection for the pornographer in the *Invincible* CD's liner notes. After his thank-you's to his children and Elizabeth Taylor, and right before Uri Geller, Jackson wrote: "Marc Schaffel . . . thank you for all of your help . . . I love you . . . Michael."

Thus, the story of Jackson and Schaffel hit the press. Barresi had waited for the right time, and then leaked the Jackson porn connection to the legal division at Sony and then to Sony Music head Tommy Mottola's office, and the mainstream media (including *USA*

Today) gratis. Then he slipped the suspect video of Schaffel cajoling young Hungarian dudes on tape to *Hollywood, Interrupted*. In turn, we dropped the dime on Schaffel and Jackson to NBC's "Dateline." The network rushed to extend their heavily hyped show about Jackson's facial rearrangement from one hour to two hours, thereby competing against the friendlier Jacko-Doc that the Fox network had planned as counterprogramming to the far from flattering British documentary made by Martin Bashir. You know, the documentary in which Jackson admits that he sleeps with children.

Jackson's flack, Klores, stated to *USA Today*: "The minute Michael and his advisers found out about Schaffel's background, they cut the cord immediately. This was months ago. (Schaffel) has nothing to do with Michael Jackson, doesn't represent him in any way, shape or form, and has been told this repeatedly by Michael's attorneys."

Yet the Fox program featured behind-the-scenes footage of the scandalous British program, featuring children enjoying themselves at Neverland—footage that was produced and mediated by none other than pornographer Fred Schaffel. Peter Pan had picked a porn producer to be his private videographer in Neverland. *Nice.*

"Dateline" aired the footage we delivered of Schaffel shooting porn with young guys in Hungary, but, regarding the pop star's relationship with the gay pornographer, the NBC show host shrugged, and accused Jackson of being guilty of only "bad judgment."[18] In a phone call to Fox News columnist Roger Friedman, he actually defended Jackson's right to carry on with the likes of a gay pornographer. So be it, but if exercising better judgment is the moral of this fairy tale, then the collective media responsible for letting Wacko off the hook again ought to get their heads examined. Also due for some serious therapy are the parents who would turn a blind eye to the fact that their own children were videotaped at Neverland by a gay pornographer with a Handicam.

Eddie Murphy, Good Samaritan

Almost a year to the wee hour of Eddie Murphy's world famous late night mercy date, the very pretty Samoan transsexual hooker, Atisone Seuli, died in a fall from her apartment house on Berendo Street in

Hollywood. Her body was found in a pool of blood, clad only in a black bra padded with silicon pouches and a black leather bikini thong. The young he/she struck the pavement with such force that her nasal bone was driven through her skull into her brain. Fingernail scrape marks trailed eerily down the building's facade.

Eddie Murphy picked up more than he bargained for when he gave a predawn ride to the transvestite hooker. Almost the entire sisterhood of sleaze began spinning tabloid tales of strange dalliances with the comedian. *The Globe* paid a tranny named Tempest $1,500 for her tale of Murphy's toe-licking habits, with a description of his cologne and underwear tossed in for good measure. In the *Enquirer*, another transsexual, self-described Diahann Carroll look-alike Sylvia Holland, "boasted of two sex encounters with the star—once in an alley, and the second time in his car."

About his Seuili encounter, Murphy—in the midst of making the child-friendly *Dr. Dolittle*—told *People* magazine: "This is an act of kindness that got turned into a f---king horror show." "I love my wife and I'm not gay," he declared on "Entertainment Tonight." Before pledging to "never, ever, ever play good Samaritan again," Murphy offered up this tidbit from his personal instruction manual on the art of being a john: "If I was soliciting, I would have picked this girl up and pulled over to some dark corner or dark alley and did whatever I was going to do."

Murphy did not respond to the tabloid stories. Instead, he sicked his attorney Marty Singer on them. They say Hollywood has a "built-in forgetter," but Murphy's damage-control lawyer, Marty "The Pitbull" Singer, audaciously hired the very guy who smeared his erstwhile client John Travolta in the tabs to make the Murphy tabloid problem go away. He hired Barresi as an investigator, using his underworld connections, to round up the chorus line of squawking transgendered hookers and performers to come into his law offices and retract all the Eddie Murphy–related stories of sexual indiscretion they'd been selling to the tabloids for years. Enticing these he-shes with "consulting fees", Barresi got several of them to change their Murphy stories. Upon receipt of traceable five figure sums from the corporate account of Lavely & Singer, they all declared in sworn videotaped depositions that they'd never had sex with the movie star.

Barresi succeeded in silencing the Murphy scandal. That is, until the comic's Samoan charity case was found face down in a pool of blood.

Smelling foul play, *Hollywood, Interrupted,* in the form of *New Times Los Angeles* reporter, began investigating a possible murder, and instead discovered a story about how far Hollywood will go to protect the image of a star. To the man/woman, each transgendered hooker interviewed freely admitted that, urged by Marty Singer's hired gun Barresi, they changed their tabloid tales, although Barresi says he never told Singer he was coaching the trannies to lie, nor did the attorneys ever order him to get perjured testimony. Singer says, "If I had known that Barresi wanted to suborn perjury or get false statements I never would have used him."

Nevertheless, armed with his shaky testimony from his out-to-lunch cast of hookers, Singer staged a lawsuit war on the tabloids. On behalf of Murphy, the lawyer filed multimillion-dollar complaints against the *Globe* and the *Enquirer,* and then—just as quickly—dropped them. In the *Enquirer* case, Murphy actually had to pay the tabloid's legal fees. In the case against the *Globe,* Singer dropped it so quickly that the tabloid didn't have time to answer. Singer refused to discuss his motives for withdrawing the lawsuit, saying only, "We made resolutions that were satisfactory to my client." He added, "When we interviewed these transvestites, reliability is not one of their strong suits. . . . You give them a sandwich, they'll tell you anything. You don't have to give them $5,000; you can give them lunch."

Call it Murphy's law, but continued litigation against the tabs would have brought more hurt than healing to the star's reputation. Murphy's suit against the *Globe* actually contains the damning statement that he "has not paid for sex with transsexuals for more than ten years."[19] Yikes! Who knows how many happy hookers were in line to sell their Murphy stories? Regardless, in large thanks to Barresi, Singer had effectively silenced the scandal. That is, until Barresi discovered that celebrity quickie-book author Frank Sanello, was working on a book about Murphy and his she-male troubles.

Barresi charmed the gay author Sanello into revealing the name of his publisher and the contents of the author's tome, which began with a Hollywood drag queen's tale of another "good deed" by Murphy. Barresi believed that such damning info would get him another payday from Murphy's legal team. But Barresi says that Singer & Company unceremoniously cut him loose. Had they given him more work, or "thrown him a bone," Barresi says, "They certainly would have had my allegiance forever. But in the same way that they demonstrated that they had no respect for me, that's how I felt about them." In turn, Barresi, receiving no compensation whatsoever apart from having his story told, turned his entire file (interview transcripts, memos, and paychecks) on Murphy over to us.

A memorial service for Seuili was held at a Hollywood mortuary. "Two grieving transsexuals who called themselves Chocolate and Visa filed past Atisone's open casket as soft church hymns filled the air," reported the *Globe*. "Visa softly touched Atisone's hand and commented how pretty she looked in a simple white gown."

Eddie Murphy, ex-good Samaritan, did not attend.[20]

INTERMISSION

LOVE MEANS NEVER HAVING TO SAY YOU'RE COURTNEY

My mother is a good mom. I'm not scared of her, and she takes
really good care of me. She's always been a good mom."
— Frances Bean Cobain, 2003

The seamless transition of Courtney Love from juvenile delinquent
to stripper and junkie, to rock star wife, to merry widow, to rock
star, to award-winning actress, to acclaimed fashion icon and erratic
bon vivant illustrates the ease with which people with issues *and* arrest
records can *now* achieve success in the entertainment industry—just
as long as they're willing to hire a cadre of craven lawyers and spin-
meisters to skew it.

Love, a trust-fund brat with a penchant for self-aggrandizement
coupled with what seems to be a healthy dose of narcissistic personality disorder, claimed in a *Vanity Fair* interview to have shot up
heroin while pregnant, and she scored tabloid points by romancing

music executive Jim Barber away from his pregnant wife and child,[1] followed by a night of hard drinking and poetry writing with rage-aholic Russell Crowe that culminated in a post-Oscar screaming match.[2]

In an industry that condones—if not outright rewards—pathological behavior, the former Mrs. Cobain ranks with among the most troubled and twisted alumni of the entertainment industry annals of fame and its many discontents, encompassing so many versions of insanity chic that she simply deserves special examination.

Road Rage

The blond, fortyish woman flying high in Virgin Airline's first class cabin was a mess—her make-up smeared, speech slurred. She loudly, obnoxiously demanded that a "friend" who was in economy class be moved up to sit with her. The flight crew, by policy, denied her request. So, the grotesque celebrity—who has disgraced the cover of dozens of magazines, all the while bragging that she is "grossly over-famous"—called the flight attendant a "bitch"; she refused to put on her seatbelt, attempted to peel off her underwear, and caused such a ruckus that the pilot radioed ahead and alerted ground police, who boarded the plane on arrival and escorted the trashed, Golden Globe–winning singer/actress off to jail on February 4, 2003.

In a statement to the press a Virgin spokesperson stated, "The safety of all our passengers and crew is of paramount importance. We will not tolerate disruptive behavior by passengers on board any of our aircraft, always report it to the authorities and always push for prosecution." But since the person involved was a rock star, prosecution was never truly an option.

Nine hours after landing at Heathrow Airport, Courtney Love was released from law enforcement custody and given a warning for "causing harassment, alarm and distress" on a transatlantic flight. She gaily arrived at a benefit hosted by Kevin Spacey at the Old Vic Theatre the day after her release, performed a song with Elton John, and was bussed by Virgin Airlines' flamboyant president Richard Branson.[3]

Branson suavely spun: "Virgin Atlantic was built thanks to the rock industry, so I like to think we are a bit more understanding than most airlines. . . . Courtney was a little out of order on the flight over and apologized to me. We are looking forward to flying her back to LA." He joked, in conclusion, "Perhaps Virgin's new slogan should be that 'Rock stars swear by us.'" To Branson's credit, his soft spot for Courtney stiffened when the singer/actress demanded that the flight attendant she battled with be fired. In an act of bravery seldom seen by corporate celebrity wranglers, Branson drew the line and banned Love from Virgin. He went on to describe the air-raging, aging rocker as "disturbed" and said he never should have let her fly on his airline.[4]

Oh, that the rest of us would be so well treated for in-flight terrorism, especially in a post-9/11 world. This wasn't Courtney Love's first act of insane behavior in the skies. In 1995 she was arrested for disrupting a Qantas Airlines flight to Australia.[5] In April 2002 she was escorted off a plane at Los Angeles International Airport in a wheelchair after passing out from "food poisoning."[6]

Love's trail of abuse is legendary—in 1998 she punched Los Angeles entertainment journalist Belissa Cohen, who covered the local Los Angeles underground and glitterati for years, as a columnist for the *Los Angeles Weekly*, when the writer tried to snap a photo of her at a party, then gloated, "I just hit Belissa Cohen and it felt *sooo* good." At a news conference, Cohen's attorney, Gloria Allred, reminded the assembled press that Love pleaded guilty in 1995 to attacking fellow singer Kathleen Hanna and was ordered to seek anger-management counseling. Part of Love's comically miscalculated sentence in that case was that she refrain from threats or violence for two years.[7] Unfortunately for Cohen—who claimed to have had her hair pulled, her face slapped, and her groin kneed by the unlovable Love—Love's play-nice probation period had ended six months earlier.[8]

> *...I will haunt you two fucking cunts for the rest of your goddamn life ...you're gonna pay and pay and pay and pay out your ass, and that's a fact. Your fucking list of enemies is gonna be longer than you can wrap your fucking finger around, and you're gonna be so fucking humiliated this time next week, you're gonna wish you'd never been born....*
> —Message allegedly left by Courtney Love
> on journalist Victoria Clarke's phone machine, 1992.[9]

Belissa Cohen got off easy; actually, she was paid off, her suit settled out of court for an undisclosed sum. Love ran into journalist and unauthorized Nirvana biographer Victoria Clarke in a bar and, according to her, Courtney "sort of grabbed me and attacked me with something. I think it was a glass. And I ended up covered in beer and on the ground. And she pulled me along the floor by my hair and tried to get me outside. It was quite a scary thing."[10] Clarke and her writing partner Britt Collins' home was also burglarized, and many music biz insiders gossiped[11] that Love and her hostaged husband Cobain were somehow involved with the break-in. *Entertainment Weekly* covered the burglary and the writers' claims that Kurt and Courtney were behind the break-in, something their management obviously and strenuously denied.[12] Clarke and Collins had written the banned-in-the United States *Flower Sniffin', Kitty Pettin', Baby Kissin' Corporate Rock Whores,* which painted Nirvana in a less than favorable light.[13]

In 1992 *Vanity Fair* magazine author Lynn Hirschberg wrote a 7,000-word, unflattering article on Love and Cobain, published in the magazine's September issue. Then pregnant with their child, and the subject of a bidding war between several record labels, Love splayed her fat lips and bared her soul to Hirschberg. She wallowed in the potential publicity, treating the reporter like a new best friend. She showed off the couple's filthy apartment, complete with nodding husband. She declared for the record that she had done heroin in her first trimester of pregnancy—though later back-flipped saying she didn't know at the time that she pregnant. Love went shopping with Hirshberg during an earthquake and spewed stream-of-conscious character assassinations freely. Prepublication, Love was happier than a truffle hog after the rain. Then, the *Vanity Fair* article dropped.

Blabbermouth Courtney and her placid, narcotized husband weren't the only people interviewed by Hirschberg; few of the journalist's plentiful sources had anything loving to say about Love. Many chose to speak anonymously, partially because Love's rage was legendary and partially because they had a heavy investment in Love, or more likely, her husband. Someone "close to Nirvana" said that "Courtney always has a hidden agenda, and Kurt doesn't. He's definitely being led." Hirschberg should have realized the reason why so many people spoke "unattributed."[14]

Advance copies of the article were faxed out, and Love went ballistic. The published "rape," as Courtney described it,[15] was indeed lurid, and painted her as a gold-digging opportunist junkie/stripper who had latched onto a star and was doing her best to pull a Yoko Ono, using heroin, rather than art as bait. In other words, it was a portrait free of much of *VF*'s usual celeb fluff and sugar-coated hype. And worse yet, there was the ghastly photo of Love, very pregnant, grisly, and washed out, clutching what would have been a cigarette if editor Tina Brown hadn't ordered the offending coffin nail airbrushed out. Oh, it was fine, telegraphed Brown, for Love to admit to heroin use while pregnant, but to smoke—never! The Cobains paid the photographer a reported $25,000 (or possibly $50,000) for an exclusive on the negatives.[16] Love's misguided mea culpa had her admitting that if she hadn't "taken drugs in the first place," she would have been "lucid enough to see what [Hirschberg] was about." But now that the damning article was making the rounds and Love was severely prenatal, she staged an unparalleled hormone-fueled attack on Hirschberg. According to Hirschberg, Love phoned her at all hours, threatening her and threatened to have her dog killed. She fax-bombed *Vanity Fair* and other media sources, and she did not let up.[17]

In 1995 at Miramax's Academy Awards party, a spaced-out, tiara-wearing Love sat next to Hirschberg for a full 15 minutes blathering obliviously to the rest of her dinner party, which included filmmaker/bad actor Quentin Tarantino. Finally, she turned her gauzy gaze on the woman and asked for a cigarette. Hirschberg said she didn't smoke and Love focused her bleary eyes for a moment. "Do I know you?" asked Love. "Yes, you do", replied Hirschberg. "Do I like you?" Love queried. "No," was Hirschberg's reply. "There's only one person I hate, and that's Lynn Hirschberg. If she were here, I'd kill her with this Oscar," threatened Love as she fondled Tarantino's statuette. The director diplomatically distracted Love, and Hirschberg hastily fled the table.

Once an embarrassed Love realized she'd failed to identify her foe tête-à-tête, she took to the media grapevine with relish. According to Love's mired memory, Hirschberg ran away from Courtney and hid under a table, where Jodi Foster burned her backside with a cigar she was smoking. Luckily, Love and Foster had the same publicist, so the story went unchallenged. Two years later, Hirschberg was still so disturbed by Love's vendetta that she refused to be interviewed for Nick Broomfield's provocative 1997 documentary, *Kurt & Courtney*.[18]

Love's publicist was (and as of 2003, still is) super celebrity flak Pat "The Pit Bull" Kingsley of the powerhouse spin control center PMK/ HBH, whose other clients include the heterosexual Tom Cruise. "I'm her charity case," contended Love at one point;[19] however, the general consensus is that Love was paying PMK close to $10,000 a month to both secure positive and squelch negative stories about her. Few in Hollywood were surprised when in June 1995, Love scored the cover of her former nemesis *Vanity Fair*, lovingly photographed wearing angel wings, stepping out of a frame. The occasion was her role as stripper/junkie Althea Flynt in the Larry Flynt bioflick *The People vs. Larry Flynt*, for which she would be nominiated for a Golden Globe award. It wasn't much of a stretch for Courtney to play a junkie stripper who married well; she'd been Method-acting that part for over a decade.

Director Milos Forman would cast her again as Andy Kaufman's wife in *Man in the Moon*, and she would appear as junkie philosopher William Burrough's wife in *Beat*. Love has made her mainstream acting career, in fact, her entire publicity-grubbing life, playing wives of doomed men, so it's a no-brainer that she's been cast as Lady MacBeth in the Luc Besson–produced *Miss June*, which began filming in late 2003.[20]

Who was the "friend" who was so important to Love that she threw the airborne tantrum, yet not so important for her to purchase a companion upgrade? He was a celebrity babysitter, who, according to the self-proclaimed "potty mouth" Love, "travels with fucked-up rock stars to make sure they don't take drugs." Love continued, "He's like a policeman who sees to it that certain people can't get to me." She declined to name him or give other details. "Every woman in America is on [the prescription anxiety-reliever] Xanax," exaggerated Love. "You can go to a taco stand in LA and get it. It's the No. 2 drug in America, and it's completely addictive." At the time she was arrested at Heathrow, Love claimed to be halfway through a 60-day program for her Xanax addiction. She had, she boasted, also been off the fashionable painkiller Vicodin for 50 days. Love rationalized her need for a "therapist guy" by saying, "since I'm traveling all the time, I can't always make rehab meetings."[21]

Courtney Love had spent the Friday before her Virgin dust-up in Hawaii, where she reportedly rang up designers including Dolce & Gabbana, Alexander McQueen, Givenchy/Christian Dior's John Galliano in Europe, and New York and "even Lebanon and Israel." Wanting to look good, she claimed, because the "fucking Queen of

England" was going to be in the audience at the Old Vic, Love is said to have babbled on and on, keeping the frenzied hotel operator busy as she lit up the switchboard of Maui's Four Seasons. One person Love spoke with that day said, "I can only say, I hope she wasn't sober. If she was sober, she is most certainly crazy."[22] Crazy Courtney had made a spectacle of herself in London late 2002 at a photo shoot for inclusion in *Q* magazine's 200th issue. The singer/actress/human toxic waste dump, spent hours amusing her entourage with her antics which included pouring champagne on herself. She set things on fire, trotted about nude in the street, and lounged naked in a taxicab. As a precursor to her near somnambulant streaking, the woman who claims to be "pretty on the inside" reportedly got a bikini wax in a room full of people.[23] Not that getting naked in public is anything new to Love.

For a number of years Love supplemented her small trust-fund income by stripping (her maternal grandparents were partial heirs to the Bausch & Lomb fortune), but the money Love received was apparently never enough to fill her soul holes. Her tour of duty included a stint in Japan to which she's added fascinating tales of the Yakuza and her escape from "white slavery" by making a dash for the American embassy. She also ran out on a three-month contract to strip at Brandy How's marine airbase–adjacent flesh parlor in Guam. Love alleges that she was chased through the airport by enforcers from the topless club, attempting to prevent her departure from the island territory.[24]

Love Child

Courtney Love Michelle Harrison Rodriguez Menely Moreland Cobain, AKA Courtney Love, is the most stunning indictment of 1960s hippie liberal parenting ever launched on Hollywood and the music world. Courtney Love was born in 1964 after her parents—rock band hanger-on Hank Harrison and square trust-fund debutante Linda Risi—met at a pot party for Dizzy Gillespie. The groovy couple married when they discovered Linda was pregnant, and Courtney Love spent her formative years surrounded by drug-frazzled members of the Haight-Ashbury elite, including musicians who would become the drug-enthusiast band The Grateful Dead, growing up in a house her wealthy maternal grandparents gave the young couple. Her parents split up, her mom remarried, Courtney got a new last name, and the family moved to another commune.

Courtney, who had begun therapy at age two, became an angry, aggressive, hostile child, despite, or because of, tasting every trend from transcendental meditation to transactional analysis. She has repeated allegations that her father gave her acid at age three or four. When the family relocated to Eugene, Oregon, Linda decided that studying psychology and becoming a therapist herself could help her deal with her increasingly difficult child. The whole family went through an obviously flawed therapeutic regimen. Love became aggressive towards her younger half-siblings, and both Linda and her husband began affairs. They divorced, and Linda latched onto river rafting guide David Menely. In an interesting show of family values, she insisted that he adopt all of her children, awarding Courtney yet another identity quick-change.

The cobbled-together family unit moved to Marcola, Oregon, into a large timber house with packed wood floors. In interviews Love has characterized that home as full of "wrangly-assed hippies" indulging in "group encounters." And while the commune members seemed concerned with purity of thought and mind, they neglected to bathe or launder, and Courtney was mocked in school, nicknamed "Pee Girl."[25]

Sick of America and weary of her oldest child, Linda packed up her husband and her four other children and moved to New Zealand, abandoning eight-year-old Courtney to a therapist friend in Oregon. The problem child quickly alienated her guardian, who shipped her overseas to her parents. She was sent back to the States again, and eventually her mother, now divorced again, returned to Oregon. Courtney, however, lived apart from mom, and it was during this time, at age 13, she was caught shoplifting and put on probation. She violated her probation and was sent to Hillcrest, a state institution for the criminally inclined, where she wallowed until she was 15. During her incarceration, her biological father Hank Harrison took her out on a day pass and gave her pot, which she smoked with her fellow inmates. She would not see him again for several years.

When father and daughter reunited in Dublin, Ireland, the juvenile delinquent Love child had already done a tour of self-demeaning duty, stripping in Portland's sleazier strip clubs, the ones that didn't bother to check the age of the performers. She also worked as a stripper in Japan, and when she returned stateside, she glommed onto local and touring musicians, using her Bausch & Lomb trust fund money, sex, and drugs in an effort to impress them.[26]

Fascinated by the emerging punk scene, Love split to England for a spin at groupie-dom. Described by singer Julian Cope and his brother Dorian as "so ugly" that not even the sluttiest band member would shag her,[27] Love began to hang around him and his New Wave band Teardrop Explodes, moving into his house and doing acid with him, or so claims Love.[28] Julian Cope later took out a full-page ad in the British music press that read "Free Us (The Rock'n'Roll Fans) From . . . Heroin A-Holes Who Cling To Our Greatest Rock Band And Suck Out Their Brains."[29]

In April of 1994, Kurt Cobain, lead singer for the platinum-selling grunge band Nirvana, injected himself with a hot shot of heroin, put a shotgun in his mouth, pulled the trigger, and blew out his brains, leaving behind a two-year-old child and his wife, Courtney Love. The interim decade had seen Courtney act in two movies, work as a stripper, develop a heroin habit, marry twice, and divorce once; she would later ask that her first marriage, to singer song-writer James Moreland, be annulled, after they had divorced. Moreland, now a transvestite who works as a copy editor for the left-wing *Los Angeles Weekly*, allegedly burned out the engine of his Volkswagen driving his then-wife to and from substance abuse programs, and produced her first single. It's said that she dropped him when she discovered the he-she wasn't as rich or as successful as she had originally thought.[30]

With her force of multiple personality, Love put together the band Hole, and released a record. *Pretty on the Inside* garnered a bit of attention from the record industry, due in part to her association with high-powered attorney Rosemary Carroll, hence affiliation with Carroll's husband Danny Goldberg. Goldberg was the head of Gold Mountain Management and chair of the Southern California chapter of the American Civil Liberties Union. Gold Mountain managed Nirvana, and then Hole, and Goldberg would transition to become the head of Warner Music Group, and later Mercury Records and Artemis Records.[31]

Kurt and Courtney's relationship was stormy from the start, built on violence and drugs; when they first met, they slugged each other and fell wrestling to the floor of a nightclub. They got high on opiates at their next meeting. Love got pregnant, the couple got married, and then *Vanity Fair* came calling.[32]

After the birth of their child, the Love-Cobain relationship quickly devolved into deeper drug use and disillusionment. Kurt, in rehab for his heroin habit, left the facility one day and dropped by Geffen Records with a handwritten note saying he wanted to quit the business. He was dissuaded from following through.[33] Child Protective Services hovered about, and the couple's child, Frances Bean Cobain, was placed with Courtney's half-sister, who moved next door to the inebriated couple.[34] Robert Hilburn of the *Los Angeles Times*— ridiculed by brethren journalists and rock fans alike for his inability to avoid mentioning Bruce Springsteen at the drop of a power chord—was enlisted to write a flattering profile of Kurt and Courtney for the paper's Calendar section[35] while Love performed solo at Largo, a small club in Hollywood. The gig was ostensibly a fundraiser and voter registration drive, but Love wasn't being purely altruistic by donating her services; she realized that the press would be on hand to study her every move. She, in fact, became the centerpiece of the evening, drawing attention to her singing and songwriting; one of the songs she played, *Pennyroyal Tea,* would end up on Nirvana's *In Utero* album, furthering the allegations that Kurt had written much of his wife's hit album *Live Through This*, unfortunately released just days after his suicide.[36]

Returning to Seattle, the love-poisoned couple began to battle even more. Courtney yearned for the designer clothes, fancy cars, and the arriviste trappings of celebrity, while Cobain wanted to hide out from the world and abandon his rock 'n roll life style. At one point during a domestic disturbance the police arrived, and guns were confiscated. Cobain then refused to do Lolapalooza, a major festival; Nirvana's appearance was worth over $9 million dollars. There were rumors of an impending divorce, Cobain was sent to rehab in Los Angeles, escaped, and killed himself. Love wore black for months after his death, carrying his ashes around in a teddy bear backpack.[37]

In Hirschberg's *Vanity Fair* article, an unnamed music executive sighed and predicted, "She's going to be famous and he already is, but unless something happens, they're going to self-destruct." The industry giant was almost right. Something did happen in less than two years after his quote was published—Kurt Cobain was dead and Courtney Love was a star, playing the part of the merry widow while beginning to self-destruct on a very public forum, the Internet.

Love's album was a hit, and she suddenly appeared on the cover of music magazines around the world. Many felt that Love's success was because she had married a rock star, but they also contended that she acted as though she felt as if Cobain's death had interfered with her plans, had overshadowed the release of her album, and made it impossible for her to achieve success on her own terms. Many people, including Tom Grant, a private eye she had hired, in a fit of morbid spin control, to locate Cobain during his deathscapade, felt she was responsible for his suicide.[38] El Duce, of the "rape-rock" band the Mentors boozily claimed in print and on camera that Love had tried to hire him to off her husband for $50,000,[39] a story disputed by a close friend of El Duce's who said the singer made up the story for cash.[40] Duce did, however, pass a polygraph test.[41] El Duce is no longer available to clarify matters; he was killed shortly after his interview with *Kurt & Courtney* filmmaker Nick Broomfield—passed out drunk on the tracks, he was run over by a freight train.[42]

Throughout Nick Broomfield's Courtney-boycotted documentary *Kurt & Courtney*, the widow of Kurt Cobain is described in such terms as "harpy" and "vampire." Her biological father has nothing nice to say about her; an ex-musician boyfriend stated, "She thought the only way she could achieve stardom was through a man... I would have ended up like Kurt.... Shoving a gun down my throat...." All of this could have been dismissed as sour grapes from past hangers-on, except for one revelatory segment.

Broomfield approached Love at the Southern California ACLU's Torch of Liberty dinner, honoring filmmaker Milos Foreman. Love, who starred in two Forman films, was to present him with the award. Love's lawyer, Rosemary Carroll, is married to the Southern California ACLU's now-president and former chair Danny Goldberg, and at the time they were both godparents to Frances Bean Cobain (Carroll has since ceased representing Love, and Drew Barrymore is now godmother)—all a very cozy liberal Love-in.[43] Then Broomfield cornered a very high glam Love as she wandered the hall outside the event.

> *Nick Broomfield: "Courtney—what does ACLU mean to you?"*
> *Love: "Well, it's a lot like my parents, very liberal. And it's about everything from the anti-death penalty—I mean, it favors stuff sometimes we all don't like."*
> *Nick: "But Courtney, why do you constantly threaten journalists in the past?"*
> *Love: "Have I threatened them?"*

At this point Love seemed to realize that the ACLU supports the Constitution, which grants certain rights, so she misguidedly invokes her civil liberties, saying, "Well, because it's my right to do it. It's not against the law."

The woman that once claimed to be Jesus and that her lawyers were the 12 Apostles[44] then shifts gears. "But it doesn't mean I'm gonna take them to court. Unless they lie." She smirks. "Don't lie," she intoned menacingly.

At this point the inarticulate Love pulls the sympathy card, hoping the filmmaker will relate to her muddled thinking: "And when I was really young, you know, I didn't know that like—was weird. I grew up with hippies, so I never knew that like, you know, I was bugging anybody. So, when I kinda got crap for it, it freaked me out. But I don't wanna talk about it, because I am so happy. . . . "

Broomfield presses on, "But what about death threats. . . ?"

The ACLU's star attraction storms off.

The British auteur Broomfield pressed on, jumping on stage after Love fumbled through her prepared speech. Hijacking the live microphone, he boomed out across the crowd of lawyers, lefties, actors, managers, and industry titans, "I don't want to appear to be a party-poop, but in the interest of free speech, I wanted to ask a couple of questions. I think Hollywood always has a problem distinguishing reality from myth or image, and unless it is considered appropriate behavior to threaten, or cajole or manipulate journalists—esteemed journalists who have written unflattering reviews—I find it a strange decision on the part of the ACLU to choose Courtney Love as a special guest here tonight. And to Courtney Love, I would like to ask Courtney Love...," ...at which point his stage microphone is cut but not before civil libertarian Danny Goldberg exercises his freedom of speech and paucity of vocabulary, telling Broomfield to "get the fuck off the stage."[45]

Though legally blameless for her husband's death, Love has not been opposed to capitalizing on the tragedy, and has been picking clean the bones of his corpse for nearly 10 years. In 2002 she sold his journals for a sweet seven-figure sum. Interestingly, the diary was shy of unflattering references to the widow.[46] Cobain's suicide was the main focus of her "Now you're a star" Barbara Walters interview. Her notoriety gave her entrée to fame—she went from being a sloppy-dressing millionaire's "kinderwhore" who proved that it cost a lot of money to look so cheap, to a VH1 fashion plate and Versace clotheshorse in the span of a year.

While making her second record for Geffen Records, according to several new sources, Love began an affair with her A&R man, the guy assigned by the label to make sure she got the project finished and that it didn't suck. It seems Love decided that WASPy Jim Barber was the man for her. The conservative sweater-wearing, respectable, and upright Barber was a distinct change from Courtney's former sweetie, Lemonhead's lead singer, dopey Evan Dando (who was handled by Barber for Geffen), and edgy, leather-clad Trent Reznor, the front man for Nine Inch Nails (in whose arms Courtney had briefly consoled herself after her husband's death). Her efforts to land ex-boyfriend (pre-Kurt) Smashing Pumpkin's Billy Corgan as a mate had fallen flat, though the married Corgan did produce several songs on Celebrity Skin. Presumably, the tiny fact that Barber was married, and that his wife was pregnant with their second child, played no part in Courtney's love decision.

Barber quit his job at Geffen and became her manager and her live-in boyfriend. Barber was on hand tending to Love's wounds in late 2000 when his wife Lesley allegedly ran over Love's foot with a Volvo. Love sued Mrs. Barber for over $1.5 million, claiming that her injury made it impossible for her to act in John Carpenter's movie *Ghosts of Mars*. The lawsuit stated that Love had been the "victim of a 20-month campaign of stalking" and harassment waged by Lesley Barber that included private eyes, spying on Love, prank phone calls, and threats. Love also accused Lesley Barber of assault, battery, trespassing, infliction of emotional distress, and invasion of privacy—stunts reflecting the rock star's modus operandi in her own rise to fame.[47] Within weeks of this lawsuit's filing, Barber, in court papers filed in the custody battle with his ex-wife, stated that his "social life" with Love had ended.[48]

When Love decided that she didn't want to record for Barber's former employers (Geffen/Universal Vivendi), she took a stance. She claimed that the California labor laws were being violated by record companies who could keep artists under contract for longer than the seven years allowed by California law, and filed a lawsuit to be released form her contract. She spoke before California lawmakers; she rallied other artists.[49] But all of this was simply for Love.

Her label, Universal Vivendi, to whom she owed several records, was also her late husband's label, and they wanted to release a Nirvana compilation. Love, against the wishes of her husband's bandmates, blocked the release until Universal capitulated and released her from her contract and gave her master recordings of songs they had paid her to record.[50] Despite Love's vitriolic attacks on the corporate system, in July 2003 the former stripper-singer-songwriter signed a deal with Virgin Records, a division of the EMI music conglomerate. During the acrimonious Nirvana lawsuit, lawyers for her husband's bandmates, Dave Grohl and Kris Novoselic, filed a motion that Love be examined by a psychiatrist to see if she was "incapacitated."[51]

"UMG, they are following me around using some guy in a black SUV, and it's terrifying, and I feel like Jeffrey f---ing Wigand. Listen to me being paranoid, dude. I've been taking pictures of the car for court. I think they're trying to bug me."[52]

On a popular music industry Internet forum, the Velvet Rope, Love, or someone claiming to be her, posted:

"I employ a gentleman.. the gentleman is a computer specialist- an older guy, not a young hacker type, but a real mensch whose been in the computer business since punch cards. He is a Private Detective, very well respected who works in tandem with...an old and dear friend of mine.

What my gentleman does is this; He comes here to this site- and on occasion that a Universal Employee writes something defamatory about a Universal artist he achieves the distinction of getting that persons URL and ID, by legal means. at any point in my tenure and the tenure of any artist of "geffen, a and m, and Interscope" my gentleman friend prints out said defamatory posts and puts them in a little file. well- its actaully a large file in your employment contracts you will find a clause preventing you from making defamatory and slanderous statements about any artist on your "label" Look closely—its in there."[53]

Love beat the "incapacitated" rap. Despite her distaste for "defamatory" rants, she took pleasure in unleashing some barbs of her own on her web site, www.hole.com, now known as http://kittyradio.com/soapbox/. When her comments were reposted at www.velvetrope.com and on www.rocknerd.com, letters from Love's attorneys were sent out, and the sites had to content themselves with summaries of her less-than-lucid ramblings.[54]

Courtney here acknowledges that she has an authority problem in a very misspelled and rambling kind of way. She characterizes a manager as a shill who does deals for you while you supervise them. She calls [former record exec and manager Gary] Gersh and [former Hole and Nirvana manager John] Silva some unpleasant names. She lets us know that she has an excellent memory and is capable of reciting the contents of a 70's Billboard Magazine backwards. She reminisces briefly about her time at a school for troubled girls. She says that Gary Gersh landed his job at Capitol based on the premise that he found and brought in Nirvana, but that in fact, Sonic Youth were responsible for bringing Nirvana to Geffen. She says that in eight years at Geffen Gary Gersh did not have one platinum artist. She bad-mouths Gary Gersh's wife. She adds that she does not hate Gary Gersh. She calls Silva a clown, & says he spoke unkindly of Kurt behind his back and liked Courtney better than Kurt. . . . She calls [uber-manager to The Eagles and Don Henley, and Giant Records head Irving] Azoff her patron . . . She says he is helping her to terrify GAS, Gersh and Silva's management company. She says she is proud that she would not be manageable by a low-end outfit like GAS. She calls the person who started the thread to which she is now responding a drooling spastic. She says that everyone at the RIAA and John and Gary will go down.[55]

In 2002, Love was sued for failing to pay rent on her Beverly Hills mansion. And though she invoked the California labor code to protect artists form the evil Goliath of the record industry, Love's employment record shows she cares not a hoot for the "little people." According to reports filed with the California Labor Commissioner's Division of Labor Standards Enforcement, her butler, her nanny, and her estate manager each claimed that Love had not paid them their salary, overtime, and/or severance. All disputed salary cases were decided against Love.[56]

Love appeared in the press during the Winona Ryder shoplifting trial as "a fairly well known musician," referred to as C.L. and Mrs. C-L-C in the report made by the California Medical Board with regard to Dr. Jules Lusman, who was relieved of his license December 6, 2002, for gross incompetence and repeated negligent acts, including improperly providing drugs to Courtney Love and Winona Ryder.

When the report was made public at www.thesmokinggun.com, Love threatened to sue to have it removed, not realizing that this was public information, and that by raising such a stink, she was in fact admitting that she was the doctor-shopping, pill-head junkie described in the report. The courageous Smoking Gunners refused to comply with Love's demands. "My client, who is not shy about asserting her legal rights, has authorized the commencement of all necessary litigation if the Story is not immediately removed from your website," wrote attorney Paul Karl Lukacs.[57]

Love also cropped up as a "famous female rock star" in Winona Ryder's probation report. Allegedly the two, who had become as thick as thieves—they were photographed smooching at a gallery opening in New York and Courtney, who had allegedly referred Winona to pill-pusher Lusman, tried on some clothes at a fashion show, and when the duo left, the clothes could not be found.[58]

Throughout her life Courtney Love strove to become famous, beautiful, and fabulous. (She succeeded on the fame level.) She remolded and remodeled her body and her history to suit her goals, but the center doesn't hold. She has declared herself a feminist, but has come to fame through men, and committed the ultimate antiwoman sin of stealing another woman's husband. Although propped up as symbol of free speech, she has threatened and assaulted journalists. She spoke out for an antidrug campaign, but is a notorious drug abuser who uses her addictions as an excuse for her insane behavior.[59] And though claiming to champion the worker, as demonstrated by her lawsuit against Universal Vivendi, she abuses flight attendants and her own employees. And now her career is stalling again. She has gone, as one industry wag commented, "From being Sally Kirkland to being Sylvia Miles." Despite the Versace dresses, the hobnobbing with Chelsea Clinton at fashion shows, her Golden Globe, and her high-priced publicists' best efforts, Courtney Love is living proof that, with apologies to the late Dorothy Parker, you can lead a whore to culture, but she's still going to stink.

As if to prove *Hollywood, Interrupted*'s point, in the fall of 2003 Courtney was arrested outside her ex-boyfriend's (Jim Barber) home after breaking windows, and charged with being under the influence of the controlled substance, oxycontin. The Department of Child and Family Services awarded custody of her daughter to Frances' grandmother, dead Kurt's mom, Wendy.[60]

THE LEFT WING

PART V

Jennifer Aniston calls Bush names and taunts daughter Jenna.
Hollywood embraces Castro. The culture wars.
South Park hates Rob Reiner.

11

"I am not disturbed by Ronald Reagan's Alzheimer's. You know, there's not a lot of cleaner pictures of karma in the world. I mean, it's not a very Christian way of thinking. I do stray sometimes. But I go right from him mocking the farm worker and eating grapes on television during the boycott to him dribbling today. And I feel a sense of justice."[1]

—Sean Penn

No, it's not just you. A large swath of the celebrity class has begun morphing into obnoxious vessels of unequaled political vitriol espousing a religious zeal for extremist politics and exposing a Taliban-like hatred for anyone who might disagree. In the process these entertainment commodities risk alienating large chunks of their audience—and the insulated stars living in elitist enclaves like LA, Manhattan, the Hamptons, and in Penn's case, Marin County, don't seem to know, mind, or care. That is until they are faced with oncoming free speech traffic.

Dare we call it "hate speech?" We do.

During the 2000 presidential campaign "America's Sweetheart" and high school dropout Julia Roberts weighed in with her political veiwpoint: "Republican comes in the dictionary just after 'reptile' and just above 'repugnant.'"[2] At a 1996 Hollywood fund-raiser for Bill Clinton (were there any other kind?) "Queen of Nice" Rosie O'Donnell coined the winning slogan "Dole sucks!"

Already heard the *Vagina Monologues*? How about something a Dick (Dreyfuss) would say: "Bush is for welfare mothers getting their welfare taken away if they have a drug arrest. If he were elected president, he'd be on the federal dole. The only difference is: He wasn't caught."[3]

Something to dance to? On his website Moby composed this little ditty: "Oh please remember, everybody, these Republicans are horrible people with a horrible agenda. Republicans (henceforth known as 'the devils party') are going to do bad things. I don't mean this as random hyperbole, but the next four years could be really bad."[4]

You won't *believe* what Cher had to say before the elections: "Has everyone lost their fucking minds? Doesn't anybody remember the illustrious Reagan-Bush years when people had no money and no jobs? What has happened to people's memories? It's like they have Alzheimer's or something."[5] (Memo to the famous: That's two Alzheimer's cracks now. The political correctness manual that many of us lesser souls are reminded to live by states explicitly on page 48 "to not mock people with diseases or handicaps.")

HBO darling Sarah Jessica Parker is beside herself with worry: "I'm very, very concerned about the Bush presidency. I'm worried about the kind of cuts he might make in domestic programs that mean something to a lot of people, including people in my family who depend on certain things from the government."[6] (Note to Ms. Parker: Perhaps you could float some "Sex" money to tide them over until Hillary Rodham Clinton comes to their rescue in 2008.)

Need a "Friend"? "Bush is a fucking idiot," exclaimed Jennifer Aniston in a *Rolling Stone* cover job that proved timing is everything as it hit news racks the week of September 11, 2001. In a totem to celebrity goodwill, rumored potheads Aniston and husband Brad Pitt[7] at talent management company Brillstein-Grey taunt 2001 summer intern Jenna Bush: "We'd pass her in the hall and Brad would say, 'Heyyyy, Jenna, wanna beer? I got one in the truck!'"[8]

Speaking of a "president" with a problem child—Martin Sheen: "George W. Bush is like a bad comic working the crowd, a moron, if you'll pardon the expression."[9]

Did someone say, "bad comic"? Try Janeane Garofalo on for size: "Our country is founded on a sham: our forefathers were slave-owning rich white guys who wanted it their way. So when I see the American flag, I go, 'Oh my God, you're insulting me.' That you can have a gay parade on Christopher Street in New York, with naked men and women on a float cheering, 'We're here, we're queer!'—that's what makes my heart swell. Not the flag, but a gay naked man or woman burning the flag. I get choked up with pride."[10]

"When I see an American flag flying, it's a joke," declared director Robert Altman while in England filming *Gosford Park*. "This present government in America I just find disgusting, the idea that George Bush could run a baseball team successfully—he can't even speak! I just find him a embarrassment... I'd be very happy to stay in London. There's nothing in America that I would miss at all."[11]

The trend even became a phat literary seller thanks to Michael Moore's *Stupid White Men... And Other Sorry Excuses for the State of the Nation*! "[Bush's] been a drunk, a thief, a possible felon, an un-convicted deserter and a cry baby... for the sake of all that is decent and sacred take leave immediately and bring some honor to your all-important family name."[12]

Jessica Lange gave an Oscar-worthy performance at the San Sebastian Film Festival in Spain. The actress, who won an Academy Award for her antinuke love letter *Blue Sky*, sank in a sea of vitriol, vehemently stating, "I hate Bush. I despise him and his entire administration—not only because of its international policy, but also the national. Today it makes me feel ashamed to come from the United States—it is humiliating."[13]

Apparently, Bush bashing helps pass *The Hours*. "Being a man," a juiced Ed Harris philosophized, "I have got to say, that we got this guy in the White House who thinks he is a man, who projects himself as a man because he has a certain masculinity. He's a good old boy, he used to drink, and he knows how to shoot a gun and how to drive a pickup truck. That is not the definition of a man, God dammit!"[14]

Pint-sized flame-thrower Spike Lee clocked in that Charlton Heston should be shot "with a .44-calibre Bulldog."[15] A considerably larger blowhard, Alec Baldwin, lamented, "I believe that what happened in 2000 [the Presidential election] did as much damage to the pillars of democracy as terrorists did to the pillars of commerce in New York City."[16]

Will stars *Say Anything*? "Bush means Dick Cheney, Tom DeLay, and all these fucking crypto-fascists are gonna get in and start carving up the pie and handing in all their markers to the Republican Party that's been itching to get back into power," professed John Cusack, close pal of former Clinton attack guru and *Government by Gunplay: Assassination Conspiracy Theories from Dallas to Today* author Sidney Blumenthal.[17]

George Clooney confessed to his dangerous mind and went full tilt boogie from dusk til dawn with a series of tired swipes at the Grand Old Party, "Let's face it: Bush is just dim."[18] While talking politics with Charlie Rose, the beetle-browed lothario commented, "The government itself is running exactly like the 'Sopranos.'"[19] His observation on Newt Gingrich was less sound bite savvy and more antediluvian. Peacemaker Clooney called the ex-elected official a "dinosaur...the man has no arms."[20] In front of the National Board of Review, the ex-good doctor with a well-reported bedside manner joked, "Charlton Heston announced again today that he is suffering from Alzheimer's."[21] (That's three Alzheimer's strikes now, Hollywood. Is "Hollywood Square" Bruce Villanch running out of material?)

The shrill star-powered rhetoric against a certain sector of the American political debate at times sounds like a call to arms. And that's something Sheryl Crow would never countenance. "I think war is based in greed," she said backstage at the American Music Awards while wearing a trendy "War Is Not the Answer" sequined T-shirt, "And there are huge karmic retributions that will follow. I think war is never the answer to solving any problems. The best way to solve problems is to not have enemies."[22] A sentiment that Hollywood, with its hatred of so many of her fellow Americans, should take to heart.

Weapons of Mass Hypocrisy

The segregated political lunch counter at the Hollywood commissary—industry grunts, the grips, gaffers, Teamsters, and other craftsmen who represent a broader sociopolitical spectrum, prefer the multicultural Taco Bell across from the Warner Bros. lot—features an assorted menu of nonelected spokespeople with one-sided, histrionic sloganeering, and field trips to totalitarian countries; "Rock the Voters" who don't vote; petition-signing junkies fixated on freeing murderers; sniveling expatriates on parade; and green-lighted Marxist vanity projects—as side dishes to go with the all-you-can-eat cognitive dissonance.

Artists of all stripes make secular pilgrimages to Hollywood to pursue their professional goals, usually forgoing higher education and escaping the drudgery of middle-class life, and, upon achieving success, invariably act as unelected representatives sending messages to the world through the entertainment media decrying the very system that affords them their opportunities.

Some take their U.S.-generated capitalist pig loot and head for the hills in the south of France. Rare is the celebrity who doesn't hesitate to cram his or her ideological views down our collective throats, not seeming to realize that celebrity gives them entrée to a soap box to which no one invited them. Practically extinct is the one who argues America is primarily an agent for good around the world—not that anyone asked in the first place.

Not satisfied with their disproportionate input on the culture vis-à-vis the nonstop conveyor belt of artistic product (movies, television, books, music, talk shows, merchandising, etc.), celebrities force themselves on the body politic with dramatic and often laughable posturing almost exclusively of the extremist slant. And since entertainment, designed primarily by those Americans who so publicly seem to dislike the United States, and the industry's byproduct, celebrity, form America's second largest export ($14 billion in 2000)[23] and a top domestic product, it's no wonder anti-American hysteria runs rampant both at home and abroad. What AIDS is to Africa, ingratitude is to Hollywood—both viruses require drastic behavioral modifications to stop the spread, while the deep cultural prejudices within their respective cultures make the task impossible. As long as super rich pseudo–role models openly exploit America's vast freedoms to spread broad-brushed and dire messages that undermine them, the pop-culturally driven nihilism will only fester.

The cycle of hypocrisy among the entertainment elite simply cannot hold up to public scrutiny. The Hollywood wings of the vast loony conspiracy have feathered their nests with capitalist spoils: They live more opulently than most royalty; reside in more segregated neighborhoods than Trent Lott; hire private armies to protect their properties; send their children to $20,000/year private schools; uphold culinary apartheid in the city's top dining rooms; drive Lincoln Navigators in the nation's smog capital (Ed Begley Jr., Cameron Diaz, and Leo DiCaprio notwithstanding); receive around-the-clock cheap labor from undocumented and untaxed foreign workers and wear sweatshopped designer jeans and cross-trainers; use their status to garner free clothing, travel, food, and seats to major entertainment events; exploit the wares of easily duped Hollywood aspirants known as "assistants"; wield black belt accountants to cut through the burdensome tax code they vociferously support; and adhere to casting couch and nepotistic hiring practices over affirmative action—yet put a microphone in front of their faces and they channel the spirit of Che Guevara. They don't call it acting for nothing.

Free Speech for Me But Not for Thee

"The early signs are this administration could go further, shutting down information, not allowing certain truths to get out. And all you've got to do is look at history to see what that led to. The McCarthy era." —Robert Redford[24]

Perhaps Redford is referring to the Clinton Administration (1992–2000), which acquired hundreds of its political enemies' FBI files, openly threatened independent reporters and prosecutors pursuing certain truths, hid evidence, obstructed justice, and intimidated witnesses in judicial proceedings.

Or perhaps he means Fidel Castro—a dictator with whom the actor/director has had the gratuitous celebrity-dictator face-to-face.[25] Neither. Of course, he's talking about George W. Bush.

"Freedom of expression is our most precious virtue," the tow-headed American ski resort mogul told the *Ottawa Citizen*.[26] Exactly what the United States needs—another U.S.-based actor fueling anti-Americanism abroad—and to Canada, no less, the country that nurtured Orwellian political correctness into its national fabric.

Considering that Redford is a man whose every political utterance is dutifully recorded by a free American press, his admonition of an impending McCarthyism seems more like laughable propaganda than fearful reality. Redford, like many in Hollywood, is perpetuating a baseless talking point he hopes when said enough will become accepted as the truth.

Ditto Susan Sarandon, who cries, "It's terrifying to me to feel the fear that exists now in the United States to even question anything for fear of being labeled anti-American."[27] Nothing Sarandon says in the public arena can take away from the genius of her breast rubdown in Louis Malle's *Atlantic City*, that brilliant topless scene opposite Brooke Shields in *Pretty Baby*, or her unforgettable vampire lesbian sex with Catherine Deneuve in *The Hunger*, a scene that could explain her ageless beauty. Art is art—as any straight adolescent male with pay cable will attest. But the naked truth behind Sarandon's Age of Aquarius meets WPA political vaudeville act with lover/father of some of her children Tim Robbins is that when not acting on her back, she is every bit as demagogic and intolerant as those she so loudly despises.

Bloviating bleeding hearts like Sarandon and Redford have some nerve complaining that their right to dissent is under fire when their access to fame and celebrity has come from within a system that promotes ideological conformity and quashes political dissent. Celebrities who disagree with Hollywood's establishment exist in an ideological Siberia where publicly disagreeing with David Geffen, Steven Spielberg, and their Democratic National Committee-supporting clone-like minions translates into something akin to career suicide. Hollywood elitists brook no dissent—or criticism—of their views.

What celebs are hearing now is the legitimate populist feedback from New World media like the Internet and talk radio. Absurd proclamations by actor, director, model, and singer alike get immediate pickup by noncorporate news outlets on the Web, sparking discussion on the AM talk radio circuit. Likewise, the emergence of the Fox News channel on the all-important television dial has driven activist celebrities mad as hatters. Their ideological monopoly on the celebrity soapbox has met a formidable challenge by articulate, informed political commentators, and even regular Joes.

The Elephant in the Living Room

When Bo Derek publicly discussed her status as a Republican in Hollywood, she told Bill O'Reilly, "It's really tough to have a nice, open conversation.... And they treat me as though I'm some hateful monster."[28]

Patricia Heaton of "Everybody Loves Raymond" explained how her politics were met with open scorn before she established her career: "I wore a Bush-Quayle button, and literally people would stop and look at the button, then look at me, give me dirty looks and say nasty things to me."[29]

Rosie O'Donnell famously broadsided Tom Selleck on her mercifully discontinued soccer mom indoctrination hour for his support of the Second Amendment. Said Selleck, "What disturbs me and I think disturbs a lot of Americans is the whole idea of politics nowadays, which seems to be, 'If you disagree with me, you must be evil.'"[30]

Shannen Doherty also met with scorn for reciting the pledge of allegiance at the Republican National Convention in Houston in 1992. (Why the RNC thought the notoriously erratic Doherty a PR coup is another question altogether.) "I got a lot of flak," she said, "but they're my beliefs. If you're going to talk to me, be prepared to hear a very conservative viewpoint."[31]

A sad episode in the real life of former "NYPD Blue" actress Sharon Lawrence supports claims of unfair treatment of those in the ideological minority. Lawrence, a lifelong Democrat and Al Gore supporter, suffered the fate of appearing on the same page as George W. Bush and other well-known Republicans in a *People* magazine photo spread.

When confronted by peers on the streets of LA, barraged by negative e-mail, and threateningly asked by one producer, "Are you really a Republican?," Lawrence decided to take her story to gossip columnist Liz Smith.

"We are ashamed of our fellow Yellow Dog Democrats in Tinseltown who would seek to ostracize others—perhaps even deprive them of employment—because they are members of the Grand Old Party. That's not the American way," the liberal Smith bravely wrote.

Aside from Smith's commentary, no swoons of moral outrage poured from canary-in-a-coalmine civil libertarian wannabes Redford or Sarandon, or Norman Lear's venerated People for the American Way. "If one is even perceived to be a Republican in Hollywood," Lawrence concluded, "there can be an excluding reaction, and people genuinely resent you!"[32]

What the Hollywood crowd is now experiencing is the end of a different kind of McCarthy era, one in which they're the ones behaving like the fascists they so volubly claim to despise.

The Keystone Cop-Outs

Established stars know even better than their less famous peers to respect the unspoken political boundaries of Hollywood. In 1999 Warren Beatty told Matt Drudge at a Hollywood dinner, "Since having children, I am pro-life." When asked why he does not publicly declare his beliefs, rhythm-Method actor and former Casanova Beatty feebly admitted, "I can't."[33]

Jack Nicholson dares not risk his iconic status advocating his unpopular abortion position either. Nicholson became pro-life when he found out that the woman who raised him was his grandmother, and, in a scene straight out of *Chinatown*, the person he thought was his sister was his mother.[34]

"I don't have the right to any other view," Nicholson conceded. "My only emotion is gratitude, literally, for my life. If June and Ethel May had been of less character I would never have gotten to live. These women gave me the gift of life. As an illegitimate child born during the Depression to a broken lower-middle-class family you're an automatic abortion with most people today."[35]

Outspoken leftist activist Martin Sheen, whose public campaigning against war, the death penalty, and nukes knows no civil disobedient extreme, refuses to even whisper his antiabortion position on the set of "West Wing." The devout Roman Catholic quietly offered a trust fund and a house to wild child son Charlie's then-girlfriend, the aptly named Paula Profitt, as incentive not to abort their child. "Abortion was suggested," explained Sheen at the time. "I don't believe in abortion, and neither does my wife."[36] Yes, Sheen is pro-life, but will he advocate against abortion on the network record? Not this season. Like Beatty and Nicholson, he knows which side his bread is buttered on.

One person in Hollywood who does publicly stray from the pro-choice teleplay is Patricia Heaton, who heads Feminists for Life. Asked why she risks her career taking such an unpopular stand, Heaton said, "As a Christian, it will not be Barbra Streisand I'm standing in front of when I have to make an accounting of my life."[37]

The Vast Hollywood Hypocrisy

Exalted celeb role models want America to follow in their thought processes, yet they themselves are for the most part highly dysfunctional. Their family structures reek of serial divorces and out-of-wedlock, often discarded children; open drug use runs rampant. Religion is based more on a "feel good" ethos rather than a challenging theology with a moral ground, and their politics can be summed up in two words: "Viva Castro."

While John Wayne jingoistic fare ended up in the dustbin of history, Oliver Stone propaganda gets the green light. Films dealing with partisan struggle always draw on the saintly JFK Democrat archetype, while portraying Republicans as creepy Nixonian villains.

Conversely, films dealing with traditional American constructs like faith in God and love of country are invariably treated with contempt or crass manipulation. No one is arguing Hollywood can't bash America—uh, "dissent." In fact its her right, and sometimes its well deserved. But if the tables were turned, and if Hollywood were dominated by religious propagandists or right-wing ideologues, there'd be nothing short of a bloody civil war in America. And that's saying nothing of the randomness of it all: Why should we Free Tibet, Mr. Gere, but not some less trendy totalitarian hellhole like Afghanistan, Iraq, or North Korea?

Our representatives answer to us, but our nonelected, self-appointed Hollywood "politicians" are held unaccountable—especially by the politically correct entertainment media. The Hollywood revolutionary (on and off camera) provides a nonstop public service announcement to the world proclaiming the American Dream nothing short of a nightmare, while the genuinely oppressed from around the world still risk life and limb to come to the United States—even if it means becoming Woody Harrelson's indentured hemp weaver.

In October 2002 Harrelson (*Natural Born Killers*) showed why he was a perfect vessel for Oliver Stone's cinematic Nam- and drug-enabled flashbacks when he summed up his own historical delusions in an antiwar, anti-America piece for Britain's left-wing newspaper, the *Guardian*. Entitled "I'm an American tired of American lies," the "Woodman" argues that the United States "killed a million Iraqis since the start of the Gulf war," that George Bush Sr. supplied nerve gas to Saddam Hussein, and that his son is trying to take over the world. "This is a racist and imperialist war. The warmongers who stole the White House—(you call them 'hawks,' but I would never disparage such a fine bird) have hijacked a nation's grief and turned it into a perpetual war on any non-white country they choose to describe as terrorist."[38]

This Baby Boomer–driven, post-Vietnam–era megatrend—the orgy of fringe politics and fairly decadent entertainment from "Friends" to any of Oliver Stone's most recent oeuvres—paints and exports a nasty, often conspiratorial picture of the American way, demoralizing shell-shocked audiences at home and fomenting hatred abroad. And what makes this so galling to so many in the fly-over states is that the people advocating radical political and institutional change can't even seem to govern their own lives.

There is the occasional ray of opposition to Hollywood's cookie-cutter dissent, something that does not occur with any frequency in the pliant and like-minded entertainment press, nor arises anywhere with regularity in the celebrity lifestyle. Rare hip conservative Gary Oldman and his manager Douglas Urbanski stepped up to the dais and pointed out bias, claiming the film they were coproducing with Dreamworks, *The Contender*—a Lewinsky scandal critique that portrayed a female Democrat vice president hounded by a Republican over a sex scandal— had been hijacked by the Dreamworks' political machinery and timed for release for the 2000 presidential election. "If your names are Spielberg, Katzenberg, and Geffen," Urbanski declared, "you can't have a film with a Republican character who is at all sympathetic—being released on October 13 [three weeks before the election]."[39]

Actually, it seems that if you want to work regularly in Hollywood at all, you can't be the sort of character who publicly sympathizes with the conservative half of the American population.

The Last Party

At the height of his Hollywood deification (Best Actor nominee in 1992 for *Chaplin*) and at the peak of his private self-destruction, high school dropout Robert Downey Jr. became defined as a thoughtful voice of conscience in post–Brat Pack Hollywood. Only the late, uber-sentient vegan River Phoenix cared more for Mother Earth and her impoverished children.

Acting as tour guide of the ironically titled documentary, *The Last Party*, Downey weighed in on youth political indifference in America using the backdrop of the 1992 presidential campaign, as the actor gained full access to both party's national conventions by virtue of his fame.

Downey and comrades Sean Penn, Mary Stuart Masterson, Billy Baldwin, Oliver Stone, and Spike Lee form a diverse focus group indeed as Democrats are portrayed as do-gooders caught in a corrupt system, while their ideological counterparts are represented by reliable GOP piñatas Jerry Falwell and Oliver North. The Malibu-based Benz-driving populist then found the courage to mock Wall Streeters for their materialism, and posited America a big dysfunctional family.

In the film's high point, Downey's father, also a victim of the Hollywood grind, expresses regrets for smoking pot with his children when they were young. And together father and son imagine noninhaler Bill Clinton as the candidate best poised to heal the dysfunctional

American family. Move over *Rocky Horror*. Take a seat John Waters. High camp cinema has a new crack-head king!

The Fidel Fetishists

Since the end of the Cold War, Hollywood's flirtation with socialism manifests in the virtual Cuba celebrity tourism bureau led by such luminaries (and usual suspects) as Robert Redford (*Havana*), Spike Lee, Robert DeNiro, Christopher Walken, Sidney Pollack, Woody Harrelson, Johnny Depp, Francis Ford Coppola, Danny Glover, Ed Asner, Shirley MacLaine, Alanis Morissette, Leonardo DiCaprio, Kevin Costner, Oliver Stone, and *Schindler's List* director and supposed moral icon Steven Spielberg.

If celebrities can peddle soap by the truckload, imagine their influence in selling the mystique of 42,804 square miles of tropical property located just 90 miles south of the continental United States. Never mind that the country hasn't had a free presidential election in over 40 years. Never mind that HIV-positive homosexuals are sequestered from the rest of society. Never mind that Castro quashes the very freedoms artists thrive on.

Clinton-era State Department spokesman Jamie Rubin put it bluntly in *Entertainment Weekly* when confronted with the trend: "We don't think it's chic to go and meet with someone who imprisons his own people, denies them the right to pursue the basic freedoms that entertainment figures have come to expect."[40] But celebrities turned a deaf ear to these sentiments expressed by an official in the administration they helped elect. The facts didn't match the trompe l'oeil workers' paradise sought by the jet setters laden down with Vuitton luggage, conspicuously unstamped passports, and success-induced, guilt-ridden emotional baggage fostered by hypocritical socialist drivel.

Spielberg, a man who has made hundreds of millions of dollars exploiting America's constitutionally protected freedoms, and captured an Oscar for illuminating the horrors of the Holocaust, reportedly described his November 2002 tête-à-tête with the murderous Castro as "the eight most important hours of my life."[41] (Stephen Rivers, the man who organized the junket, and who is not Spielberg's official press agent, claims the Cuban press made up the quote. Yet Spielberg—who once went out of his way to distance himself from an alleged pro-Bush quote—has yet to publicly deny the much attributed comment himself.)

Cuban émigré Gloria Estefan, whose father was a political prisoner of the Castro revolutionaries, says, "Fidel has control over the money, over the people, he runs an oppressive and terrorist government."[42] "It would be a great betrayal to go there," concurred Andy Garcia, one of the few Hollywood experts on the subject—his family escaped when he was five. "I obviously think about going back all the time, but it's like asking a Jew to go visit Nazi Germany...I hope that one day democracy will exist and [Castro] will no longer be there."[43]

Yet Kevin Costner, after his jaunt to Castro's Potemkin *casitas* echoed Spielberg, calling his meeting with Castro the "experience of a lifetime."[44] When models Kate Moss and Naomi Campbell sojourned to Castro's garden of delights, Campbell described the cuddly dictator as "a source of inspiration to the world."[45] And at Earth Day 2000 in Washington, D.C., not ready for late night talk show host Chevy Chase declared, "Sometimes socialism works...Cuba might prove that."[46]

Robert Redford's flirtations with the dictator ("[Castro] was very friendly, very gracious and kind to me, and in good shape")[47] led him to host a star-studded fund-raising dinner that raised $25,000 for Cuba's International Film School.[48] Created in 1986 by Castro and author Gabriel Garcia Marquez, the school is directly overseen by the Cuban Institute of Film Art and Industry, an outfit that actively seeks to promote the regime's point of view and wields censorious powers over works not in line with the regime's thinking. "I guess I expected that as soon as the political winds shifted against Cuba, and with Castro going into trouble, that the school would go into trouble, too," fretted Redford as the unfortunate fall of the Soviet empire put a crimp on Soviet subsidizing of the film school.[49] Strangely, when it comes to freedom of expression concerns north of Havana, the sixty-something self-proclaimed human rights activist possesses a rare vision. At 2003's Sundance Film Festival, Redford lamented oppression of dissent in post-9/11 America. "I got a little uneasy when I started to see there was a hint of this notion that normal parts of a democratic process were being treated differently, like it was unpatriotic to ask questions."[50] True to form, Redford was dead silent in April

2003 when his physically fit dictator pal began rounding up Cuban dissident writers and other democratic reformers for questioning *his* political order.

Comandante, Oliver Stone's deep, wet kiss to Castro, serendipitously debuted at Redford's festival—on the same weekend Cuba held uncontested elections for 609 fortunate Communist candidates. "We are perfecting our revolutionary and socialist democracy," Castro told a crowd of "extras" outside a polling place.[51] Meanwhile, Redford's movie market masquerading as an "independent" festival debuted Stone's AOL-Time Warner and HBO–financed and uncontested look at Castro's 40-plus-year experiment in "democracy." When confronted at Sundance, the narcissistic Stone mused, "I can't tell you what this film really is. Is it a documentary? Is it an essay? What is it? It's a little bit about me, isn't it?"[52]

In the film, Stone tells Castro he has the right to say, "cut" when the director inadvertently strayed from the *comandante*. The obviously charming (aren't all cult leaders?) dictator comes off as an American pop culture buff who enjoys pirated American videos like *Titanic*— James Cameron's syrupy Oscar-winning paean to class warfare.

"Due to the recent alarming events in Cuba, we decided not to air the film in May [2003] as originally scheduled," an HBO spokeswoman said, understanding that Castro's concurrent dissident crackdown made the cable network look like a world-class propagandist. "Had we aired the film in March, I don't think we would have had an issue with it. But now, the arrests and trials are an important piece of what's going on in Cuba. And the film's incomplete."[53] The problem with HBO's laudable response is that the damage control pretends that Castro's misdeeds are a new chapter in his dictatorial playbook.

If celebrities were morally blind to the human rights abuses committed by well-intentioned Marxists, one would think they'd at least be concerned over the mass video piracy of Hollywood product. Particularly since they have complained so bitterly about market "boycotts" of their products based on their war protests. Also on Stone's whitewash of history docu-docket: Yasser Arafat and Kim Jong Il.[54] No kidding.

With regard to Cuba, Hollywood's cognitive dissonance and hypocrisy are nowhere more apparent than in its slavering adoration of *Before Night Falls*, the story of Cuban poet and author Reinaldo Arenas (played by Javier Bardem, who was nominated for an Oscar in this role). Arenas, a member of Castro's rebel troops, came out as openly gay and openly critical of the very government he helped create. His dissent outraged Castro, who jailed the poet for two years in a cramped prison cell so small it did not allow him to stand upright. During that time—while his human rights were continually violated by the leader so revered by Hollywood's free speech, Amnesty International advocates—Arenas wrote letters for other prisoners along with poetry and a novel that was smuggled out of Cuba. Leaving Cuba during the Mariel boatlifts, the writer lived stateless and impoverished in Manhattan until his death in 1990. When asked why he wrote, Arenas offered a one-word reply, "Revenge."[55]

Les Expatriates

For some of Hollywood's more respected artists, the vagaries of living in the United States become too much to bear, while others threaten to expatriate if the electorate does not bend to their political whims. Case in point: John Malkovich and Johnny Depp cowered off to France. Alec Baldwin, Robert Altman, and Eddie Vedder threatened to move in 2000 if Bush were elected. Oh, that we were so blessed. As of 2003, they are still stateside.

While Malkovich and Depp both maintain especially private lives by modern celebrity standards, both have taken public swipes at the homeland that still provides them the resources to live a fantasy life abroad. Malkovich moved to the south of France in the mid-1980s and has since lived there with his girlfriend Nicoletta Peyran and their two children. "America is crippled by fear," the accomplished Illinois-born actor observed in the pages of *Playboy* a year before 9/11. "Twenty percent of the population is part of what's known as the re-ligious right and is crippled by the word 'fuck.' Then there's the Tipper Gore crowd. If Dr. Dre writes a song about bitches and whores, they don't look for the genius in the work. America is a big, wild country where lots of bad things come to pass, and from the minute my children were born I was determined that they not grow up there."[56]

These dramatic stream of conscience sound bites show a certain cognitive dissonance specific to the self-ascribed cognoscenti wherein songs about "bitches and whores" and the word "fuck" support fine values; however, the country itself is big and wild, and a lot of bad things come to pass to here, things that some would say are caused by the very permissiveness that Malkovich celebrates. However, one can assume, all rhetoric aside, that Monsieur Malkovich's girlfriend's Gallic roots played a vital role in his decision-making process to live in France. Working off the same script, Johnny Depp moved to France to live with his French girlfriend Vanessa Paradis and their daughter Lily-Rose Melody Depp. "I mean, little kids going into school and shooting up their pals and killing people," self-proclaimed "wine-a-holic" Depp[57] exhorted to the press. "I have a little girl who's almost two years old. I don't want her to grow up with that kind of thing in her brain."[58]

Among the traumas Lily-Rose should avoid while living abroad is her father's legacy to the American experience. Available at the local Blockbuster, Depp's body of work possesses the nihilistic flair that would have appealed to Columbine killers Dylan Klebold and Eric Harris. First there was his star turn in *Nightmare on Elm Street*, not to mention the nightmare of *Edward Scissorhands*. Then there was the syco-phantic homage to drug-addled gonzo journo Hunter S. Thompson, *Fear and Loathing in Las Vegas*. By removing a throat-slashing scene, *From Hell* avoided an NC-17 rating, yet *USA Today* still described it as "an opium-stoked, blood-soaked, class-conscious descent into the bowels of Victorian-era madness."[59] Summing it up best, a Canadian newspaper critic wrote of Depp's global import *Nick of Time*: "It makes you wonder anew about the mental health of a culture that would produce such a movie and the culture that would pay to see it."[60] Considering the film grossed a negligible $8,175,346, it looks like the American public had the good sense not to affirm Francophile Depp's worst assessment of them.

Upon his divorce from Nicole Kidman, the heterosexual Tom Cruise agreed that his American-born ex-wife's adopted homeland, Australia, would be a better place to raise his children. "I think the US is terrifying and it saddens me," said the witless all-American boyish actor. "You only have to look at the state of affairs in America. I do worry about my children. As a parent you are always concerned. I just want them to be in a place where they are going to be strong enough to be able to make the right choices. Unfortunately we're in a position where people are so irresponsible that human life holds such little value to them."[61] Based on statements like this, one can only assume that Cruise, Kidman and kids Conor and Isabella escaped a bloody tenure in a cramped one-bedroom tenement in the Bedford-Stuyvesant section of Brooklyn. No doubt, with a pickup in his flagging career, this worried paterfamilias will make better living arrangements for his brood while living bicontinentally. Divorced.

In 2000 the German media attributed quotes to Kim Basinger that she and her husband Alec Baldwin would flee the United States if George W. Bush were elected. "I can very well imagine that Alec makes good on his threat," Basinger allegedly told *Focus* magazine. "And then I'd probably go too."[62] Under intense talk radio fire, Baldwin denied the report and placed blame for the brouhaha on the "Drudge Report" for linking to an Associated Press story on a slow news Sunday.

"Kim did indeed speak to a *Focus* magazine," Baldwin later admitted. "It was during a press junket. When you do those junkets, the studio forces you to do dozens of interviews with people you never heard of. And *Focus* was one of the interviews she did. But my wife and I never said unequivocally that we would leave the country if Bush won."[63] Baldwin, of course, didn't leave America after Bush won, but he did leave Basinger.

Similarly, Robert Altman denied reports that he would flee America after a Bush win—but only after talk radio and the Internet mocked him, offering one-way tickets to France for him and his petulant peers.

The Wingnuts

"Freedom of the press is limited to those who own one."
—A.J. Liebling

When Liebling, a respected cultural critic of the mid-twentieth century, wrote those famous words he had not seen the future of Aaron Sorkin—a man with a television show whose power to shape public opinion ranks up there with being owner of *The New York Times*.

As producer of NBC's high-rated "The West Wing," Sorkin has crafted an hour-long weekly drama that acts as a shadow presidency, dispensing finely crafted and entertaining story lines that boil the complex American political experience down to one simple truth: Republicans are the primary source of the world's woes. As head writer Sorkin appointed notorious extremist waxwork Martin Sheen to play the American president—a role he has since assumed off camera. Sheen spoke at actor Mike Farrell's antiwar press conference and imparted his presidential wisdom tempered with a bit of New Agey psychobabble: "I think he'd [Bush] like to hand his father Saddam Hussein's head and win his approval for what happened after the Gulf War. That's my own personal opinion. I don't know if that's true. I hope it's not, but I suspect it is."[64] Assorted vocal Democrats like Rob Lowe, who performed so brilliantly on videotape at the 1988 Democrat convention in Atlanta, and actor/antiwar activist Bradley Whitford rounded out the inaugural cast.

When asked by *Playboy* magazine whether West Wingers could even fathom devising a televised presidency around a Republican administration, Sorkin admitted, "I don't know if I could, and I know that I wouldn't." Sheen agreed: "I would like to believe I could, but my heart wouldn't allow it." Rob Lowe echoed the party line: "I wouldn't have done it. When I read the script, the characters inspired me. I doubt I would have been inspired by the story of a conservative White House. How dreary."[65]

The candor of the "The West Wing" actors does not take away from the tragedy of their sentiments. Sorkin, like the Hollywood establishment, genuinely and consistently conveys—that there is only one side to an argument. "The West Wing" used the bully pulpit to advocate for, among other political ideas, campaign finance reform—legislation that limits the paid political advertising of those who might disagree with Sorkin.

Nonelected opinion makers like Sorkin and Sheen justify their unchecked power in the belief they speak on behalf of the oppressed. "I can say I stood with the people who were nameless. And I gave voice to the people who were voiceless," President Sheen told *USA Today*.[66] But those are BMW commercials in between those divisive "The West Wing" vignettes.[67] If the show is written for the downtrodden (or the vanishing American autoworker), why is the show trying to sell $75,000 foreign automobiles?

When in 1989 the Malibu Chamber of Commerce appointed Martin Sheen to the ceremonial position of honorary mayor, he immediately offered the following unilateral proclamation: "I hereby declare Malibu a nuclear-free zone, a sanctuary for aliens and the homeless, and a protected environment for all life, wild and tame." When busloads of homeless people took him up on his conspicuously compassionate offer, Malibu residents publicly seethed. "The community is pretty upset," said the chamber's executive vice president Mary Lou Blackwood. The Malibu Inn featured the marquee "Dump Martin Sheen."[68] In February 2003, a year before the New Hampshire primary, President Bartlet, a.k.a. Martin Sheen, became the first celebrity to endorse a candidate, in this case predictably, ex-Vermont governor Howard Dean. Dean's staff happily pointed out that the fictional Bartlet, like Dean, is a former governor of a New England state and a Democrat. Both also are married to physicians. "People are familiar with the show: a New England governor whose wife is a doctor. That is our story line," said Susan Allen, Dean's campaign press secretary.[69]

"The West Wing" vet Rob Lowe, whose public fall from Brat Pack grace came (and came again) in 1988 while horsing around in home movies, at the Democratic National Convention in Atlanta, admitted life in Sorkin's art imitates life. "I'd come home and watch "Crossfire" and go, 'You know, [I] have to talk to [the White House staff] about that the next day,' Lowe recalled. "You really (start to think) that you're actually working there."[70]

Lowe, a working father of two young children, and the show's token conservative consultants Peggy Noonan, Frank Luntz, and Marlin Fitzwater, were unceremoniously dumped from the make-believe "The West Wing." "They dropped us because they decided they didn't want a conservative viewpoint anymore," Fitzwater said.[71] Job cuts, of course, are mean—when they are done by venal bottom-liner Republicans, but not when they are done by pot-toking 1960s idealists like Sorkin.

Not content with just one one-hour DNC filibuster, NBC ordered up "Mister Sterling," another heavy-handed political advertisement promoting such maverick ideas as banning offshore oil drilling, promoting proabortion legislation, supporting farm worker unions, and other boilerplate Democrat issues. And this is fine—broadcast companies, TV studios and executives, writers, and actors can create whatever product they want and sell it. But apparently conservative issues will not be sold on broadcast TV. The celebs bemoan Fox News Network not seeming to realize that it is almost the only television option for conservatives.

Celebrity Felon-Identification Disorder

Death penalty–opposing celebrities—that would be most of them—reflexively lend their names to petitions that often go beyond trying to remove convicts from death row. In the case of convicted cop killer Mumia Abu Jamal, celebrity illumination on his open-and-shut case (three eyewitnesses testified seeing Jamal shoot Philadelphia police officer Daniel Faulkner five times with his own .38-caliber gun, including an execution-style shot between the officer's eyes) has turned the former cab driver into a superstar of Cabernet-sipping celebrities.[72]

Being given the honor to address the miniscule hemp haven Evergreen State College's 1999 commencement ceremony with a 13-minute taped speech proved the value of having the likes of Paul Newman, Joanne Woodward, Susan Sarandon, Tim Robbins, the Beastie Boys, Rage Against the Machine, Ossie Davis, Ed Asner, Alec Baldwin, Spike Lee, Oliver Stone, John Landis, Naomi Campbell, Sting, Whoopi Goldberg, David Byrne, and Michael Stipe on your side.[73]

Tucker Carlson's damning 1995 piece "Mumia Dearest" in the *Weekly Standard* chronicled how big names came to sign a petition calling for a new Jamal trial that was placed as an ad in *The New York Times*: "There is strong reason to believe that as an outspoken critic of the Philadelphia police and the judicial and prison systems, Mumia Abu-Jamal has been sentenced to death because of his political beliefs."

Gloria Steinem had once seen popular author William Styron talk about the case, and that was good enough for her. "Wasn't there some question about his brother? And weren't there no witnesses?" queried the former Playboy bunny/feminist. Fellow petitioner and scribe of the great social commentary *Beyond the Valley of the Dolls*, Roger Ebert explained, "Basically, my position is, I'm opposed to capital punishment, so it was a real easy call for me because I didn't even have to think about the merits of the evidence."[74] Bob Stein, a businessman who helped gather the celebrity signatures, admitted, "If you asked them about the particulars of the case, they might not know enough about them to feel comfortable speaking about it."[75]

But even prominent progressive journalist Marc Cooper of *The Nation*, an anti–death penalty activist, sees the folly in the Mumia movement, stating bluntly, "I've had it. If I go to one more lefty event and see one more Free Mumia poster, I might just have to switch sides on this one. What collective affliction has overcome my fellow pinkos? You haven't had enough defeats and embarrassments these past two decades? Now you want to take the deathly serious issue of capital punishment and tie it to some flaky cult member like Mumia Abu-Jamal?"[76] For his dissent, Cooper was the object of a demonstration outside his Pacifica radio talk show by his former radical peers.[77] Over 20 years since the murder, trendy celebrity support of Jamal's politically inspired drama has forced slain Officer Faulkner's widow to constantly relive the nightmare as she has been reluctantly conscribed to counter the discordant disinformation spread by Rage Against the Machine and Co.

The anti–capital punishment troika of Tim Robbins, Susan Sarandon, and Sean Penn unwittingly made the greatest contribution to the death penalty movement—the Oscar-winning propaganda piece *Dead Man Walking* was accidentally received as the futile last words of the anti–death penalty lobby when many audiences cheered as Penn's reprehensible character, who admitted to murder, received his lethal injection. Ooops.

Other celebrities hit the switch with more precision. Glenn Close, who played the psycho bunny-boiler in *Fatal Attraction* opposite repentant alcohol abuser, Michael Douglas,[78] helped secure the freedom of Precious Bedell, a woman with a history of drug addiction convicted of murdering her two-year-old daughter. The original prosecutor in the case, Richard Hennessey, credits the actress's star power as the driving factor that freed Precious on a technicality (Bedell had not been allowed to accompany the jurors to the crime scene during the trial). "A celebrity shouldn't be able to redo what the criminal justice system has done," Hennessey lamented.[79]

The New York Post described the Free Bedell movement as part of a "star-studded epidemic of lunacy. Like mold, they're popping up everywhere—famous people eliciting sympathy, and sometimes winning freedom, for convicts and miscreants. This pathological need to unleash violent creeps on those of us who can't afford bodyguards amounts to a disease. Call it Celebrity Felon-Identification Disorder," wrote the tabloid of record.[80]

In 1975 Leonard Peltier, an Oglala Lakota and Turtle Mountain Ojibwea tribe member, was convicted of murdering two FBI agents. His cause has been embraced postcoitally by ex-mates Johnny Depp and Winona Ryder, along with Peter Coyote and musicians Robbie Robertson and the band Rage Against the Machine. Ryder has become a trustee of the American Indian College fund, as well as an impassioned Free Peltier-ist, and supporter of the American Indian Movement. Some conspiracy hunters have speculated that perhaps winsome Winona's persecution, um, prosecution, for shoplifting was politically motivated payback for her AIM activism.

In early January of 2001, "Clinton called our house for Winona Ryder," said Tom Cook, a Mohawk tribe member who lives in Chadron, Nebraska, with his Oglala wife Loretta Cook, according to an October 31, 2001 interview in the *Lakota Times/Indian Country Today*. Cook recalled that the actress "talked for about five minutes and said Clinton would give her one hour on his schedule, but no press, no delegation and no gift."

The waifish actress's charms were apparently lost on celebrity lover Clinton, who denied her plea for the convicted murderer's release. Perhaps swayed by a petition signed by 9,500 law enforcement officers, coupled with a 500-G-man march on the White House organized by FBI officers, Clinton rejected freeing the celebrity-endorsed assassin. Or perhaps the president recalled another incident that tarnished the star-studded parole movement.[81]

In 1981 Norman Mailer, Hollywood's favorite bad boy literary icon, helped win parole for convicted murderer Jack Henry Abbott based upon the quality of his prison letters—which Random House published in the best-selling *In the Belly of the Beast: Letters from Prison*. "This guy isn't a murderer, he's an artist," vouched *The Executioner's Song* auteur. "Not only the worst of the young are sent to prison, but the best—that is, the proudest, the bravest, the most daring, the most enterprising and the most undefeated of the poor."[82]

Powered by the fuel of celebrity activism, Abbott won freedom based upon artistic potential and immediately became a media cause célèbre appearing on "Good Morning America" and in the pages of *People* and *Rolling Stone* magazine. Six weeks after his release, Abbott butchered 22-year-old café manager Richard Adan, who refused the con access to the restaurant's staff bathroom.

Said the late novelist Jerzy Kosinski (*Being There*): "I blame myself again for becoming part of 'radical chic.' I went to welcome a writer, to celebrate his intellectual birth. But I should have been welcoming a just freed prisoner, a man from another planet who needed to know how to control negative emotions. He was emotionally imbalanced. Easy love and easy hate. You could sense this in the man."[83]

Today, Stormin' Norman Mailer is not so contrite and lends his name to the Free Mumia celebrity juggernaut.

Congressional "Sideshows"

Actors asserting their First Amendment right to make fools of themselves do so most amusingly when speaking as experts before Congress on subjects unrelated to the rigors of show biz. Ed Asner, Jack Klugman, Julia Roberts, Christie Brinkley, Denise Austin, and even Muppets Elmo and Kermit the Frog have joined the growing list of stars who have unwittingly transformed C-SPAN into episodes of the "Surreal World."

In 1985, when the so-called farm crisis hit America's heartland, Democrats on the House Agriculture Committee summoned millionaire actresses who had just portrayed farm wives in a slew of orchestrated farm subsidy advocacy films. Jessica Lange (*Country*), Sissy Spacek (*The River*), and Jane Fonda (*The Dollmaker*) appeared in tears before the committee while Sally Field's (best actress Oscar in *Places of the Heart*) written statement was read before the congressmen, all promoting Soviet-style farming solutions to the situation.

Fonda, a.k.a. the former Mrs. Tom Hayden, simplified the crisis in the narcissistic terms of a Hollywood head-case, orating, "The reason we are here is to underscore the gravity of the crisis that is leading to the bankruptcy, humiliation and banishment of farmers from their lands at a rate not seen since my father (Henry Fonda) made *The Grapes of Wrath*."[84]

The folly perhaps reached its nadir when the Backstreet Boys' Kevin Richardson spoke before the Senate Environment and Public Works subcommittee to argue against mountaintop removal mining. "I am not a scientist," the teeny-bop sensation admitted before Congress, "but I know what I've seen in flights over the coal fields." Sen. George Voinovich (R-Oh), refusing to be part of the spectacle, walked out of the conference room, voicing his outrage to reporters, "It's just a joke to think that this witness can provide members of the United States Senate with information on important geological and water quality issues. We're either serious about the issues, or we're running a sideshow."[85]

Robin Hood Was Right

During the halcyon nights of the Clinton presidency, showbiz players—big and small—gained unlimited access to executive power and turned Washington into a big-budget Hollywood production, replete with the requisite struggle to avoid an NC-17 rating. Movie star, producer, diva, and sitcom actress alike spent countless evenings at the White House, and, at times, even policy was discussed.

Leon Wieseltier, former cultural editor at the *New Republic*, frowned upon the burgeoning Hollywood/D.C. orgy, "The idea that these insulated and bubble-headed people should help make policy is ridiculous. Hollywood actors are even more out of touch than elected politicians."[86]

Seeking to avoid tabloid-fueled embarrassment and East Coast snobbery, top celebrities have taken to hiring political gurus culled from Clinton-era mixers to lend their political dabbling a modicum of respect. The Creative Coalition began as a result of Clinton indulging celebrities in their pet projects. "A celebrity is expected to have an issue now as much as he or she is expected to have an agent," the coalition's Robin Bronk admits.[87] According to the *Los Angeles Times*, "The salary range for the new political experts ranges from

$75,000 to $175,000 for those who oversee charitable foundations and above $250,000 for those who count political outreach among their duties at a major Hollywood corporation." Hollywood political consultants represent the folly that arises from celebrities looking to buy a conscience.

When Richard Dreyfuss hired Donna Bojarsky as his "personal political consultant," a position that landed her a nice office on the Paramount lot, the ex–coke fiend Dreyfuss, like so many industry train wrecks, soon gained access to the Lincoln Bedroom. Robert Redford uses Joyce Deep, a former aide to Jimmy Carter, Walter Mondale, and Michael Dukakis, to coordinate his political networking. Norman Lear keeps former National Endowment of the Arts spokeswoman Cherie Simon on staff as his round-the-clock politico. Rob Reiner hired a twenty-something Clinton operative who helped him during the filming of *The American President* (written by Aaron Sorkin, who employs a slew of former D.C. politicos himself).[88]

Former antiwar activist and head of VISTA (Volunteers in Service to America) during the Carter administration Margery Tabankin, who festoons her Culver City office with political buttons like "Robin Hood Was Right," is the best known of the bunch. Her biggest clients, Barbra Streisand and Steven Spielberg, give her power to oversee million-dollar political foundations. Morgan Fairchild and Mary Steenburgen made their way on to CBS's "Face the Nation" as a result of her connections.[89]

Tabankin, a huge figure behind the scenes, also headed the now-defunct Hollywood Women's Political Committee, a political action committee open only to industry bigwigs. The HWPC set a strict litmus test for membership that required supporting publicly funded abortions, social welfare programs, nuclear disarmament, and affirmative action, as well as being a woman both highly placed and visible in the industry, or hypocritically, married to a suitably important, wealthy, liberal-thinking man. Dues were steep, amounting to over a month's wages for the majority of women employed in the industry as assistants, production staff, and other low-level personnel. To join, you had to be sponsored by a member.[90]

Locked out by this cultural sectarianism, punk rock singer Exene Cervenka from the critically acclaimed band X, along with a group of over 50 like-minded alterna-chicks who worked in various Hollywood fringe jobs, formed the Bohemian Women's Political Alliance.[91] While on the surface their agenda barely differed from that of HWPC, the BWPA did manage to make an impact and have sense of humor while doing it; along with registering voters at a concert featuring Courtney Love, they raised thousands of dollars for breast cancer research by staging a strip-a-thon-cum-burlesque show and an autographed celebrity bra auction (including a multicolored boob-sling from Madonna with the size tag removed and a rather plain supporter from Courtney Love), outraging as many feminists as it attracted breast lovers.

Perhaps Streisand should have employed one of the BWPA in her political war room; she might have gotten more for her money. In the period between September 26 and October 16, 2002, Streisand was in high gear to help the Democrats get control of the House and maintain control of the Senate. Among her efforts that turned her web site, barbrastreisand.com, into a political sweatshop was a star-studded Los Angeles fund-raiser in which she would, once again, come out of retirement to perform.

Unfortunately for Babs, the "Drudge Report" was paying attention to her and Tabankin's operation. In September Streisand caught controversy when she faxed a spelling error–ridden memo to Missouri congressman Dick Gephardt, asking him to resist Bush's Iraq moves.[92] Streisand blamed the mistakes on a "new employee."[93] Blaming the help. How Hollywood.

Then in October, Drudge revealed that, at the big Hollywood gala, Streisand fell for an Internet hoax in which she falsely attributed a quote to Shakespeare in an attempt to castigate President Bush for his position on Iraq. "Beware the leader who bangs the drums of war in order to whip the citizenry into a patriotic fervor, for patriotism is indeed a double-edged sword."[94] Sounds more like a Baldwin brother than the Bard.

"It was just called to my attention, but it doesn't detract from the fact that it is powerful and true and beautifully written," the Funny Girl, uh very smart woman, told *The Washington Post*. "Whoever wrote it is damn talented. I hope he's writing his own play."[95]

Soon thereafter Drudge reported that in 2000 the Streisand Foundation, through its investment adviser, had bought and traded 800 shares of Halliburton, a company she had blasted on her web site because Vice President Dick Cheney was once its chief executive."[96] And in a final blow, on October 16, in a "truth alert" on her web site, Streisand called Iraqi leader Saddam Hussein an "Iranian" dictator.[97]

Whose fault was it this time? Another assistant? Streisand herself? Drudge, for pointing it out—again? Us, for laughing? Or could it be Tabankin and her ilk, for enabling celebrities' delusions of grandeur and positioning them as somehow more important than regular citizens by helping them gain access to places regular citizens dare not dream of going? Or maybe politically large Marge is just following Robin Hood's lead—pilfering from her rich celebrity clients and laughing all the way to the bank.

Strike a Pose, There's Nothing to It

In 1990 Madonna unwittingly kicked off the Clinton decade with a provocative seminaked public service campaign encouraging disillusioned young voters to the polls. Prancing in front of her preening backup dancers, she made the case draped in an American flag and red panties, "If you don't vote, you're going to get a spankie."[98]

Millions of citizens, some who probably secretly longed for a spankie from the sexually voracious singer, heeded her advice, but Madonna was later shown to not have cast her vote in that or many previous elections. Ten years and a lifetime of "Rock the Vote" public service announcements later, Benjamin G. Affleck took to the American road with Helen Hunt, Martin Sheen, and Rob Reiner to reinforce the importance of youth voting (Democrat, that is).[99]

The future Mr. B-Lo lectured crowds in California, Florida, and Pennsylvania on civic responsibility. "One of the reasons that I'm here is to demonstrate that no matter who you are going to vote for...I think it's important to get involved and get out and vote." On Election Day, Affleck told Rosie O'Donnell's audience, "I'm about to go vote. I am personally gonna vote for Al Gore."[100]

Thesmokinggun.com, a web site famous for embarrassing celebrities with public documents, found that Affleck lied to Rosie and to the American youth; he had not voted in the 2000 do-or-die Bush/ Gore fight-off, and according to records in Boston, New York, and

Los Angeles, the actor had voted only once as far back as 10 years. Spokesman David Pollick confirmed the report and blamed a bureaucratic snafu at the polls.[101]

An equal opportunity offender of J. Lo suitors, The Smoking Gun also exposed Rap the Vote's Sean "P. Diddy" Combs for failing to get it up to vote after imploring an East Hamptons political pow-wow, "I'm here to support the young vote and to reach the young audiences to get them to go out and vote. We need this vote. It's a positive thing to change the world."[102]

Which leads to the obvious question—are their politics for real or just for show business?

12

BLUE COUNTRY HAZE

Political Correctness n.: conformity to a belief that language and practices which could offend political sensibilities should be eliminated.[1]

Politically Correct adj. Abbr. PC : 1. Of, relating to, or supporting broad social, political, and educational change, especially to redress historical injustices in matters such as race, class, gender, and sexual orientation. 2. Being or perceived as being overconcerned with such change, often to the exclusion of other matters. (from the American Heritage Dictionary)[1a]

Political Correctness n.: A Hollywood affliction in which troubled souls present themselves as entertainers but instead use entertainment media as a means to promote a dysfunctional moral and political agenda. (from the Hollywood, Interrupted Lexicon)

As difficult as *political correctness* is to define in lay terms, perhaps Supreme Court Justice Potter Stewart's famous definition of hardcore pornography applies best: You know it when you see it.

PC is addressing stewardesses or stewards as flight attendants, actresses as actors, women as "womyn" (eliminating "men" from the designation), and blacks as African-Americans, even if they're Dutch. PC is designating the handicapped as the "handi-capable," short people as the "vertically challenged," and junkies as "substance abusers." The chronicling of the past is no longer history, but *her-story*. Political correctness twists language inside out and turns ideas upside down— all in the pursuit of a vaguely utopian cause using an even more vague sense of language.

On college campuses, political correctness brings First Amendment– trampling "speech codes" and narrow academic disciplines such as Gay Theory, Gender, Chicano, and African-American studies, which encourage students to see themselves and others only as members of oppressed factions. PC's underlying tenet is that those individuals in groups that do not constitute the majority—read: white males—are at all times the object of overt or covert prejudices and conversely the cause of all prejudice. And PC is the means by which the playing field is to be leveled—by any means necessary. In government, political correctness seeks to strip individual rights in lieu of a group's right, for example, hate-crime laws.

Political correctness has become the primary weapon used by those in *Blue Country* (Hollywood, elitists, Democrats, mainstream media, academia, multiculturalists, et al.) to squelch the ideas and speech of those in *Red Country* (Middle America, conservatives, Republicans, and yes, NASCAR fans), creating a uniform social consciousness that appears to celebrate diversity and tolerance, but rejoices only in its own narrow and condescending perspective.

But if you really want to see political correctness run amok, turn on the Lifetime or Oxygen television network, or take a trip to the local movie multiplex, where political correctness, the manifestation of Orwell's deepest warnings, is brought to you in Technicolor and THX.

Hollywood: Ground Zero of the Culture War

With the possible exception of compulsory celebrity alcohol and drug problems, no Hollywood affliction over the last 20 years has been as obvious and odious as full-blown PC. Careers have been built on its very premise (See Goldberg, Whoopi), and whether they'll admit it or not, studio executives, actors, and the rest of Hollywood's elite hierarchy use political correctness as an illegitimate and undemocratic method to ram their narrow, dysfunctional, condescending moral and political values down the rest of our throats in a very un-American way.

Once upon a time entertainers entertained, actors acted, singers sang, and comedians cracked jokes. Those born after Boy George may not remember this innocent era; history books will hopefully reflect its brief life. But political correctness put an end to the run.

Now, built into the DNA of the Hollywood decision makers—from producers to screenwriters to actors—is a fundamental belief in their superiority over the average audience member. Save a few fringe entertainment commodities, our mass-consumed entertainment product has become a vessel for unapologetically allegedly safe and sane messages constructed to transform the unwashed masses into enlightened souls—as defined by the media elite.

Enter Rosie, PC's Trojan Horse.

Revenge of the Latchkey Kid

The year was 1996, September to be exact, and the *borderline* comic, who at one time hosted a dreary comedy revue on VH1 called "Stand-up Spotlight," was appointed by Time Warner Inc. to compete with Oprah Winfrey in the race to bend the malleable minds of midday's television-viewing masses. Faux-comedienne Rosie was presented by the mega-corporation with an afternoon talk show and put on the cover of *Newsweek*, framed as the "Queen of Nice."[2] Nice if you agree with her particular brand of K-Mart emblazoned sensitivities. Not nice if you are a National Rifle Association member like Tom Selleck.

Like most PC stars of her era, Rosie tapped the resources of her imperfect upbringing as the primary source of her creative inspiration: She grew up on Long Island, and as she is not shy to divulge, lost her mother to cancer when she was only 10 years old. It was "the defining event of my life, and it remains so," she told television columnist Gail Shister in 1996.[3] As the story goes, her father was "never a parental figure,"[4] refusing even to discuss the tragic loss of his wife with his five children, thus pushing Rosie into a life of relying on television to teach her life's large lessons. The one-eyed monster provided Rosie with vivid daydreams of bigger-than-life maternal surrogates like Bette Midler, Carol Burnett, Dinah Shore, and Barbra Streisand, while Mike Douglas and Merv Griffin countered her uncommunicative father as perfect male archetypes.

The inevitable friendship between Madonna and Rosie hinges on both having come of age during the early 1970s without mothers, relying on pop culture as an all-purpose crutch. "When I saw *Truth Or Dare*, I thought, I understand what this is about. I know what it's like to go to your mother's grave and see your own name," O'Donnell told the *Toronto Star*. "I knew that if I met her we would be friends."[5]

Madonna has put restraining orders on people for less, but in the aristocracy of showbiz an admitted sycophant like Rosie was able to make her bubblegum wishes come true. As PC vessels, Madonna and Rosie have sent not so subtle messages to their adoring public. Neither seems to care who their children call father, nor whether *he* will be a constant in their lives. And similarly, both have built their acts around pushing primary life lessons they apparently missed out on as young children, compelling everyone to travel with them on their very public erratic spiritual odysseys.

In Rosie, Time Warner found a willing and able accomplice happy to promote a never-before-seen level of gluttonous consumerism, on the one hand, while she hammered away at *mean* things like the Second Amendment, certain Judeo-Christian principles, the tabloids, assorted Republicans (Rudy Giuliani, George W. Bush, and Bob Dole, to name a few), smoking, Howard Stern, and all those things she grew up learning to hate, while obediently taking her cues from the TV set.

Rosie even incorporated tragicomic Paula Poundstone (a contributor to *Mother Jones*), her cerebral better and a like-minded progressive Republican hater, into the daytime mix. Sadly, fellow pants-wearing comic Poundstone didn't have her demons in check and became Rosie's evil doppelgänger, arrested for endangering her brood of foster kids as she drove drunk with the kids in the car to fetch some ice cream.[6] Rosie's *nice* show had all the Orwellian markings of trying to start a clandestine cultural revolution—sponsored by the nation's second largest national retailer.

During this time, Rosie attempted to inoculate herself from mainstream criticism by building her comedic persona around conspicuous philanthropy. Concept: Cure raises money for breast cancer research; Freshly Squeezed seeks to find homes for hard to adopt kids; and $10 per sale of the Rosie O'Doll goes to her all-purpose charity For All Kids. Toys for Tots and a cystic fibrosis group also receive her attention. She's also noted for publicly offering a lifetime supply of diapers to those sextuplet births played up on the "Datelines" of the world.

In her first major fit of using her pop cultural cachet to push PC objectives, Rosie pressured Kmart, which had hired her on as a spokesmodel, to stop carrying weapons and ammunition. And then she went on to found the Million Mom March, a couple *thousand* strong yenta stampede on Washington that prompted a flurry of NRA membership sign-ups from a few thousand disgruntled husbands across the land.[7]

"I think the only people in this nation who should be allowed to own guns are police officers," ranted Rosie on one occasion. "I don't care if you want to hunt, I don't care if you think it's your right.... You are not allowed to own a gun and if you do own a gun, I think you should go to prison."[8] "A fear of weapons," Sigmund Freud once observed, "is a sign of retarded sexual and emotional maturity."[9] Near-definitive proof that Dr. Freud was a very smart man.

Rosie's attempt to shove her agenda down the throats of Americans was foreshadowed before she had her own television show. In 1994, while performing as Rizzo in *Grease* on Broadway, O'Donnell staged a smoke-out, an overt PC public relations stunt embraced at the time by the media as high-minded and not challenged by her peers as an act of creative cleansing. "I've never tried a cigarette," she said at the time. "I'm repulsed by it."[10] So what? The playwright penned her character as the bad girl of the bunch, and the cigarettes helped convey that.

As the host of her supposedly nice show, O'Donnell attacked Mayor Giuliani and his policy that required the homeless to work for their shelter or possibly lose custody of their children to the foster care system. O'Donnell called Giuliani "out of control," and asked her audience members to call his office to complain. Dutifully, they did. "Since when are we justified in separating children from mothers and fathers because they are poor, when we should be helping to make a family stronger and offer that child and his or her parents a real future?" O'Donnell said. "My concern is a humanitarian one, not a partisan one."[11]

Other mid-day talk shows of the time, like Jerry Springer and Ricki Lake, excluded big name guests because exploiting everyday folk was far cheaper and easier from a booking standpoint. So celebrities looking for a soft interview to promote themselves found in Rosie a more than willing enabler. The Queen of Nice stuck in television's craw because she fell over herself desperately wanting to be loved by her idols, like Bette Midler and Barbra Streisand, whose performance on her show made her cry. Rosie is the television viewer who knows her idols in the entertainment world are her betters.

O'Donnell, a lesbian even to the untrained eye, presented herself as the girl next door's unattractive friend who spent her days dreaming about the unattainable heterosexual Tom Cruise. Comfortably lying on such a big issue, O'Donnell continued to expertly deceive her audience, using her show to push her own utopia.

"When Rosie O'Donnell (whom I liked as a stand-up comedian but whose work as a schmaltzy talk-show host I find brittle and fake) called for a one-year boycott of the tabloids by readers who want to honor Diana, I was so outraged that I immediately bought copies of both the *Enquirer* and *Star* in protest," all-star culture critic Camille Paglia vented in her "Salon" column two weeks after the princess's death. Paglia continued, "O'Donnell was hypocritically using Diana's tragic death to grind her own axes: Omitted from her histrionic appeal was the inconvenient fact that the prior week's splashy *Enquirer* cover story (with just a small inset photo of Diana on her Mediterranean vacation) was about the motorcycle-straddling O'Donnell's alleged affairs with two lesbian lovers. Sugar-sweet, all-American Miss Rosie has a shadowy closet the size of Greenland. And folks, backstage she bites."[12]

O'Donnell's barely concealed sexuality became politicized when after years of gleefully collecting millions in corporate paychecks as "straight Rosie," she then decided to leave the building as a lesbian activist pushing the cause of gay adoption. Having for years deceived her public, presuming the worst of its antigay prejudices, O'Donnell decided to spend her falsely accumulated moral capital on what the *Advocate* magazine calls "Rosie's Crusade."[13]

"America has watched me parent my children on TV for six years. They know what kind of parent I am," the shameless Trojan horse said to Diane Sawyer, and soon thereafter the ABC News talking head received The Gay & Lesbian Alliance Against Defamation (GLAAD)'s "Excellence in Media Award" for raising awareness of gay adoption.[14] Journalists as advocates. Entertainers as activists. Welcome to the new media order. Just shut up, sit down, turn on the TV, and become more enlightened.

In O'Donnell, America has its first proto-pop culture politically correct humanoid. Her values are an amalgamation of every single public service announcement and after-school special aired on television but delivered by a humorless oracle based in falsehood. Daytime television, always ground zero for the re-education process, may have lost a large pedagogue when Rosie retired, but the leading lady of sob-sisterhood, Oprah, reigns on.

The Story of O: Billionaire Queen of PC

Not only is political correctness a tool for Hollywood stars to ram their arcane values down our throats, but it is also a means for them to celebrate their dysfunction and supposed victimization, all in the service of their narcissism and need for self-promotion.

Political correctness is the framework by which Hollywood's esteemed now openly rave about their life difficulties—from race to rickets, SARS to sexuality, and multiple personality disorder to menstrual difficulty. In the era of the model/actress, or worse, the *reality* star, PC has given merely genetically endowed celebrities a crutch that allows them to appear talented, while coming off as morally and intellectually superior. As a result, it's far more common to see a celebrity kvetching on TV than performing. So whether stars intend it or not, PC serves the dual purpose of perpetuating their endless desire to be loved while marketing their goods. Just ask Oprah, the billionaire queen of PC.

Oprah Winfrey and Rosie O'Donnell, among others, building upon beta-man Phil Donahue's robust PC legacy, have redefined the daytime talk show terrain with cause-driven programming focusing on the assumed victimhood of the majority female audience, all the while keeping them glued to commercial breaks filled with Cheer commercials rather than *empowering* them.

Celebrities now hawk their wares by exposing emotional baggage in a never-ending stream of woe and redemption. Woman-as-victim is a cottage industry selling books via clubs, movies, TV shows, diets, lifestyles, and workout routines to the terminally oppressed and depressed.

The success of the touchy-feely "Oprah Winfrey Show" illuminates how PC has permeated the celebrity promotion process. In the age of Johnny Carson, or even Mike Douglas, Merv Griffin, and Dinah Shore, celebrities came on talk shows to entertain us via singing, dancing, comedy, and witty discourse. Now Hollywood stars hold court with Queen Oprah, candles burning in the background, as they humorlessly share their raw hurt with millions of strangers as a means to achieve politically correct redemption.

The time-tested Oprah formula is now a permanent part of our culture: self-promotion mixed with bathos/pathos kitsch. The famous come on "Oprah" to confess they have been to hell and back. To prove it, invariably, they have a book describing the trek. Most amazingly, the moment the injured luminary appears on "Oprah." life is now nearly idyllic. Perhaps they are buoyed by the prospect for robust Amazon.com preorders or a flurry of Starbucks book buys. The "Oprah" story arc, real or imagined, demands that the melodrama play out with an uplifting or informative ending—ready to be optioned by Lifetime or possibly Oprah's very own network, Oxygen.

Under the auspices of "raising awareness" of a particular malady or social beef, stars tap the ripe vein of victimhood or downright wretchedness. Want to feel their pain? Check out these representative Oprah show descriptions:

> *The high cost of fame for singer/actress Brandy: Brandy discusses her rise to fame as a teen-ager, her breakdown in 1999, her future with a new husband, a new CD and a baby on the way.*[15]

Brandy's contribution to improving society was her 2002 foray into reality television, "Brandy—Special Delivery"—in which the young songstress gave birth before the MTV cameras. Did her core inner-city fans really need added incentive to become teen mothers?

> *Life lessons from funny people: Several actors and comedians give examples of what they've learned throughout their lives.*[16]

Too bad Oprah couldn't get insights into Chris Farley, John Belushi, Sam Kinison, Lenny Bruce, and Phil Hartman's magical lives before they left us. Or Richard Pryor and Eddie Murphy, all of whom obviously have their acts together. Thanks for not noticing the obvious, O: Comedians are doomed.

> *Mariah Carey: Singer Mariah Carey talks about her breakdown and recovery, and about her new CD.*[17]

Dear Valued Viewer: Please take the gun out of your mouth, log on to Amazon.com, click on the "Oprah's Picks" icon and purchase Mariah's exultant comeback! We promise it will make the pain go away. Sincerely, Your Friends at Harpo, Inc. P.S. We're sorry for recommending *Glitter* the last time she was on.

> *Kelsey Grammer discusses his career, family and conquering his drug and alcohol addictions; cast members of "Frasier" discuss the show and its 200th episode.*[18]

God bless, Kelsey. Really. As anyone who follows *EW* or *People* knows, almost all of his loved ones have been maimed or murdered, and he has overcome *other* great personal odds. If that wasn't enough, his lovely wife, Camille, suffers from and is a spokesperson for irritable bowel syndrome. Leave it to Oprah to figure out the perfect way to celebrate 200 shows of epic "Frazier" comedy!

> *People who are afraid of people: Jamie Blyth of "The Bachelorette" and Ricky Williams of the Miami Dolphins discuss their battles with social anxiety disorder.*[19]

Pity the poor near-celebs and their hard times interacting with their fellow human beings. They're shy, just not camera shy.

*Rock star Bono's mission to save the world: Bono talks about his efforts
to help the people of Africa; Chris Tucker and Secretary Paul O'Neill
discuss their trip with Bono.*[20]

Like a less divisive Jesse Jackson, Bono wields his celebrity to force
political change through guilt and intimidation. Bono has successfully
lobbied First World countries to forgive Third World debt, incidentally giving the First World no incentive to lend them money ever
again. Yet, decent tickets to U2 concerts will still set back rock fans
from the Third world a few hundred bucks—no small change in *any*
world. Republicans are most vulnerable to Bono's PC charms, as
George W. Bush's former Treasury Secretary hoped some of the "I
Care" cool could rub off on his terminally un-hip party. It didn't.

*Adoption stories: Actress Melissa Gilbert discusses being adopted and
hosting the show "Adoption," which gives a candid look inside the process
and emotions of adoption.*[21]

Gilbert's show, however, will not expose how unmarried celebrities
jump to the head of the adoption line ahead of qualified married
couples that have been waiting for years. When will a celebrity "raise
awareness" about *that* troubling issue?

The original Oprah Book Club—decaffeinated literature served up
at Starbucks—was a testament to the hurt. Adoptive hurt. Cheated-on
hurt. Female hurt. Religious persecution hurt. African-American
hurt. Did we say female hurt already? How many Toni Morrison novels can a suburban soccer mom read before she drives into oncoming
traffic? Enough with the guilt. Take our houses. Take our cars.
Forgive our Third World debt. Anything. Just make it stop!

In the age of celebrity, even presidential aspirants, the ultimate reality stars, must go through the Oprah turnstile and bleed. When Bush
came on, he chatted movingly about his love for his daughters and
presented himself as a man off the bottle. "Alcohol was beginning to
compete for my affections, compete for my affections for my wife and
my family. It was starting to crowd out my energy and I just had to
quit," Bush told her.[22] Immediately after the show aired, Bush's standing in the polls jumped. When Gore came on, he appeared stiff and
didn't emote much.

"It's become a disgusting spectacle," Camille Paglia told the *Los Angeles Times*. "The idea that you now have to kiss the ring of Oprah Winfrey or act like a buffoon on a television show to win the U.S. presidency is something that should concern all of us."[23]

Oprah's success provides a paradox wherein she ostensibly promotes female empowerment and the pursuit of individual achievement and life fulfillment, but whether she pushes a book, a movie, or even a presidential candidate, millions of followers chained to their TV sets during the middle of the workday seem to march lockstep behind their billionaire guru.

Cause Célèbre

Political correctness serves Hollywood's narcissistic need for self-promotion. Celebrities, most of whom chose not to attend college, mimic PC conventions rampant in postmodern academia as a means to appear smarter and more humane than they actually are (see the rest of this book). Using the vast entertainment media to promote their careers, celebrities cloak themselves in an air of social and philanthropic superiority in order to cling to the slippery reins of fame and fortune.

Nearly all of cause-happy Hollywood suffers from *narcissistic personality disorder*. Obsessed with appearing empathetic, modern celebrities make top-tier PC carriers as they appoint themselves our secular saints anointed to overlook and protect the rest of us from our nasty, uncouth selves or any organized religion not in line with their PC values.

The less raw talent or tangible human qualities a celebrity possesses, the *Hollywood, Interrupted* corollary goes, the more PC PR CPR he or she needs. That's why supermodels are so drawn to causes that supposedly prove how warm, caring, and morally upstanding they are, like the People for the Ethical Treatment of Animals (PETA) movement. The vapid and the shallow need all the positive publicity they can get to offset their wanton designer drug-fueled jet-set lifestyles.

"Today's stars make astronomical amounts of money in a time of vast media conglomerates," NYU media professor Mark Crispin Miller told the *Christian Science Monitor*. "They all need a way to atone for their success. These celebrities need opportunities to show they're well-meaning and committed."[24]

It's all mildly humorous to a point, but when someone like Rob Reiner can push to enact laws (such as California Children and Families First, which earmarks 50 cents from cigarette pack sales to various state-funded toddler programs) form-fitted to his parochial brand of politics, and sell them by saying he's doing it "for the children," PC's all-purpose catch phrase, then the regular guy is doomed because he— or she!—cannot match the size of his soapbox nor counter the power of celebrity rhetoric.

Even actors and stars who know better are forced by the Hollywood machinery to toe the line and pick a cause for the betterment of their image and career. Actress Alley Mills recounts the heady days in which she got her big break when she was cast in 1987 as the angelic mother on "The Wonder Years." In the whirlwind of the hour, Mills found herself at a high-powered Los Angeles public relations firm assigned to help craft her public image.

"You should associate yourself with a cause, they told me," Mills recounted. "And that way we can do an immense amount of public relations based upon your cause." "Pick something I don't know any-thing about?" Mills replied. "And they said, 'Yeah, it doesn't matter. Because we can do publicity for you as the spokesperson of the cause instead of you just being the mother on the 'The Wonder Years.'"

"Pick something I don't care about so I can go to their events and talk about it on the 'Tonight Show?'" she asked incredulously. "It was freaky because it all seemed so disingenuous. There were a lot of interesting things in my life at the time that I would have liked to use the 'The Wonders Years' as a platform to help, but I didn't want to turn them into a PR stunt. And that's when I realized what many celebrity causes are: getting dressed up in a gown and going to a chicken dinner and aggrandizing one's self. That's how the PR machine works."[25]

Extreme narcissism and fashionable activism go hand in hand in modern Hollywood as benefit events, film festivals, and the ever-increasing number of award shows dominate the social calendar. At these year-round love-ins, celebrities and aspiring artists jockey for social standing by making hollow political or social gestures, all the while trying to cozy up to King Harvey [Weinstein] and Queen Sherry [Lansing].

The cavalcade of award shows serve as little more than fronts for Hollywood to showcase its PC values and conspicuous philanthropy as means to mask its sickening narcissism. Award shows provide celebrities ample camera time to promote themselves *and their pet causes*—as long as the issues they adopt pass PC muster.

The Oscars, PC's night of nights, puts Hollywood ego on display. Films and celebrities portraying hobbled or disadvantaged souls make their way to the head of the contender list (*Rain Man* to *My Left Foot* to *Born on the Fourth of July* to *Boys Don't Cry* to *A Beautiful Mind*, etc.). Self-congratulation and racial sensitivity PC met head-on at the 2002 event when Denzel Washington and Halle Berry won in the Best Actor and Best Actress categories, and Sidney Poitier received a well-deserved, well-timed Honorary Award. The night became less a victory for blacks in film than an industry self-congratulation for whites honoring blacks in film.

As the number of award shows has increased to feed Hollywood's narcissistic personality disorder, so has the need to offset the meness of it all with hollow gestures of solidarity with the afflicted and the allegedly oppressed.

What Color Is Your Ribbon?

Witness the ascent of the red AIDS ribbon beginning at the 1991 Tony Awards. The fashion-cum-political statement did not happen within a vacuum. The backdrop of the event was the aftermath of the Gulf War. At the time the nation was showing support for the troops in the form of yellow ribbons inspired by Tony Orlando and Dawn's hackneyed song about a returning convict, *Tie a Yellow Ribbon Around the Old Oak Tree*. Worn by regular folks all around America, the ribbon was a warm and true gesture.

While the country was awash in patriotic spirit, Hollywood showed no overt support for the troops at the 1991 Academy Awards held at the height of the soldier's return on March 25, only three weeks after the war ended. Not comfortable with national attention averted from the concerns of the *artists*, Hollywood took its cues from extremist activist group Visual AIDS. After all, how many celebrities even know a single soldier? "If *we* could show this kind of concern for a war abroad," said Visual AIDS founding director Patrick O'Connell, "why not for this war at home?"[26]

We? But nary a representative from the Hollywood community even wore the yellow ribbon during the 1991 Oscar ceremony. The people wearing those ribbons and exhibiting the telltale signs of jingoism, to the consternation of the artistic community, were the middle- and lower-middle-class denizens of flyover country, a.k.a. Red country, whose communities were more affected by soldiers being put in harm's way.

Incidentally, that year the historical revisionism of oppressed Native Americans, the PC *Dances with Wolves*, edged out the PC diseased-are-people-too screed, *Awakenings*, for Best Picture. The stable of Best Actress nominees that year, Kathy Bates, Julia Roberts, Joanne Woodward, Angelica Huston, and Meryl Streep, presented the face of the emerging social awareness.

That year's Tony Awards host Jeremy Irons is credited as the first celebrity to wear the red ribbon, and later in the year at the Emmys Jamie Lee Curtis made a plea that was then followed by an ad placed before the 1992 Grammy awards by Columbia Records: "Wear this ribbon tonight. Let's all do more tomorrow."[27]

The ribbon became a predictable fashion statement when festooned at the following year's Oscars by PC stalwarts Whoopi Goldberg and Billy Crystal and a sea of artsy lemmings. Richard Gere, the Dalai Lama of Hollywood PC, made an overwrought speech à la Jamie Lee to a national audience at this point starting to see the dark comedy in a national tragedy. Elizabeth Taylor, no longer an actress but a billboard for PC causes, incorporated the ribbon into her repertoire.

Proving that Hollywood should rarely be taken seriously, once the ribbons no longer carried any social status, they simply disappeared. "AIDS hasn't gone away," LA stylist Kim Bowen told *People* magazine, "but the ribbons have just sort of phased out."[28]

Since charities are now associated with celebrity, the charity organizations, be they pink ribbons for breast cancer or violet ribbons for artists against racism, must fight one another for positioning. My ribbon is bigger than your ribbon. Even empathetic regular citizens can get into the act and wear a black and blue ribbon signifying concern for the disease that celebrity has become.

The two perennial charity juggernauts in PC Hollywood are AIDS and animal rights groups, and in 1996 the two met head-on prior to the Oscars in an ethical debate well beyond the town's ability to grasp.

The AIDS activist Americans for Medical Progress Association took on celebrities' other "pet cause" in a full-page ad placed in *Daily Variety*, the industry's must-read trade newspaper. Addressed to People for the Ethical Treatment of Animals (PETA) spokesman Alec Baldwin, the letter began: "When you help PETA, this is who you hurt the most. . . . The red ribbon that you wear tells the world that you've made a choice: a cure for AIDS over animal rights. . . . When a cure for AIDS is found, it will come through research with animals. You can't be for AIDS research AND animal rights."

The text was accompanied by an image of a baby on life support. Baldwin, a noted peace activist, responded with a letter of his own threatening to sue AMP president Susan Paris "until [she is] bleeding from the eyeballs."[29]

Oliver Stone, Mary Tyler Moore, Lily Tomlin, Woody Harrelson, Hugh Grant, and Antonio Banderas sided with PETA, while in the AIDS corner stood Demi Moore, Paul Newman, and the town's AIDS point person Elizabeth Taylor. Caught in the middle of the PC charity tug-o-war, among others: Bette Midler, Whoopi Goldberg, Robin Williams, Elton John, Tom Hanks, and Susan Sarandon.[30]

Miles of PC cause ribbons and the spectacle of dueling interest groups cannot obscure the fact that the Hollywood product and its producers are rarely worth rewarding anymore.

Taking the Task Forces to Task

Political correctness fuels Hollywood's narcissism, and also encourages institutional censorship and ridiculous examples of special treatment for supposedly aggrieved groups. PC operates insidiously, proposing that the majority white heterosexual, primarily male, oppressor class owes select historically aggrieved classes a series of remedies. Central to this reimbursement is that certain groups get the kid glove treatment in mass culture.

Hence, Tom Clancy's *The Sum of All Fears*, which featured Islamic extremists in the novel, ended up with European neo-Nazi terrorists once it hit the big screen. The Council on American-Islamic Relations successfully lobbied Paramount Pictures to change the villains to *another* group for the film adaptation, and in the end much-feared neo-Nazis drop the bomb instead. We wouldn't want to create an un-realistic portrayal of Islamic extremists acting as agents of terror, now would we? Notice how the film's producer, Paramount Studios, shows no concern for portraying whites as villains. Apparently stout European folk can take a broad-brush negative portrayal, while Muslims, Allah forbid, must be protected from the fictitious portrayal of the *truthful* behavior of some of their coreligionists. "In these politically correct times, there's no question that the studios and networks and their corporate owners hate being surprised by bad publicity upon release of a film or launch of a TV program," wrote Josh Spector in the now defunct "Inside.com."[31]

The un-PC Christian Coalition can protest until it's blue in its face, and Hollywood is not going to stop negatively portraying that faith and their faithful. But groups representing the American Indian, Arab-Americans, Chinese-Americans, gay Americans, et al. have the ability to stop production, get shows taken off the air, and force press release apologies from networks and studios airing anything not flowery and uplifting pertaining to said groups.

Examples of group protest and corporate acquiescence abound in the PC age, a dynamic that ultimately neutralizes commercial art's ability to say anything. If the artists were artists first and activists second, third, or fourth, then maybe things could change.

What is Disney thinking when it removes the black Centaur in the classic *Fantasia*? Did Alfre Woodard call and say it offended her or something?[32]

Basic Instinct met with protest during its filming and at its release because the ice-pick-wielding antagonist played by Sharon Stone resided on the island of Sapphos half of the year. C'mon. Everyone loves attractive lesbians—especially bisexual ones![33] "Everything's so repressive now," recovering addict and *Basic Instinct* costar Michael

Douglas said at the time. "It's like the No generation. You can't do anything, you can't eat anything, you have to abstain."

How about *Pocahontas*, in which history is revised for a PC agenda? According to the Disney-fied revision of American settlements, the colonists arrived to strip mine, a blatant fabrication that is approximately 300 years off in its veracity.[34]

Schlockmeister Michael Bay's *Pearl Harbor* twisted history by making sure thousands of American GIs were never shown smoking cigarettes—a hideous misrepresentation of an era when Lucky Strikes were as plentiful as bullets and were not culturally vilified by a health-obsessed, censorious elite.[35]

For *Saving Private Ryan,* Steven Spielberg was lauded for portraying the gory realities of war, yet he conspicuously protected audiences from hearing American soldiers slurring the Nazi enemy as "krauts" or "jerries." The selective use of editing—vivid war realities juxtaposed with dulled cross-cultural animus—brings to mind whether Spielberg was trying to make the ultimate antiwar movie, while at the same time soft-pedaling the racial and nationalistic schism so not to offend an 80-million-plus-person film market that now resides in the former Third Reich. The question arises: Would the beloved Spielberg really manipulate the historical record to further his political ends? For those who saw Dreamworks' *The Contender*, the question has already been answered.[36]

Albinos, or rather the pigmentally challenged, were pissed off they were the bad guys in *Matrix: Reloaded.* If society can't have a good laugh at our translucent brothers and sister, then who in God's name can we laugh at? And after all, they are evil white men, so what's the problem? They really need to lighten up, er, relax!![37]

Curiously, Israeli-Americans and Cuban-Americans are not given the same protective umbrella since neither seems to play the game by positioning themselves as oppressed victims of an unfair societal order. As Orwell wrote in his prescient *Animal Farm*, "All animals are equal but some animals are more equal than others."

The 1990s were filled with more exposure of minority groups, both real and imagined, than previously—but they were portrayed as helpless and pathetic, in need of laws and art to protect them. Their separate but equal status was emphasized, while at the same time these groups were marginalized. And the business of Hollywood did everything it could to uphold this tragic new politically correct dynamic. Oddly, no one saw the irony of the industry's paternalistic doctrine, which rendered real diversity and empowerment down to a paper tiger.

Most noticeably, black popular culture gets a free pass from PC consideration. Hip-hop culture, which rhythmically demeans most notions of human decency (bitches, 'hos, gangstas, murder, etc.)' is somehow acceptable despite its emphasis on un-PC weaponry like Glocks. Black comedians can recklessly explore the unsettling regions of race and express deep-seated rage against Korean liquor store owners or even their own mothers, or your mother.

White pop culture, however, is crazily policed. By self-appointed rights groups that speak on behalf of certain groups (NAACP, NOW, GLAAD, etc). By media bigwigs scared senseless of any protest, boycott, or publicized backlash. And by the artists themselves who proactively seek to be portrayed as *sensitive* citizens of the world.

Though it may sound innocuous, PC has the cultural effect of stifling dissent, something you'd think would stoke the fires of selective free-speechers Martin Sheen and Janeane Garofalo. PC is to discourse what the left says McCarthyism was to politics. It stifles free speech so much so that it is routinely wielded by Hollywood as a tool to squelch any views but those held by her elite.

There is no piece of shock art crafted to offend the sensibilities of pious, church-going folk, often at state expense, that won't be defended by Alec Baldwin on some A&E special. And media conglomerates like Time Warner and Viacom are so concerned not to offend at any cost that they embed PC into an economic reality, giving "the oppressed" the artistic equivalent of 40 acres and a mule.

This Faustian bargain, wherein Hollywood seeks to soothe the aggrieved, may win points with a certain sector of the audience that believes art should reflect the moral and political goals of a political movement, but overall untold millions are sick of being hit over the head with the authoritarian hammer.

THE DEATH OF COMEDY

Stars and entertainment execs not attuned to the politically correct way of thinking cower from dissent, fearful of being called racist, sexist, homophobic, anti-Mongolian, or any other all-purpose impossible-to-defend slander. Even the accusation of operating outside the boundaries of political correctness is enough to put a damper on one's professional life.

Just ask the comedians—particularly Andrew "Dice" Clay.

Remember him? During the 1980s, Clay developed a raunchy and over-the-top dirty limerick–spouting Guido *character* that took the country by storm. Man and woman alike, black and white, packed 5,000-plus auditoriums to hear Clay deliver obnoxious dirty limericks and ethnic jibes. Clay's *character* seemed to conjure a bygone era, like he was the Fonz with a more treacherous mouth.

"I was in *The Adventures of Ford Fairlane* [with Clay]," fellow comedian Gilbert Gottfried recalls. "It wasn't being judged as a movie: It was just considered a terrorist attack. The National Organization of Women were picketing the theaters and spraying graffiti over the posters. And what got me about that is that, in the course of the film, one man is poisoned to death, another man is shot . . . another man is set on fire . . . . I get electrocuted, and the critics were all saying, 'This movie prides itself on violence against women,' and I was thinking: 'Where? How?' "[1]

Organized protests of Clay forced him into a tearful televised apology on the PC "Arsenio Hall Show" after (unfunny) Nora Dunn and (confused soul) Sinead O'Connor boycotted his "Saturday Night Live" hosting stint.

No Comic Relief

As the plight of Andrew "Dice" Clay illustrates, nowhere has political correctness had a more devastating effect than in the formerly healthy field of stand-up comedy.

In the boom years of the 1980s, a new generation of comedians took to the stage with reckless abandon at nightclubs such as the Improv and Comedy Store in Los Angeles and Caroline's and Catch a Rising Star in New York. Among the stars that sprouted from the fertile comedy soil were Richard Lewis, Jay Leno, Roseanne Barr, Judy Tenuta, Sam Kinison, Dennis Miller, Steven Wright, Paula Poundstone, Ellen Degeneres, Garry Shandling, Richard Belzer, and Eddie Murphy.

The explosive success of stand-up spawned a national trend, as comedy clubs with silly names like Yuk Yuks and Giggles popped up at strip malls across the land. *US News & World Report* claims that 320 clubs existed in the United States in 1988 when there were only a dozen 10 years before.[2]

Caroline Hirsch of New York City's Caroline's Comedy Club proclaimed, "Comedy is the rock-and-roll of the '80s." Cultural indicators like *Rolling Stone, Time,* and *Newsweek* magazines concurred.[3] Home Box Office, Cinemax, and Showtime jumped on the bandwagon, offering a steady stream of comic revues and one-man shows. Then, without warning, stand-up comedy's bright future was ruined by the PC brigade. Cue Whoopi, Robin, and Billy.

Inspired by the Farm Aid and Live Aid phenomena, writer-producer Bob Zmuda, best known for collaborating with Andy Kaufman, launched "Comic Relief" in 1986 as a means to offer economic assistance to those referred to, in the PC parlance, as "the homeless" and to show the world that "comics care," like their new breed rock star brethren.[4]

Nearly 50 comics appeared on HBO's telecast of the first "Comic Relief" pledge-a-thon, hosted by the reliable milquetoast triumvirate of Robin Williams, Whoopi Goldberg, and Billy Crystal. "Comic Relief" sought to use humor as way to raise awareness, and to transform stand-up comedy into the folk music of the 1990s, with the power to teach and heal us all. Unfortunately, the only lasting consequence of "Comic Relief" was to extinguish stand-up comedy's wildfire expansion, and to reforge comedians into little more than mouthpieces for Hollywood liberalism and political correctness.

An uncharitable *Washington Post* review of a "Comic Relief" skit with Williams as a homeless vet: "This material was so patently meant to 'enlighten'...I was grateful when it was over."[5] Television critic Tom Shales wrote in 1990, "'Comic Relief' serves as a voluntary initiative to help the homeless and as an annual love-in for show-biz liberalism."[6]

From the beginning in 1986, the "Comic Relief" partisan troika transformed the event into a nonstop pillorying of conservatives and the Reagan administration, and in doing so "Comic Relief" turned off a lot of the telethon's potential donors. The event's organizers showed their cards at a high-profile press conference two weeks before the inaugural show, where yet-to-be-tried-for-vehicular-manslaughter Sen. Edward Kennedy (D-MA) blamed President Reagan for ignoring the homeless issue as he introduced the show's hosts.

Whoopi Goldberg, née Karen Johnson, a self-described former "welfare mother," took an immediate swipe at the president, saying facetiously that anyone, *including* "Mr. R." could become homeless. Robin Williams then cracked: "I just want to invite Mr. Reagan to throw out the first piece of cheese"—an allusion to the administration's surplus cheese handouts.[7]

"Comic Relief" developed a simple formula: Offer stand-up routines by safe comics that reflect the anti-Reagan zeitgeist (Paula Poundstone, Rita Rudner, and Louie Anderson, for instance), interject tear-inducing videos in between the quasi laugh-making to elicit the guilt-induced phone dialing to the 800 number, and then when all the cash is collected, watch Whoopi, Robin, and Billy dole out the cash in photo-ops with top Dem politicians across the nation. Massachusetts governor Michael Dukakis was among them, a stunt perfectly timed to give a high-profile boost to his presidential campaign.[8]

Come the first "Comic Relief" show at the apex of the Reagan years, Los Angeles Democratic Mayor Tom Bradley told the crowd that homelessness is a "*new* phenomenon."[9] Bradley, who lived through the Great Depression, was not intentionally trying to elicit laughs.

That evening, Robin Williams did his mean-spirited Reagan nod: "Well, Nancy and I believe the homeless are basically people between homes." He then handed Mayor Ed Koch of New York, also a Democrat, a check for $139,500 and asked, "Where's Mr. Reagan's name? Nowhere to be found."[10]

Come year two of the event, this type of routine became routine: Industry ass-kisser Richard Belzer interviewed Reagan as played by impersonator Jim Morris: "I saw myself on the news. I must've done something today. I've said it before, and Ed Meese has said it before, the homeless choose to live where they live, just as I choose to live in the White House."[11]

When Hollywood's favorite talker, Bill Clinton, came into office, the "Comic Relief" franchise predictably fell apart, although homelessness only got worse during the Clinton years. "We saw more homelessness in the 1990s than we did in the 1980s," said Patrick Markee, senior policy analyst for the Coalition for the Homeless.[12] Yet the few shows that aired during those years occurred under far less fanfare and with no jokes alluding to the administration's tepid response to the cause. The *Village Voice* took *The New York Times* to task for a similar double standard.[13] Homelessness remained a serious problem during the Clinton years, yet the paper and social satirists of record couldn't see fit to hold their Baby Boomer president accountable—at the expense of the people in need.

In 1992's "Comic Relief" presentation, in the aftermath of the Los Angeles riots, Goldberg offered a monologue entitled "From Clarence to Daryl"—allusions to all-purpose liberal whipping boy Supreme Court Justice Clarence Thomas and Los Angeles Chief of Police Daryl

Gates.[14] In the arcane rules of PC, it is okay to demean or to excoriate a black man, if and only if he is politically conservative. Comics like Goldberg were at the forefront of making the dignified Thomas a national punch line. And for it, they have literally no shame. Crystal then took to the stage with a minstrel show rendition of a black man caught up in the turmoil of the riots in the heart of South Central LA.

By "Comic Relief VI" in 1994, six years after Ronald Reagan left office and the first Clinton-era show, Goldberg joked, "Like the Reagans," Goldberg said, "the homeless have not gone away."[15]

Goldberg, who during the 1996 election said, "Will someone please introduce Lorena Bobbitt to Bob Dole?," opined to *Playboy* in 1997: "As far as I'm concerned the Reagan years did more to destroy the fabric of the nation than anything. Dismantling a lot of those programs with no safety net destroyed the morale of folks who were working so hard and struggling so long to make something happen." Robin Williams offered a similar hell-in-a-hand-basket world view in 1992: "We're raising a nation of overweight, unintelligent people."[16]

If Whoopi, Robin, and Billy cared the slightest about the bottom line, they'd realize that according to the Generosity Index (http://www.catalogueforphilanthropy.org) the fat, stupid rubes in flyover country that voted for Reagan twice donate more of their income per capita than do those in the supposed enlightened states like Massachusetts, New York, and California, and that framing the issue as "us versus them" would turn a lot of them off. And, more importantly, the trio of do-gooders would realize it sucked to be homeless as much during the groovy Clinton years as it did during the reign of their much-loathed president, Ronald Reagan.

Had the Internet or talk radio existed at the turn of the 1990s, "Comic Relief" would have undergone a full-out populist deconstruction, exposing its organizers as partisan hacks. Instead, Zmuda and company were saved by a pliant media that mainly presented the philanthropy as another example of showbiz selflessness.

In-the-know Hollywood hipsters, like the "Comic Relief" crowd, now use art to re-educate the masses and inculcate PC values—creating an alternate *conformist* environment, this time emphasizing the ideals adopted by the reigning class, the fatuous Baby Boomers. As a result, comedy routines, network sitcoms, and films now routinely patronize the audience with PC messages. When things get more controversial, as with the "Def Jam Comedy Hour," the outrageous commentary is tailor-made by an aggrieved minority for an aggrieved minority.

The "Comic Relief" alumni association is a Who's Who of Baby Boomer elitists who, when confronted, usually show their intentions as truly political. "I hated Bush [the father] and what he did during his years in office," tragicomic Paula Poundstone said in 1992. "It's taboo to express your political beliefs on TV, but I don't care. I'm excited about Clinton."[17]

"I was at *Schindler's List* and [Rush Limbaugh] started the wave," Brett Butler said at "Comic Relief VI."[18] Butler also entertained the working press at the event, telling them she would participate in any charity as long as the name "Republican" is not in it. There's nothing a Yankee likes more than a Southerner who goes out of his or her way to demean the South, and any perceived alliances associated therein. That was part of Butler's charm, and the same formula that Clinton used to woo the American electorate.

The "Comic Relief" altruistic alignment of social consciousness raising with the anarchistic spirit of stand-up, beginning with the first show in 1986, started a domino effect, making comedians who walked the line of good taste fearful of organized protest and the shunning of peers. And comedians that toed the "Comic Relief" line ushered into the 1990s a form of comedy that bordered on the pathological. And boring.

Who Killed Sam Kinison?

Comedians signing on to "Comic Relief" not only received great national exposure, but also were written up by the national media as *caring*. The 1990s filled up with touchy-feely comics, comics with cancer, feminist comics, and a you-name-it slew of *alternative* comics armed with more causes than one-liners, the kind of comic you could take home to Oprah.

The growing alternative comedy scene included the morose comedic stylings of Ben Stiller and Janeane Garofalo, who helped define the genre by making even straightforward cracks appear to be inside jokes. Generation X may have had a positive effect on rock and roll, but its stand-up legacy is lagging.

Those not invited to participate, or who chose not to join the "Comic Relief" festivities, end up looking like Scrooges, or pariahs. If maximizing aid to the homeless was the main goal of "Comic Relief," Andrew "Dice" Clay and Sam Kinison—true rock stars of the 1980s comedy boom—could have come and put most of Skid Row up in the Hilton for a year. But Clay and Kinsion were the whipping boy "misogynists" of the new politically correct mindset. Even their peers took stabs at them publicly. Paula Poundstone decried their ilk, "You know, what's been popular over the past years sadly is incredibly racist, incredibly provoking material. To me, the lesson in this whole thing has a lot to do with responsibility."[19]

Sam Kinison, no doubt, would have had a field day over Poundstone's idea of responsibility—drunk behind the wheel driving her kids to get some Jamoca Almond Fudge. Or Robin Williams leaving his wife and running off with the nanny. But they belong to a protected class—because their hearts (and political affiliations) are in the right place.

Arguably the funniest comic of the 1980s, Kinison was a "Comic Relief" no-show simply because of his take on the homeless subject in his act: "I bought two homes just to piss the homeless off," Kinison would roar.

Kinison's famous rant on African hunger also wouldn't go over too well at the "Comic Relief" nice zone: "You want to stop world hunger? Stop sending these people food. Don't send these people another bite, folks. You want to send them something? You want to help? Send them U-Hauls. Send them U-Hauls, some luggage, send them a guy out there who says, 'Hey, we been driving out here every day with your food, for, like, the last thirty or forty years, and we were driving out here today across the desert, and it occurred to us that there wouldn't BE world hunger, if you people would LIVE WHERE THE FOOD IS! YOU LIVE IN A DESERT! YOU LIVE IN A FUCKING DESERT! NOTHING GROWS OUT HERE! NOTHING'S GONNA GROW OUT HERE! YOU SEE THIS? HUH? THIS IS SAND. KNOW WHAT IT'S GONNA BE A HUNDRED YEARS FROM NOW? IT'S GONNA BE SAND! YOU LIVE IN A

FUCKING DESERT! GET YOUR STUFF, GET YOUR SHIT, WE'LL MAKE ONE TRIP, WE'LL TAKE YOU TO WHERE THE FOOD IS! WE HAVE DESERTS IN AMERICA—WE JUST DON'T LIVE IN THEM, ASSHOLES!'"

"In the 1990s, it's OK to do comedy about the Chernobyl disaster or the Space Shuttle blowing up," Kinison complained to the *Los Angeles Times*. "It's acceptable to ridicule the Pope or the president of the United States, but God forbid you do a joke…about gays…. Just because I do a few comedy bits about gay people, that does not mean I'm out there promoting some anti-gay cause. I'm a comedian and my comedy has never endorsed violence towards gays."[20]

Sam Kinison, unjustly treated as a vessel of hate, died an untimely death in a head-on car collision in the California desert, leaving Howard Stern as the sole purveyor of uncensored humor. Lack of industry support for Stern has made him a huge favorite among working-class stiffs who regard patronizing celebrities and their pet causes as the bane of their existence.

Presumably, stand-up audiences are looking for a break from pedagogic life lessons, and want in their performers a temporary reprieve from, say, fending off beggars every day on the way to work. A joke against the homeless is not necessarily an endorsement of hate toward the afflicted, but instead a healthy means of dealing with life's many traumas, of which homelessness is one. If done artlessly, the stand-up comedian risks being heckled, so the stakes are high to walk the line without crossing it.

The appeal of a Sam Kinison routine is not that it affirmed our collective humanity in the way *Schindler's List* did, but that it offered collective exhaustive relief from a culture run amok. Don Rickles made a fortune in Vegas mocking the obvious ethnic, gender, and other cultural distinctions of his audience members. People, believe it or not, actually came to his show to drink booze, smoke cigarettes, and be insulted—three cardinal sins in the neo-puritanical age.

He slammed people with dignity in live shows. Always reserving a slot at the end of each show to thank his victims, slant-eyed or otherwise, for being "good sports." And he'd thank them by name.

You think these PC comics today even *care* whether or not their audiences *have* names? The limo is waiting right outside the celebrity exit for the PC comics of today.

"The comedian serves as a counter-cultural model that expresses a lot of the anti-social or sociopathic sentiments that people have," Larry Mintz, a professor of American Studies at the University of Maryland told the *The Record* (New Jersey). "The angrier, the nastier you can be, and get away with it is what comedy has been, going back to the Middle Ages," he said.[21]

Of course, there's nothing wrong in principle with the idea of an idyllic world of social politeness, a world where no one ever feels offended or disrespected. But when the rigid rules of political correctness make honest communication nearly impossible, and demonize and censor free expression in the arts, there's no justification for supporting them.

Niggahs with Latitude

Today's black, uh, African-American comics get it.

"I was so impressed with Don Rickles, the way he can just come in and just destroy an entire room," Bernie Mac told NPR—of all places. "And I was not offended as a young boy watching this guy and some of the things he said about Jews, blacks and the Chinese. I mean, he tore you up, but you knew it was a joke. I got it right away. I was not offended. I was not saying, 'Did you hear what he said?' He was funny."[22]

Yet with "Def Jam Comedy Hour," "Showtime at the Apollo," and *The Original Kings of Comedy*, the stages are as fertile for honest comedy as they are segregated. And this PC double standard has only helped to separate the races.

Take Chris Rock's famous "nigger" routine: "Everything white people don't like about black people, black people don't like about black people," Rock begins. "It's like our own personal civil war. On one side, there's black people. On the other, you've got niggers. The niggers have got to go. I love black people, but I hate niggers. I am tired of niggers. Tired, tired, tired.

"Niggers always want credit for some shit they're supposed to do. They'll brag about stuff a normal man just does. They'll say something like, 'Yeah, well, I take care of my kids.' You're supposed to, you dumb motherfucker. 'I ain't never been to jail.' Whaddya want? A cookie? You're not supposed to go to jail, you low-expectation-having motherfucker!"[23]

And for this kind of material he is amply rewarded. *Vanity Fair*, *Time*, *Rolling Stone*, you name it: Chris Rock is the funniest man in America! And, he might well be, but the competition has been pushed off the field. Instead of winning on merit, he shines by default. "What Chris Rock is saying is what would ruin any white performer's career," long-time comic Gilbert Gottfried says. "But it's coming from a black kid so you think, it's OK."[24]

Like their hip-hop musical counterparts, black comedians are given unlimited latitude to make their points—no matter how crude or off-putting. Martin Lawrence, like Rock, knows well that his hysterical explorations into race issues could not be executed by his white counterparts, who are too busy trying not to be offensive—through self-deprecation (Jeff Foxworthy, Ray Romano) or by playing with props (Carrot Top, Gallagher). Innocuous material served up for dwindling audiences.

And those white cultural critics who find Howard Stern, Sam Kinison, and Andrew "Dice" Clay deplorable, and go so far as to stage economic boycotts, rarely hold black comics accountable because of the liberal racist tendency to not hold minorities to the same standards of the rest of society, particularly white society.

In 2002 a black-produced movie with a mostly black cast, *The Barbershop*, met with controversy when civil rights shakedown artist Jesse Jackson and the NAACP protested jokes within the script at the expense of Rosa Parks and Jesse Jackson himself. This Clarence Thomas moment, wherein the black establishment tries to use the institutional tools of political correctness to keep fellow blacks on the plantation, had little effect. *The Barbershop* shined at the box office ($70 million) on its own merits, defiant of the boycott threats—perhaps a small sign that the PC era may be coming to an end.[25]

Title IX Gripers

We don't need any more menstrual cycle jokes. Period. At one point Sandra Bernhard was a shining star on the stand-up circuit, but a desire to mix it up—acting, cabaret, and sucking up to those more famous then her—sidetracked her from truly achieving greatness. Joan Rivers, no doubt, had her moment in the sun, not to mention the plastic surgery to repair the rays' damage. And Roseanne Barr was literally a giant before she hit it big with her eponymous sitcom.

However, for the most part, women have been a disaster on the comic stage, not tapping into the universal plight of humankind but focusing instead on the woes of womanhood alone. Yet in the 1990s that's what we got, in ultra-strength doses. Those comedians not filled with black pride tended to be of the angry feminist stripe, each one seemingly trying to make up for historical lost time. Rosie O'Donnell, Janeane Garofalo, Margaret Cho, and Elayne Boozler held court at the comedy tent at the Lilith Fair touring women's empowerment festival—each one telling a similar tale.

Ellen Degeneres, on the other hand, was, in essence, a female Jerry Seinfeld, a club-traveled veteran who just happened to be a woman, until the point when her closeted lesbianism became an issue and she and Anne Heche moved out of town declaring LA gay-unfriendly. That was funny, actually.[26]

Behind each routine, whether it be the back story of Degeneres, O'Donnell, and Cho's openly mixed-up sexuality or Garofalo and Boozler's barely containable antimale rage, lurked a strong sociopolitical message: We can hang with the boys, whether they like it or not. This comedy as feminism theme hit obnoxious heights with Eve Ensler's *The Vagina Monologues,* a one-woman show that has touched the funny bone of such PC vets as Jane Fonda, who waxes gynecological about the power derived from joking about her genitals.

"[*The Vagina Monologues* is] a brilliant piece of empowering theater," she confessed to fellow vagina possessor Barbara Walters in an explanation that sounded like an outtake from open-mic night at Wesleyan University.

"You can't talk about vaginas, and not talk about this remarkable ability that they have, to give birth. It is awesome. If penises could do what vaginas could do, they'd be on postage stamps. There would be a 12-foot one bronzed at the rotunda in Washington. I mean, vaginas are just absolutely extraordinary. It's the most important part of our lives, and no one can say the word. You can't say it. There are so many young girls, grow up only hearing 'down there,' talked about as nasty, and this, you know? So they think there's no problem giving it away, it's a nasty thing."[27] Howard Stern, for some reason, does not receive the same kind of rave media reviews over his *empowering* penis talk.

No matter how Ensler or her sisters try, feminism will never be funny, and as long as the hope of aspiring female comics is to prove something to men, or to demythologize historical patriarchal wrongs, the pinnacle of the female comedian will either be yammering on about what stars are wearing at the Oscars on E!, or like Whoopi Goldberg these days, sitting in the center square on "Hollywood Squares."

Melanie Graham, a former staff writer on "Saturday Night Live" and creative director of the L.A.-based comedy troupe Groundlings, says it's not the case that men are superior comic minds. "As long as women are forced into the role of lecturing school marms," she told *Hollywood, Interrupted*, "they will leave the crowd wishing these bitches would just go home and wash the dishes."[28]

One current exception to the rule, a thirty-something Jewess from New Hampshire named Sarah Silverman, ably uses her meek and attractive visage to throw the audience with an intentionally offensive, ethnic barrage. In July 2001, on NBC's "Late Night with Conan O'Brien," Silverman experienced the PC backlash from a joke she delivered. Silverman was telling O'Brien how she wanted to get out of serving on jury duty after getting a court notice.

The following exchange got her into hot water: "My friend is like, why don't you write something inappropriate on the form, like 'I hate chinks.'" Silverman continued that she didn't want anyone to think she was racist, so instead she explained: "I just filled out the form and I wrote 'I LOVE chinks'... and who doesn't?"[29]

Unfortunately for Silverman, Guy Aoki, president of the Media Action Network, a Chinese-American media watchdog group, saw the routine and complained to NBC, calling the bit "offensive" and "inappropriate." "I'm a fan of Conan's and Sarah Silverman's, but I was disappointed when she started using that word," Aoki told "E! Online." "They don't have to use slurs like that. They're distancing themselves from fans. They wouldn't do that with 'nigger,'" Aoki said.[30]

Aoki said "nigger!" Aoki said "nigger!" Call the sensitivity police, Aoki said "nigger!" If the selectively indignant Aoki is such a Sarah Silverman fan, he should have known her entire repertoire flies in the face of all PC conventions, and effectively uses the offensive as a means to render genuine racism less potent. In all likelihood, Silverman's many Holocaust jibes (when correcting her niece who adds an extra zero to the end of the number of Jews Hitler killed, Silverman informs the audience, "*60* million would be unforgivable") are not intended to traumatize her fellow members of the tribe.[31]

"If it were just 'chinks,' I would wonder, but . . . it's the fucking New McCarthyism!" fellow SNL alumnus Colin Quinn told the *New York Observer*. "There's no irony in anybody when it comes to these things!"[32]

For her sin, NBC, whose head of programming at the time happened to be Asian-American, issued an apology: "The joke on 'Late Night with Conan O'Brien' was clearly inappropriate and the fact that it was not edited by our Standards and Practices department was a mistake. We have reviewed our procedures to ensure such an incident does not reoccur, and we will edit the joke out of any future repeats of the show."[33]

Silverman, who has since defiantly taken her routine to edgier heights, points out how so-called civil rights groups can hold a major company like NBC economic hostage if they don't acquiesce to PC pressures: "The truth of the matter is, it's not a moral issue in terms of the network. They may put this façade on that it is, but it's about advertisers and the F.C.C. and pleasing them. It has nothing to do with morals; they are void of morals. It's all about money. It's all about money."[34]

Sacred Cow Meets Wascally Wabbit

The only reliable source of Anglo-American risk taking during the incorrectly politicized years has been cartoons created for adults. "The Simpsons" (Fox, 1989–present), "Beavis and Butthead" (MTV,

1992–1996), "King of the Hill" (Fox, 1997–present), and "South Park" (Comedy Central, 1997–present) have bucked the PC system and provided a rare sustained escape from the sensitivity training seminar that entertainment has become today. Bugs Bunny would be proud.

PC bureaucrats have had little success containing such cartoon mayhem since they witnessed the carnage when their brother in censorship, the Rev. Jerry Falwell, came out on the losing end of a battle with a purple Teletubbie.[35] As such, cartoons have been able to fly under the radar of the PC culture warriors, who realize how silly it looks to pick a fight with a cuddly children's toy, or a Shmoo, or even Scooby Doo.

Pacific Northwesterner white man Matt Groening's seminal contribution to the cause, "The Simpsons," transformed the American nuclear family experience into a window into our Chernobyl meltdown pop culture—and now is the longest-running animated show in network television history. Father Homer and son Bart are the stupid white men PC fearmonger Michael Moore warns his readers about, and a greedy white industrial titan (Mr. Burns), a Middle Eastern convenience store manager (Apu), and a Christian zealot (Ned Flanders) round out the cast. In the cartoon town of Springfield stereotypes abound, and no group is spared. Somehow we survive.

"Beavis and Butthead," created by Texan white man Mike Judge, showed that the best way to make truly outrageous statements is to put the words into the mouths of laughably drawn animated adolescents who don't know any better. Judge followed that phenomenon with "King of the Hill," a sentimental, yet honest look at Middle-American life—beer bellies, human prejudices, and all.

But white men Matt Stone and Trey Parker from Littleton, Colorado (yes, the home of Columbine High School), have gone waaaaaaay further with "South Park," a show, given the times, that should not be on the air. "South Park" flies in the face of the PC zeitgeist and mercilessly mocks the Hollywood and elite establishment for creating a world as mockably conformist and reactionary as the Eisenhower 1950s.

In one episode Cartman, the show's most un-PC representative, and that's saying something, throws a rock at a black kid named, appropriately, Tok(k)en, and is arrested on federal hate crimes charges:

Prosecution lawyer: "He is African-American, and so, you decided to pick him out!"

Cartman: "I did?!"

Prosecution lawyer: "The rage built and built inside your head until it became too much, because you hate African-Americans!"

Cartman: "No! I hate hippies!"

Prosecution lawyer: "What?!"

Cartman: "I hate hippies, when they're always talkin' 'bout protecting us and they're drivin' 'round on these cars that get poor gas mileage and wear those fuckin' braces! I hate 'em! I wanna kick 'em in the nuts!"

Judge: "I am making an example of you, to send a message out to people everywhere! That if you want to hurt another human being, you better make damned sure they're the same color as you are!"[36]

When *Hollywood, Interrupted* met up with Stone and Parker at their Marina Del Rey studio, there was no Pellegrino water offered to us and no tales of a recent soul-searching trip to a Third World country. Instead, the two irreverent satirists laid out a serious set of grievances against the self-satisfied Hollywood establishment. Apparently, Comedy Central doesn't do background checks.

Trey Parker (TP): *When we started out, we didn't know anything about political correctness. We were just two guys from Colorado, and it was because we didn't know any better that we did the kind of humor we did. We like being rebellious, and we like flying in the face of what people think we should say.*

Hollywood, Interrupted (HI): Much of the anti-PC material out there is in the form of cartoons created by those outside of the Hollywood elite.

Matt Stone (MS): *It takes someone like Matt Groening, who's from Washington, or Mike Judge, who grew up in Albuquerque. The really creative shit always comes from the middle of the country. People in Hollywood are surprised it's all a smash hit, but the shows represent the point of view of most of the country—just not here. Hollywood keeps coming out with these sitcoms with two gay Jewish guys in New York. Where we're from, no one's interested in that shit. That's been done to death, and it's just not funny.*

HI: How do you think Hollywood feels about its audience, the regular people in the country?

TP: *People in the middle of the country do not matter* AT ALL *to the entertainment people in LA and New York. People in the entertainment industry are by and large whore-chasing drug-addict fuck-ups, right? But they still believe they're better than the guy in Wyoming who really loves his wife and takes care of his kids and is a good, outstanding, wholesome person. Hollywood views regular people as children, and they think they're the smart ones who need to tell the idiots out there how to be.*

HI: PC Hollywood treats regular people like children, but also doesn't believe they can understand or appreciate smart jokes or irony.

MS: *We see that all the time. Early on in 'South Park,' we would have Cartman say, 'Shut up Kyle, you're a dirty Jew.' Cartman is a little racist, and he just heard that someplace. Kyle always tells him to fuck off. In the beginning we were told you can't do that because there would be a lot of people out there that would repeat it without irony. That somehow they'll think it's okay to say, 'You're a dirty Jew.' And we'd say, no they're smart in the middle of the country, they get it. In Hollywood, there's a whole feeling that they have to protect Middle America from itself. We can all laugh at Jew jokes and gay jokes, and I can make a black joke because I'm enlightened here in Hollywood, but don't put that on TV because when people in Nebraska hear it, they're going to yell the 'N word' at the next black person. Political correctness started from there, with the idea that the middle of the country can't handle sophisticated jokes. And that's why 'South Park' was a big hit up front, because it doesn't treat the viewer like a fucking retard.*

HI: Hollywood uses political correctness as a tool to save and heal the unenlightened masses.

MS: *And PC Hollywood feels the need to pass laws because the rest of us can't take care of ourselves. The smoking ban is a perfect example. It's bad to smoke, but that's irrelevant. If people want to do it to themselves, then that's fine. If you don't want to go in that bar with the smoke, don't go in that bar. Rob Reiner is like one of the most evil people on the earth. That guy's completely evil in his intentions if you look at the way he's passed the cigarette taxes, which are the most aggressive taxes in the world. Let's punish the poor people. He always sells it on the back of some children's program, which is fucking bullshit. He just hates smoke. Somebody blew smoke in his face one time, and he fucking hates it, and he has to start using his celebrity power. When Rob Reiner needs to take a break, he can go to some fucking spa in*

Arizona for five days, but your average Joe may only have his cigarette. He's probably got a fucking hard job that's shitty and thankless, and at the end of the day, he wants to hang out with his friends and have cigarettes. And Rob Reiner is saying, 'I hate that.' The guy probably hasn't been in a bar in 10 years, but he's telling everyone what to do. Whoopie or Billy Crystal or Rob Reiner, they talk about all that stuff, but they're the last people in the world who would want to be around any of the people they're trying to save. Do you think fucking big Rob Reiner wants to hang out with anybody regular?

HI: Political correctness has now infected comedy. 'Comedy Relief' tried to use comedy as a means to enlighten America and preach a cause, instead of simply making people laugh.

MS: *Comedy should be observational, but its job is not to preach to people or make some important statement. Usually our statement is 'Go fuck yourselves, all of you.' That's basically the end of every show, but people in Hollywood think it's amazing satire. People thought it so brave we did a show with Osama bin Laden and people watching CNN right after 9/11. It was six weeks after 9/11, and that's all we had been thinking about, and we're supposed to sit down and do a show about something. It has to be about 9/11, our thoughts and feelings about it have to come out. And everyone in Hollywood thought it so brave because they would never touch that. Why not? What's wrong with you?*

HI: 'South Park' has always been anti-Hollywood and anti-celebrity.

TP: *'South Park' was based on our hatred and loathing for Hollywood, that's what we were doing when we created it in college. We were in Colorado thinking, 'Fuck those celebrities, they are big douches and evil.' Having celebrities on the show was all about the deconstruction of celebrities. Take Winona Ryder. In the* South Park *movie we did a bit with her and some Ping-Pong balls. It had nothing to do with the real Winona Ryder. We've never met her and have no idea what kind of person she is. It was just the idea of her celebrity. Just ripping on her celebrity, not on her personally. People wonder why we rip on celebrities, when all around there are pages of shit glorifying celebrities like Winona Ryder. And celebrities view themselves as the fucking Mozarts of their time. Even fucking Ray Romano thinks he is an enlightened individual. These people all think they are enlightened artists and therefore speak for the country. But I haven't met one celebrity who wasn't a little bit fucked up. Actors and actresses are the worst, because they are just fucking monkeys. Half the people in this country can do what they do, but for some reason they think their opinion matters.*

HI: A number of celebrities who felt their opinion mattered to the country, like Martin Sheen, Sean Penn and Janeane Garofalo, were compelled to speak out against the Iraq war.

MS: *I honestly think that Janeane Garofalo went way overboard with her crusade. She's well-meaning and believes in what she's doing and she's not an evil person, but I think people watched her with the same macabre sense of wonder that they watched Michael Jackson. I think most people watched her with a bit of sadness and not hate, thinking, 'That poor girl, she really thinks she's doing the right thing.' But she's so out to fucking lunch. If she is writing jokes about the war, fine, that's what she's good at. But the idea of her instantly becoming a real analyst and politico, that is insane. You see a celebrity who has lived in a bubble too long. She is insane to think everyone is going to listen to her talk about the war. I watched Sean Penn on Larry King with my mouth open, wondering whether Penn really thought people were watching him talk about nuclear nonproliferation and listening with any bit of seriousness. Poor fucking guy. It happened with Alec Baldwin. He started talking shit, and no one wants to see him anymore even though he's a brilliant actor. He's fucked up his career. Again, some of it comes from a good place. There were a lot of celebrities who wanted to help after 9/11. They were affected like everyone else, and wanted to help out. But some felt the world's attention had turned away from them. Whenever anything big happens, celebrities have to get their noses in there because that's their job. They're the people on TV, so if there's a war, they've have to be a part of it somehow. But they cannot really be a part of it, so they have to protest it, because they have to be on TV.*

HI: Politically correct, liberal celebrities always act like they know what's right for the country, and always seem fearful of any conservative idea.

TP: *We are often asked to speak at anticensorship events, and it's always the Hollywood liberals because they think right-wing religious leaders like Falwell are trying to stop the show. And it's not true. We started making a cartoon in college, came out here, and people started throwing money at us. We did a kid in a wheelchair and people threw money at us. We've never been told to shut up, and we have only gotten richer the more insane it has become. The left wants to think that the right is out there trying to shut us up, but that pressure is completely nonexistent. The Clinton administration put much more pressure on Hollywood than Bush. The only time we hear about people being oppressed is from the political correctness–conscious left: 'Hey, you can't make a black joke like that. You can't make a gay joke like that!' Rob Reiner, wanting to make it so if there is any smoking in a movie, it's rated R. He actually submitted that to the MPAA. Jack Valenti shot it down, luckily, but that's insane. That's control from Rob Reiner.*

The Final Frontier

With these few exceptions, most comedians sit passively as PC pressures continue to sanitize the entertainment genre. But once upon a time, before PC sensitivities destroyed comedy's soul, brave minds like Lenny Bruce stood up against censorship efforts.

At the height of the conformist 1950s, social commentator and humorist Bruce took to kibitzing about taboo subject matters such as politics, sex, and organized religion. And like most trailblazers, he paid the price. "I am busted not for my obscenity but for my *attitudes*," Bruce said at his trial, which had all the elements of the modern courthouse spectacles exploited in today's cable news cycles.[37]

Although the conflict between Bruce and the law made for good front-page copy and controversial stage material (Bruce would often just read from his court transcripts on stage), the beleaguered social commentator came out on the losing end; he died of a morphine overdose soon thereafter, devastated, penniless, and broken. In a Pyrrhic victory for comedy, the ruling was overturned by an appeals court shortly thereafter and no such prosecution in the United States has been tried since.

Rodney Smolla, a First Amendment expert at the University of Richmond, describes Bruce's courtroom travails as "one of the important free speech lessons in our history—an example of what can go terribly wrong when we do not protect the words of the renegade heretic who dares to shock and disturb."[38]

Said David M. Skover, a law professor at Seattle University and the coauthor of *The Trials of Lenny Bruce, The Fall and Rise of an American Icon*, "It's really Lenny's legacy that he opened up the comedy club as the greatest free speech zone in America."[39]

Bruce's refusal to back down, and determination to fight for his right to vent uncensored on stage, provided comedians a Rosa Parks–

like figurehead and laid the path for the likes of comic geniuses Richard Pryor and George Carlin in the 1970s. "Lenny Bruce opened the doors for all the guys like me," Carlin attested. "He prefigured the free-speech movement and helped push the culture forward into the light of open and honest expression."[40]

So much for a movement toward open and honest expression. Today, political correctness is killing comedy and helps to Balkanize the races, sexes, religions, etc., in the name of some vague supposedly higher cause. The PC police are not in the comedy clubs to laugh and enjoy themselves, but to judge whether a comedian has crossed any relevant sociological lines. And if an act is deemed offensive, call NAACP, NOW, PETA, PTA, or any other group with an active emergency red phone looking to create a media mountain out of an off-color comic molehill.

PC-sanctioned comedy is simply a means for Hollywood to promote its twisted values, and the political correctness mission has altered the relationship between comic and audience. No longer does stand-up act as an artistic exhaust system for a culture run amok, a means by which people can vent and laugh constructively.

"I think the final frontier for comedy gets back to what it was back then—it's the truth," said Robert Weide, the director of *Lenny Bruce: Swear to Tell the Truth*, a 1999 documentary aired on HBO. "Telling the truth and keeping it funny. And I think Lenny was just telling the truth the way he saw it."[41]

Hopefully future generations of comic truth tellers will emerge, joining Dennis Miller, Sarah Silverman, and Norm McDonald, to name a few, unafraid to buck the status quo, and unafraid to stand up against the scourge of political correctness. Until that time arrives, however, maybe we can all just have a good laugh knowing we lived through an era in which the most manifestly troubled among us took it upon themselves to teach us how to become better and enlightened citizens.

LIES, MORE LIES, AND VIDEOTAPE

PART VI

B-list actors ply pans. Is that a documentary or
the real thing? Hollywood's own Jayson Blair.

14

Another Monday morning finds a handsome, young LA actor angling through a trail of dirty laundry toward the bathroom mirror. The honking of a chauffeur-driven black sedan outside his Hollywood rental knocks the sleep from his eyes and—overnight bag slung over his gym-defined shoulder—he's out the door. His buddy, an up-and-coming young movie director, greets him from the back seat. The driver knows the destination: Los Angeles International Airport, if you please.

At the LAX ticket counter, the Hollywood A-Team flash their frequent-flyer cards, and sweet talk the rep into first-class seat upgrades. Next stop? Any given city in America, where a star-struck hotel desk clerk is charmed into magically turning single rooms into deluxe suites for the boys. It's on.

Dinner reservations are made wherever the fattest steak can be found. Backslapping local good old boys deliver directions to the nearest strip joint, or casino—wherever the boys can hold court as the actor-director team, in town on a short stint, doing research for an upcoming movie to be shot in town. Fully in character, these boys with B-list credits are babe-magnets taking numbers—designing the evening's debauchery.

Morning comes quickly, and actor boy opens his eyes to a buxom beauty—sometimes more than one—wrangled willingly from a club just before last call. The ringing phone shatters any chance of a repeat performance. Director dude has him up and her out the door in 10 minutes. The studs don their Diesel jeans and accessorize with hints of gold—maybe a Rolex purchased with a residual check from long ago, maybe a gold chain over black T-shirt. Definitely leather jacket. It's show time.

But it's not the show you're expecting—and it's certainly not the show these B-boys were expecting, either, when they came to Hollywood. But it's all they've got—and they'll take it as long as they can.

Now Watch This

Approaching the revolving doors of Any City's convention center, these guys look and move like those money dudes from *Swingers*, or maybe a couple of strays from *Reservoir Dogs*. They're all business as they stride the hallway. As they adjust their headsets—careful not to muss the hair—they enter a great hall, abuzz with sticky hairspray and pent-up estrogen. The actor and the hot young director are about to take Middle America by storm. They just know it. They hear applause piping through their earpieces. They are superstars now, amped on adrenaline and caffeine, shouldering their way through the crowd to a curtained-off booth. Director eyes actor and beckons him to "Get on the box." The actor winks and steps up on a pallet. Director calls, "Now, pour the milk!"

Huh? Just what kind of a set is this?

The actor gathers a crowd by thrusting his hips and jacking his jock—then purrs into his amplified mouthpiece: *"Now, I'm gonna burn a little milk."*

Hungry housewives assemble at crotch level as the actor waves a frying pan in front of their glazed eyes; his Cheshire Cat–grinning partner mans a credit card machine. He zeroes in on a brown-eyed Betty carrying a bit too much weight on her spandexed thighs and hips.

"You ever get your bread bag a little too close too the toaster? Says 'Roman Meal' on the side of it?"

The Betty cracks up laughing with the rest of the entranced home show klatch, but she knows he's winking directly at her.

"I was in your kitchen last night. That's how I know that. I was making a sandwich. I hope you don't mind."

More laughter from the ladies.

"And I found these!"

He rabbit-out-of-the-hats a pair of rancid, bent, and scratched-up frying pans, and bangs them together—causing a concerned commotion amongst the crowd. Then he schools them.

"Now, this is Teflon. You scratch this, or overheat it, it's gonna flake into your food. You're gonna eat it. It's a poison. That's why restaurants can't use these."

Back to his glistening pan, through a gleaming smile.

"Now, our surface is ceramic titanium."

Once the buzzwords have sunk in, he fires up another one of his pans on an electric burner. Unfortunately, our handsome Hollywood hunk isn't making a movie, or even an infomercial. And he's not on the "Today" show or "Good Morning, America" touting his latest cookbook. Nope, he's demonstrating cookware at a trade show. Let's tune back in:

"Now, I'm gonna make you my gourmet, grilled cheese sandwich."

He slaps a chunk of bright orange cheddar into the pan, asking no one in particular:

"Now, when you make your grilled cheese at home, do you put butter on the bread?"

The crowd nods knowingly, enthusiastically.

"Why do you do that?"

A lady in the back yells, "Because it tastes good!"

"Absolutely. Tastes great. I love it. Any other reasons?"

Another lady shouts, "So it doesn't stick!"

"That's right. And that's why they call us the health pan."

He's rolling now, as he points to a sign posted in back of him—right above the "Not Teflon" banner and "Ceramic Titanium Reinforced"—that reads, "Approved by Weight Watching Groups."

"Weight Watchers endorses all of our cookware, because you cook in all of our of our cookware without any butter, oil, grease, fat, or nonstick sprays. Ever again!"

He pauses dramatically, surveying his bevy of buyers. He zeroes in on Betty again.

"Eating healthy? Low-fat? Low-cholesterol?"

Betty blushes, while he blithely tosses a breast of chicken and vegetables into a second pan on the burner. He smiles at Betty. She's blushing, but she's sold. Director guy is ready to process her credit card.

"Now, I'm gonna take a piece of bread. Now, watch this."

He puts the bread on top of the cheese in the pan, and starts moving it around.

"Can everybody see that? Look—it doesn't stick. Can you imagine the mess it's gonna make in your cast iron and your stainless steel?"

The crowd is absolutely mesmerized by his slight of hand magic in the pans.

"Now, you've got yourself a gourmet, Mel Tormé, grilled cheese sandwich."

He takes them back to school, over the nicely browned sandwich and delectable chicken plate, the scents of freshly cooked food stimulating their sales response.

"Now, what's the most expensive way to buy a set of cookware?"

Someone asks, "Piece by piece?"

"That's right. That's why the crazy *deal is on the box set. Now, in this set, you get your two-quart and your three-quart saucepan—sauces and gravies, rices and vegetables. And you've got your eight-quart Dutch oven—not your standard five- or six-quart. That's why it looks a little bigger and deeper."*

He finds the hottest chick in the crowd.

"Do you have anything that deep at home?"

She nods, smiling.

"I'm not talking emotionally, darling Feel it. It looks heavy, but it's not."

If they feel, they buy. He passes it to the hot chick. She's surprised by the lightness!

"Pass that around. Everyone gets a free feel at my booth. Tell your friends."
The crowd of hopeful homemakers is rolling with laughter now.

"Now, that's the set. Now, if you wanna get the set outside the home show, say, mail order? Lotta money. $599 just for the seven-piece set. Get the set today, and we're gonna do three things: Number 1—$200 comes off, and it's now $399. Second thing—which piece do you like? The chicken fryer with the long handle, or without?"

The hot chick points to the long handle; he gives it a lingering, suggestive stroke.

"I thought so."

Laughter all around. He takes them all in for the end of the ride.

"Get the set, and you have your choice of either piece . . ."

He drops the long-handled chicken fryer into the eight-quart pot with a loud "bang."

". . . FREE! Third thing I'm gonna do . . ."

He glides his hands over an array of frying pans.

"Get the set right now, and I'm throwing in all three for free."

Like a three-card monte shark, he deftly places the entire set together again in an orderly fashion. He points almost accusingly at Betty.

"You wanna do the set?"

Beet-red, and bursting out of her knickers, she nods enthusiastically. Credit cards appear, and actor-boy ushers the eager crowd to kid director at the money box for the all-important "close."

Oh, how the mighty have fallen.

Flash in the Pan

Not unlike the off-season Borscht Belt comics known as "tin men," who plied the aluminum siding scam in the 1950s and 1960s, the pan men are largely out-of-work actors, directors, comedians, and Hollywood writers—the fringe players who have sipped from too short a cup of success.

The charming young director Mars Callahan made a movie released in 2003 called *Poolhall Junkies*, featuring the indisputable talent of Christopher Walken, Chaz Palmentieri, and Rod Steiger in his last film role. The movie was released but quickly disappeared, failing to live up to its hype. Comic Paul Hughes brings his biting bits of aggressive comedy to open-mike nights around Hollywood, and even set up shop with his own regular showcase at the world famous Comedy Store on the Sunset Strip. Lawrence Crimlis has starred in plays, hung with stars like Leonardo DiCaprio, and is in postproduction on his own very personal film called *Creep*. Another pan slinger had a successful multiseason run as a star in a cable television cop series. All four of these cats relentlessly hang on to their dreams of stardom, but to finance such pricey delusion, they've collectively digressed to the lowest common denominator. Ironically, what they do to make ends meet is not so different from what the fat cats calling the shots in this town without mercy do: They are hucksters. They are carnies. They are the pan men.

The Hollywood pan men are looking for fast cash and cheap thrills selling inexpensive cookware at home shows, state fairs, and military bases throughout the United States and Canada—and they're coming to a town near you.

There's a million sales schemes originating in this city, but the cookware game is the perfect hustle suited for the out-of-work struggling Hollywood artist. Why wait tables, when a couple of grand net from a weekend home show is not uncommon?

What is unusual is the recruiting ground for potential pan men. These handsome hucksters aren't culled from the classified ads that scream "toner pros," or "closers wanted." And while the typical salesman winds down the day's grift at happy hour, the majority of cookware cowboys out of LA end their workday in poorly lit rooms with uncomfortable chairs and bad coffee. Many of these pan men (not necessarily those mentioned above) are wrangled from the local 12-step recovery network. Okay, we're talking Alcoholics Anonymous here.

While AA chapters throughout the world provide a strength to millions in need, the LA AA circuit has a long history of sleazy sales scams that originate in its cloistered halls—boiler-room "toner" sales operations representing the most heinous of rip-offs. One captain of that nefarious industry, known in AA circles as "Ferrari Joe" for the car he bought off bilking others, became an unsuccessful talent agent, and then put a bullet in his head several years ago. One of his sales managers—also recruited from the AA program—dosed himself with a shot of heroin strong enough to drop an elephant.

The theory here is that for an alcoholic or addict, to drink and/or use drugs is to die; to stay clean and sober, one must adhere to a set of 12-step principles stressing, above most else, "rigorous honesty." There's a clear conflict involved when you're duping small businesses into purchasing copy machine toner at a 600 percent mark-up. For one actor caught up in cookware, it was the "little lies" of cookware that drove him back to drink.

The base of operations and actual physical distributorship for the cookware is a San Fernando Valley company, fittingly located right in the heart of the multibillion-dollar pornography industry. Stressing that salesmen are independent "retailers," the owner confirmed that the previously listed personalities sold his product, and credited himself with writing the original pitch parroted at home shows, state fairs, and military bases across the country.

Tall, wiry Philadelphia-born Lawrence Crimlis moved to Los Angeles from New York City in 2000 to pursue his acting/writing career, but he was mostly seeking geographical cure from his hand-to-mouth, discontented partying lifestyle.

"I say it was about acting and writing, which is partly true," Crimlis muses. "But I think there was something greater motivating it." That something was a desire to get his act together on some level. A drunk-driving incident that should have landed him in jail was a sign that he needed help. At the urging of friends who had come to sobriety, Crimlis began attending an informal, men's 12-step meeting held daily at a restaurant in seaside Santa Monica.

"The guys there all had careers," says Crimlis. "They were fun guys, they were all loving life. They were exciting, and I thought, 'Here it is. These guys are really cool and they have what I want. I get it now. This is what I've been looking for. I went, and I loved it, and I got sober.'"

Soon his life improved. Along with his newfound sobriety, he quit smoking and joined a gym. "I was doing everything right, I was feeling really good," he explained, even though he'd just gotten fired from a waiter job. And his newfound salesmen friends from fellowship meetings were there to help on the employment front. They shared road stories of the hot women and fast money to be made hustling cookware, and in no time he signed on as a "prat," or apprentice, with a guy named Nick.

Together Nick and Lawrence drove to a 10-day state fair in San Jose, where—in a booth in front of a slogan-laden banner—Nick taught Crimlis the basics of the trade. "I went, he showed me how to set up, showed me what to do," explains the actor. "I set everything up and he basically got on a pallet that they used to ship the cookware, and he pitched. He sold cookware. And I was the guy who rang them up."

Though Crimlis didn't cotton to the subservient aspects of being a "prat," or "plebe," he was hooked into the cash possibilities. He was hurting for money and Nick was paying him $100 a day plus bonuses on the cookware he sold from the palette. On his second show in Phoenix, he walked with $2,500 after 18 days.

Financial prospects were brightening. Crimlis now knew that full-on salesman made $100 on a $400 cookware set, and he wanted a taste of that action. He jumped when comedian Paul Hughes called him up to the big leagues. "He liked me," explained Crimlis. "He saw that I could be good. He let Nick train me a little bit and then stole me, with the idea, 'Dude, do you want to do better shows? Do you want to make more money? Do you want to be treated like a rock star? This is where you come. You're lucky to be working with us.'" On a weekend show in Phoenix with Paul Hughes and two other salesmen, he saw sales of almost 80 sets of cookware and grosses of $8,000.

"They were cool," says Crimlis of his new partners in cookware. "They were fun, they were these cool guys." And the standard of road life was certainly better than slumming it at state fairs with Nick. "You know, it's always the best. They stay in these nice hotels, they go out and have these fat dinners. Strip joints, they talk to chicks, they get laid, they're partying and they have a blast." While Nick would "nickel and dime everything" on the road, these guys were staying in Marriott hotel suites and renting Cadillacs. They were cookware cowboys, rolling from Phoenix to Salt Lake City, and winging to Honolulu.

Out of the Frying Pan...

Problem was, Crimlis was sober and trying to live by the 12-step principles stressing honesty. The only catch is that the principles of Alcoholics Anonymous don't really fit with the pan man scheme.

Rigorous honesty is stressed in AA as a foundation of sobriety, and soon Crimlis learned that his pitch was inherently dishonest.

One night a fellow prat tipped him off that the "ceramic titanium" pots and pans he'd been banging were in fact coated with the chemical that makes up Teflon. Crimlis went to Paul Hughes, and Hughes brushed it off, urging Crimlis not to worry about it. "You're selling cookware. Don't get caught up in that," advised the senior salesman. But Crimlis was caught up in it; he felt that selling lies was contrary to what he had learned in recovery. At the first opportunity, he asked a senior salesman about the make-up of the pans he was shilling at $399 a set.

The salesman told him, "It's not Teflon. Don't worry about it," but when Crimlis pressed him further, the quintessential sales guru admitted, "Well, there's a little polytetrafluorene in there. Basically polytetrafluorene is Teflon. But no—it's ceramic, but there's just a little bit of Teflon in there—a flake, mixed in."

And here's where it got tricky for Crimlis. The claim that all the pan men made was the pan was not Teflon, and while they weren't lying, they weren't actually telling the truth, either. Besides, the banner they sling pans in front of in public clearly touts the cookware as "Not Teflon." Teflon is a registered trademark for the polytetra fluoroethylene made by DuPont. The substance coating the pan man product is polytetra fluoroethylene. According to a report from lab director Bruce Sauer at OCM Test Laboratories in Anaheim, the coating on the cookware "mirrors the chemical make-up of Teflon to a T."

Sauer points out that the pan man pitch is semantically correct. "I'm sure they could say it's not Teflon because they didn't get it from DuPont," but, "although not all TFE is Teflon, all Teflon is TFE, just as not all colas are Coca Cola, all Coca Colas are cola." And a major part of the pan man pitch is based on playing on America's fear of and bashing of DuPont's product. The lab director concludes: "If the sales ploy of those selling this frying pan is to claim that this nonstick surface does not contain Teflon, then they are misleading the consumers who purchase this item."

Explains Crimlis, "What we do is we talk about Teflon. And we're telling people we're selling it to how bad Teflon is—'It's poison. It's a carcinogen. It scratches—it flakes into your food. That's why restaurants can't use it.'" Crimlis was distraught when he realized that he was selling the same substance he was bashing in his pitch, and sought out others in recovery groups, hoping to find help in the fellowship. But since most of the people he knew in the fellowship were also pan men, instead of comfort he got a cold shoulder. He was told, "I don't want to know about it," or "Let it go."

The coating wordplay became especially difficult for Crimlis because, "All these people were in [recovery]—relying on principles of honesty and truth."

Then there was the cheese deal. In order to enhance the nonstick coating and impress the "dreck" (as pan men refer to the buying public), a sliver of sharp cheddar cheese would be wiped inside a pan on the burner during the demonstration. The hot pan would release some of the fat from the cheese, coating the pan and creating the crisp, browned bread for the grilled cheese sandwich. An egg would then be fried in the leftover grease, then magically rolled out of the pan—further wowing the rubes.

And the pans' coating and cheesy fibs weren't the only games being foisted on hopeful housewives; the "titanium" so lovingly described by the pan men turned out to be aluminum.

Crimlis's handsome face falls when he continues describing the slight of pan in which he participated. "Ultimately, we wanted to steer clear of aluminum, because people get afraid of aluminum. They think it causes Alzheimer's. And we make sure to point out that the handle is 'solid nickel steel, triple riveted.' So, when you say that, we're allowing them to believe that the whole pan is solid nickel steel, when, in fact, it's aluminum. And we say, 'It's not aluminum. It's an aluminum manganese alloy.'"

Crimlis is right, the pans are aluminum. According to testing done by Durkee Labs of Paramount, California, the pots and pans are solid aluminum alloy. The report states that the pans are "an aluminum grade called 3003, an alloy containing a trace amount of titanium resulting from the refining process—standard for all aluminum. It's not an added addition to the sample, just a trace residual amount always present in aluminum. One one-hundredth of a percent." And Chemistry Lab Supervisor Bob Lafferty concludes,

"There is nothing to say that it's titanium-enhanced or titanium-based material."

That negligible amount of titanium was the final straw for Crimlis. "We're saying that you're never cooking on aluminum, because the ceramic is baked on—so you're never really cooking on the aluminum itself. It's not ceramic, there's no baking on it—it's just a coating of Teflon. You're always cooking on aluminum. All these word games. It's insidious. You can rationalize all these points in your head, but the truth is, it's all a lie."

. . . Into the Fire

And that's not all there is to the pan man pitch. From the box, many pan men announce that Weight Watchers endorses their product. It does not. One pan man verbally advertises that Chef Emeril Lagasse of the Food Channel uses their product. He does not. Lagasse uses All Clad. And on, and on, and let's not forget—No Teflon!

Despite his success in sobriety, despite making thousands of dollars a month, Crimlis couldn't live with himself and the profitable prevarication. But he was hooked on the pan man life style; instead of quitting home shows, he quit sobriety. After all, it was not drinking that had got him hooked on falsehoods.

Crimlis rationalized his drinking as a way to rationalize his lying to would-be Martha Stewarts. "I felt betrayed by AA. I just felt like a liar. And once I removed myself from AA and once I started partying again, I rationalized it all. It was almost like—I don't have to worry about honesty any more, because I'm not in AA any more. I don't have to deal with it any more."

But the camaraderie of Alcoholics Anonymous brought Crimlis briefly back to meetings, and the lure of lucre kept him pitching pans. Then, on a trip to New Orleans with an independent film-director-cum-pan man, despite the strippers, despite the gambling, despite the naked babes in his bed, Crimlis was revolted.

"It's like, all that stuff that I perceived to be all that fun—I mean, it was to a certain extent, but it was really hollow and empty, and I almost got sick. It was sickening. Because of all the gambling and strippers and throwing money around and . . . and lying. It was all about the lies. All about the lies." And those lies went deep to the core of his identity as a salesman. Assuming that no self-respecting stripper would pander to a pan salesman, the director donned surgical scrubs and actually claimed to be a plastic surgeon so he could grope the gals.

And of course, there was the big Hollywood lie—"'We're writing a script, that's why we're here. We're doing research. We have a meeting with producers for this film—blah, blah, blah.' All lies. All lies." Crimlis groans. And then at the home shows he'd have to explain to the buyers, once their credit card had been charged with a sale, that it's better to hand-wash the pans. The dubious coating that he had just pitched as "dishwasher safe" and not "peeling, chipping, flaking, cracking, or sticking" can peel and flake with repeated machine washings. And metal utensils he used as another sales ploy should not be used on it, and that yes, there's a 25 year warrantee, only you have to pay to ship the defective product back to the manufacturer in order to get a replacement.

But like a junkie who just can't quit, Crimlis doesn't know how to get off the pseudo "ceramic titanium" spin. He's making thousands of dollars for only a few days work; he's able to pursue his acting and writing, having starred in a play during his nonstick sales career. And far from the celebrities-in-recovery circuit, the booze flows freely on the road.

"Consciously, I'm grateful that I made money and I can pay my bills. And my big thing is, I guess, writing a script." But he's still distraught over his financial and creative freedom coming with such a huge price. "At my core, when I get to the truth of what's going on, and I get past the rationalization and all that stuff—it feels like I'm being ripped apart. It feels like I'm being eaten alive right now. . . . In a microcosm, this cookware is representative of our society, of Hollywood. And you realize that, you realize that everybody is lying to a certain extent, and you want to be one of the few that's not."

He sighs, and sips his coffee, thinking of the acting gigs he wants, as opposed to fibs he throws to strippers about researching a nonexistent movie. "I want to be truthful . . . but—what am I gonna do instead? That's the dilemma. And it's that balance—'Just one more time. Lemme do it one more time.' And it sucks knowing the truth that in order for me to go back to where I want to go and who I want to be, I need to leave that. How do I leave that?"

Before you count the pan men as classic Hollywood road-kill, in a fitting postscript, these guys (including newly clean and sober Crimlis) have made the move to capitalize on their own insane downward spiral. Under the direction of fellow pan man Neill Barry, Crimlis, Hughes, and the TV star turned the camera on themselves and their sorry state of affairs. Ensemble, they are all participating in a film about a one-time television star reduced to selling cookware.[1]

15

When Is a Documentary Real?

doc·u·men·ta·ry: Presenting facts objectively without editorializing or inserting fictional matter, as in a book or film.

On the surface, the "groundbreaking" HBO channel appears as an antidote to the reality television dross. But when we look closer, we discover that the awards and plaudits heaped on the pay channel for its original programming come at the price of credibility.

It can be argued that Sheila Nevins, the doyenne of documentary programming at HBO for over two decades, is responsible for indirectly bringing reality programming to television. Yet she denies it. Nevins claims that she's "never done a reality show," going on to argue that "her documentary programming is pure.... We'd never put anyone where they're not supposed to be.... If you manufacture it you don't learn anything."[1]

Where, we ask, is the Nevins-branded purity in HBO's messy visit to a Nevada brothel, "Cathouse," aired as part of their documentary series, "America Undercover"? Most of the participants in this gratuitous sex-for-ratings quest were, in violation of documentary protocol, paid for their on-camera self-debasement. And we've discovered that an entire segment, "Two Brothers" (presented as fraternal kinfolk soliciting sex with a sex worker) was fabricated, top to bottom. The "brothers" depicted in "Cathouse" are not even remotely related. In fact, they are performer/producers in their own right—responsible for an underground video called *Brawlin' Broads* featuring topless, white trash females duking it out in a makeshift trailer park ring. And of course, these jokers also were paid for their participation. Not only that, but before HBO picked up on his story, Dennis Hofs, the owner of the cathouse in question (the Moonlight Bunny Ranch), had been unsuccessfully trying to sell his whorehouse story as "the 'Osbournes' of Sex" to other networks.

So, while we argue that sex has virtually destroyed Hollywood from top to bottom—via cheesy, pseudo-documentary programming like "Cathouse," their largely pornographic "Real Sex" series, and, of course, the blight of their otherwise stellar Sunday night lineup, "Sex and the City"—gratuitous sex is also soiling HBO.

Another area of concern regarding HBO's playing fast and loose with facts and peoples' feelings would have to be their mind-numbingly-boring "Project Greenlight" series—an ill-conceived project also broadcast as original "documentary" programming. Presented as a blow-by-blow video journal of what happens to contest-winning neophyte filmmakers in their quest to realize their projects to the screen, "Project Greenlight" has now successfully passed its sophomore season. Sex is not the lynchpin for attracting a viewership here; it's Hollywood's other favorite reality show pastime—*cruelty*.

The celebrity that is the notorious "American Idol" judge Simon Cowell admitted to the King of Cruelty Howard Stern that it was, in fact, "cruelty" that made the "Idol" show such a huge hit. "American Idiot" has since spawned countless imitators including the study in child abuse that is the similarly themed "daddy-make-me-a-star" Fox fiasco "American Juniors."[2] Cowell has only Sheila Nevins and the HBO cruelty camp to thank for pioneering that particular kink.

Herewith, we give you this exclusive report on the origins of HBO's Sunday night freak show, "Project Greenlight."

For Pete's Sake

In 1997, former production assistant Alex Keledjian found himself frustrated by the fact that movie stars on films he was laboring on "were making $20 million for some stupid movie that no one's gonna like anyway." He theorized, you "could take a million bucks and give it to 20 guys, and have the odds of making all that money and a lot more, while discovering new talent." The enterprising grunt pitched his idea to the newly formed television division of Miramax, and the plan for "Project Greenlight"—a purported "HBO Documentary Series"—was hatched.

With shiny Miramax money magnets Matt Damon and Ben Affleck attached to produce, and Damon's Harvard buddy Chris Moore on board to round out the troika, a nationwide screenwriting contest was launched online, drawing over 8,000 submissions into a web of electronic democracy. From there, the "Project Greenlight" online community narrowed the field down to 250 scripts, and then 30 from which the dream team selected 10 finalists. Then, the TV series commenced, depicting the finalists edging closer to the once-in-a-lifetime opportunity for one talented writer to make his movie courtesy of a $1 million budget put up by Miramax. The catch was that the final selection process and "making of" the movie was to be captured on videotape for what proved to be the immensely popular "Project Greenlight" series.

Keledjian's original premise for the show called for what he thought might be indicative of a lot of independent directors he knew: "Crazy, self-involved, self-indulgent, arrogant, sleeping with the actress, getting drunk, and showing up late." "Clearly," laughs the show creator, the contest winner, Pete Jones, "is not that guy." The Chicago-bred, rosy-cheeked Irish Catholic father of two is, as Keledjian describes him, "a sweet, even-keeled mensch."

So, where's the drama? To be sure, Jones's winning screenplay, *Stolen Summer*, and his resulting film about family and faith, featuring kids on a quest to change the world, has enough laughs, pathos, and heart-warmth to imbue the "Hallmark Hall of Fame." But the drama the cable TV moguls sought for their show had to be *created*—thus blurring the line between documentary television and ruthless "reality" programming.

The first order of "scripting" the "Project Greenlight" on-set soap opera was to surround first-time director Pete Jones with a relatively inexperienced crew—ensuring that the "bad guy" characters cast as producers would have plenty to bitch and moan about during production. On-set producers and a studio spy in the guise of a "development executive" would put the pressure on Pete. "Pressure that is unnecessary for a first-time director," reports *Stolen Summer* star Aidan Quinn in the movie's production notes.

According to his costar Kevin Pollak, Quinn wisely wrested contractual control of how he was portrayed in the series, but his costar, Bonnie Hunt, arrived on set off-guard. Her agency reps failed to warn her about the attendant TV show, but she went along with it after the Princess Machiavelli-in-charge-of-production, co-executive producer Liz Bronstein, allayed her concerns. "We're not going after the actors," Bronstein assured Hunt. "We're going after Pete." And sure enough, the majority of the 11-episode HBO series depicts Pete Jones as an ungrateful, at times petulant, bumbling doofus, who—for the sake of "dramatic arc"—seemed doomed for failure in the first 10 episodes.

Of course, by the series' triumphant finale, Pete Jones has made it to the Sundance Film Festival with his movie *Stolen Summer*. Though solid in a tear-jerky after-school special sort of way—were it not for the festival's financial partnership by way of sponsorship with HBO and Miramax, and the questionable "indie cred" of Damon and Affleck—the saccharine film had no business at Sundance. The ex-insurance salesman Jones admits he was an oddball in Park City. "I can't grow a goatee, I don't wear a beret, I can't be that edgy cynical guy—that's just not who I am," says the neophyte director. Nonetheless, the nonindustry festival crowds embraced Jones, and heartily enjoyed this post-9/11 comfort film.

One admiring audience member leaped up at the Q&A session with the director: "I just wanted to let you know that a lot of my friends at work have responded negatively about the making-of project, and one of my buddies just called me and said, 'Hey—did you see that dumb film?' And I go, 'Yeah—it was the best film I've seen at Sundance.'"

Plaudits were music to the puffy Pete Jones' ears, but no symphony of praise could deflect the damage done to his integrity by the makers of "Project Greenlight." At the festival screening he acknowledged to the audience that "[they've] seen the bad things on HBO," but hoped out loud that the "good things" would show up in his finished product. His advice for would-be filmmakers was: "I'd recommend not having a documentary crew following you around."

At Sundance, Jones seized the opportunity to mingle with other filmmakers, and learn that they all went through their share of trials trying to get their little movies made, but later, he shares his lingering resentment: "This period has been frustrating for me with all the press HBO is getting, because I've been so much wanting it to be about the movie, and, in my opinion, they edited that [the "Project Greenlight" series] for drama."

"Specifically," explains Jones, "there's a situation where Chris [Moore] and I kind of go at it, mainly Chris goes at it with me, saying that I sandbagged a shot. Then they cut to an interview with me sitting on a couch, saying 'Well, I wrote this script in my boxers at three in the morning.'" "Well," he continues, "the incident with Chris took place on May 17th, the interview took place on March 15th, and the question in the interview was, 'Where are you going to get your confidence as a director?'"

What Jones was trying to say in that wildly out of context–placed dialogue was "The only confidence I have is I wrote the script, so I know it. And, the way it's edited," explains Jones, "it looks as if I'm saying 'Chris, get out of my face. I wrote this script.' It's an answer to a question that has nothing to do with where they're showing it, and it took place two months before."

"I understand if Pete feels that that interview happened before the scene happened," says producer Moore, "and I don't actually know, but—if it did, then that's a little bit sketchy."

Another *Stolen Summer* star, actor-comedian Kevin Pollak, believes that the TV series was cast as "Shakespearean drama." He feels that the show was about "seventy percent bullshit," created in editing, and he too was the victim of a back room scissors assault. Lifted from a trademark Pollak comic monologue intended to "take down" every-one on the movie, was a snippet where he bags on costar Aidan Quinn's acting methodology. Quinn and Pollak agree that, in the show, it appears like a personal attack on Pollak's friend and colleague, Quinn.

Pollak views the whole "Project Greenlight" drama as a "classic conundrum," whereby the series ultimately promotes the movie—a product in which he has a financial stake. However, he also thinks the TV show embraces the tabloidish mentality of American audi-ences who "view movies as royalty," yet—when it comes to behind-the-scenes mythology—tune in for the negative stuff, especially if a good man is knocked down. No doubt, the "Greenlight" producers knew they'd get some vicious laughs showing Jones falling down a hill after he was already red-faced from the berating he swallowed for choosing a location beneath a rumbling railroad trestle. "It hap-pened," shrugs Moore, lamely defending his documentary approach and the skewed facts therein.

In Jones's movie chronicling the relationship between a young Catholic character named Pete (Adi Stein) and a cancer-stricken Jewish boy, Danny (Mike Weinberg), Pete informs Danny: "I'm Catholic." Danny asks: "What's that like?" Pete deadpans: "Noisier." That's great dialogue lifted from Jones's winning script, but louder than any over-head Chicago "El" train is the director's objection to a personal shot fired by the "Project Greenlight" producers.

In an on-set scenario dovetailing off the above-outlined con-tretemps between producer Chris Moore and Jones, Jones was filmed filming a young boy trying to catch a baseball. Moore berated the director for "stealing the shot," thereby holding up the production. To illustrate how Jones wasted time, producer Liz Bronstein chose a succession of cuts for her story only showing the kid dropping the ball, when, in fact, the boy caught the ball half the time. The boy was Jones's nephew. "Listen," he said to Bronstein later off-camera (of course), "If you're trying to illustrate my failures as a director, trust me, I've given you other shots to do it with." "So," he pleaded, "could you throw my nephew a bone and show them that he caught it, so he could show his friends that he's on HBO catching a ball?" He sighs, "And they didn't do it. And that, to me, that little scene right there, is a microcosm of what that show is about. To me, that encapsulates everything they've done."

When asked to explain why she chose to humiliate the kid on the ball field for the sake of the story, Bronstein (who has a bio-pic on Jaclyn Smith to her credit) snaps: "The scene was about the relationship between Pete and Chris, and the shot. It wasn't about showcasing whether or not a small kid can catch a ball. I understand if it was his nephew, or whatever, but these aren't Pete Jones's home movies."

In a Fall 2003 *Fade In* magazine[3] report on the second season of "Project Greenlight," writer Nelson Handel discovered that little has changed on the faux documentary series: "After [Project Greenlight] season one's participant lambasting, getting professionals to agree with season two was no easy task...." If anything, they have been more egregious. According to Handel, many of the keys scenes that set the tone and character of the principals were manipulated.

To place a classic Pete Jones quote from the "Project Greenlight" series squarely out of context, "I guess you're supposed to take it in the ass, and like it." Welcome to Hollywood, Pete.

Stealing the Faith

Stuart Blumberg, Yale class of 1991, would seem to lead a charmed life. His first screenplay, *Keeping the Faith*, the story of a priest and a rabbi who fall in love with the same woman, was directed by fellow Yalie and former New York roommate, actor Edward Norton, for which Blumberg was paid $650,000 against $1 million once it was produced. He has no less than six high-profile projects currently in development. He has cameo roles in both *Keeping the Faith* and Norton's last film, *Fight Club*—ironically as a used car salesman who provokes a passing priest with a water hose. He was even able to land the same TV agent as *American Beauty* screenwriter Alan Ball on little more than his Yale connections. In fact, it might seem that's all it really takes to make it in show business. But look closer.

After moving to Hollywood in early 1996, Blumberg approached college acquaintances Andrew Reich and Ted Cohen, successful writers and supervising producers for "Friends," asking to borrow one of their sample scripts to learn the craft. Reich and Cohen lent him an unproduced "Frasier" episode they had penned. But somehow, the same script mysteriously wound up on the desk of a television development executive, now sporting a single writer's credit on the title page—that of Stu Blumberg. Recognizing it as a writing sample he had read, the executive immediately notified the agents of both parties.

"If I was shocked at anything," recalls the TV executive, who is adamant that his name not appear here, "I was shocked at the stupidity. I mean, he knew the guys he was stealing from, didn't he?"

For the record, writers Reich and Cohen refuse to be interviewed, preferring that the matter be dropped. Their agent confirms the incident, but doesn't want her name mentioned ("I have kids," she shakily explains). And Blumberg's agent, Todd Kerner, formerly of Writers and Artists, maintains it was his client's original "Friends" spec script that initially caught his attention. But then how exactly did the purloined "Frasier" script wind up on a development exec's desk?

"I never thought I'd hear myself say this," Kerner claims, "but I have no comment on that."

Amazingly, this isn't the only brush with alleged "appropriation" that Blumberg's reputation has survived. Sometime after the writer had landed a staff writing job at the Fox Television sketch comedy show "Mad TV," a New York City-based sketch comedy duo—Eric Slovin and Leo Allen—submitted a packet of sketches to the show. Their sample package included their signature sketch, something called "Turkey Slapper" ("a silly, absurd sketch about deli meat"). When their manager followed up, he was informed that his clients had submitted an identical sketch to one Blumberg had already submitted for the show. "We didn't want 'Mad TV' to think that we were plagiarists," says Slovin guardedly. "But we didn't really worry about it, because everybody knew we created the bit."

Soon after, in early 1997, a blind item ran in the *Los Angeles Magazine* "L.A. Raw" column alleging that "Mad TV" was harboring an unnamed plagiarist. Rancor ensued among the show's writing staff, mainly because an innocent staff writer was taking the heat—inadvertently sharing the same initial by which the accused had been identified in print. Another writer took it upon himself to confront Blumberg, suggesting that he sign a letter admitting to the infraction and announcing his remorse.

"It was a moral twilight for him," states the writer, who again requests anonymity—because he feels that any additional publicity will only further Blumberg's career in a sinkhole like Hollywood. "There was the pretense of 'I'm so sorry and I feel bad,' but he seemed more concerned about his career. That's what made me blow up and made it personal. I asked him, 'Doesn't it drive you crazy that you're making money off your friends' labor and creativity?' Then he tried a different tack: 'I'm such a victim; my parents are getting divorced.' He tried to equate himself with someone going through some real problems. We all looked like shitheads. Couldn't he just resign?"

After what is described as a "mini-Mexican standoff" between Blumberg and "Mad TV"'s executive producers, Blumberg finally resigned from the show without admitting any wrongdoing. Disgraced, he disappeared from Hollywood circles for a year, only to return in 1998 with the completed script for *Keeping the Faith*. And, perhaps inevitably, rumors began to circulate just as quickly about the authenticity of that project as well.

In a phone interview, the then 30-year-old Blumberg contritely admits that he stole the Reich and Cohen script in an effort to get representation. "Yeah," he explains, somewhat prosaically, "With one of their writing samples, and my writing samples, I tried to pass it off to get an agent. I own up to it. It was a very big mistake, and I regret it completely. I'm really sorry that I did it. I mean, it's something that I've dealt with for a long time. I still deal with it, and I tried to make amends, and, you know, that's really all there is to it."

Blumberg could not recall whether Reich and Cohen had accepted his amends. Nor does he recall being confronted by his fellow writers on the "Mad TV" set, and denies stealing the "Turkey Slapper" sketch. "That was something I had developed before," he asserts haltingly. "I mean, I heard it was familiar, but that was something I had come up with before. It involved, I think, a chicken."

Then in the middle of the interview, unprovoked, he makes an odd request. "Actually, can we talk about the other thing really quick? The *Keeping the Faith* thing? I think you were going to touch on that, too?" When asked if there is any question as to the veracity of *Keeping the Faith*, his answer is forthright: "That's completely unfounded. I mean, I heard that someone claimed that I took the idea or something, but it's completely unfounded."

The wild card in all of this is Ed Norton, whose reputation in film circles is that of a fundamentally decent guy. And although movie stars falling prey to bad advisors is certainly nothing new, it was Norton who recut *American History X* when director Tony Kaye was removed from the project, it was Norton whom no one wanted to alienate when they cast his then-girlfriend Courtney Love in her post-*People vs. Larry Flynt* roles, and it was Norton who first came to prominence in *Primal Fear*—as a polite southern convict revealed by movie's end to be a ruthless sociopath. Although asked to comment specifically on the allegations, Norton, in a prepared statement, reiterates his long-standing relationship with the writer, and not much else.

"Stu's first draft of *Keeping the Faith* was one of the funniest most multilayered scripts I had read in a long while. . . . We have known each other for 12 years and worked together for probably 10. The thing that's great about our collaborations is that they are always very organic, and there has never been any pressure from either of us to work together. . . . But we know that we can always consult each other and get perspectives from someone whose taste we trust, which is invaluable."

And did you hear the one about the priest and the rabbi?[4]

AMERIKA ONLINE

PART VII

Where the stars go and what they do when they virtually get
there. From fringe players to big stars—sex online, all the
time. The media Berlin Wall falls. America talks back.

16

HOLLYWOOD CAN'T GET ONLINE

There are thousands of corporate Hollywood web sites clogging up bandwidth on the Internet, accomplishing very little in terms of enhancing the bottom line. No wowie-zowie online movie trailer or strategically placed advertorial can successfully sell a movie to a wired America jaded by Hollywood's tired marketing ploys. The almighty entertainment industry can't even protect their copyrighted, password protected, and encrypted product from being ripped off by teenagers armed with modems. So what is to prevent young Hollywood wannabes from infiltrating the lives of the actual players lurking behind online screen names? Not much.

We've discovered the real online action pervading between disparate characters trying to break into Hollywood with a high-speed or dial-up connection and the utterly debauched cyber-reality of the stars, the deal makers, and other various and sundry "creative types."

The result is not pretty.

In this ugly, Hollywood-infected electronic world, all lines of propriety are crossed via the wires of the Internet. Although it may be a cliché to refer to the ubiquitous casting couch of the twenty-first century, we can say and cite for certain that modern technology has paved the way for virtual foreplay and its real-life consequences.

Sex, Lies, and Gigabytes

America Online: The link-up of a global village? An electronic campfire for fact finding and the exchange of ideas? Hardly. Ultimately, AOL is pornography central and, via chat rooms, an ego-feeding ground for semianonymous Hollywood players who—at the end of the day of promoting their sexual prowess online—are all virtually alone. Welcome to Hollywood online, in the Hollywood Café chat room.

The few success stories notwithstanding, Café players and their cyber sycophants' online lives and offline reality got tangled into a cyber soap opera we'll fittingly title *As the World Scrolls*. Sure, those early Hollywood AOL chatterers may have included some of the people we read about in *Entertainment Weekly*, and they may have breast implants and cellular phones, but they're no better than their nerdy *Star Trek* geek counterparts. Actually, they are people who are so submerged in the spiritual decay that is Hollywood, where every day is an identity crisis, they decided to waste hours of time and energy within the confines of their computer. They decided to sign on, and turn off. Let's meet the players.

Meet "Anamorph," a successful young director who reflects on the Café as "completely the place to go to feel better about your sucky position in Hollywood." He chose to stay up all night—sometimes for eight hours at a sitting—on his computer, reaming producers with whom he had worked, and chatting up a bevy of eager film geeks and girls.

Meet "Badger97," a below-the-line movie industry transportation professional who took his laptop on the road with him, from location to location, arranging liaisons with chatty AOL ladies willing to put out in real time, offline. He claims he never enjoyed receiving "a ton of porn via e-mail," yet admittedly downloaded every prurient online interaction and dirty picture to his hard drive.

Meet "Pumpkin599," a thirty-something writer, who spent much of her online time gossiping with her girlfriends and trashing people. She thinks that the AOL chat experience was "a giant waste of time," yet she continued "talking" to people on AOL for years—people to whom she'd never give a moment's notice in real life.

At a Studio City watering hole, the players, having spoken online for over a couple of years, met face to face in a desperate attempt to make sense of their rapidly wasting lives on the wires of AOL. They talked cyber psychobabble and sexual deviancy, going through Hollywood Café history, scandal to scandal.

In that the Café was a rather remote destination online, it was a word-of-mouth promotion that brought people there. (That inherent exclusivity lent a cachet of legitimacy for working people in Hollywood, hence, a bit of danger, because, as Anamorph put it: "If you go in there and mouth off, there's a chance of getting caught. But then, if you do get caught, you can go 'Fuck you! What are you going to do to me, Mr. Spielberg?'")

Until word of mouth made its way to the Café, the chat room was populated by a precious few: "Cheuton," a journalist/screenwriter who actually got a movie deal with her writer husband, monikered "MKWord;" "Wendox," an online-addicted art director; and "RevaSplicer," an anonymous film editor who disappeared from the Café scene sometime after she took a gig on the box office disaster that was *Waterworld*.

That kilowatt klatch's Kaffe Kafka didn't last long. Enter Pumpkin599 and her friends, who unwittingly took the Café lowbrow with its first celebrity scandal. Having discovered that Christian Slater and his ex were in the process of breaking up online, Pumpkin would goad the couple by quoting from *Mobsters* and other awful Slater vehicles. So, the electronic sideshow of the Café became the fracturing of that fairy-taled couple, and pretty much the end of the Café as the place for the elite to meet. Instead, there were pathetic appearances by Johnny Depp's ex-wife, Lori Depp ("Addictina"). Ms. Depp was followed by her ilk of disgruntled ex-wives like Donya Fiorentino Fincher Oldman (a.k.a. "Myself5169")—a Hollywood photographer who has made a cottage career out of collecting celebrity surnames.

Who else?

Sandra Bullock, a.k.a. "SandyB," was rumored to lurk online, but she wasn't quite nailed down. Anamorph claims a certified Jamie Lee Curtis celebrity cyber sighting, describing her as "acerbic and fast"; legendary film scribe William Goldman lurked in the Café on occasion as "AlienMind," and Quentin Tarantino sent underlings online as "BandApart" to check his reputation in Hollywood.

Director Robert Rodriguez ("ChangoBeer") used up his 10 free hours online and vanished after catching the brunt of a *From Dusk 'Til Dawn* reaming that blazed through the wires until that picture found a suitable home in 99-cent grind houses.

Enter a new set of Café regulars (whose real names are withheld and online screen names altered), most of whom knew nothing about film and were mainly in search of celebrity fodder. Of course, there were indeed Café habitués with knowledge of cinema. For instance, a cat screen-named "Dole" showed promise as a movie buff, but quickly got caught up in online intrigue. In an attempt at playing Hollywood-style himself, Dole coaxed a Bay Area wretch screen-named "Missy-Brando" to jet into his hometown of Kansas City, only to decide that he didn't like the face on the girl he'd been cyber-sexing for months. He put her on a plane back to San Francisco the next day.

Too much time on their hands?

As unsettling as this online/offline nightmare sounds, it's the kind of thing that went on all the time in and around the Hollywood Café, and elsewhere online, because computer communication among the stars and starry-eyed breeds, well, miscommunication.

Which brings us to the question: Is America Online, behind their Chuck E. Cheesey promotions as a family online service, simply hiding a cash cow in online's favorite four-letter word, "chat"? Sifting through the embers of the Hollywood Café, it's pretty clear that chat leads to sex, scandal, miscommunication, and, certainly, addiction.

Anamorph says: "They [America Online] are certainly making an incredible amount of their income off people in there trying to get off. Yes." But for him the chat room was "more about tension than just plain old having cyber sex. The reality is that it's about the tension of the possibility." Yes—the tension of the possibility that you can indulge that tension through sexual innuendo online. Then you can go giddy over the possibilities likened to ordering a call girl with the inherent mystery of not knowing who or what is going to show up at your door once you take your flirtations offline, into your real world.

Pumpkin599 lamented: "I am a nice girl. I did not go on there for the sex dynamic...and in the end I do feel that's the prevalent dynamic. But that's what it is, it's a sexual playground."

Anamorph was less inclined to admit that online chat was a bad thing, as was Pumpkin599, who saw it as personally damaging. She declared: "The online chat experience should not be a constant in your life. It promotes delusional behavior and projection, neither of which can be good things."

But Badger97 feigned innocence: "I've never been a predator, and I think that everyone is on there for sex as much as it is that everyone in the Hollywood Café is trying to get a job in the film business."

Of course, in true Hollywood Café form, the round table dissolved into accusations. Pumpkin599 accused Badger97 of being a hypocrite who had indeed been sloughing sexual innuendo to women online; Anamorph told Pumpkin599 that her reason for being online was because she wasn't happy in her own life, while admitting to not being satisfied in his. The evening out ended in discord, but, of course, they all saw each other on the computer later.

It's no coincidence that, as the 1990s came to a close, the Hollywood Café was promoted by America Online as "the Hollywood Café: Tinseltown's Online Hot Spot." However, the Café was primarily populated by unhappily married movie industry men, sad single women, sexual deviants, and a lot of folks whose main concerns in life were their careers, and to get off sexually in presumed anonymity.

E-Girl

This is the story of how a Midwestern teenager named Heather Robinson learned the innermost workings of America Online, and became new best friends with the biggest stars and lowest life scum in the world. Though she supported all her claims with her America Online employment records, computer printouts, taped conversations, and additional sources, most of the cast of Hollywood characters she collected online will remain anonymous. For now...

Heather Robinson is still only in her mid-twenties, but she never thought she'd live this long. She claims she was recently rediagnosed with cancer, which had been in remission since she was 19.

She was searching for an identity in a generation that's supposed to be obsessed with the Internet, and she found herself increasingly anonymous, incapable of leaving even the tiniest mark on the world. Her parents were divorced; she had kind of a dark, damaged childhood and had been in trouble with the law—maybe she was trying to find herself, and this is how it happened. Or just the fact that it happened—she says it *did* happen, and figures that it is somebody else's job to make sense of what it all means.

Or maybe it was that she was among the first generation of frontline workers at America Online. According to Robinson, despite what they may tell you on their relentlessly cheery corporate web site, it can be used as an insidious surveillance mechanism by its employees. And as a foot soldier in the first wave of AOL's faltering global domination, working eight-hour shifts in the darkened cubicles of an office tower in Tucson, Arizona, for minimum wage, she says she was given the keys to the kingdom—access to internal security codes, partial financial and credit information, internal passwords, and most disturbingly, records of online traffic—for potentially all of their millions of customers. This means that for anyone in the AOL database—private citizens, political patrons, celebrities big and small—she could track them online, no matter how private or anonymous they believed their surroundings.

But however it happened, or whatever it all means, Robinson has spent roughly the last seven years involved in online confidential relationships with some of the biggest stars in Hollywood, the sports world, popular music, and politics. And she can prove it—she's got (and shared with *Hollywood, Interrupted*) everything saved, every e-mail and private letter, and notes on every phone call and private interaction.

From what Robinson can tell, celebrities are sitting ducks. Since an early age, all they've wanted was to achieve a level of recognition that matched their inflated sense of self or anointed sense of destiny (or, conversely, to make up for the very lack of it). And ever since they achieved that fame, power, and wealth—whatever their internal yardstick was calibrated to—they've had people to take care of all their needs. So what you have are mostly outgoing, Type A personalities, sitting up behind the locked gates of a mansion in the Bel-Air Estates or the Colony in Malibu, cut off from simple human contact by the price of fame, and bored out of their skulls because of it. People of questionable stability to begin with, who likely scuttled any moral framework in the service of ambition long ago, now made more paranoid by the embers of conscience and the unreasoning mania with which most people seem to pursue them, and without even the coping skills of anyone who has to cook their own food or pay their own bills. And then suddenly, down the pike comes this brand new technology which promises them unlimited access to strangers, guarantees to protect their identity, and offers them the one thing they can never ever have again—the chance to be a regular person.

However unlikely it may seem, Robinson claims (and turned over the paperwork to back it up) she has met online and begun correspondences with dozens of people whose celebrity names you already know. She says that she developed relationships with some in the real world. According to Robinson, a lot of them were just friendships, but a lot—with both the men and the women—were, frankly, sexual. She's often talked them through central dilemmas in their lives—ones she then would see veiled references to in the pages of magazines or on TV.

Robinson says she has provided celebrities with a sounding board in a way that virtually no one else could—because no matter how trusted or indebted the people around them were, these people would always know their true identities. In the same way that we are often tempted to open ourselves up to people we meet in foreign places or strangers in a bar or temporary lovers, Robinson claims, these public figures would often open up to her, because they met her at their most unguarded. And because no matter what they confessed to her, in their minds there was no way she could ever connect it back to their public selves.

I'll Be There for You

According to Robinson, a major female movie star and our E-Girl became good online friends for a time. Robinson met the star in a dog chat room where she knew she hung out. She had read that the star was interested in a golden retriever puppy, so she started out by saying that she was thinking of buying one, and soon they were chatting. In two months, they were IM (instant message) buddies, and then they would chat twice a day—about boy troubles, dating, typical woman stuff. The star was like a big sister to her. Then after eight months or so the star disconnected from AOL and that's the last she heard from her.

She worked through a pregnancy scare with a television starlet. She had cybersex with another small-screen siren in a lesbian chat room. She and a major comic actor had a little online fling—graduating from instant messages to phone chats—until his wife picked up the extension and got really mad and wanted to know who she was. He just said, "Gotta go," and hung up, and then called her back an hour later. Two weeks later, she heard he was getting a divorce.

She claims she talked to drug addict comic actor Chris Farley right before he died. He was high and wanted her to come see him. But she didn't want to. A week later she heard that he had died.

Robinson says she got to know a troubled television actor over a long period of time, which included his various drug dependencies and rehab stays. She first met him by mass-mailing everybody back when some celebrity forgot to blind copy his e-mail list, and then he started attacking her, only jokingly. Before long, she was calling him Joe Fox and he was calling her Kathleen Kelly, which were the character names in *You've Got Mail*. They spent a lot of time on the phone. Later she saw him through rehab, and once even smuggled in cigarettes to him at the celebrity entrance of the detox ward at Cedars Sinai Hospital.

And Robinson says it suddenly gave her the thing she'd never had before: She was popular. The most popular kids anywhere liked her. In her real life, she wasn't very pretty; she was overweight, and she resented the world around her. Everybody else had the things she wanted—things which it was somehow decided she would not be entitled to, before she was ever born. Then suddenly, with this fantastic new toy, Robinson says she was able to make herself into anyone she wanted to be. And there were things about her which celebrities were drawn to.

In this way—completely by accident, except that she worked very hard for a very long time to make it happen—in a country and century obsessed with fame, Robinson may have enjoyed a privileged intimacy with the famous that is unrivaled in the history of the media. She was an 18-year-old recent high school graduate from the Midwest, making pennies above minimum wage, who was in the right place at the right time, and who recognized the power of a brand new social force long before its official overseers and the so-called experts. And because she had the power to become what these people wanted her to be: She could be their new best friend.

The Pyramid and the Eye

Not for nothing did America Online adopt as its corporate logo what looks like a pyramid with an eye in the center of it—the same mysterious symbol that shows up on the back of the dollar bill and has hinted at 400 years of Masonic conspiracy at the heart of American government. If people only knew, this would seem innocent by comparison.

At 17, Robinson answered an ad in the newspaper for something called an MSR, or Member Service Representative at AOL. These are the low-level grunts that answer subscriber questions—as opposed to computer techs—and have greater access than other positions. Initially, she would reset passwords if customers forgot theirs, check authorizations, and handle billing. And very quickly she realized that everyone's information is available at the touch of a keystroke.

By the second of day of training, Robinson says she had basically figured out that this was potentially incredibly valuable information. "They even use celebrity names as examples of people to look up when they teach you the system," says Robinson.

Meanwhile, according to Robinson, AOL treated workers like they were idiots. As far as they were concerned, they were trained monkeys. That's probably why they were so lax about security. Because no one imagined employees could ever be enterprising enough to figure out the wormholes in the system. These workers were like telephone operators, but without even a union to protect them, so they were paid minimum wage. On the day shift, supervisors wandered the aisles, looking over shoulders to make sure workers weren't surfing porn sites or something. If they caught you doing something you weren't supposed to, you got one warning, and then they fired you on the spot.

But on the night shift, Robinson recounts, they didn't even bother to do that because the supervisors weren't making much more than the hands-on workers were. The corporate climate was a mixture of greed trickling from the top down, utter contempt for the clientele (except for the celebrities, who everybody thought were pretty cool), a sense of paranoia they tried to instill in the workforce, and ultimately, a pervasive apathy that rendered the other three toothless.

Robinson says her first celebrity call was from legendary comic actress Goldie Hawn. She needed her password reset. Hawn was really cool, and then they stayed in touch afterward. The star reminded her of her Mom—funny, a little ditzy. Maybe she would play her Mom in the movie version of Heather's life. (LOL. That means Laughing Out Loud.) From there she shifted into overdrive. She started filling steno notebooks full of screen names she copied down out of the AOL database.

Robinson then started buying *People* magazine and watching TV shows for the list of credits, and then looked them up at work. She worked the graveyard shift, so things were usually quiet after midnight, with no one looking over her shoulder. If she found a number for someone at a film studio or talent agency—Warner Bros., for instance, or the William Morris Agency perhaps—she would print out all the other phone numbers in sequence, and soon enough she had a working contact map for these companies. She went to the American Film Institute and Writers Guild of America web sites and compiled lists of officers and alumni.

Eventually, she had notebooks full of this stuff—about 4,000 names, more than she could ever use. Nobody around her had any idea what to do with this information—they'd have, say, Lisa Kudrow on their Buddy List, or somebody from Metallica, but that was about it. And the thing with celebrities and AOL is that they often get a free lifetime membership. AOL gives these away in gift baskets at the Golden Globe Awards and the like. So they had just about everybody that was anybody.

Robinson says she started by contacting a working screenwriter—because she wanted to test her skills out with someone who wasn't that important in case it backfired. So rather than a big producer or actor, she chose a writer. Because what's the worst that could happen? She told him she was an airline pilot for United, on layover. She had been in a chat room one time and a female pilot came in, and the guys went berserk over her. Plus she knew all about flying from her family and airbase experiences. She had a fake picture of herself that she circulated—a Midwestern girl, slightly older than her, pretty but not too pretty, with a nice smile. She pulled the image off the Internet.

It was like that movie *What Women Want*: As Robinson explains, she knew who these guys were and what they wanted, but they didn't know she knew. And so it seemed like she could read their fortunes—they were just astounded. It's very easy to figure out who people want you to be, even online, even when you've never met them before. And if you can become that person—well, these are people with finely honed imaginations; let's just say they would meet you more than halfway. From the summer of 1999 through the fall of 2001, she was carrying on sexually charged online romances with two prolific, middle-aged Hollywood producers, a septuagenarian Academy Award–winning screenwriter, and a young movie studio executive.

The Dark Side of Innocence

There was also a dark side to all this, and Robinson says it came to a boiling point on one of her trips out to Los Angeles. A lot of the guys she would meet online—midlevel studio executives and movie producers, especially—were only interested in one thing. At first, that was okay. She was 18 and they were often 45 or 50, and she really liked the power she had over them. When the communication turned sexual, it wasn't especially provocative for her, but she enjoyed the command she had of the relationship. It was a new feeling and ultimately fascinating.

One high-profile producer in particular was very graphic in what he wanted and expected of her. Whenever she would talk to him, it almost immediately became sexual, and then dominating, controlling. For example:

Subj: No subject
Date: 8/22/99 4:22:52 AM Pacific Daylight Time

From: [Producer]
To: HooterR [Heather Robinson's AOL screen name]

Heather,

I really do want more pictures of you. Is it possible? I want friendly ones, innocent ones, sexy ones, professional ones, bad hair ones, fat ones, skinny ones, naked ones, funny ones, sad ones and even posed ones. OK? And e-mail. Words with pictures. Poetry of the net. Send it. And I have a request. This one you'll have to think over. Will you be mine in LA? Absolutely and utterly mine? I'm clean and I don't believe in pain or humiliation. It will be fun. If not, you can make me stop with the magic words: "Stop . . . You are an old fart." Until then, no joke. Mine. At my command.

According to Robinson, this producer had explicit fantasies of breaking into Robinson's house, of finding and then raping her. She played along with these in instant message chats and over the phone. They were a game at first. He would send her huge bouquets of flowers or gift certificates from the Victoria's Secret catalogue. Once she even had him convinced she was in LA, and led him all over Bel-Air on a wild goose chase to meet her while he was on his car phone.

About a year after she finally moved to LA, Robinson says she agreed to meet him at a restaurant in Westwood. Her mother and her friends advised her not to go because he had been such a sleazebag online, but she let her curiosity get the best of her. When she saw him, Robinson recalls, he was 50, really small and scrawny—he looked like a male ballerina. She knew that he was expecting someone who was much prettier than her, and she thought that would probably be the end of it right there, but she wanted to see what would happen. When he arrived, though, it was exactly the opposite. He didn't care what she looked like. They talked for a while, and then he said, "Let's go for a ride."

He told her he was going to a friend's house for coffee. He had a black two-door Lexus, and almost as soon as she got in, she could sense that something wasn't right. His eyes had kind of glazed over, and his breathing got very shallow. In almost no time at all he had exposed himself and in short order pulled into a deserted parking lot at UCLA and stopped the car. He said, "Now we're going to make up for the time we've missed." She figured if worse came to worse, she'd let him masturbate and that would be the end of it. In a way, she had asked for it, teasing him online and everything.

But instead, he reached over her and flipped the seat back, and then he was on top of her. And she couldn't stop laughing. She was going to get raped now, maybe even murdered, because of this whole stupid plan of hers, and there was nothing she could do about it. He ripped open her blouse and she had on a red satin bra, and he said, "You wore this just for me?" She said, "I didn't wear this for you, you idiot."

Then he said, "You shouldn't have lied to me online." She said, "Can we go now?" and he said "No." Then he got back on top of her and pushed her head down really hard, and this time she could see he was starting to get mad. She could tell this time she was going to get hurt, so she kicked him as hard as she could and kept kicking until he opened the door and fell out of the car. Luckily, a UCLA campus cop drove by right then, and she ran out and tried to flag him down. He didn't see her, but the producer took that as his cue to get back in his car and drive away, and she walked back to her car. Robinson says she never talked to him again. But she still has the shirt he ripped open and ejaculated on.

A Cry for Help

And then there are the stories that Robinson can't really believe herself, and is reluctant to reveal. She doesn't want to hurt anyone. But then again, she says it happened. She corresponded with a Republican government official and a Democratic politico, both with pornographic screen names. The most amazing relationship Robinson had was with one of the biggest stars in the world. She met him in an "Ebony for Ivory Men" chat room, which means black women who want to meet white men. She only knew him by the screen name indicating a designer brand of denim wear.

This person had a serious shoe fetish, and he wanted to bid on a famous pair of Marilyn Monroe's white pumps at an auction and buy them for her. She kept declining, until finally the shoes arrived in a zip-lock plastic bag. Also in the package was a videotape of him. He is sitting facing the camera with a baseball cap obscuring most of his face. A hand-lettered sign in the back says "Hi Heather." He begins to masturbate, and just before he climaxes onto the shoes he turns the brim of the baseball cap around. At that point, you can very clearly make out his true identity.

Here is a sample of one of her online conversations with the movie star:

ILuvShoes:	Hey!
HooterR:	HEY!
ILuvShoes:	how are you, hon?
HooterR:	BOUT TIME YOU SAID HI TO ME! ;D
ILuvShoes:	where are u?
HooterR:	Innnn COLORADDDDOOOOO!!!! Been flying the LAX to DEN route. It's cold here.
HooterR:	You know what happens when it gets cold?
ILuvShoes:	what?
HooterR:	My nipples get hard! Then I need you to come warm them!
ILuvShoes:	when are u coming out here . . . it's warm here . . . You know I would love to warm your nipples.
	. . .
ILuvShoes:	so when are you here??? I want to buy you something You have been so good to me when I needed someone.
HooterR:	I am there ALLLL Of October!
ILuvShoes:	really? where are you staying?
HooterR:	In Beverly Hills Holiday Inn on 405.
ILuvShoes:	cool. oh that's ner brentwood. If u r lucky I might cum visit you.
HooterR:	did you call me this afternoon?
ILuvShoes:	. . . yes I tried you from my car phone . . . . Did you get my pictures?
HooterR:	. . . The pictures of the shoes? Yes I did. Uhm thanks.
ILuvShoes:	what makes you wet sweetheart? I want to watch you cum on my shoes I get at the auction. That is if I get the pair I want.

HooterR:	hmmm. well if you make a video for me of you doing it I just might ;-) xox
	. . .
ILuvShoes:	i want to take you flying. I want to make all of this a reality someday. do you understand that?
HooterR:	but how can AOL be a reality. For all I know you could be married with 12 kids.
ILuvShoes:	no way,11 kids :-)
ILuvShoes:	i meet women all the time. But your interests are the same as mine. You're smart, sexy I want you
HooterR.	ok, well
ILuvShoes:	answer the phone
HooterR:	ok.

Robinson claims that the movie star sent both the shoes and the tape to her in the hopes that she would get herself off with the shoes, climaxing on them, and send them back to him. She currently claims that she has both in a safe deposit box, yet—despite repeated queries—has not yet shown us the evidence.

That's just a small sampling of the people Robinson has met through doing this. She has shared with us incriminating printouts or electronic files of everything, because she compulsively saves things. She still has everyone's e-mail address, many of them still active, many of whom she is still in touch with.

In a fitting touch (and too clichéd for us to have made it up!) to E-Girl's story, she recently sold the movie rights to *The Perfect Man,* an original story based on Robinson's experience in creating an imaginary man for her mother. Little girl idol Hilary Duff is set to star in the film.

For better or worse, that's it.[1]

17

The Best Laid Plans of Microsoft and Geffen

You can imagine Hollywood meetings in the mid-1990s, the halcyon days of the Internet. Top entertainment players, from producers to talent agents late to the dot-com trough, summon *their people* into a boardroom to ask everyone from secretaries to story editors what they know about the Internet.

"Let's hire *the best* people from Silicon Valley to come down here and we'll put movies on the Internet!

"Let's create *interactive* chat rooms where stars can talk to *millions* of their fans!

"We'll *own* the Information Highway!

"Fran, call Bill Gates in Seattle. Tell him I need to talk to him *yesterday....*"

A sense of wonderment seized Hollywood over this new interactive medium that, on its interface, appeared perfect for promoting product and creating relationships with the people who devour it.

Silicon Valley geeks and pimply college graduates with basic HTML skills lunched with high-powered industry moguls who boasted of recreating the world by merging the powerful sectors of technology and entertainment—the ultimate synergy. This webalopolis was given a few names: "Siliwood" and "Hollyweb."[1] Empires were imagineered. Capital was raised. And in a few short years, it all went *poof.com.* Oops.

Icebox.com, which produced moderately humorous cartoons of the "Ren and Stimpy" stripe, was one of the vaguely amusing, yet seriously misguided web-based operations to come out of Hollywood. But with 106 employees and no logical means to generate income commensurate with their production and distribution desires, the nascent content provider closed doors in February 2001, having blown through $14.3 million in little more than a year.[2]

Then there was Pop.com, the bad dream work of Steven Spielberg, Jeffrey Katzenberg, and David Geffen, along with Ron Howard and his partner Brian Grazer, who got Microsoft billionaire Paul G. Allen to cough up $50 million to get the ball rolling.[3] Katzenberg envisioned "the capability not only to offer a variety of entertainment options, but to tap into an as yet undiscovered talent pool that is as global as the Internet itself."[4] With a dozen episodic programs and over 100 minifilms in the can featuring the likes of Spielberg, Noah Wyle, Matthew McConaughey, and Drew Barrymore, the site folded two weeks before its planned launch.[5]

Boys Gone Wild

However, it was the ballyhooed Digital Entertainment Network, a D.E.N. of decadence hatched by alleged boy molester Mark Collins-Rector, his dilettante partner in crime Chad Shackley, and a creepy 17-year-old former child star named Brock Pierce that made Hollywood the laughingstock of the dot-com fall.

Created ostensibly to make easily downloadable short films and serials, the Santa Monica–based D.E.N. became best known for its overpaid employees (executives making seven-figure salaries at an Internet start-up), its opulent Santa Monica workspace, its under-developed business plan, and, most notoriously, the precipitous fall of its three founders.

"For a start-up to succeed, you need to work your ass off," D.E.N.'s former online marketing director Afshin David Youssefyeh observed. "These Hollywood guys just don't want to get their hands dirty. It's against everything they're about."[6]

Among the atrocities Digital Entertainment Network attempted to put on your monitor were "Tales From the East Side," a "Beverly Hills 90210" set in the barrio, and "Chad's World," featuring the life and turbulent high school days and nights of a gay teenager—a show filmed often on location in Encino at Mark Collins-Rector and Chad Shackley's multimillion dollar love shack, otherwise known by local schoolboys as the "M & C Estate." In hindsight, the location for film-ing "Chad's World" was less about saving on production costs than incorporating Hollywood's infamous casting couch, er, bunk bed, into the online Hollywood milieu.

The freewheeling company's house of marked cards began to fall in 1999 when Collins-Rector's past came back to haunt him. He was at once sued for allegedly molesting a 13-year-old New Jersey boy who had worked for him during his days as founder and CEO of Concentric Networks, an Internet service provider. Then he went on the lam after three underage D.E.N. employees accused him of assault and rape as well.

Digital Entertainment Network's long awaited IPO, intended to replenish big-name investors like NBC and Microsoft, was uncere-moniously halted when cofounders Shackley and Pierce were also named in suits alleging assault, rape, and even making death threats.[7] The two were later arrested in Spain, allegedly on the run from their U.S.-based legal nightmares, held under the suspicion of possessing child pornography.[8]

Ironically, those who suffered the most as a result of the attempted Hollywoodification of the Internet were the below-the-line technicians and other grunts of the trade. Perhaps symbolically, however, many were saved from poverty when Hollywood's loss became the San Fernando Valley's gain. The booming online porn industry—one of the few entertainment-based business model successes on the Internet— ended up hiring many who had lost their jobs. Although not paid as much as they were over the hill in glitzy Hollywood, at least they could earn an honest buck and finally get their dignity back.[9]

U.S. versus Them

They're mad as hell, and *we're* not gonna take it any more! That's the clear and present message on the Internet of a real and increasingly frustrated America—and the world, for that matter—reacting to Hollywood's blind and unapologetic descent into lunacy two and a half decades after the release of *Network*. In Paddy Chayefsky's prescient Oscar-winning movie from 1976, Howard Beale, a vener- ated yet soon-to-be-deposed network anchor, starts unraveling on air while his bosses, envisioning a ratings boon, keep him on the air. Beale's madness is exploited to feed the media monster. Sound familiar, Viacom?

They (the Hollywood elite) are mad because they capitalize on human weakness rather than inspire us. They're mad because they take the audience for granted. They're mad because they set a terrible example in their public and private lives while telling the rest of us how to live ours. They're mad because they don't take responsibility for their increasingly erratic behavior. They're mad because, well, most admit they're mad—in $27.95 tell-all books. Their product is mad, their contempt for their public is mad, their lifestyles are mad, and you can be damn sure that their politics are mad. And on and on and on. . . .

And we (including "flyover country," as Hollywood snidely refers to its bread-and-butter target audience) are finally in a position to do something. Since the advent of the commercial Internet in the early 1990s through its dot-com boom and bust and into the digitized 2000s, hundreds of millions of flyover boys and girls have been given the means to broadcast to the rest of the planet. This is no small feat, and the effect on the formerly controlled media establishment has been revolutionary. And it's not all been to their liking.

In Hollywood, the capital of the media industrial complex, the Internet has served more as a massive migraine than the panacea they envisioned, which was to create a useful vehicle to promote product and develop further revenue streams. From breaking up bogus business practices via the antiseptic of sunlight to venting frustration on online posting boards to locating embarrassing arrest records of wayward stars, the Internet has become ground zero for America's revenge on the Hollywood beast.

Payback is bitchy. Power to the people didn't come through consciousness raising. It didn't happen as a result of a sit-in, Internet for Kampuchea, a riot, or any elected official, Al Gore's claims to the contrary notwithstanding. It happened as a result of technology. Pure and simple.

Saturday Box Office Numbers

Hollywood's Internet troubles began back in 1995 when the "Drudge Report" started posting Friday night's embargoed movie box office numbers on Saturday mornings. Ignoring cease and desist letters from studio brass, Matt Drudge gave the public a look into the raw data that were being used to spin a movie's bottom line.

In the olden days, way back in 1994, regular folks couldn't get a gander at the data until Monday when the numbers were published in the town's trade papers—two-day-old bread for those who actually gave a damn. "Only Matt Drudge tells [the box office numbers] to the plebeians on Saturday morning—at the same time as all the big shots are calling each other to whisper them," tuned-in LA politico Susan Estrich, whose ex-husband Marty Kaplan is a screenwriter, told *Slate* in 1997. "I used to go to parties on Saturday night where people would trade the numbers, like we traded exit polls."[10]

Drudge's numbers' peddling prompted the all-powerful movie industry into overdrive, trying frantically to stop this democratizing practice in its tracks. But that would have required figuring out where the CBS gift-shop-manager-turned-Internet-news-icon was getting the numbers in the first place. That would never happen.

Drudge has since grown tired of posting box office results. "It's the same silly people going to the same silly remakes every week," he told *Hollywood, Interrupted.* Drudge now admits that he got his hands on an internal William Morris Agency phone number that was made available exclusively for its stable of talent agents. Power to the people—populist anticorporate troublemaking courtesy of the Web's best-known radical in the tradition of Ben Franklin!

Now the insider trading of movie numbers is a chapter for the history books, although it's unlikely Drudge will get his due from faux-populist historians. Online mischief making has taken a tidal turn, and box office results can now be seen by anyone with an Internet hook-up at "Box Office Mojo" (http://www.boxofficemojo.com/daily/).

There, daily dollar estimates are posted along with the number of theaters the film is playing in, per theater averages, and the percentages (up or down)—comparing a film's daily take with prior day's numbers. These variables may seem esoteric, but they portend whether or not a film is going to sink or rise above the crowd. And with that type of data now out there for the taking, some unlikely entertainment muckrakers took to the Web to create new headaches for the media-industrial complex.

A Wireless Armageddon

Turn on your Palm Pilot, the party's over. The coveted teen demographic, which has long been crassly manipulated to buy like trained monkeys, are now turning the tables on their corporate masters. By instantly flashing spot reviews of films to friends ("*Gigli* sucked!")—via Clies, Treos, Blackberries, and Internet-capable cell phones—teens are creating a real-time word-of-mouth chain reaction that reaches critical mass when a consensus is made on Internet chat rooms and posting boards where in-the-know reporters troll for the latest ideas.

The *Los Angeles Times*, hardly considered an aggressive industry watchdog, every now and then hits a triple with its coverage of entertainment business trends. An August 17, 2003, article by Lorenza Muñoz, "High-Tech Word of Mouth Maims Movies in a Flash," is one such case.[11]

Muñoz points out that, according to box office tracking firm Nielsen EDI Inc., movies widely released in the summer of 2003 dropped off an average of 51 percent between their first weekend and their second. In 1998, that drop-off averaged only 40.1 percent. "In the old days, there used to be a term, 'buying your gross,'" Miramax chief operating officer Rick Sands said. "You could buy your gross for the weekend and overcome bad word of mouth, because it took time to filter out into the general audience. Those days are over. Today, there is no fooling the public."

The biggest victims of the unofficially T-Mobile–sponsored summer of 2003 were Ang Lee's *The Incredible Hulk* (69.7 percent drop from week 1 to 2), *Charlie's Angels: Full Throttle* (62.8 percent drop), and the abominable *Gigli* (81.9 percent drop). Not only are the kids all right, they've effectively learned to close a movie that deserved zero big screen time in the first place. On the other hand, as word got out, *Pirates of the Caribbean: The Curse of the Black Pearl* rose 17.3 percent from Friday to Saturday—a word-of-mouth triumph. "Make a good movie and you win," Oren Aviv, Disney's marketing chief said. "Make a crappy movie and you lose."

The joy of watching a piece of celluloid garbage crash and burn over the course of an opening weekend is a perk of the new media age, and a sign that movie studios can no longer manipulate the marketplace through hype alone. Apparently, we have pimply-faced, hardwired teens to thank.

Revenge of the Online Movie Nerds

Matt Drudge's homespun populism, in which he implored a frequent tipster to "Go online, young man," prompted an obese, red-headed college dropout named Harry Knowles to start "Ain't It Cool News" (http://www.aintitcool.com). Since 1996 Knowles has disseminated geek-friendly insider information previously corked by the formerly airtight entertainment monopoly. Although his site looks and often reads like something Charles Schultz would whip up in an acid trip frenzy, somehow it is must-read material for cinephiles in and out of the industry.

Among his major accomplishments, Knowles is credited for killing the box office prospects of the previously reliable franchise *Batman and Robin*, directed by Joel Schumacher, when he posted scathing prerelease pans from his network of spies of in 1997. "When the reviews of the early tests came in, people were writing about a screening where someone in the audience had stood up and screamed, 'Death to Schumacher!'" Knowles told *Index* magazine. "Then I found a review by a guy who said that he got so impassioned that he stood up and screamed during the screening."[12]

On the positive side of the ledger, "Ain't It Cool News" turned hostile prerelease *Titanic* buzz (as a result of reports of director James Cameron's on-set behavior and the film's storied budget woes) to ecstatic raves by posting prerelease reviews of the film from online spies who Knowles had tipped to see an early print of the film at a "secret" Minnesota test screening. Those early assessments ended up being picked up by mainstream publications, and, ultimately, "the Internet" was credited for turning the ship around. This is the *upside*, but it was nonetheless very much out of the hands of the Hollywood elite.

An intensely competitive online movie geek world has exploded since Knowles's pioneering venture. Likeminded, yet discernibly more industry-critical sites like "Film Threat" (http://www.filmthreat.com), "Movie City Geek" (http://www.moviecitygeek.com), and "Film Jerk" (http://www.filmjerk.com) took to muckraking Hollywood rather than slavishly adoring it.

This vibrant film dweeb universe is known almost as much for its internecine squabbles as it is for scooping the mainstream media. These battles, at their essence, serve as a necessary check-and-balance system, a self-policing meant to keep mainstream influence at bay as a means to maintain the purity of Internet truth seeking.

"Hollywood Bitch Slap"(http://www.hollywoodbitchslap.com) explains the motivation behind its puritanical movie-loving zeal: "Essentially, we got sick of being continually conned into paying to see the latest big Hollywood blockbuster franchise movies, believing the hype and coming out feeling thoroughly anally probed. We pay a heap for tickets, we pay way too much for popcorn and soda, and we expect we'll be rewarded at some point in the process with a quality film. Well, for too long these wishes have been ignored, so now we're fighting back. This is the place where Joe Public smacks the heck out of the studio execs that treat us like cattle."

At the center of many web site-on-web site battles is often Harry Knowles himself, who has been accused of whoring himself out for standard-issue industry perks usually thrown at mainstream journalists, plus some exorbitant gifts representative of his growing clout. "Hollywood Bitch Slap" took the king of online film scoops to task for becoming the very thing the Internet protected Knowles from becoming: a ward of the Hollywood publicity system. Sure, "Hollywood Bitch Slap" hits low when they compare his writing to a third grader's, but ultimately they offer a compelling list of goodies Knowles has received from the Hollywood publicity machine and call his integrity into question:

- All-expenses trip to New York for premiere of *Godzilla* at Madison Square Garden.
- Paid trip to LA for the premiere of *Detroit Rock City*, where KISS performed.
- Paid trip to the premiere of *Green Mile*.
- The bit part given to Harry in *The Faculty*—did I forget to mention that Harry's friends were given jobs as extras? And that the premiere was held in Harry's hometown of Austin? And that everyone involved was invited to attend?
- Dreamworks provided an exclusive, advanced screening of *Gladiator* for Harry in San Francisco. An *exclusive* screening, mind you. Even Roger Ebert watches the flicks he reviews with other journalists in attendance, but Harry gets an all-expenses-paid trip and a private screening.
- A set tour of *Armageddon* in Houston and a paid trip to the premiere in Florida. Harry later stated in his review that he wept at the film's conclusion. Good grief.
- Paid trip for one of Harry's writers to Los Angeles, to the set of *Mystery Men*.
- Paid trip to London to set of *The Mummy.* London!
- Tours of many film sets, including *How the Grinch Stole Christmas*, *Monkey Bone*, *Fail Safe*, and the list goes on.[13]

Knowles admitted to "Bitch Slap" that he took perks, but claims they do not affect his editorial point of view.[14] Nevertheless, such a damning laundry list, primarily meant to inflict damage on an online competitor whose laudatory reviews of said films comes into direct focus, more significantly exposes major film studios and their supposed artists as desperate to put the online genie back in the bottle. But on the Internet that's not possible, for now even the watchdogs have watchdogs, and one false move can result in a bitch-slap.

No Rules on the Internet

Countless single-voiced opinion-driven publications, some self-described as "blogs"—shorthand for web logs—and others called "e-zines," populate the Internet, creating an alternative viewpoint tapestry opposite the corporate journalism monochrome. While some citizens, sickened by the mainstream media monopoly, opt solely for these low-to-no budget publications that celebrate exuberant individualism—warts and all—an increasing mass of Information Age connoisseurs mix and match, a hopeful trend toward the emergence of a more engaged public.

One of many voices that rise above the static and that would otherwise go unnoticed, or worse be censored, but for the miracle of self-publishing is believer Jeff Rassoul, a Michigan-based writer who offers a running analysis of "Amerikan kulture" at the "J Man Times" (http://hometown.aol.com/thejman99). Rassoul serves up a heaping of literate judgment from an unwavering evangelical Christian, yet Republican-loathing standpoint that reads more like punk rock maverick Johnny Rotten than false prophets Jim and Tammy Faye Bakker.

The "J Man Times'" must-read movie review capsules and longer essays equally dole out a heaping of blame for our sad state of "kultural" affairs not only to the producers of Hollywood dreck but also to its hapless "konsumers." Rassoul offers well-thought-out contrarian thinking such as a brilliant "Fargo—Hate Film" essay that lays out a case for why the critically lauded Coen brothers' flick is "technically brilliant" yet "racist."

"To underscore their point that this film is about white culture, the filmmakers have set *Fargo* in the dead of winter in North Dakota and Minnesota," Rassoul dares to notice. "Winter's white is nearly the only color used expressively. The film opens with a scene of a blinding white snowstorm. White is seen as a malevolent force, blanketing and suffocating everything."

The J Man continues his tirade against the heretofore untouchable, critically lauded Coen tandem in his review of *The Big Lebowski*: "What could have been a mildly entertaining farce about zen and the art of bowling is ruined by the filmmakers' racist and anti-Christ beliefs. The filmmakers' hatred of Whites is a carryover from previous efforts (most notably *Fargo*). There's a kind of inverted Aryanism to the filmmakers' racial beliefs (note the *conversion* of John Goodman's Slav character) that is pitiable in the way one pities the hatred of an abused child. What is not pitiable is the filmmakers' vicious slander of the Lord Jesus Christ—no need to repeat here the filmmakers' foul mockery, but only to pray their blindness be taken away."

Pauline Kael or Roger Ebert he is not. Hallelujah!

"The great failure of the media in regard to film criticism is the reluctance of the mainstream movie reviewer to expand analysis beyond the story on the silver screen to the culture that spawned it," the J Man opined from his Ann Arbor media complex. "If one were to transport the contemporary critic in a time machine to 1934, *Triumph of the Will* would be hailed as the 'Feel Good Movie of the Summer.' Being on the Internet, with no ads to sell, no sponsors to please, I feel no hesitation in interpreting Hollywood. Movies are the Amerikan sign of the times, and the corporate media critics refuse to read them."

That media wants to make everyone feel good, or politically correct touchy-feely tingly, because they want to sell as many papers and television advertising minutes as possible. The Internet provides the opportunity for someone like the J Man with a less popular view to get the word out. "I'm a sinner," Rassoul told *Hollywood, Interrupted*. "I'm just as guilty as the specimens in my essays."[15]

Rassoul's religious purism and rejection of American consumerism, er, konsumerism, guarantees he will not get the Harry Knowles treatment from Hollywood's publicity machine. But his defiant and articulate voice will surely draw other unique voices into the opinion-making mix, and hopefully help to make Hollywood auteurs and bean counters accountable to something other than the lowest common denominator.

Smoked Celebrity with Papaya-Apple Chutney

The Smoking Gun web site (http://www.thesmokinggun.com) does something so simple yet so well that it has become an indispensable tool for watchers of the celebrity apocalypse. Started by former *Village Voice* crime beat reporter William Bastone, The Smoking Gun unearths and posts mostly embarrassing documents such as divorce papers, arrest records, mug shots, and out-of-print magazine articles whose contents come back to haunt the stars.

The Smoking Gun's exposure of the excessive backstage requirements of top musical acts got a lot of deserved play on the Internet. Christina Aguilera demands a police escort because she just can't bother to "encounter any delays due to traffic."[16] Faux-punkers Limp Bizkit require "(4) dimmable lamps—Very Important—MUST BE DIMMABLE!!!"[17] And the artist formerly known as Prince demands that "all items in dressing room must be covered by clear plastic wrap until uncovered by main artist. This is ABSOLUTELY NECESSARY."[18]

Much of The Smoking Gun's smoking guns, however, are genuinely damning—like the posting of unsealed grand jury testimony from 13-year-old Samantha Gainey, whose allegations of sexual abuse at the hands of 43-year-old Roman Polanski spurred the director to flee the United States for Europe in 1977. The transcripts of Gainey's accounts—released as the Academy feted the AWOL pedophile-cum-director for *The Pianist* in 2002—recount Polanski's allegedly methodical attempts to manipulate the child, from claiming to be taking nude photographs of her for French *Vogue*, to feeding her a Quaalude and champagne, to directing her to take off her underwear and to get into a Jacuzzi, and, ultimately, to anally raping her on a bed in Jack Nicholson's house.[19]

Lest anyone think for a moment Hollywood punished Polanski for his misdeeds, including not facing the music for his evil behavior, the unrepentant Polish-born director soon thereafter released *Tess*, starring Nastassja Kinski, who Polanski started dating when she was only 15 after he fled America. "Normal love isn't interesting," the tiny, unrepentent alleged rapist telegraphed while on the lam from his American accusers, "I assure you that it's incredibly boring."[20]

Of course, if the offline media were doing their job, the site would mostly be a repository for "old news," offering hard copy backing up hardnosed mainstream journalism. But since that Utopia doesn't exist, Bastone and company continually break news that has their alleged superiors perpetually playing media catch-up. And, again, there's nothing Hollywood publicists can do to stem the tide.

Celebrity Nudes

Perhaps the most poetic rejection of a Hollywood convention—rampant cinematic nudity portrayed as art—is the proliferation of porn sites offering celebrity nudes grabbed as screen shots from VHS cassettes and DVDs in which mostly young actresses exposed their breasts, and often more.

These sites are everywhere. Along with unsolicited generic Viagra ads and penile extension devices, celebrity nude web sites are among the most heavily spammed to unsuspecting e-mail boxes. Try a Google search for "celebrity nudes" and thousands of titles pop up. That's *titles*.

The reason for their popularity—you've got to hand it to these web entrepreneurs—has nothing to do with America's love for high art. Almost every serious film actress in the last 30 years has at one point been reduced to taking her top off in a film. Picture Coco in *Fame* undressing for a photographer who lured her into his apartment. As Coco cries, she ultimately acquiesces—as if she is resigned to the act as part of a woman's ritual indoctrination into celebrity.

Yet when a serious actress is asked about undressing on screen, she invariably claims "the role required it," and often adds for good measure that the scene was "done artistically." Talent agent Lin Milano, mother of oft-nude former child actress Alyssa Milano, started CyberTrackers in 1998 to help stop the proliferation of celebrity nudes on the Internet. Milano started tossing legal letters to offending sites as well as those that simply linked to them.

"We want the Net to be a place where celebrities can hang their images and be safe," Mama Milano told *USA Today*. "Hopefully we'll be able to set some standards."[21] Perhaps her daughter wouldn't be in the quandary she's in if a different set of standards were impressed on her growing up—like don't take your clothes off in the name of art if you don't want it to be used for prurient reasons somewhere down the road.

The celebrity nude web site phenomenon is an unintentionally populist statement—one that can set you back $39.95 a month at Uncle Scoopy's Fun House (http://www.scoopy.net), which bills itself as "the daily celebrity nudity e-zine" and boasts of possessing 290,000 images. That's a lot of "art"!

At a philosophical level the reduction of mainstream Hollywood fare down to its bare goods—frames captured of gratuitous boob shots—exposes the sad truth that a large portion of the entertainment crop is glorified soft porn. In the pursuit of "art" today's celebrity class has created a legacy of soft porn that through computer-enabled historical preservation will tell something significant about our age.

Dysentery Is Patriotic

During the Iraq war preamble, antiwar celebrities, who for the first time in the modern age started *hearing* negative feedback from the general population, started to complain that their *right* to dissent was being quashed. Among the brooding nonconformists with exquisite gourmet kitchens in their idyllic retreats, the Usual Suspects: Robert Redford, Susan and Tim, Janeane, and Sheen the president.

Snooty Hollywood even found a country act they could line dance to, The Dixie Chicks, for spewing venom overseas about George W. Bush. "Just so you know, we're ashamed the president of the United States is from Texas," Natalie Maines told a London crowd on the brink of war.[22] Country stations across the land started boycotts and web sites began popping up, mostly pillorying the Texas-based trio.

In the past, something like this might be buried in yesterday's newspapers, featuring a sufficient amount of PR damage control to avert full-fledged blowback. But the Internet has changed that dynamic for the long term.

"Free Republic" (http:www.freerepublic.com), a libertarian/conservative news forum, featured dozens of threads showing thousands of registered users blasting the "Vichy Chicks," and was ultimately blamed for orchestrating the backlash on Sony Music in an e-mail sent out to country stations. "Your company is being targeted by a radical right-wing online forum," the e-mail read. "You are being 'Freeped,' which is the code word for an organized e-mail/telephone effort attempting to solicit a desired response."[20]

The Freepers, as they call themselves, were not alone, but they did have the power to create a virtual critical mass, and soon the Dixie Chicks own web site had to shut down its public forum because the abuse became too much. (Alec Baldwin, too, was forced to shut down his user forum under similar circumstances.) Many top country radio stations spurred into action by the web site and other web-based grass roots activism either banned the top selling act from radio playlists, or had Dixie Chicks CD-crushing promotional events in their parking lots.

Similar virulently anticelebrity politics sites, mostly all of the anti-leftist bent, started popping up all over the place. "Hollywood Halfwits" (http://www.hollywoodhalfwits.com) offers the mission statement: "Exposing Ignorant, Insane and Anti-American Celebrities in Entertainment, Media and Politics." The "Boycott Hollywood" posting board (http://www.boycott-hollywood.net/) declares, "You do not speak for me." And based upon unscientific on-site polling, "Famous Idiot" (http://www.famousidiot.com), "the art of confusing fame with wisdom," offers lists of the most boycotted actors (1. Janeane Garofalo, 2. Susan Sarandon, 3. George Clooney, 4. Michael Moore) and artists (1. Dixie Chicks, 2. Barbra Streisand, 3. Eddie Vedder, 4. Madonna Ciccone).

True, celebrity bashing has become a tired trend, but no more so than the continuous stream of stars spouting one-sided vitriol that, by association, mocks the beliefs of their fandom, who, until the Internet, had no means to respond.

Poster "Scout Finch" at Lucianne Goldberg's lively news and politics posting board (http://www.lucianne.com) commented on Johnny Depp's comparison of America to a "dumb puppy" and a "broken toy" to Germany's *Stern* magazine in September 2003.

"You know, I gotta laugh when these Hollywood celebrities suck up to Eurotrash by trash-talking our President on foreign shores. When are these idiots going to realize that their words always come back to bite them in the butt as word gets 'round via the Internet? Then it's all about 'backpedal' and 'spin-control.'"

The next day, after a round of Internet-to-talk-radio-to-cable-news quote recycling, Depp backflipped and his publicists spun out of control. "There was no anti-American sentiment," Depp stated, whining about his comments being taken "radically out of context."[24]

"What I was saying was that, compared to Europe, America is a very young country and we are still growing as a nation. My deepest apologies to those who were offended, affected, or hurt by this insanely twisted deformation of my words and intent." *Stern* stood by its story.

Scout Finch over at Lucianne.com ended her post with a clever Homer Simpson rejoinder: "Actors. Is there anything they DON'T know?"

Even more obnoxious, the celebrity response to dissent of their dissent became the catch phrase, "Dissent is Patriotic." Skywriters took to the colonic wind over Hollywood, farting out similar omens: "Beware the New Censorship!" Soon, "the new McCarthyism," was the talking point echoed by dyspeptic celebrities on prime talk radio and cable news air space. The irony of the supposed dissent crackdown being broadcast to millions every night never sunk in—with them, at least.

Robert J. Thompson, a professor of media and popular culture at Syracuse University, says the expansion of the media world via cable television, talk radio, and the Internet is the driving force behind the heightened debate. "There's plenty of time to have a long, drawn-out discussion about whether Sean Penn should have visited Baghdad or Janeane Garofalo should keep her mouth shut," he told *The New York Times*. "The reason this gets talked about so much is that there are so many more places to talk about it."[25]

But these histrionics are not new, nor are they relegated to politics alone. Celebrities, with their highly tuned egos, demand not only the right to express their opinions and their art, but they also demand the right to be affirmed. What they have come to expect is glowing praise for their slightest achievements—artistic, philanthropic, and, if you've read much of this kind of tripe—even for taking out their garbage.

Stars—They're Just Like Us!

What annoys celebrities is the fact that the Internet feeds talk radio, and that one-two punch matches in intensity what was once the sole domain of actors and other entertainers who had carte blanche to use the public airwaves to get their points across. Celebrities are not upset that their dissent is being quashed. They are upset that yours isn't. The people have finally taken on the people who have long claimed to speak for them. Celebrity egalitarianism and populism have been exposed as a patently fraudulent stunt.

The failure of Hollywood to harness the Internet and to transform it into an extension of its vast entertainment empire was the first sign that the times are a changin'. Conversely, the freedoms found on the Internet have provided countless ways for an unorganized network of independent-minded reporters, filmmakers, self-styled critics, teenagers, housewives, and sundry entrepreneurs to challenge the old Hollywood order.

And the current crop of celebrities and clueless executives is just the first to feel the pain. Given their ability to distort reality, their outlandish salaries, and their access to Dr. Feelgoods ready to prescribe them pain medication, *Hollywood, Interrupted* thinks they'll survive. Just barely.

EPILOGUE

MarkEbner59: Are we done yet?

Bodiaz: Hardly. As if her drug-fueled rock throwing spree weren't enough, *People* magazine reports: "Wild rocker Courtney Love said today she tried to make her recent drug overdose 'fun' for her 11-year-old daughter..."

MarkEbner59: How sweet.

Bodiaz: "...Love was booked for being under the influence of a controlled substance, then released..."

MarkEbner59: Lemme guess... OxyContin?

Bodiaz: "Once home, she says she took at least 20 mgs of OxyContin 'to be knocked out.'"

MarkEbner59: Frances Bean! Mommy's home! <thud>

Bodiaz: "When Love got sick, Frances made her green tea and kept her company, along with a nanny, until

an ambulance came. 'That's the only time my daughter
has ever, ever, ever pitched in on one of my little
crises,' Love says. 'I made it fun. I said it was
going to be gross and I was going to have to make
myself throw up, but it was going to be okay.'"

MarkEbner59: In one "little crisis" Miss Hole manages
to act out a synopsis of this book.

Bodiaz: Bad parenting!

MarkEbner59: Nannies! The mystical, healing properties
of green tea!

Bodiaz: And celebrity *pain* medication! We could turn
this into a Broadway musical!

MarkEbner59: Yeah. We can get Rosie O'Donnell to
produce.

Bodiaz: We'll call it "Weekend at Courtney's" with
Frances Bean singing selections from Hole's "Live
Through This" album while dragging her comatose mommy
around like a rag doll.

MarkEbner59: Ouch.

◻ ◼ ◼

Drawing from the doomed domain of rock and rollers "hoping to die
before they get old," Courtney Love has thrust insanity chic into the
body of Hollywood royalty. The vicious cycle of elevated entertainers
mimicking woebegone inbreeds hoping to get their 15 minutes on
daytime trash TV sparks the question: What came first: The chicken
or the egg? Or more specifically, who is to blame for the catastrophe
that is celebrity culture: The stars who misbehave, or society at-large
that savors every twisted plot point? There is no simple answer.

As long as overpaid stars continue to hold their demographic in
contempt by demeaning their middle class lifestyles and politics, or
presenting themselves as unaccountable role models, the audience
will continue to derive a sick satisfaction from watching their in-

evitable public downfalls. The most extreme example of this *schaden-freude* on a morbid scale has been unleashed on the Internet in the form of "celebrity death pools." On web sites like www.stiffs.com the public predicts batches of potential celebrity deaths and gain points upon their correct choices. At the end of the year the person with the most points draws winnings from a cash pool. The aged and the supremely self-destructive celebrities provide a lower bounty than their more healthful counterparts. Courtney Love would net far fewer points than, say, the ostensibly upright Lisa Kudrow, but legend has it that some schmo in Rapid City, South Dakota made a cool $500 on a Chris Farley/Phil Hartman perfecta. The King of Pop, given his current situation, wouldn't net a single point were he to exit Neverland prematurely, and permanently.

☐ ◼ ◼

Bodiaz: CNN has learned Michael Jackson has hired Mark Geragos, who has been representing Scott Peterson in a high-profile California trial, as a paid legal consultant.

MarkEbner59: Geragos? Does that mean that Jackson will be found guilty?

Bodiaz: Well, we watched Geragos botch Winona's case.

MarkEbner59: True. And look at how at least one of the top Hollywood fixers we've mentioned in this book (Bert Fields) is now popping up in the Anthony Pellicano illegal wiretapping fiasco. Jacko has to resort to Geragos--the guy whose sole defense to save Winona Ryder, the pill-popping stealing beauty, was to try and destroy the low-wage Sak's store workers who caught the thief in the first place. Look how that backfired.

Bodiaz: If Jackson is found guilty, I guess that means his next comeback tour would have to comport with Megan's Law with concerned neighborhood parents passing

out flyers outside the Staple's Center as the morally
depraved offer the gloved one instant redemption
upon his work release.

◻ ◼ ◼

While insanity chic metastasizes, the media invents greater ways to present in-your-face celebrity overkill as actual news. Celebrity is big business and in the 300-channel cable-sphere there are not enough talented writers to fill the programming bill. So, there's no forecast for correction.

Van Gordon Sauter, producer of "The CBS Evening News with Dan Rather," once conjectured after one of his star news anchor's more public aberrations: "Prolonged exposure to that little red light on the television camera can cause clinical insanity." Maybe he knew something the rest of us are only now discovering.

Too bad the scandal class hasn't realized a downside yet. The superstar *du jour* can revel in his or her pitiful private torments and shameful public behavior, play out whatever twisted psychodrama they want in the press, and know full well that *People* and *Entertainment Weekly*, "Larry King Live" and "Oprah," *Vanity Fair*, and "E! True Hollywood Stories" among others will be there as a safety net to let them down easy, reward them for their facile contrition, and feed them as much fast-food fame as their bodies can absorb.

◻ ◼ ◼

MarkEbner59: What do we do next, Andrew?

Bodiaz: I don't know Mark, but it's been great writing
this book with you. Now I have to go tuck in my
children and read them Madonna's best-selling Kaballah-
inspired children's book, *Mr. Peabody's Apples*.

MarkEbner59: Are you joking?

Bodiaz: It's either that or my daughter's favorite by Spike Lee--*Please, Baby, Please*.

MarkEbner59: **Interesting. What else is on the Breitbart baby bookshelf?**

Bodiaz: Well, we've got Jamie Lee Curtis's *I'm Gonna Like Me: Letting Off a Little Self-Esteem*, and Katie Couric's *The Brand New Kid* is enjoyed by the entire family. Believe you me. And we're all really looking forward to Jay Leno's *If Roast Beef Could Fly*--coming this summer from Simon & Schuster. We pre-ordered at Amazon.com!

MarkEbner59: **Whoa. We've really got to save the next generation from this cradle-to-grave indoctrination into the cult of celebrity.**

Bodiaz: I've got it! We write a book for children! That's our next project.

MarkEbner59: *Don't Touch the Stars; They'll Burn You.*

Bodiaz: *Goodnight, Stars.*

MarkEbner59: ☺

Bodiaz: ☺

NOTES

Introduction

1. "Harrison Ford Delivers Oscar to Polanski," Associated Press, September 9, 2003.
2. Chris Wright, "Harrison Ford blasts US Iraq policy, "video game" films," Agence France Presse, August 27, 2003.
3. Jonathan Storm, "U.S. TV has mixed impact on the rest of the world," *The Philadelphia Enquirer,* October 17, 2001.
4 "Smut king seeks throne in California," Reuters, August 5, 2003.
5. "Papa was a creep, she says," *The Miami Herald*, May 26, 1996; "Flynt's daughter: Carville behind father's bounty hunt," John Godfrey, *The Washington Times,* January 8, 1999.
6. "Flynt Testifies He Was Hustler Publisher in 'Name Only'," Associated Press, July 27, 1983.

Chapter One

1. Karen S. Schneider, Ken Baker in Hailey, Irene Zutell in Los Angeles, Ward Morehouse III in New York City, Jane Walker in Madrid, and

bureau reports, "Turning point: Separated from Bruce Willis for 14 months, Demi Moore savors life in the slow lane—with her kids and a new companion," *People*, September 6, 1999.

2. Jamie Portman reports from Century City, California, "Spacek returns to the limelight: Sissy Spacek is delighted that her career is again flourishing. But the Oscar-winner says that acting has always played second fiddle to marriage and family," *The Ottawa Citizen*, (Ottawa, Canada) February 26, 1999.

3. Cheryl Johnson, staff writer, "Jessica Lange feels eyes of stargazers at home in Stillwater," *Star Tribune* (Minneapolis, MN), October 22, 1995.

4. Cynthia Sanz, "Love and marriage '98: Happily ever after: These star couples prove lasting love can be more than a Hollywood fantasy," *People*, June 22, 1998. To find the full *USA Today Weekend* quote, go online at http://www.valotte.com/usa_wknd2.htm.

5. Interview by Paul Semel, *Maxim*, August 2003.

6. Meg James, "Reality bites back as VH1 counter-sues Minnelli, Gest" and "Network says Gest's erratic behavior and costly demands led it to cancel the couple's show," *Los Angeles Times*, February 7, 2003.

7. ABC News Transcripts, "Good Morning America" (7:00 AM ET) ABC, August 6, 2002, "Anna Nicole Smith: Anna's New Reality Television Show."

8. Nellie Andreeva, "Smith will bare daily life for E!," *The Hollywood Reporter*, May 29, 2002.

9. Ibid.

10. Lois Timnick, staff writer, "Brando ends silence, defends son. Court: Christian Brando's bail in murder case is reduced to $2 million. Marlon Brando criticizes prosecutor, press," *Los Angeles Times*, August 10, 1990.

11. "Tuesday, Cheyenne Brando sent to Tahiti," *The Gazette* (Montreal, Quebec), November 19, 1991.

12. Ian Katz, "Godfather of despair: It started and ended in the paradise island of Tahiti, where Cheyenne Brando finally succeeded in taking her own life. Ian Katz traces the tragic paths of Brando's children," *The Guardian* (London), features page, April 19, 1995.

13. Charles Feldman, "Blake's lawyers offer audio tapes of dead wife, Actor Robert Blake leaves home on May 5," CNN, May 14, 2001.

14. Review by Tony Kaye, "My beautiful secretary sat next to Marlon Brando, 78 years old and 18 stone. He began taking off her clothes. She just smiled," *Mail on Sunday* (London), January 12, 2003.

15. "Larry King Live," CNN, April 5, 1995.

16. Lois Timnick, staff writer, "Brando ends silence, defends son. Court: Christian Brando's bail in murder case is reduced to $2 Million. Marlon Brando criticizes prosecutor, press," *Los Angeles Times*, August 10, 1990.

17. "No hard feelings: Putting years of acrimony—and his cancer scare—behind them, ex-lovers Farrah Fawcett and Ryan O'Neal go public as friends," *People*, April 14, 2003.

18. "The sorry life of Ryan," *The Daily Telegraph* (Sydney, Australia), February 25, 1997.

19. Richard Thomas, "Women: Whatever happened to Tatum O'Neal? She was the famous daughter of a famous father, the Oscar-winning child star who became the famous wife of a famous husband. And now? Richard Thomas reports," *The Guardian* (London), February 3, 1997.

20. Michelle Tauber, Todd Gold, and Lorenzo Benet in Los Angeles and K.C. Baker in New York City, "To hell and back: An Oscar winner at 10 and an addict by 20, Tatum O'Neal lived for years in the shadows. Now, angered by ex-husband John McEnroe's new book, she's speaking out and fighting back," *People*, July 8, 2002.

21. George Gordon, "Ryan's son accused of beating up lover; He threatened to shoot me, says terrified actress," *Daily Mail* (London), September 11, 1992.

22. Ibid.

23. Ibid.

24. "Ryan O'Neal's son sentenced to drug program," United Press International, December 10, 1992.

25. *Newsweek*, December 4, 1978.

26. Perry Brothers, "Mary Tyler Moore reveals her wounds," *The Cincinnati Enquirer*, January 28, 1999, Thursday East Edition, TMP, p. 5C.

27. John Carmody, staff writer, *The Washington Post*, April 18, 1995, The TV Column.

28. Dennis Romero, "New facts emerge in Matthew Ansara death probe," *City News Service*, July 13, 2001.

29. Associated Press, "Carrie Hamilton, 38, actress and writer," Los Angeles, January 21, 2001.

30. Spotlight Health, Thursday, July 24, online chat. For an online transcript go to http://www.spotlighthealth.com/morbid_obesity/carnies_story/ cws_trans_brians_daughter.html.

31. Chad Jones, "Holy dullsville! Aquaman and beach boy dive into troubled 'State': Two stars—surf bored," *The Oakland Tribune* (Oakland, CA), Friday, March 1, 2002.

32. "The worst father in the world," *The Sunday Telegraph,* (Sydney, Australia), November 11, 2001.

33. Ibid.

34. Graeme Hammond, "The world's most dysfunctional families: fractured families," *The Sunday Telegraph* (London), April 21, 2002.

35. Liz Braun, "Life rich with incident: Deuces Wild's Balthazar Getty was both a movie star and a heroin addict at 17," *The Toronto Sun* (Toronto, Canada), May 1, 2002.

36. Jeannie Williams, "Final Edition, Life: Jeannie Williams," and "AIDS grips Liz's ex-daughter-in-law," *USA Today*, Thursday, November 14, 1991, p. 2D, 357 words.

37. Interview with anonymous LA-based journalist.

38. Drew Barrymore, *Little Girl Lost*, Pocket Books, (February 1991, reissue).

39. Rebecca Eckler, "For richer, for poorer 'til two years are up: A look at marriages that last as long as a good muffler," *National Post* (Canada), July 30, 2002.

40. Dana Kennedy, "In a restless family of talent and tragedy, another star is born," *The New York Times*, March 4, 2001.

41. Elizabeth Snead, "Another Phoenix rising: Shy Joaquin makes his mark in 'To Die For'," *USA Today*, October 5, 1995.

42. http://www.river-phoenix.org/quoting/loving/page3/.

43. Barry Wigmore, "River Phoenix was a missionary in his mother's crusade to change the world. Now his brother Joaquin has inherited her hippie dream," *Sunday Herald Sun* (Melbourne, Australia), October 1, 2000.

44. John Glatt, "Lost in Hollywood: the fast times and short life of River Phoenix," *Cosmopolitan*, April 1995 v218 n4.

45. Barry Wigmore, *Sunday Herald Sun* (Melbourne, Australia), October 1, 2000, "River Phoenix was a missionary in his mother's crusade to change the world. Now his brother Joaquin has inherited her hippie dream."

46. A Mother's Note on Her Son's Life and Death," *Los Angeles Times*, November 24, 1993.

47. David E. Van Zandt, "Living in the Children of God," *Kirkus Review:* 1991 "Escaping a Free Love Legacy; Children of God sect hopes it can overcome sexy image," Don Lattin, *The San Francisco Chronicle,* February 14, 2001.

48. Ibid.

49. John Glatt, "Lost in Hollywood: the fast times and short life of River Phoenix," *Cosmopolitan*, April 1995.

50. Ibid.

51. Ibid.

52. "One Big Hippy Family: River Phoenix and Company Move Into Hollywood," *Life*, August 1987.

53. John Glatt, "Lost in Hollywood: the fast times and short life of River Phoenix," *Cosmopolitan*, April 1995.

54. Ian Parker, "Wasted: How on earth did River Phoenix, purest of all child stars, sensitive, clean-living and eco-friendly, end up dead from a

drug overdose at the age of 23? The answer lies in a secret life that was shocking even by the notorious double standards of Hollywood," *The Independent* (London), December 5, 1993.

55. Aljean Harmetz, "How 4 Boys in 'Stand By Me' Became a Film Team," *The New York Times*, September 16, 1986, *NYT* special from Hollywood.

56. Barry Wigmore, "River Phoenix was a missionary in his mother's crusade to change the world. Now his brother Joaquin has inherited her hippie dream," *Sunday Herald Sun* (Melbourne, Australia), October 1, 2000.

57. John Glatt, "Lost in Hollywood: the fast times and short life of River Phoenix," *Cosmopolitan*, April 1995.

58. Shelley Levitt, Lorenzo Benet, Lyndon Stambler, Johnny Dodd, and Joanna Stone in Los Angeles and Don Sider in Gainesville, "River's end: Actor River Phoenix was young, idealistic and full of promise. His death at 23 stunned friends—and revealed a dark side that few knew existed," *People*, November 15, 1993.

59. Eva Simpson, "Winona is so hot—This won't harm her career," *The Sun*, November 8, 2002.

60. Joan Smith, "Winona Ryder's ascent from adolescence to idol essence," *The San Francisco Examiner*, March 6, 1994.

61. Eva Simpson, "Winona is so hot—This won't harm her career," *The Sun*, November 8, 2002.

62. Neva Chonin, "Ryder In the Storm: Winona plays mental patient in 'Girl, Interrupted' and recalls her own bout with depression," *The San Francisco Chronicle*, January 16, 2000.

63. Joan Smith, "Winona Ryder's ascent from adolescence to idol essence," *The San Francisco Examiner*, March 6, 1994.

64 Simon Hattenstone, "Alive and Kicking," *The Guardian* (London), February 28, 1997.

65. Interview with Rosanna Arquette, *Playboy*, October 1985.

66. Holly Millea, "Shooting Starr," *Premiere Magazine*, December 1998.

67. Lawrie Masterson, "Out of the closet," *Sunday Herald Sun* (Melbourne, Australia), September 8, 2002.

68. "'I am going to take my clothes off in this movie': The cover girl of the Tarantino generation talks about motherhood, family—and her naked ambition," *The Independent* (London), January 26, 1997.

69. Interview with Rosanna Arquette, *Playboy*, October 1985.

70. Diane Werts, "Loving a Man Who Wants to Be a Woman: Two upcoming TV films look at romance that transcends gender," *New York Newsday*, March 13, 2003.

71. Liz Smith, Producing Laughs, *Newsday*, June 2, 2003; "Matrix full of mystic powers," Terry Mattingly, Scripps Howard News Service, *Deseret News* (Salt Lake City), November 1, 2003.

72. *The Smoking Gun* online at http://www.thesmokinggun.com/archive/wachowski1.html.

73. John E. Yang, Ann Devroy, "Quayle: 'Hollywood doesn't get it': Administration struggles to explain attack on TV's Murphy Brown," *The Washington Post*, May 21, 1992.

74. Federal News Service, "The Vice President's office, Office of the Press Secretary prepared remarks by Vice President Quayle to the Commonwealth Club of California," May 19, 1992, San Francisco, California.

75. Rick Du Brow, "'Murphy Brown' wins Emmys: Quayle chided: Television: 'Northern Exposure' captures six awards. Candice Bergen takes best comedy for third time," *Los Angeles Times*, August 31, 1992.

76. Judith Michaelson, staff writer, "'Murphy': Off deadline," *Los Angeles Times*, April 13, 1998.

77. Ivor Davis, "Parenthood, Hollywood style," *The Washington Times*, May 23, 1996.

78. Ibid.

79. John Stossel, "Single moms: Why does Hollywood celebrate them?" "20/20," ABC, February 22, 2002. To read the transcript, go online at http://abcnews.go.com/sections/2020/2020/GMAB_020221_adoption.html.

80. Marcus Errico, "Jon Voight: Angelina needs help," *E! Online*, Aug 1, 2002.

81. Barbara Walters, "20/20,", ABC, July 11, 2003.

82. Michelle Tauber, Todd Gold, "And baby makes two: Swearing her wild days (and Billy Bob) are behind her, Angelina Jolie says she was saved from chaos by the love of a good man: her adopted son Maddox, now almost 2," *People*, August 4, 2003.

83. "The Ultimate Badass: Angelina Jolie," interview by Randy Christenson, *Cosmopolitan*, June 1, 2001; "Fantasy Made Flesh," Andrew Gumbel, *The Independent* (London), June 30, 2001.

84. Bill Hoffman, "Smoochy Jolie and bro too close for comfort—Fans," *The New York Post*, March 28, 2000.

85. Barbara Walters, "20/20," ABC, July 11, 2003.

86. Ibid.

87. Ann Oldenburg, "Tattoos leave indelible impressions," *USA Today*, July 6, 2001.

88. Barbara Walters, "20/20," ABC, July 11, 2003.

89. *Access Hollywood*, August 2002.

90. Barbara Walters, "20/20,", ABC, July 11, 2003.

91. Michelle Tauber, Todd Gold, "And baby makes two: Swearing her wild days (and Billy Bob) are behind her, Angelina Jolie says she was saved from chaos by the love of a good man: her adopted son Maddox, now almost 2," *People*, August 4, 2003.

92. *San Francisco Chronicle,* December 23, 2002.

93. David Gardner, "Bing: Liz is dodging DNA test—Exclusive 'I want to know if I'm the father.'" *Sunday Mirror* (London), June 16, 2002.

94. Tanya Talaga, "Why more women choose Caesarean," *Toronto Star*, November 19, 2002.

95. "Yeah, Baby, Yeah! Elizabeth Hurley welcomes son Damian Charles. Next stop: determining Pop," Samantha Miller, Pete Norman in London and Alison Singh Gee in Los Angeles, *People*, April 22, 2002.

96. *People in the News,* Knight Ridder Newspapers, January 11, 2003.

97. Colin McDowell, "Picture proves Hurley has shed the baby pounds," *The Evening Standard* (London), September 16, 2002.

98. Janet Wu, "'Designer c-sections' in vogue with celebrity moms," KNTV, July 7, 2003. To read this story in full, visit http://www.nbc11.com/health/2316421/detail.html.

99. Vicky Allen, "A new technique promises a caesarean section in 20 minutes, meaning yet more mothers will opt for the surgery. The natural childbirth lobby is horrified but, asks Vicky Allan, is it really such a bad thing?" *The Sunday Herald* (London), January 26, 2003.

100. Antonella Lazzeri, "Zeta puts medics on standby at Oscars," *The Sun* (London), March 10, 2003.

101. George Rush and Joanna Molloy with Suzanne Rozdeba and Rebecca Louie, "Keeping the Faith?," *Daily News* (New York), August 22, 2002.

102. Janet Wu, "'Designer c-sections' in vogue with celebrity moms," KNTV, July 7, 2003. To read this story in full, visit http://www.nbc11.com/health/2316421/detail.html.

103. Samantha Critchell, "Garden variety of gowns at Golden Globes," *Associated Press Online*, January 19, 2003.

104. Anne Marie Owens, "Pregnant celebrities 'too posh to push': New mothers choose surgical delivery in bid to get fit and toned," *National Post* (Canada), February 10, 2003.

105. "Bruce/Demi, Los Angeles," *City News Service*, February 2, 1998.

106. "Bruce Willis and Demi Moore v. Ex-Nanny Kim Tannahill," January 28, 1998, U.S. District Court, Boise, Idaho.

Chapter Two

1. http://www.hollywood.com/news/detail/article/1712835 and http://www.courttv.com/trials/tommylee/verdict_ctv.html.

2. http://www.courttv.com/talk/chat_transcripts/2003/0414lee-ryan.html and http://www.wfor.com/artman/publish/article_104.shtml.

3. http://xtramsn.co.nz/news/0,,3772–2277231,00.html.

4. http://www.courttv.com/trials/tommylee/verdict_ctv.html and http://xtramsn.co.nz/news/0,,3772–2277231,00.html.

5. http://www.att.eonline.com/News/Items/0,1,11588,00.html?tnews and http://www.courttv.com/trials/tommylee/041403_ctv.html and www.courttv.com/talk/chat_transcripts/2003/0414lee-ryan.html.

6. http://www.courttv.com/talk/chat_transcripts/2003/0414lee-ryan.html and www.att.eonline.com/News/Items/0,1,11588,00.html?tnews.

7. http://www.hollywood.com/news/detail/article/1712835.

8. http://www.imdb.com.

9. http://www.imdb.com and http://www.hollywood.com/news/detail/article/1712835.

10. Interview with author.

11. Interview with author.

12. Suzanne Hansen, *You'll Never Nanny in This Town Again*, Ruby Sky Publishing, 2003, pp. 129–131.

13. Interview with author.

14. Interview with author.

15. Interview with author.

16. Interview with author.

17. Suzanne Hansen, interview with author; and Sunny, interview with author.

18. Interview with author.

19. Suzanne Hansen, *You'll Never Nanny in This Town Again*, Ruby Sky Publishing, 2003, p. 95, 97.

20. Suzanne Hansen, interview with author.

21. Suzanne Hansen, *You'll Never Nanny in This Town Again*, Ruby Sky Publishing, 2003, p. 99.

22. Suzanne Hansen, *You'll Never Nanny in This Town Again* Ruby Sky Publishing, 2003, p. 133.

23. Suzanne Hansen, *You'll Never Nanny in This Town Again*, Ruby Sky Publishing, 2003, pp. 127–128.

24. http://www.childbirth.org/articles/whatis.html.

25. Suzanne Hansen, *You'll Never Nanny in This Town Again*, Ruby Sky Publishing, 2003, p. 137.

26. Suzanne Hansen, *You'll Never Nanny in This Town Again,* Ruby Sky Publishing, 2003, p. 134.

27. Suzanne Hansen, *You'll Never Nanny in This Town Again*, Ruby Sky Publishing, 2003, p. 48.

28. Interview with author.

29. Interview with author.

30. Interview with author.

31. Interview with author.

32. Interview with author.

33. Interview with author.

34. Interview with author.

35. Suzanne Hansen, *You'll Never Nanny in This Town Again*, Ruby Sky Publishing, 2003, p. 97.
36. Interview with author.
37. http://www.macrobiotics.co.uk/sugat.htm.
38. Interview with author.
39. Interview with author.
40. Interview with author.
41. Interview with author.
42. Interview with author.
43. Suzanne Hansen, *You'll Never Nanny in This Town Again*, Ruby Sky Publishing, 2003, pp. 48, 77.
44. Suzanne Hansen, *You'll Never Nanny in This Town Again*, Ruby Sky Publishing, 2003, p. 219.
45. Suzanne Hansen, *You'll Never Nanny in This Town Again*, Ruby Sky Publishing, 2003, pp. 24, 218–219, and Suzanne Hansen, interview with author.
46. Suzanne Hansen, *You'll Never Nanny in This Town Again*, Ruby Sky Publishing, 2003, p. 219, and Suzanne Hansen, interview with author.
47. Suzanne Hansen, *You'll Never Nanny in This Town Again*, Ruby Sky Publishing, 2003, pp. 222–225, 268.
48. Suzanne Hansen, *You'll Never Nanny in This Town Again*, Ruby Sky Publishing, 2003, pp. 222–225, 229 and Suzanne Hansen, interview with author.
49. Suzanne Hansen, interview with author.
50. Interview with author.

Chapter Three

1. The names in the following story have been changed at the participants' request for privacy.
2. http://www.santa-moncia.org/cityclerk/council/agendas/1995/.
3. http://www.helpguide.org/mental/morgan.htm.
4. "Actor Brian Keith commits suicide, police say," *E! Online News*, June 24, 1997.
5. Taken from court records.
6. "Plane crash: California crash victims identified," *Las Vegas Review Journal*, June 10, 2003.
7. http://www.xrds.org.
8. "Erin Hamilton dancing as fast as she can," *The Advocate*, May 14, 2002.
9. Steve Gorman, "Actor Rob Lowe leaving 'The West Wing,'" *Reuters*, July 24, 2002.
10. "Actor Brian Keith commits suicide, police say," *E! Online News*, June 24, 1997.

11. http://www2.amw.com/site/thisweek/C/CooperZeke/CooperCAP.html.
12. Information in this chapter was based on extensive interviews with former students and faculty including alum Richard Rushfield, alum Ali Rushfield, alum Jack Black, alum Victoria Sellers, alum Jessica Kaplan, alum Eric Kessler, Headmaster Roger Weaver, Crossroads film instructor Jim Hosney, alum Jason Blumenthal, alum Jim Gibson, former Crossroads faculty member Jack Zimmerman, the late director of the Crossroads upper school Jack Jacobusse, Crossroads drama instructor/Mysteries coordinator Peggy O'Brien, former student Caleb Goddard, alum Gary Coleman, alum and studio executive Amy Pascal, alum and motion picture director Michael Bay, and other alumni who prefer to remain anonymous. Crossroads curriculum material, news reports including the *Los Angeles Times*, school yearbooks, and additional school brochures and curriculum material, and a published eulogy all served as source material.

Chapter Four

1. For further information, go online and view the Mental Health History Timeline at http://www.mdx.ac.uk/www/study/mhhtim.htm.
2. Ibid.
3. "Psychiatry and film: A fatal attraction," 1997, http://www.cchr.org/art/eng/page05c.htm.
4. W. Arnold, *Shadowland,* McGraw-Hill, 1978.
5. Ibid.
6. Ibid.
7. Review of *Shadowland, Penthouse,* July 1978.
8. W. Arnold, *Shadowland,* McGraw-Hill, 1978.
9. Ibid.
10. Leonard Maltin, *Leonard Maltin's Movie Encyclopedia,* New York: EP Dutton, 1994.
11. W. Arnold, *Shadowland,* McGraw-Hill, 1978.
12. Ibid.
13. Jack El-Hai, "The Lobotomist," *The Washington Post,* February 4, 2001.
14. Ibid.
15. W. Arnold, *Shadowland,* McGraw-Hill, 1978.
16. "Nurses say 'Frances' inaccurate," *Seattle Post Intelligencer,* January 26, 1983.
17. "Biography for Frances Farmer," Internet Movie Database, http://www.imdb.com/.
18. "Biography for Vivien Leigh," Internet Movie Database, http://www.imdb.com/.
19. A. Edwards, *Vivien Leigh,* Simon & Schuster, 1977.
20. Ibid.

21. Ibid.
22. "Biography for Vivien Leigh," Internet Movie Database, http://www.imdb.com/.
23. A. Edwards, *Vivien Leigh,* Simon & Schuster, 1977.
24. G. Lambert, "Vivien Leigh: internal struggle," http://www.dycks.com/vivienleigh/articles/article1.htm).
25. David Bloom, "I love trouble," *Variety,* September 16, 2002.
26. David Bloom, "Time to play attack-a-flack," *Variety,* September 11, 2000.
27. David Bloom, "I love trouble," *Variety,* September 16, 2002.
28. "Biography for Judy Garland," Internet Movie Database, http://www.imdb.com/.
29. Leonard Maltin, *Leonard Maltin's Movie Encyclopedia,* New York: EP Dutton, 1994.
30. "Biography for Judy Garland," Internet Movie Database, http://www.imdb.com/.
31. Ibid.
32. K. Gabbard and G. Gabbard, *Psychiatry and the Cinema,* University of Chicago Press, 1970.
33. Ibid.

Chapter Five

1. "Hollywood drug casualties mount...," News, *Chicago Tribune*, August 21, 1996, p. 9.
2. Ibid.
3. Michael Fleeman, "The doctor, the movie producer...," Associated Press, September 8, 1996.
4. Ibid.
5. Chuck Phillips and Carla Hall, "Fatal attraction," *Los Angeles Times*, October 23, 1995.
6. Michael Fleeman, "The doctor, the movie producer...," Associated Press, September 8, 1996.
7. Graham Brink, "Questions raised about expert," *St. Petersburg Times*, December 7, 2000.
8. "Judge won't drop weapons charge against celebrity private eye," Associated Press, June 30, 2003.
9. Ibid.
10. Michael Fleeman, "The doctor, the movie producer...," Associated Press, September 8, 1996; and interview with Nomi Fredrick.
11. Interview with Frank Snepp, and interview with Chuck Phillips, *Los Angeles Times.*
12. Michael Fleeman, "The doctor, the movie producer...," Associated Press, September 8, 1996.

13. Michael Fleeman, "The doctor, the movie producer…," Associated Press, September 8, 1996; and Matt Kelley, "118 Gov't doctors punished," Associated Press, April 14, 2002.
14. Chuck Phillips and Carla Hall, "Fatal attraction," *Los Angeles Times*, October 23, 1995.
15. Michael Fleeman, "The doctor, the movie producer…," Associated Press, September 8, 1996.
16. Interview with Nomi Fredrick
17. Michael Fleeman, "The doctor, the movie producer…," Associated Press, September 8, 1996.
18. Michael Fleeman, "The doctor, the movie produce r…," Associated Press, September 8, 1996; and Chuck Phillips, "Prescription for an epidemic," *Los Angeles Times*, September 18, 1996.
19. Chuck Phillips, "License of Late Producers…," *Los Angeles Times*, March 4, 1999.
20. Michael Fleeman, "The doctor, the movie producer…," Associated Press, September 8, 1996.
21. Chuck Phillips, "License of Late Producers…," *Los Angeles Times*, March 4, 1999.
22. Interview with Nomi Fredrick.
23. Interview with Nomi Fredrick.
24. Interview with Nomi Fredrick.
25. Chuck Phillips and Carla Hall, "Fatal attraction," *Los Angeles Times*, October 23, 1995.
26. Interview with Nomi Fredrick; and Chuck Phillips, "Embattled psychiatrist…," *Los Angeles Times*, October 26, 2000.
27. Interview with Nomi Fredrick.
28. Chuck Phillips, "Prescription for an epidemic," *Los Angeles Times*, September 18, 1996.
29. Chuck Phillips, "Embattled psychiatrist…,"*Los Angeles Times*, October 26, 2000.
30. Interview with Nomi Fredrick; and Chuck Phillips, "Embattled psychiatrist…," *Los Angeles Times*, October 26, 2000.
31. Ibid.
32. Interview with Nomi Fredrick.
33. Interview with Nomi Fredrick.
34. Mathew Heller, "The doctor and the showgirls," *Sunday Mail* (Australia), June 8, 2003, p. 54.
35. Ibid.
36. Ibid.
37. Mathew Heller, "The doctor and the showgirls," *Sunday Mail* (Australia), June 8, 2003, p. 54; CBSNews.com, December 10, 2002, "Doctor to the Stars Loses License."

38. Mathew Heller, "The doctor and the showgirls," *Sunday Mail* (Australia), June 8, 2003, p. 54.
39. Taken from court records; and Mathew Heller, "The doctor and the showgirls," *Sunday Mail* (Australia), June 8, 2003, p. 54.
40. http://imdb.com/.
41. Find the Texas State Board of Medical Ethics at http://imdb.com/ www.tsbme.state.tx.us.
42. http://imdb.com/.
43. Ibid.
44. "Playing doctor" *SPY*, January/February 1995, p. 30–31.
45. http://imdb.com/.
46. Gina Kolata, "Diet pills: allure and risk," *The New York Times*, July 16, 1997.
47. Ibid.
48. http://www.smokedefense.com.
49. Ian Markham-Smith, "Why Hollywood stars . . .," *The Evening Standard*, (London) November 21, 2000, p. 18.
50. Ibid.
51. http://www.cbsnews.com/stories/2000/06/14/48hours/printable205736. shtml.
52. Mark Ebner, "The hepoisie," *Seed*, January/February 2003.
53. Mark Ebner, "Hep-C generation," *Details*, October 1999.
54. Mark Ebner, "The hepoisie," *Seed*, January/February 2003; and Mark Ebner, "Hep-C generation," *Details*, October 1999.
55. "Information about herbs, botanicals and other products," Memorial Sloan-Kettering Cancer Center. Visit the article at http://www.mskcc. org/mskcc/html/11571.cfm?RecordID=523&tab=HC.
56. *Rolling Stone*, August 7, 2003.
57. Mark Ebner, "The hepoisie," *Seed*, January/February 2003.

Chapter Six

1. http://www.lyricstime.com/lyrics/37129.html.
2. http://abclocal.go.com/wls/news/entertainment/120302_en_whitney.html.
3. Nancy Mills, "The harder they come," *New York Daily News*, March 23, 2003.
4. Read "Polanski the predator" at http://www.thesmokinggun.com/archive/polanskicover1.html.
5. Read "'Ally McBeal' will finish season without Downey," April 24, 2001, at http://www.cnn.com/2001/LAW/04/24/downey.arrested.02/.
6. Kari Mozena, "Clean & sober: the essential guide to drug rehab centers," *Los Angeles Magazine*, April 2002.
7. http://www.aabibliography.com/aaphotonewhtml/obituary_of_bill_ wilson_co.html.
8. http://www.passagesmalibu.com.

Chapter Seven

1. http://www.encyclopedia.com/html/t/tantra.asp and http://www.salon.com.
2. http://www.cultnews.com; http://www.rickross.com; *Dallas Morning News*, April 7, 1998; and *USA Today*, April 20, 2003.
3. Rick Ross, interview with author.
4. Rick Ross, interview with author; and http://www.rickross.com.
5. Ibid.
6. Rick Ross, interview with author.
7. Rick Ross, interview with author; and Pauletter Cooper, *Scandal of Scientology*, Tower Publishing, 1971.
8. Peter Washington, *Madame Blavatsky's Baboon*, Schocken Books, 1996, pp. 277–end.
9. Ann Charter, ed., *Portable Beat Reader*, Penguin USA, 1992; and Alan Watts, *Zen and the Beat Way*, Charles E. Tuttle, 1992.
10. http://www.churchofsatan.com; and Sammy Davis Jr., *Hollywood in a Suitcase*, William Morrow, 1980.
11. Marilyn Manson and Neil Strauss, *Long Hard Road Out of Hell*, New Jersey: Plexus Publishing, 1998.
12. "Scandal of Scientology", *The New York Times,* December 9, 1969, p.104.
13. http://www.cielodrive.com; Ed Sanders, *The Family*, A K Pr Publishing, 1989.
14. http://www.eonline.com; Ed Sanders, *The Family*, A K Pr Publishing, 1989; and Vincent Bugliosi and Curt Gentry, *Helter Skelter*, W.W. Norton, 2001.
15. http://minet.org/mantras.html.
16. *National Post* (UK), February 9, 2000; http://www.watchman.org; and http://www.ocweekly.com, June 18–24, 1999.
17. http://www.eonline.com, February 8, 2000; http://www.rickross.com; http://www.salon.com; *San Francisco Chronicle*, December 29, 1995; http://awog.editthispage.com; http://www.natural-law-party.net; *Dallas Observer*, October 5, 2000; and Insight on the News, http://www.insightmag. com, August 21, 2000.
18. http://www.pfaw.org.
19. ABC News, March 8, 2001; Fox News, March 8, 2001; and *New York Daily News*, March 14, 2001.
20. BBC News, April 20, 2000; and *The New Yorker*, April 2000.
21. http://www.nationalreview, February 11, 2003; http://www.credopub. com, March 1999; http://www.hollywood.com, January 2000; and Associated Press, August 25, 2000.
22. http://www.christiancourier.com, October 8, 1998; and Ted Turner, speech to National Family Planning and Reproductive Health Association, February 16, 1999.

23. *The Guardian*, June 18, 2002.
24. Ted Turner, speech to National Family Planning and Reproductive Health Association, Feb 16, 1999; http://www.nationalreview, February 11, 2003; http://www.credopub, March 1999; and http://www.hollywood.com, January 2000.
25. http://www.tibet.com; http://www.christiancourier.com; October 1, 1999; and http://www.touchstonemagazine, November 2000.
26. http://www.newsmax.com; and *Marantha Christian Journal*, August 2000.
27. *Marantha Christian Journal*, August 2000; http://www.episcopalchurch.org; and http://www.hinduismtoday.com.
28. http://www.beliefnet.com; http://www.newsmax.com; *Marantha Christian Journal*, August 2000; http://www.millenneumpeacesummit.com; http://www.touchstonemagazine, November 2000; and http://www.episcopalchurch.org.
29. *Los Angeles Times*, September 7, 1997; and http://www.chopra.com.
30. *Entertainment Weekly*, October 3, 1997.
31. Televised broadcast.
32. *Esquire*, October 1997; http://www.tibet.dk; http://www.eonline.com; http://www.ananova.com; http://www.thesmokinggun.com; "Steven Seagal gets a shot at stardom," Patrick Goldstein, *Los Angeles Times*, February 14, 1988.
33. Tina Turner and Kurt Loder, *I, Tina*, Avon Books, 1987.
34. Dominick Dunne, *Justice: Crimes, Trials and Punishments*, Three Rivers Press, 2002, pp. 1–45; Dominick Dunne, *Another City Not My Own*, Ballantine Books, 1999; and Lisa Derrick, interview with author.
35. "Open letter by Susan Cohen, an exploited follower," http://www.rickross.com, August 31, 2002; *The Montreal Mirror*, May 23, 1991; and *The Roanoke (Virginia) Times*, August 3, 1991.
36. *The Roanoke (Virginia) Times*, August 3, 1991.
37. *New York Post,* August 21, 2002.
38. http://www.cultnews.com; *USA Today,* February 13, 2002; and http://www.style.com.
39. http://www.observer.guardian.co.uk; http://www.timesofindia.com; *New York Post*, August 24, 2002; VH-1 News; http://www.cultnews.com, http://www.rickross.com; and http://www.my.webmed.com.
40. http://www.rickross.com; United States District Court Northern District of California United States of America v. Albert Ellis and Gurujot Singh Khalsa AKA Robert Alvin Taylor, Magistrate Case No. 388 0144 FW.
41. http://www.rickross.com; and http://www.cultnews.com.
42. http://www.eonline.com, September 18, 1998; http://www.vh1.com.
43. *Philadelphia Inquirer*, July 13, 2003; and *Hello Magazine*, May 26, 2003.
44. *Hello Magazine*, May 26, 2003.
45. "The red string squad," Melena Z. Ryzik, *New York Daily News*, October 16, 2003.

46. MSNBC, January 9, 2003.

47. http://www.kabbalah.com.

48. *Star Magazine*, January 26, 1999.

49. *Los Angeles Magazine*, December 1998.

50. *New York Post*, August 13, 2003.

51. This is London, http://www.thisislondon.com, July 10, 2002.

52. *Las Vegas Weekly*, September 6, 2003; *New Times Los Angeles*, April 27–May 3, 2000

53. http://www.wtps.co.uk; http://www.archive.salon.com; *Associated Press*, February 3, 2000

54. *Las Vegas Weekly*, September 6, 2003; http://www.kabbalah.com; http://www.borders.com; and http://www.barnesandnoble.com.

55. *The Scotsman*, December 26, 1997; and http://www.kabbalah.com.

56. http://www.kabbalah.com; and *Spin*, April 1999.

57. According to Sharp Sword's Prophet Watch (http://sharpsword.tripod.com/prophet-watch3.html). IRS records of TBN, the network and Paul Crouch have reported over $400 million in revenues between the years 1993–1996.

58. http://www.apologeticsindex.org; http://www.endtimedeception.com; and http://www.cephasministry.com.

59. *Los Angeles Times*, November 4 and 7, 2001; and *Orange County Register*, http://www.ocregister.com, May 31, 1998–June 2, 1998.

60. *Los Angeles Times*, December 17, 2001; and *Orange County Register*, http://www.ocregister.com, January 1, 2002.

61. http://www.tbn.org.

62. Ann O'Neill, "God's party of the first part," *Los Angeles Times*, September 11, 2001

63. Ibid.

64. http://www.gpdcandu.com; and *Los Angeles Times*, July 8, 2001.

65. *Los Angeles Times*, Aug 14, 1988; http://www.john-roger.org; and http://www.msia.org.

66. *Orange County Register*, http://www.ocregister.com, Oct 29, 1987.

67. *The Guardian*, June 9, 1997.

68. *Los Angeles Times*, December 5, 1986; and *Cosmopolitan*, August 1991.

69. *Seattle Post*, October 4, 2000.

70. Associated Press, *Seattle Post-Intelligencer*, October 10, 2000.

71. http://www.johnedward.net.

72. Penn and Teller's television program, "Bullsh*t."

73. *New York Times Magazine*, July 29, 2001; *Time*, March 6, 2001; *Skeptical Inquirer Magazine* November/December 2001; Katherine Ramsland, *Prism of the Night: A Biography of Anne Rice*, E.P. Dutton, 1991; and "Anne Rice: Birth of the Vampire," BBC Television and Lifetime Television, 1994.

Chapter Eight

1. *The Australian*, December 24, 1998.
2. Christopher Reeve, *Nothing Is Impossible: Reflections on a New Life,* New York: Random House, 2001.
3. *Los Angeles Times*, August 27 and 29, 1978; *Wall Street Journal,* December 30, 1997; and *New York Times*, March 9, 1997.
4. "Church of Scientology pays $8.7 million to Ex-member," Reuters Wire, May 11, 2002.
5. http://www.factnet.org; http://www.xenu.net; and *St. Petersburg Times*, June 7, 2001–August 20, 2003; www.lisamcpherson.com.; "Scientology seeks millions as punishment," Robert Farley, *St. Petersburg Times,* August 20, 2003.
6. *Mean Magazine*, June 2000; and John Carter, *Sex and Rockets: The Occult World of Jack Parsons*, Feral House, 2000.
7. Paulette Cooper, *The Scandal of Scientology*, Belmont/Tower, 1971, pp. 99–105; and *The San Diego Union-Tribune*, February 15, 1998.
8. *Rolling Stone*, August 1983; *The Australian*, December 24, 1998; http://www.scientology.org; and http://www.whatisscientology.org.
9. http://www.vh1.com; http://www.whatisscientology.org; WENN, November 20, 2002; *National Enquirer*, March 8, 2002 and August 7, 2002; *Hello Magazine,* August 12, 2002; MSNBC, August 13, 2002; *Newsday* August 12, 2003; *Rolling Stone,* April 2003; and Fox News, January 22, 2003.
10. http://www.cchr.org; *Washington Post*, August 25, 2002; and *People*, September 27, 2002.
11. MSNBC, October 1, 2002.
12. http://www.cchr.org; *Washington Post*, August 25, 2002; and *People*, September 27, 2002.
13. *Freedom Magazine*, February 2003.
14. *Boston Herald*, February 9 and 10, 2001; *Los Angeles Times*, July 29, August 1, September 18 and 23, 1997; *Sacramento Bee*, June 8, 1998; and *Now Magazine Toronto*, December 10, 1992
15. http://www.studytech.org and *Boston Herald*, March 2 1998
16. MSNBC, February 5, 2001; *The Boston Herald*, February 10, 2001; *Sacramento Bee*, June 8, 1998; and *Boston Herald*, March 2, 1998; *Los Angeles Times*, September 23, 1997; http://www.studytech.org; and ACLU, press release, August 6, 1998.
17. http://www.lrhubbardprofile.org; http://www.studytechnology.org; *Boston Herald*, March 3, 1998; and *I.F. Magazine*, January/ February 1998.
18. http://www.worldliteracy.org/faq.html.
19. http://www.cchr.org; *Washington Post*, August 25, 2002; and *People*, September 27, 2002.

20. *Spy Magazine*, February 1996; and http://www.celebritycentre.org.
21. http://www.whatisscientology.org; *Newkirk Herald Journal*, Newkirk, Oklahoma, August 17, 1989; and http://www.lronhubbard.org.
22. http://www.whatisscientology.org.
23. http://www.cchr.org.
24. L. Ron Hubbard, *Basic Study Manual*, Bridge Publications.
25. *The Dominion Post*, Morgantown, West Virginia, March 1, 2003
26. *People,* July 12, 2003; Fox News, July 14, 2003; and *National Enquirer* August 7, 2003.
27. Associated Press, July 11, 2003; http://www.nida.nih.gov; http://www.msn.com; *Irish Examiner*, July 21, 2003; http://www.interdys.org; and *National Enquirer* August 7, 2003.
28. Based on statistics compiled from Scientology's own publication, *Advance* magazine, issues dated 1966–1996.
29. Based on most current prices for Scientology services at Scientology's Saint Hill Organization as published in the monthly Scientology journal, *The Auditor.*
30. http://www-2.cs.cmu.edu/~dst/OTIII/; http://www.apologeticsindex.org; *New Times Los Angeles*, various, 1996; Robert Minton, "Demystifying Scientology's Fundamental Reality—The BT's," http://www-2.cs.cmu.edu/~dst/OTIII/minton-essay.txt; Declaration filed April 9, 1993 in connection with civil case 91-6426 HLH (Tx), Church of Scientology International v. Steven Fishman and Uwe Geertz, US District Court for the Central District of California, pages 76–100 containing the text of OT III; Lafayette Ronald Hubbard, Operating Thetan Section III, (1968), handwritten manuscript available online courtesy of Andreas Heldal-Lund; and *The San Diego Union-Tribune*, February 15, 1998.
31. L. Ron Hubbard, "A Manual on the dissemination of material," *Ability, the Magazine of Dianetics and Scientology*, 1955.
32. "Scientology Suit Against *Post* Dismissed," *The Washington Post*, November 29, 1995. Charles W. Hall.
33. For his story, "Scientology: The Cult of Greed," *Time* magazine reporter Richard Behar won the 1992 Gerald Loeb award for distinguished business and financial journalism, the Worth Bingham prize, and the Conscience in Media Award from the American Society of Journalists and Authors; "Judge Dismisses Church of Scientology's $416 Million Lawsuit Against *Time* Magazine," Business Wire, July 16, 1996.
34. Author's and other journalists' personal experience.
35. http://www.scientology.org.
36. HCO Policy Letter of October 18, 1967, "Penalties for Lower Conditions," Hubbard Communications Office.
37. Issue #18. *High Winds: the magazine of the Sea Organization* (undated, copyright claim 1995), "The Sea Org—Handling Suppression on the 4th Dynamic."

38. http://www.freedommag.org, http://www.whatisscientology.org; and http://www.scientology.org.
39. *Los Angeles Times*, May 2, 2001 and May 14, 2001; *Santa Barbara News Press*, March 31, 2002; *Mercury News*, September 10, 2001; *Los Angeles Times*, March 26, 2003; and *US News and World Reports*, May 28, 2001; "High Profile Couple Never Pair Church and State," *St. Petersburg Times,* December 13, 1998; *The Los Angeles Times,* December 21, 2001.
40. Flag Order 3323, May 9, 1973.
41. *Buzz Magazine*, March 1998 and Fox News, September 15, 2001.
42. *Celebrity* magazine.
43. Affidavit of Andre Tabayoyon, section 131.
44. Article by former Scientologist Michael Pattison, sent to author in 2002.
45. "Brainwashing in Scientology's Rehabilitation Project Force (RPF), academic paper, presented at the Society for the Scientific Study of Religion, San Diego, California, November 7, 1997 by Dr. Stephen Kent, University of Alberta, Canada.
46. Affidavit of Andre Tabayoyon, section 146; and written accounts by Robert Vaughn Young, September 24, 1997, http://www.holysmoke.org.
47. "Ownership," *Professional Auditor's Bulletin*, May 27, 1955, number 53.
48. L. Ron Hubbard, "Politics," Hubbard Communications Office Policy Letter, February 1965.
49. L. Ron Hubbard, "Department of official affairs," Hubbard Communications Office Policy Letter of March 13, 1961.
50. *San Francisco Chronicle*, October 13, 1994; *Salon,* Internet magazine, Daily Clicks, February 25, 1997; *The San Diego Union-Tribune*, February 15, 1998; and *The New York Times*, "Scientology Faces Glare of Scrutiny After Florida Parishioners Death," Douglas Frantz, December 1, 1997.
51. L. Ron Hubbard, *Scientology—A New Slant on Life*, Bridge Publications, p. 76.

Chapter Nine

1. http://www.plasticfantasy.com/products-as.htm.
2. *Snowboarder Magazine,* August 14, 2000.
3. *Business Week Online,* September 7, 2001.
4. Lovely ladies meeting places identified and based on first person experience of one *Hollywood, Interrupted* reporter and others.
5. Interviews, real estate records and first-hand accounts.
6. Based on the interviews and participatory experience of journalist Andrew Vontz.
7. *Crain's Chicago Business,* May 26, 2003.
8. "Playboy Buys Back from Vivid Three Hardcore Cable Channels," *Adult Video News,* September 2001.

9. "Blow For Freedom," *The Guardian* and *The Observer*, Sunday April 28, 2002; Linda Lovelace, *Ordeal*, Berkley Publishing Group, 1981; and *http://www.farinc.org/PETA and Pornographic Culture II.*

10. Sharon Waxman, "The Playboy After Dark," *The Washington Post*, October 10, 1999.

11. http://www.askmen.com/women/actress_100/102c_shannon_tweed.html.

12. *Hugh Hefner: Once Upon a Time;* http://www.playboy.com/worldofplayboy/hmh/hefmedia/onceapon.html.

13. Dave Thompson, "Hef's reality," http://www.TheBookLA.com.

14. "The Playboy After Dark," Sharon Waxman, October 10, 1999, *The Washington Post.*

15. Hef: A Viagraphy is largely based on "Hugh Hefner: What the Butler Saw," by Mark Ebner, as originally published in *Arena* magazine, October, 2001.

Chapter Ten

1. "Michael's money meltdown," *New York Daily News,* June 7, 2003.

2. Don Crutchfield, "Confessions of a Hollywood P.I.," http://www.pi4stars.com/confess.shtml.

3. *Spy Magazine*, May-June, 1992.

4. Tania Branigan, "Jackson still lets children sleep in his bed," *UK Guardian,* February 4, 2003.

5. http://www.thesmokinggun.com/archive/mjcivil1.html.

6. http://bushlibrary.tamu.edu/papers/1992/92050101.html.

7. Reuters, 1993; and http://www.anc.org.za/anc/newsbrief/1993/news1209.

8. "Jackson's sister says she believes he is a molester. . .," Jim Newton, *Los Angeles Times,* December 9, 1993.

9. http://www.btinternet.com/~Ptwebsites/mj/latoyaint.txt.

10. "Michael Jackson's lawyer said he shared bed—not sex—with boy," Associated Press, December 7, 1993.

11. http://www.lukeford.net/profiles/profiles/anthony_pellicano.htm.

12. The Bagman section is largely based on a series of interviews with Paul Barresi, backed up by research notes, interview transcripts, court documents, and photographs provided by Barresi.

13. http://www.paulbaressi.com.

14. Los Angeles Superior Court, BC148692; and http://www.entlawdigest.com/story.cfm?storyID=771.

15. http://www.reviewjournal.com/lvrj_home/2003/Mar-07-Fri-2003/news/20839203.html.

16. http://www.adultvideonews.com/archives/199905/bone/ by0599_024.html.

17. http://www.usatoday.com/life/music/2002/07-15-jackson.htm.
18. http://www.msnbc.com/news/873878.asp.
19. "The Bagman," Mark Ebner and Jack Cheevers, *New Times Los Angeles,* April 26, 2001; interviews with the transvestites in question and a review of their documentation; interviews with the *Enquirer* and *Globe* attorneys, and Marty Singer.
20. Mark Ebner and Jack Cheevers "The Bagman," *New Times Los Angeles,* April 26, 2001.

Intermission

1. "Then she sued the cuckolded Mrs. Barber for assault," *New Times* (Los Angeles), December 1999; *Rolling Stone,* January 5, 2001; and www. eonline.com, January 5, 2001.
2. http://launch.yahoo.com, November 28, 2001, http://www.nationalenquirer. com, May 10, 2001; and WENN, March 25 and 27, 2001.
3. http://news.bbc.co.uk/2/hi/entertainment/2724499.stm and (bbc news February 5 & 6, 2003); www. launch.yahoo.com, February 6, 2003; and *Sunday Times* (London) February 9, 2003.
4. http://www.worldonline.co.za/musi/musi_center_music_.579506.html, February 12, 2003; http://www.dotmusic.com/news/February2003/news28259.asp, February 2003; and http://seattlepi.nwsource.com/people/ 108154_people12.shtml, February 12, 2003.
5. *The Straits Times* (Singapore), February 2, 1995; *Sydney Morning Herald,* January 24, 1995; and Poppy Z. Brite, *Courtney Love: The Real Story,* Simon & Schuster, 1997, pp. 203–205.
6. *National Enquirer* April 17, 2002. For photo, visit http://www. nationalenquirer.com/stories/feature.cfm?instanceid=28499.
7. *Courtney Love: Queen of Noise,* p. 247.
8. http://www.eonline.com/News/Court/9806.love.html.
9. *Seattle Times,* November 6, 1992, *Kurt and Courtney,* directed by Nick Broomfield.
10. *Kurt and Courtney*, directed by Nick Broomfield.
11. Anonymous industry source.
12. *Courtney Love: Queen of Noise,* p. 158.
13. Melissa Rossi, *Courtney Love: Queen of Noise,* Pocket Books, 1996, pp. 136, 158; *The Seattle Times,* November 6, 1992; and Poppy Z. Brite, *Courtney Love: The Real Story*, Simon & Schuster, 1997, p. 144–145.
14. "Strange Love," *Vanity Fair,* Lynn Hirschberg, September, 1992.
15. *Courtney Love: The Real Story,* p. 137, Poppy Z. Brite.
16. Ibid; *Courtney Love: Queen of Noise,* Melissa Rossi, Pocket Books, 1996, p. 128.

17. *Vanity Fair*, September 1992; *Courtney Love: Queen of Noise*, pp. 120–129; and *Courtney Love: The Real Story*, pp. 137–139, Poppy Z. Brite, Touchstone Books, December 1998.

18. *Courtney Love: Queen of Noise*, pp. 242–243, Melissa Rossi, Pocket Books, May 1996.

19. Jim D. Rogatis and Bill Wyman interview with Love on radio station WKQX in 1995; *Courtney Love: Queen of Noise*, p. 146.

20. http://www.imdb.com.

21. *New York Daily News*, February 20, 2000.

22. *New York Post*, February 3, 2003.

23. *The Sun*, January 31, 2003, London, U.K.

24. *Courtney Love: The Real Story*, pp. 85–86.

25. Ibid, pp. 19–25.

26. *Courtney Love: Queen of Noise*, pp. 19–85; and *Courtney Love: The Real Story*, pp. 19–66.

27. According to an anonymous source, friend of Dorian Cope.

28. *Courtney Love: Queen of Noise*, p. 35.

29. Ibid, pp. 34–35; and *Courtney Love: The Real Story*, pp. 52–56, 142–143.

30. According to an interview with an anonymous source; *Courtney Love: Queen of Noise*, pp. 89–90; and "New York Rock," November 1997 at http://www.angelfire.com/tx5/brookesalbumcovers/holebio.html.

31. *Kurt & Courtney*, Nick Broomfield, director; www.artemisrecords.com; and www.votenader.com/campaignevents.

32. *Courtney Love: Queen of Noise*, pp. 87–117; and *Courtney Love: The Real Story*, pp. 98–118.

33. Interview with anonymous source.

34. *Courtney Love: Queen of Noise*, pp. 130–131; *Courtney Love: The Real Story*, p. 141.

35. *Los Angeles Times*, September 21, 1992.

36. Interview with Nipper Seaturtle, *Courtney Love: Queen of Noise*, p. 247.

37. *Courtney Love: Queen of Noise*, pp. 223; and *Courtney Love The Real Story*, p. 183.

38. *Courtney Love: Queen of Noise*, p. 223; and *Courtney Love: The Real Story*, pp. 188–189.

39. http://www.salon.com/media/1998/02/25media.html, August 14, 2003; *High Times*, April 1996; *Globe* magazine, April 2, 1996.

40. http://www.velvetrope.com April 1997; and interview with anonymous source.

41. *Kurt & Courtney*, Nick Broomfield, director, 1998

42. http://www.justiceforkurt.com/investigation; *Mojo* magazine, May 1998; *Willamette Week*, April 8, 1998.

43. http://www.ez-entertainment.net/Barrymore_Drew.htm; http:// www.actresstrivia.com/drew_barrymore.html.

44. *Courtney Love: Queen of Noise,* p. 146.
45. *Kurt & Courtney,* Nick Broomfield, director.
46. *Rolling Stone,* August 26, 2002;
    http://www.vh1.com/artists/news/1452631/02262002/nirvana.jhtml;
    http://www.knotmag.com/?article=488; and
    http://search.barnesandnoble.com/booksearch/isbnInquiry.asp?
    isbn=157322359X&itm=3&pwb=2.
47. http://www.eonline.com, January 5, 2001; http://www.cbsnews.com
    January 5, 2001; *Rolling Stone,* January 5, 2001.
48. http://eonline.com, May 21, 2001.
49. *Los Angeles Times,* February 28, 2001; and http://www.eonline.com,
    February 28, 2001.
50. http://www.thestranger.com/2002–10–10/music3.html; and
    http://www.cbsnews.com October 1, 2002.
51. http://www.thesmokinggun.com.
52. "Courtney Love", *Entertainment Weekly,* March 29 2002, Love is a
    Battlefield, By Holly Millea.
53. "Courtney Love", http://www.velvetrope.com.
54. http://www.velvetrope.com; http://www.rocknerd.com
55. http://www.velvetrope.com, synopsis of C. Love post summarized by
    J.G. Flash as a courtesy to the webmaster of http://www.hole.com.
56. http://www.thesmokinggun.com.
57. Ibid.
58. Ibid.
59. Calliope Foundation/MAP Press conference, 1996.
60. Hollywood "Bad Girl" Courney Love Battles to get daughter back,
    Agence France Presse, November 7, 2003.

Chapter Eleven

1. James Kaplan, "Give it up for Sean Penn," *The Observer,* May 6, 2001.
2. Mitchell Fink and Helen Kennedy, "Al reels in celeb supporters," *New
   York Daily News,* September 15, 2000.
3. Lloyd Grove, *The Washington Post,* September 17, 1999, the Reliable
   Source column.
4. Read Moby's Online Journal for February 1, 2001 at http://www.
   mobyonline.com.
5. Amy Reiter, Salon.com, November 3, 2000,
   http://archive.salon.com/people/col/reit/2000/11/03/npfri/.
6. Lloyd Grove with Beth Berselli, *The Washington Post,* December 21,
   2000, the Reliable Source column.
7. "Brad and Jennifer caught in drug scandal," *Star* magazine, January 24,
   2001.

8. Mark Binelli, *Rolling Stone*, September 2001.

9. "Sheen slates 'bad comic' Bush," BBC, February 13, 2001.

10. Trish Deitch Rohrer, "Don't tread on Janeane," *Buzz* magazine (now defunct but a 1993 or 1994 date is likely); http://www.hollywoodinvestigator.com/2002/garofalo.htm.

11. Stephen Dalton, "It's no walk in the park," *The Times* (London), January 21, 2002.

12. Michael Moore, *Stupid White Men*, New York: HarperCollins, 2002.

13. Jeannette Walls, "Scoop," gossip column at MSNBC.com, October 1, 2002.

14. Greg Pierce, *The Washington Times*, January 23, 2003.

15. Spike-Lee-Guns, *Broadcast News*, May 26, 1999.

16. Robert Hardt Jr, "Bush league Baldwin in 9/11 insult," *The New York Post*, March 9, 2002.

17. Mitchell Fink with Lauren Rubin, "Apparently, being John Cusack means being really mad at Bush," *New York Daily News*, June 7, 2001.

18. "Clooney haunted by old fling," *The New York Post*, December 18, 2002.

19. Suzanne Rozdeba and Ben Widdicombe, "Clooney isn't joining Dubya's gang," *New York Daily News*, January 20, 2003.

20. "Clooney haunted by old fling," *The New York Post*, December 18, 2002.

21. "George takes a stand," *Newsday* (New York), January 19, 2003.

22. Diana West, "Sheryl Crow; and the Franco-German union," *The Washington Times*, January 24, 2003.

23. Jonathan Storm, "U.S. TV has mixed impact on rest of the world," *The Philadelphia Inquirer*, October 7, 2001.

24. Jay Stone, "Sundance still relevant," entertainment section of *The Vancouver Sun* (British Columbia, Canada), January 21, 2003, p. F4.

25. "Redford's trip to Cuba reportedly under investigation," Associated Press, August 5, 1988.

26. Jeannette Walls, "Redford fears Bush censorship," MSNBC.com, January 23, 2003.

27. Bernard Zuel, "Lights, camera, take action: Sarandon rallies the arts," *Sydney Morning Herald* (Australia), November 19, 2002.

28. Simon Davis, "Hollywood freezes out Republicans, says Bo," *Telegraph* (London), September 6, 2000.

29. "The O'Reilly Factor," Fox News Network, October 1, 2002.

30. "Rosie's etiquette lesson," *The New York Post*, May 21, 1999.

31. Jennifer Weiner, "Making nice with a part in a quirky new movie, Shannen Doherty can actually joke about her past as Brenda on '90210,' Well, sort of," *The Philadelphia Inquirer*, October 19, 1995.

32. Liz Smith, "Her white elephant," *Newsday* (New York), February 15, 2001.

33. "Beatty: I am pro-life!" "Drudge Report," September 30, 1999.

34. Lynn Hirschberg, 'Wrong verb, honey' is typical Nicholson," *The Toronto Star*, October 2, 1988.

35. Douglas Thompson, "Joker who just loves to laugh," *The Herald* (Glasgow), March 1, 1997.

36. Charles Laurence, "Guilt takes the gloss off Sheen," *The London Telegraph* (UK), July 19, 1997.

37. "The O'Reilly Factor," Fox News Network, October 1, 2002.

38. Woody Harrelson, "Real lives: I'm an American tired of American lies," *The Guardian* (London), October 17, 2002.

39. *Premiere* magazine, November 2000.

40. Jessica Shaw, "Havana good time, wish you were here," *Entertainment Weekly*, April 24, 1998.

41. "Steven Spielberg says he feels 'at home' in Cuba," Deutsche Presse-Agentur, November 6, 2002.

42. "Gloria Estefan blames Castro for Cubans' 'suffering'," Agence France Presse, August 18, 2000.

43. Cynthia L. Webb, "Five questions with Andy Garcia," Associated Press Online, February 24, 1999.

44. Vanessa Bauza, "Costner on Castro: 'He enjoyed the film,' " *Sun-Sentinel* (Fort Lauderdale, FL), April 12, 2001.

45. "Supermodels sample socialism: Campbell, Moss cozy up to Castro," Agence France Presse, February 23, 1998.

46. "'American Investigator' Earth Day Report on Chevy Chase, Donna Mills, Tom Arnold, Marc Morano," April 24, 2000, http://www. americaninvestigator.com/.

47. Chuck Conconi, staff writer, "Personalities," *The Washington Post*, May 2, 1988.

48. Deirdre Donahue, "Hollywood stars and the Cuban connection," *USA Today*, March 30, 1990.

49. Cynthia H. Craft, "Art transcends politics at Cuba film school," *Los Angeles Times*, December 31, 1992.

50. David Germain, "Redford reflects on two decades of dissent and daring at Sundance," Associated Press, January 18, 2003.

51. Anita Snow, "Castro, millions of Cubans vote in elections dissidents call a farce," Associated Press, January 19, 2003.

52. Interview with author.

53. Luisa Yanez and Glenn Garvin, "Take 2: HBO wants Stone to re-interview Castro in documentary," *The Miami Herald*, April 17, 2003.

54. "Hero Worship: Berlin's Personae Non Gratae," Stephen Garrett, *The Village Voice*, March 5–11, 2003.

55. Jeff Simon, "Closed Book: Persecuted artist is only a fringe subject," *Buffalo News* (New York), February 16, 2001.

56. Interview by Kristine McKenna, "John Malkovich," *Playboy*, August 1, 2000.

57. Press junket interview by Mark Ebner for the movie, *From Hell,* 2001.

58. "Depp: U.S. Too Violent for Daughter," Associated Press, April 9, 2001.

59. Susan Wloszczyna "The brothers Hughes," *USA Today*, October 18, 2001.

60. Susan Riley, "Improbable plot, gratuitous violence overwhelm latest Johnny Depp film," *The Ottawa Citizen*, November 22, 1995.

61. Peter Holder, Jo Casamento, and Naomi Toy, "Sydney confidential," *The Daily Telegraph* (Sydney, Australia), June 28, 2002.

62. "Baldwins will leave if Bush wins," Associated Press, September 17, 2000.

63. Mitchell Fink with Laruen Rubin, "It's Coming Into Focus," *New York Daily News*, September 20, 2000.

64. Anthony Breznican, "Celebrities endorse letter asking Bush to stop war rhetoric," Associated Press, December 10, 2002.

65. "Playboy interview: The West Wing," *Playboy*, October 1, 2001.

66. Jefferson Graham, "Martin Sheen: Positively not presidential 'West Wing' star prefers left-wing politics," *USA Today*, December 15, 1999.

67. Jean Halliday, "Carmakers leave it in neutral," *Advertising Age*, March 14, 2001.

68. Jeff Wilson, "Celebrity colony rankled by 'mayor' Martin Sheen's invitation to homeless," Associated Press, May 23, 1989.

69. Ross Sneyd, "Actor Martin Sheen endorses Howard Dean for president," Associated Press, January 30, 2003.

70. Joanne Weintraub, "As president, Martin Sheen is definitely no Bill Clinton," *Milwaukee Journal Sentinel*, August 1, 1999.

71. *The Federal Paper*, Nov. 18, 2002 (this publication is now defunct; title/author information unobtainable).

72. http://www.danielfaulkner.com/.

73. Read about the Mumia support list at the web site for Grand Lodge, Fraternal Order of Police at http://www.grandlodgefop.org/faulkner/projamal.html.

74. Tucker Carlson, "Mumia Dearest," *The Weekly Standard*, September 18, 1995.

75. Ibid.

76. Marc Cooper, "For a Mumia-free 2000," *New York Press*, January 6, 2000.

77. Judith Michaelson, "Protesters take aim at KPFK, host's statements," *Los Angeles Times*, February 2, 2000.

78. "Michael Douglas disclosed: Actor encounters difficulty with life behind scenes," Cindy Pearlman, *Chicago Sun-Times,* September 7, 1997.

79. David Montgomery, "Celebrity justice, or simply a 'star-studded epidemic of lunacy'?" *The Scotsman*, November 24, 1999.

80. Andrea Peyser, "Glenn Close's misguided crusade for killer mom," *The New York Post*, November 12, 1999.

81 Harjo, Suzan Shown, "Whither the Peltier pardon?" *Indian Country Today* (Lakota Times), October 31, 2001.

82. Terence Blacker, "In the mind and belly of the beast," *The Independent* (London), February 19, 2002.

83. M.A. Farber, "Killing clouds ex-convict writer's new life," *The New York Times*, July 26, 1981.

84. Sonja Hillgren, "Actresses see real-life farm crisis," United Press International, May 6, 1985.

85. Malia Rulon, "Stars come out on Capitol Hill, and one senator has had enough," Associated Press, June 6, 2002.

86. Maureen Dowd, "Washington is star-struck as Hollywood gets serious," *The New York Times*, May 9, 1993.

87. Michele Willens, "When celebrity hearts bleed," *The New York Times*, April 16, 2000.

88. Anne-Marie O'Connor, "Keeping stars bright politically," *Los Angeles Times*, November 1, 2000.

89. Lisa Leff, "A liberal dose of star power; Margery Tabankin links the celebrities to the cause," *The Washington Post*, December 10, 1994.

90. Interview with anonymous LA-based journalist.

91. Ibid.

92. "Streisand to 'Gebhardt': don't attaq Irack," "Drudge Report," September 26, 2002.

93. The Reliable Source column, *The Washington Post*, October 2, 2002.

94. "Now Barbra's in Shakespeare hoax: singer used phony internet quotes in war cry," "Drudge Report," October 1, 2002.

95. The Reliable Source column, *The Washington Post*, October 2, 2002.

96. "Streisand bought eight hundred shares of Cheney's Haliburton," "Drudge Report," October 3, 2002.

97. "Streisand calls Saddam 'Iranian'," "Drudge Report," October 16, 2002.

98. Chuck Phillips, "Vamping for the vote: record industry coalition pushes registration campaign," *Los Angeles Times*, October 17, 1990.

99. "Actors make appearances, calls for Gore," Associated Press, November 5, 2000.

100. "Ben Affleck, Hollywood hypocrite," "The Smoking Gun," April 24, 2001, http://www.thesmokinggun.com/archive/affleck_doc.shtml.

101. Ibid.

102. "Rap the vote," "The Smoking Gun," http://www.thesmokinggun.com/archive/rapthevote1.html.

Chapter Twelve

1. Definition taken from the Merriam-Webster dictionary. 1990.

1a. The American Heritage Dictionary of English Language: Fourth Edition, 2000.

2. Rick Marin with Susan Miller, and Jeanne Gordon, "Coming up Roses," *Newsweek*, July 15, 1996.
3. Gail Shister, "Rosie's O'Donnell breaks into daytime talk; comic actress skips demanding movie roles to spend time with son," *Austin American Statesman*, June 9, 1996.
4. *Us* magazine, February 1998, found online at http://www.geocities.com/rofaq/rofaq.html.
5. Juliann Garey, "Riveting Rosie steps from stand-up into big league," *The Toronto Star*, August 4, 1992.
6. "Comedian Paula Poundstone Sentenced to Five Years Probation." Terri Vermeulen Keith, *City News Service,* October 10, 2001.
7. Larry Margasak, "Moms demand gun safety," Associated Press, May 15, 2000.
8. "O'Donnell: admits she's no constitutional expert," "The Hotline," April 23, 1999.
9. Signmund Freud, *A General Introduction to Psychoanalysis*, Simon & Schuster, June 1920, revised edition.
10. "The roar of the paint, the smell of smoke," *Newsweek*, May 16, 1994.
11. Donna de la Cruz, "City Republican blasts Rosie O'Donnell on homeless issue," Associated Press, December 9, 1999.
12. Camille Paglia, "Boycott Rosie, not the tabloids," Salon.com, September 1997.
13. Jessica DuLong, "Rosie's crusade: could the "queen of nice" turn the tide for gay adoption rights?" *The Advocate*, April 16, 2002.
14. GLAAD Media Awards, April 7, 2003, Marriott Marquis, New York.
15. "The Oprah Winfrey Show," March 18, 2002.
16. "The Oprah Winfrey Show," November 7, 2002.
17. "The Oprah Winfrey Show," December 3, 2002.
18. "The Oprah Winfrey Show," November 12, 2001.
19. "The Oprah Winfrey Show," March 4, 2003.
20. "The Oprah Winfrey Show," September 20, 2002.
21. "The Oprah Winfrey Show," June 3, 2002.
22. Joyce Millman, "The road to the White House goes through Oprah," Salon.com, September 25, 2000.
23. Josh Getlin, "In politics of celebrity, be charming, win big," *Los Angeles Times*, September 29, 2000.
24. Gloria Goodale, "Oscar works hard for the charities," *Christian Science Monitor*, March 20, 1998.
25. Alley Mills interview by Andrew Breitbart.
26. Judith Lazarus, "The AIDS ribbons' tangled message: why some see red," *Los Angeles Times*, March 24, 1993.
27. Gaile Robinson, "A cause for conern, symbols: that once-ubiquitous red AIDS ribbon is seldom seen lately," *Los Angeles Times*, March 30, 1995.

28. "Trends of the times: what defines decades of Oscar style?" *People*, April 9, 2001.
29. "AIDS Activitists Have Some PETA Peeves," George Rush and Joanna Molloy with Baird Jones, *New York Daily News,* May 6, 1996.
30. John Beveridge, "Charity warfare," *Courier Mail* (Queensland, Australia), May 22, 1996.
31. Josh Spector, Inside.com, March 2001.
32. Peter Sheridan, "Dinsey Aladdin caves in to the Arab protestors," *Daily Mail* (London), July 12, 1993.
33. Matthew Gilbert, "Beyond villains & buffoons: gay and lesbian activists want Hollywood to broaden its portrayal of them on film," *The Boston Globe*, March 22, 1992.
34. Brian Bethune, "Pocahontas," *Maclean's*, June 26, 1995; and strip mining factoid was discovered in 1876. See topic information at http://www.kgs.ukans.edu/Extension/cherokee/coalmining.html and http://www.ascoffanscuff.com/kansas/about/Kabout-08.html.
35. Peter Whittle, "Censor humour," *Sunday Times* (London), April 20, 2003.
36. Ibid.
37. Mark de la Vina, "Films accused of stereotyping advocates say albinos unfairly portrayed as freakish evildoers," *San Jose* (California) *Mercury News*, May 18, 2003.

Chapter Thirteen

1. Andrew Breitbart interview with Gilbert Gottfried.
2. Alvin P. Sanoff, "Climbing the ladder of laughs," *U.S. News & World Report,* September 12, 1988.
3. Diane Stefani, "Comic instinct or can you learn to be funny?" *Back Stage,* April 2, 1993.
4. Douglas J. Rowe, "'Comic Relief' the TV fund-raiser becomes 'Comic Relief' the book," The Associated Press, October 11, 1996.
5. Dave Nuttycombe, "Sit down, already! TV's comic glut," *The Washington Post,* March 6, 1994.
6. Tom Shales, "Comedy that takes the low road: 'Comic Relief,' 'Saturday Night' provide little laughing matter," *The Washington Post,* May 14, 1990.
7. Susan Milligan, *States News Service,* March 12, 1986.
8. Donna Cassatta, "Bush huddles with GOP governors to map out strategy," Associated Press, May 28, 1988.
9. Lawrence Christon, "'Comic Relief' is no routine benefit," *Los Angeles Times,* March 31, 1986.
10. "City gets $139,500 from 'Comic Relief,'" Associated Press, August 19, 1986.

11. Lawrence Christon, "'Comic Relief,' an HBO tradition: comedians weave laughter into plea for homeless at amphitheatre," *Los Angeles Times,* November 16, 1987.
12. Interview with Patrick Markee, "Hannity and Colmes," Fox News Network, January 9, 2002.
13. Andrew Hsiao, Press Clips, *Village Voice*, December 8, 1998.
14. Daniel Cerone, "The show must go on: 'Comic Relief' revised for a post-riot audience," *Los Angeles Times*, May 16, 1992.
15. Mark Dawidziak, "'Comic Relief' raises lots—at Bobbitt's expense," *The Philadelphia Inquirer,* January 18, 1994.
16. "Playboy interview: Whoopi Goldberg," *Playboy,* January 1997.
17. Michael Snyder, "Poundstone's career purring along offbeat stand-up comic's career takes a leap up," *The San Francisco Chronicle*, December 27, 1992.
18. David Kronke, "Comedy review: it's no joke: $6.4 MILLION: 'Comic Relief' sets record but overdoses on Bobbitt humor," *Los Angeles Times*, January 17, 1994.
19. Daniel Cerone, "The show must go on: 'Comic Relief' revised for a post-riot audience," *Los Angeles Times,* May 16, 1992.
20. Chuck Philips, "Kinison takes a second look at his AIDS and gay humor," *Los Angeles Times*, August 5, 1990.
21. Jody Leader, "Blue comedy's back in style—but not everyone's amused," *The Record* (New Jersey), March 27, 1989.
22. "Bernie Mac discusses his career as a comedian," "Fresh Air," NPR, November 27, 2001.
23. David Bennum, "Ready to rock," *The Observer*, December 26, 1999.
24. Andrew Breitbart interview with Gilbert Gottfried.
25. Peter Whittle, "Censor humour," *Sunday Times* (London), April 20, 2003.
26. Hilary de Vries, "Company town: DeGeneres says she and Heche are quitting Hollywood," *Los Angeles Times,* December 1, 1998.
27. ABC News, "On her own: Jane Fonda discusses her new life's goals," "20/20," February 9, 2001.
28. Andrew Breitbart interview with Melanie Graham.
29. Lynn Elber, "Racial epithet used on 'Late Night,'" Associated Press, July 17, 2001.
30. Josh Grossberg, "PC police bust Conan O'Brien Show," "E! Online," July 18, 2001.
31. "Real Time with Bill Maher," HBO, February 21, 2003.
32. Alexander Jacobs, "Saving Silverman," *New York Observer*, August 6, 2001.
33. "NBC: Slur a 'mistake'," *Daily Variety*, July 19, 2001.

34. Alexander Jacobs, "Saving Silverman," *New York Observer,* August 6, 2001.

35. "Tinky Winky has been outed along with Falwell's ignorance: encouraging kids to read would be a better use of time," *Portland Press Herald* (Maine), February 12, 1999.

36. "South Park, Cartman's Silly Hate Crime 2000," Comedy Central, episode 401.

37. "Bruce's trial," *Newsweek*, July 20, 1964.

38. Ronald K. L. Collins, David M. Skover, *The Trials of Lenny Bruce: The Fall and Rise of an American Icon*, Sourcebooks Trade, September 2002.

39. Ibid.

40. Ibid.

41. Paul Brownfield, "Telling the 'truth' about Bruce," *Los Angeles Times*, August 7, 1999.

Chapter Fourteen

1. This chapter is based on the participatory experience of Mark Ebner and interviews with: the owner of the cookware company, customers, and various salesmen for the company in question, Paul Hughes, and Lawrence Crimlis—the main focus of the story. Also, interviews were conducted with and testing of the cookware in question was done by Bruce Sauer of OCM Test Laboratories in Anaheim, California, and Chemistry Lab Supervisor Bob Lafferty of Durkee Labs in Paramount, California.

Chapter Fifteen

1. *Fade In* magazine, 2003.

2. http://www.marksfriggin.com/news03/6–23.htm.

3. http://www.fadeinonline.com/.

4. Except where otherwise sourced, the material in this chapter is based on extensive author interviews with HBO "Cathouse" characters the Boone Brothers and published reports; "Project Greenlight" creator Alex Keledjian; "Project Greenlight"/*Stolen Summer* actor Kevin Pollack; "Project Greenlight" co-executive producer Liz Bronstein; "Project Greenlight," director Pete Jones, and *Stolen Summer* production notes; television show and film screenings, and published reports; screenwriter Stuart Blumberg; agent Todd Kerner; comedy writer Eric Slovin; actor Ed Norton (via a faxed statement); several anonymous sources close to the "Stealing the Faith" story, and published reports in print outlets such as *Los Angeles* magazine.

Chapter Sixteen

1. Chapter sourcing is based on interviews with the Hollywood Café players, the E-Girl, Heather Robinson, and confirmation of her past employment with AOL through her employment records, e-mails, chats, and checks of screen names (which are altered here) with their online profiles and bios and double-checked phone numbers and places of employment disclosed to her in the documented communications.

Chapter Seventeen

1. Michael Schrage, "All roads lead to new-media capital," *Los Angeles Times,* June 23, 1994.
2. Amy Vickers, "Icebox.com to close," *Guardian* (UK), February 9, 2001.
3. "Pop.com losses its fizz in less than a year," Forbes.com, September 6, 2000.
4. Claudia Peschiutta, "Shellshocked web survivors lie low: digital Hollywood picking up the pieces," *Los Angeles Business Journal*, August 12, 2002.
5. Noah Robischon, "The best and worst internet," *Entertainment Weekly*, December 22, 2000/December 29, 2000.
6. Christopher Noxon, "High anxiety: online entertainment industry hits financial turning point," *Los Angeles Magazine*, September 1, 2000.
7. Ibid.
8. "Former chairman of internet company accused of abusing teenagers," Associated Press, June 18, 2002.
9. Ralph Frammolino and P.J. Huffstutter, "Dot-com refugees find welcome in porn industry: jobs: internet shakeout and potential Hollywood strikes are good for adult entertainment companies," *Los Angeles Times*, April 23, 2001.
10. Susan Estrich and David Frum, "Matt, Bill, and Monica," *Slate* magazine, December 13, 1997.
11. Lorenza Muñoz," High-tech word of mouth maims movies in a flash," *Los Angeles Times*, August 17, 2003.
12. Jesse Pearson, "Interview with Harry Knowles," *Index* magazine, November, 2001.
13. "Harry Knowles must go: Isn't his fifteen minutes up yet?" *Oz*, April 15, 2003; and http://www.hollywoodbitchslap.com/feature.php?feature=724.
14. http://hollywoodbitchslap.com/feature=724.
15. Interview with Jeff Rassoul and quotes from his movie reviews found on his website at http://hometown.aol.com/thejman99, September 2003.
16. http://www.thesmokinggun.com/backstage/backstage.html.
17. Ibid.

18. http://www.thesmokinggun.com/backstage2/backstage2.html.
19. http://www.thesmokinggun.com/archive/polanskicover1.html.
20. "Polanski: Hollywood exile with a troubled past," Agence France Presse, March 24, 2003.
21. Arlene Vigoda and Elizabeth Weise, "Milano family sues over nudity on net," *USA Today*, April 29, 1998.
22. John Kiesewetter, "Is Dixie Chicks protest a conspiracy?" *The Cincinnati Enquirer*, March 18, 2003.
23. Ibid.
24. "Actor Johnny Depp disavows anti-American quotes," Reuters, September 04, 2003.
25. Rick Lyman, "Rich and famous man their soap boxes," *The New York Times*, March 2, 2003.

INDEX

INDEX